CAMBRIDGE

CW01510984

Official Cambridge Exam Preparation

COMPLETE

FIRST
for Schools

Student's Book without answers

B2

WITH ONLINE PRACTICE

Guy Brook-Hart, Susan Hutchison, Lucy Passmore and Jishan Uddin

ENGLISH FOR SPANISH SPEAKERS

Cambridge University Press
www.cambridge.org/elt

Cambridge Assessment English
www.cambridgeenglish.org

Information on this title: www.cambridge.org/9788490362037

© Cambridge University Press and UCLES 2019

First published 2019

20 19 18 17 16 15 14 13 12 11 10 9 8 7 6 5 4 3 2 1

Printed in the United Kingdom by Latimer Trend
Legal Deposit: M-8749-2019

A catalogue record for this publication is available from the British Library

ISBN 978-8-490-36203-7 Student's Book without answers with Online Practice

Contents

Map of the units

	Unit title	Reading and Use of English	Writing	Listening
1	A family affair	Part 6: 'From worst enemies to best friends' Part 2: 'How do you manage your money?'	Part 1: An essay: It is beneficial for teenagers to receive pocket money from their parents. Do you agree?	Part 1: Young people talking about their families and activities
2	Leisure and pleasure	Part 1: 'Ice skating – my passion' Part 4: Sentence transformations	Part 2: An article: A great way to spend your free time	Part 2: A talk by a professional footballer
		Vocabulary and grammar review Units 1 and 2		
3	Happy holidays?	Part 3: 'A bus journey' Part 7: 'Holiday surprises'	Part 2: A story: It was a trip I'll never forget'	Part 3: Five young people talking about their best holiday ever
4	Food, glorious food	Part 6: 'Are insects the future of food?' Part 1: 'How to eat sushi'	Part 2: A review: A local restaurant, snack bar or café in your area	Part 4: An interview with a young chef
		Vocabulary and grammar review Units 3 and 4		
5	Study time	Part 7: 'Making the most of your summer' Part 3: 'Exam stress for teenagers'	Part 2: The set text: The most interesting character in the book that you have read	Part 1: People talking about study and school
6	My first job	Part 5: 'My first job' Part 2: 'Voluntary work'	Part 2: A letter or email: What part-time jobs can teenagers do in your country	Part 3: Five young people talking about weekend jobs
		Vocabulary and grammar review Units 5 and 6		
7	High adventure	Part 6: 'Are you ready for a school challenge?' Part 4: Sentence transformations	Part 2: An article: A great way to keep fit	Part 2: A talk about the Duke of Edinburgh Award Part 4: An interview with someone who did a parachute jump for the first time
8	Dream of the stars	Part 7: 'Careers in film and the theatre' Part 1: 'I want your job: stunt person'	Part1: An essay: There are both advantages and disadvantages to a career as a musician or actor. Do you agree?	Part 2: A talk about unusual sports
		Vocabulary and grammar review Units 7 and 8		
9	Secrets of the mind	Part 5: 'Our month in a tech free house' Part 4: Sentence transformations	Part 2: A short story	Part 1: People talking about different influences on personality
10	On the money	Part 2: 'How I like to shop' Part 5: 'I got rid of nearly everything I owned'	Part 2: A review: Write about something you have bought or been given recently	Part 4: An interview with a student about 'Buy nothing day'
		Vocabulary and grammar review Units 9 and 10		
11	Medical matters	Part 4: 'A school science project' Part 3: 'Afraid of the dentist'	Part 1: An essay: Young people generally don't pay attention to their health and fitness. Do you agree?	Part 3: Five people talking about health problems and reasons for visiting a doctor
12	Animal kingdom	Part 1: 'Not just a hobby' Part 7: 'Animal rescue'	Part 2: A letter or email : Advice for a visitor to your country	Part 1: People talking about wildlife and conservation
		Vocabulary and grammar review Units 11 and 12		
13	House space	Part 5: 'Living in a yurt' Part 2: 'The smallest house in Britain'	Part 2: An article: My ideal home	Part 2: A talk about building a small house from a kit
14	Fiesta!	Part 6: 'Koningsdad: Europe's most lively festival' Part 3: 'The week my town goes back in time'	Part1: An essay: The advantages and disadvantages going to the cinema compared to streaming films at home	Part 4: An interview with someone who visits music festivals
		Vocabulary and grammar review Units 13 and 14		

Speaking	Pronunciation	Vocabulary	Grammar
Part 1: Speaking about your home and what it is like to grow up in your hometown	Word stress	Phrasal verbs to describe relationships Collocations with *make* and *do*	Present perfect simple and continuous
Part 2: Describing and discussing the benefits of different free time activities	Sentence stress (1)	Phrasal verbs to talk about skills and hobbies	Making comparisons Adjectives with *-ing* and *-ed*
Part 3: Choosing the best activities for a school trip	Intonation (1)	*travel, journey, trip* and *way*	Past simple, past continuous and *used to* *at, in* and *on* in time phrases Past perfect simple and continuous
Part 4: Talking about diet and healthy eating	Grouping words and pausing (1)	*food, dish* and *meal* Adjectives to describe food, meals and restaurants	*so* and *such* *too* and *enough*
Part 1: Talking about your preferences regarding school subjects	Word stress (2)	Phrasal verbs connected with study *find out, get to know, know, learn, teach* and *study* *attend, join, take part* and *assist*	Zero, first and second conditional
Part 2: Describing what people learn and enjoy about doing different kinds of jobs	Sentence stress (2)	*work* and *job; possibility, occasion* and *possibility; fun* and *funny* Collocations with *job* and *work*	Countable and uncountable nouns Articles
Part 3: Discussing different ways to encourage students to do more sport	Intonation (2)	Verb collocations with adventure activities *look, see* and *watch; listen* and *hear*	Infinitive and verb + *-ing*
Part 4: giving opinions on the importance of dance, drama and music as school subjects	Grouping words and pausing (2)	Verb collocations with *ambition, career, experience* and *job* People and the theatre Verb collocations with *ambition, career, experience* and *job*	*at, in, on* to express location Reported speech
Part 2: Describing the emotions that people have in different situations	Sentence stress (3)	*achieve, carry out* and *devote* *stay, spend* and *pass; move, cause* and *have*	Modal verbs to express certainty and possibility
Part 1: Talking about your personal life and interests	Linking (1)	*arrive, get* and *reach* Phrasal verbs connected with shopping	*as* and *like* Modal verbs to express ability
Part 2: Describing different ways to stay healthy and ways to deal with different illnesses	Intonation (3)	Health vocabulary Idiomatic expressions	Relative pronouns and relative clauses
Part 3: choosing a topic connected with animals **Part 4:** Discussion about looking after animals	Word stress (3)	*avoid, prevent* and *protect; check, control, keep an eye on* and *supervise*	Third conditional and mixed conditionals *wish, if only* and *hope*
Part 2: Describing what life is like in different places	Revision of features of pronunciation	*space, place, room, location* and *square*	Causative *have* and *get* Expressing obligation and permission
Part 3: Deciding how to celebrate an occasion **Part 4:** Discussion on festivals and celebrations	Improving fluency	Vocabulary to describe what people do Vocabulary for festivals	The Passive

Introduction

Who this book is for?

Complete First for Schools is a stimulating and thorough preparation course for school-aged learners who wish to take the **B2 First for Schools exam** from **Cambridge Assessment English.** It helps them to develop the necessary reading, writing, listening and speaking exams for the exam as well as teaching essential grammar and vocabulary. For those who are not planning to take the exam in the near future, the book provides skills and language based around engaging topics, all highly relevant for school-aged learners moving towards a B2 level of English.

What the Student's Book contains

- **14 units for classroom study.** Each unit contains:
  - an authentic exam task taken from each of the four papers (Reading and Use of English, Listening, Speaking and Writing in the B2 First exam.
  - essential information on what each part of the exam involves, and the best way to approach each task. Exam advice boxes before exam tasks explain how to do this.
  - a wide range of enjoyable speaking activities designed to increase learner's fluency and ability to express themselves.
  - a step-by-step approach to doing First for Schools Writing tasks.
  - grammar activities and exercises for the grammar learners need to know for the exam. When you are doing grammar exercises, you will sometimes see this symbol ⊙. These exercises are based on research from the **Cambridge Learner Corpus** and they deal with the areas which often cause problems for students in the exam.
  - vocabulary activities and exercises for the vocabulary you need to know for the exam. When you see this symbol ⊙ by a vocabulary exercise, the exercise focuses on words which First for Schools candidates often confuse or use wrongly in the exam.
- **Six unit reviews.** These contain exercises which revise the grammar and vocabulary in each unit.
- **Speaking and Writing reference section.** These explain the possible tasks students may have to do in the Speaking and Writing papers, and they give you examples and models together with additional advice on how best to approach these Speaking and Writing exam tasks.
- A **Grammar reference section** which clearly explains, unit by unit, all the main areas of grammar which you will need to know for the **B2 First for Schools exam**. There are also practice exercises for all grammar points.

Also available

- **Downloadable audio online** containing all the listening material for the 12 units of the Student's Book plus material for the 14 units of the Student's Book plus material for the Speaking Bank. The listening material is indicated by coloured icons 🎧(02) in the Student's Book.
- A **Teacher's Book** containing:
  - **Step-by-step guidance** for teaching activities in the Student's Book
  - A number of suggestions for **alternative treatments** of activities in the Student's Book listening material.
  - **14 Photocopiable wordlists** (one for each unit) containing vocabulary found in the units. Each vocabulary item in the wordlist is accompanied by a definition supplied by the corpus-informed Cambridge *Advanced Learner's Dictionary.*
  - **Access to extra photocopiable materials online** to practise and extend language abilities outside the requirements of the **B2 First for Schools exam**.
- A Student's **Workbook** containing:
  - 14 Units for homework and self-study. Each unit contains further exam-style exercise to practise the Reading and Use of English, Listening, Speaking and Writing skills needed in the **B2 First for Schools exam**. In addition, they provide further practice of grammar and vocabulary, which also use information about common First for Schools candidate errors from the Cambridge Learner Corpus ⊙ .
- **Downloadable audio online** containing all the listening material for the workbook.
- **A Test Generator** containing:
  - **A Grammar and Vocabulary Test** at standard and plus levels of each of the 14 units in the Student's Book.
  - Three **Term Tests** including grammar, vocabulary and First for Schools Reading and Use of English, Writing, Speaking and Listening exam tasks.
  - An **End of Year Test** including grammar, vocabulary and First for Schools Reading and Use of English, Writing, Speaking and Listening exam tasks.

B2 First for Schools content and overview

Part/Timing	Content	Test focus
Reading and Use of English 1 hour 15 minutes	**Part 1** A modified cloze text containing eight gaps and followed by eight multiple-choice items **Part 2** A modified open cloze text containing eight gaps **Part 3** A text containing eight gaps. Each gap corresponds to a word. The stems of the missing words are given beside the text and must be changed to form the missing word. **Part 4** Six separate questions, each with a lead-in sentence and a gapped second sentence to be completed in two to five words, one of which is given as a 'key word' **Part 5** A text followed by six multiple-choice questions **Part 6** A text from which six sentences have been removed and placed in a jumbled order after the text. A seventh sentence, which does not need to be used, is also included. **Part 7** A text, or several short texts, preceded by ten multiple-matching questions	In tasks 1–4 candidates are expected to demonstrate the ability to apply their knowledge of the language system by completing the first four tasks. In tasks 5–7 candidates are also expected to show understanding of specific information, text organisation features, tone, and text structure.
Writing 1 hour 20 minutes	**Part 1** One compulsory essay question presented through a rubric and short notes **Part 2** Candidates choose one task from a choice of four questions. The task types are: • an essay • an article • a letter or email • a review • a story • a task based on a set text	Candidates are expected to be able to write using different degrees of formality and different functions: advising, comparing, describing, explaining, expressing opinions, justifying, persuading, recommending and suggesting.
Listening Approximately 40 minutes	**Part 1** A series of eight short unrelated extracts from monologues or exchanges between interacting speakers. There is one three-option multiple-choice question per extract. **Part 2** A short talk or lecture on a topic, with a sentence- completion task which has ten items **Part 3** Five short related monologues, with five multiple- matching questions **Part 4** An interview or conversation, with seven multiple- choice questions	Candidates are expected to be able to show understanding of attitude, detail, function, genre, gist, main idea, opinion, place, purpose, situation, specific information, relationship, topic, agreement, etc.
Speaking 14 minutes	**Part 1** A conversation between the examiner (the 'interlocutor') and each candidate (spoken questions) **Part 2** An individual 'long turn' for each candidate, with a brief response from the second candidate (visual and written stimuli, with spoken instructions) **Part 3** A discussion question with five written prompts **Part 4** A discussion on topics related to Part 3 (spoken questions)	

1 A family affair

Starting off

1 Work in pairs. Discuss these questions.

- Which of the activities in the photos look the most fun?
- Write a list of five activities you enjoy doing with your family and a list of five activities you enjoy doing with your friends. How different are the two lists? Why do you think this is?

Listening Part 1

- In Listening Part 1, you listen to people talking in eight different situations, which may be either conversations between two or more people, or just one person speaking.

- You answer one question for each situation by choosing A, B or C. You hear each piece twice.

Exam info

1 Work in pairs. You will hear people talking in eight different situations. Before you listen, read questions 1–8 and underline the main idea in each. The first one has been done for you.

1 You hear part of a conversation between friends.
The boy says <u>the reason his father cooks most of the time</u> is because

  A the boy doesn't like exotic food.
  B the boy has too much school work.
  C the boy doesn't know what ingredients to buy.

2 You hear part of a conversation between friends.
The girl says that she enjoys spending weekends with her family because

  A her mother spends a long time researching places to visit.
  B her mother often chooses entertaining activities to do at the weekend.
  C her parents allow her to relax at home.

3 You hear a girl talking to her brother on the phone. What has her brother done to annoy her?
- **A** He hasn't done something he agreed to do.
- **B** He has bought the wrong present.
- **C** He has forgotten to buy a card.

4 You hear a boy taking part in a class discussion. His relationship with his brother
- **A** was surprisingly better in the past.
- **B** was bad because they argued.
- **C** improved because of their parents' actions.

5 You hear a girl talking to a friend. She says her sister didn't tell her mum that she had got two new kittens because
- **A** her mother doesn't like cats.
- **B** her room was too small for kittens.
- **C** her mother thought that one cat was enough.

6 You hear a boy leaving a message on his mother's phone. He is calling his mother because he wants her to
- **A** tell his relatives that he can't see them tonight.
- **B** allow him to stay at his friend's house.
- **C** help him with his project.

7 You hear an interview with a young chess champion. She says that the main reason for her success is that
- **A** her father gave her a chess set when she was young.
- **B** she has been very lucky.
- **C** her family have helped her.

8 You hear a boy talking to a friend. Why did the boy go to Denmark last summer?
- **A** He likes trying new things.
- **B** He always spends his holidays there.
- **C** The climate is better there.

2 Listen and choose the best answer (A, B or C).

02

3 Work in pairs. Correct the mistakes in questions 1–6.
1. How often you do the cooking?
2. You usually spend your weekends with your family?
3. You have yet managed to get a present?
4. Parents should limit the amount of time their children spend in front of a screen?
5. How much pets you say you had at home?
6. How you have become so successful?

Vocabulary
Phrasal verbs

1 Match the phrasal verbs (1–12) from Listening Part 1 to their definitions (a–l).

1. chill out *c*
2. come up with
3. set off
4. work (something) out
5. rely/depend on (someone)
6. fall out with (someone)
7. try (something) out
8. hit it off
9. look out for (someone/something)
10. take after (someone)
11. look up to (someone)
12. look back at (something)

a. have an argument with someone
b. immediately like each other and become friendly
c. relax and rest
d. experiment with an idea
e. be able to trust someone to do something
f. find an answer to something
g. respect or admire an older person
h. start a journey
i. think of (an idea or plan)
j. think about something in the past
k. try to notice
l. be like a parent or older sibling

2 Complete the sentences with a phrasal verb from Exercise 1 in the correct form.

1. I used to .... with my cousins all the time when I was younger, mostly because I didn't agree with their opinions, but now I'm a bit older we've started to really .... as we seem to understand each other better.

2. My mother is a really good artist. I've always .... her because I've always known she's talented. I really hope I .... her so that I can make a living out of art too.

3. I know I can .... Martin if I've got a problem because he always .... good suggestions.

4. When I think about my childhood, I .... all the silly things I did, but at least I now know what to .... so that I can avoid making the same mistakes.

5. My friend loves the weekend because she can get up late and just .... On weekday mornings, on the other hand, she's up at 7 am as she has to .... for school soon after that.

6. When Tomas has a problem, he often .... a few ideas before he finds the correct solution. It doesn't matter what the situation is, he usually .... it .... in the end.

Reading and Use of English   Part 6

1   Work in pairs. You are going to read an article giving advice to teenagers about how to get on better with their siblings (brothers and sisters). Before you read, write these adjectives in the correct column below.

> ~~caring~~ cheeky childish cooperative
> critical energetic enthusiastic hardworking
> irritating mature organised patient
> reliable responsible self-confident sensitive
> sympathetic thoughtful

usually positive	usually negative
caring	

2   Add one of these prefixes *dis-*, *im-*, *in-*, *ir-*, *un-* to each of the words to make opposites.

> ~~cooperative~~ *uncooperative* critical enthusiastic
> mature organised reliable responsible
> sensitive sympathetic

3   Work in pairs. Which of the adjectives in Exercise 1 do you think typically describe older siblings in relation to younger siblings? Why? Which describe younger siblings in relation to older siblings? Why?

4   Work in groups.

- Make a list of things teenage children sometimes say about their siblings.

  He's really irritating!

  My parents always praise her.

- Discuss what you can do to live happily with your brothers and sisters.

  Be kind to them and try to be cooperative.

- In Reading and Use of English Part 6, you read a text of 500–600 words with six gaps where sentences have been removed.
- You choose one sentence from a list of seven sentences (A–G) for each gap; there is one sentence you will not need.

Exam advice

5   Read the article opposite carefully, ignoring the spaces, and make a note of the main idea of each paragraph.

First paragraph:

Getting on with your siblings can be difficult, but it is possible to have a good relationship.

6   Six sentences have been removed from the article. Choose from the sentences (A–G) the one which fits each gap (1–6). There is one extra sentence which you do not need.

Use the underlined words in the sentences and in the text to help you.

A   It is also crucial that you are sensitive to the feelings of your siblings too.

B   Your siblings need to learn to take responsibility if they have done something wrong.

C   These arrangements will hopefully make both of you more cheerful.

D   It is only natural that these developments will affect your feelings towards members of your family.

E   But you should try not to let incidents like these have too big an effect on your relationship.

F   Indeed, it could seem impossible to imagine that you could ever be friends.

G   This could be watching a series on television, joining an exercise class or even preparing a family meal.

FROM WORST ENEMIES TO BEST FRIENDS

Everybody feels irritated by their siblings from time to time. Maybe your younger brother shows off and behaves in an immature way when you invite your friends to your house. Or perhaps your hardworking older sister gets a lot of praise from your parents, making you feel like you are not trying hard enough. At times, your brother or sister can feel like your worst enemy. **1** But your relationship can improve greatly with a bit of effort and understanding.

Sibling relationships can be especially difficult for teenagers, who are experiencing many changes to their preferences and personality. **2** For example, you may now find some of the activities that you used to enjoy doing with your younger brother childish or a waste of time. At times, the age difference can feel bigger than it really is, and this can have a negative effect on your relationship.

One way to solve this problem is to make sure you continue to include your brother or sister in your day-to-day life. Find an activity that you think you will both enjoy and suggest that you do it together. **3** If you do this activity regularly, you will soon remember how much fun it can be to spend time together, and you will start to get on better with each other. This can take some time, so it is important to be patient and enthusiastic.

Of course, it is perfectly normal for brothers and sisters to fall out with one another over small things. When you live together, it is only natural that you will get on each other's nerves from time to time. For example, if your younger sister is always borrowing your clothes without your permission and then loses or damages them, then of course it is your right to be annoyed with her. **4** It is important to learn to forgive your siblings for this kind of behaviour, just as you would forgive your close friends.

In situations like these, it is really important to let your sibling know how you feel. Rather than insulting

your sister when she takes your things, tell her that it makes you feel angry, and that you would feel much happier if she asked you first. **5** Your older brother may be more popular with your parents for his academic achievements, but he may also feel sad that he is not so popular with you. By making an effort to understand each other's feelings, your relationship will quickly improve.

Finally, it is important to learn how to compromise. It is understandable that you may not want to lend your favourite jumper to your unreliable sister, but maybe you could offer her a less valuable alternative item of clothing. Or if your brother likes to spend all his free time watching football and you find it boring, you could suggest a different sport that you follow regularly together. **6** And if you make the effort to make your sibling happy, he or she will do the same for you.

7 Work in groups of four. Two students should take the role of Brother/Sister A and two students should take the role of Brother/Sister B.

- Read the role-play cards and decide as a group what the missing / borrowed item is going to be.
- Work with the student who has the same role as you. Read your role and prepare what you are going to say.
- When you are ready, change partners and have your conversations.

Brother/Sister A

You recently received a special gift for your birthday. When you looked for it the other day, it had gone missing. You think that your brother/sister may have taken it. You are annoyed because

- they often take your things without asking
- this gift is very important to you as it is something that you had wanted for a long time.

Have a conversation with your brother/sister. Find out what happened and decide how to avoid this situation in the future.

Brother/Sister B

You recently borrowed something belonging to your brother/sister without asking them. You sometimes do this because your brother/sister never lets you borrow their things.

Have a conversation with your brother/sister. Explain what happened and discuss how to avoid this situation in the future.

Grammar

Present perfect simple and continuous

▶ **Page 162 Grammar reference**

1 Look at the pairs of sentences in *italics* and answer the questions that follow.

1 a *I've broken my personal record playing virtual tennis.*
  b *I've been playing virtual tennis all evening.*

  Which sentence (**a** or **b**) talks about …
  1 the result of an activity?
  2 the length of an activity?

2 a *I've been learning how to bake bread.*
  b *I've phoned her more than six times, but she never answers the phone.*

  Which sentence (**a** or **b**) talks about …
  1 how many times something has been repeated?
  2 changes or developments which are not finished?

3 a *I've been helping my mum while her assistant is on holiday.*
  b *We've lived in this house since I was a small child.*

  Which sentence (**a** or **b**) talks about something which is …
  1 temporary?
  2 permanent?

2 Complete the sentences with the present perfect simple or continuous form of the verbs in brackets.

1 I *'ve been visiting* (visit) friends, so I haven't spoken to my parents yet today.
2 My mum .... (ask) me to tidy my room several times.
3 I .... (clean) the kitchen, so what would you like me to do next?
4 Our neighbour .... (play) the violin for the last three hours and it's driving me mad!
5 Congratulations! You .... (pass) the exam with really high marks!
6 Adriana doesn't know many people in our town yet. She .... (only live) here for a few weeks.
7 We .... (spend) every summer in Crete since I was a child, so it'll be sad if we don't go there this year.
8 I'm really tired because I .... (cook) all day!

3 Students often make mistakes with the present perfect simple and continuous. Correct the underlined verb which is wrong in each sentence.

1 I <u>was</u> interested in it since I <u>saw</u> a film about it.

have been ✓

2 In these last three weeks, I <u>learned</u> so many interesting things which I <u>didn't know</u> how to do before.

3 This <u>isn't</u> the first time I <u>fix</u> the brakes on my bike.

4 My name <u>is</u> Hannah and I <u>play</u> tennis for three years.

5 Since I <u>started</u> the project, I <u>had been doing</u> research on someone famous from my country.

6 They <u>had been talking</u> about it for weeks, but nothing <u>has been done</u> up to now.

7 Vicky and Kostas <u>are</u> friends for many years. They actually <u>met</u> at primary school.

Reading and Use of English   Part 2

Exam info

- In Reading and Use of English Part 2, you read a text of 150–160 words with eight gaps where words have been removed. You write one word in each gap. You are given an example (0).

1 Work in pairs. You are going to read an article about how teenagers get and manage their money. Before you read, match the verbs (1–7) to the nouns (a–g) to make phrases related to getting and managing money. Some verbs may be used with more than one noun.

1	open	a	a budget
2	get	b	a bank account
3	set	c	pocket money
4	buy	d	essential items
5	receive	e	bills
6	make	f	a part-time job
7	pay	g	choices

2 Work in groups. Discuss these questions.

- Which of the phrases in Exercise 1 are related to getting money? Which are related to managing money?
- Which of the things in Exercise 1 have you done, or do you do?

I do housework every week to get pocket money from my parents.

3 Read the text quickly. How do teenagers get and manage their money?

4 Think of the word which best fits each gap. Use only one word in each gap. Make sure that you spell the word correctly.

How do you manage your money?

How (0) ....*do*........ young people manage their money? A recent survey asked teenagers (1) .... their money comes from and about their spending habits. Just over 80% of the teenagers surveyed received regular pocket money (2) .... their parents. About half of these had to (3) .... housework in return for their pocket money. Just under 10% received no money but said that their parents bought (4) .... essential items, such as clothes. A further 12% chose (5) .... get a part-time job. Reasons (6) .... seeking employment included having more money to spend, saving up for a large purchase such (7) .... a car and wanting to be financially independent; that is to say, to make their own money. When asked about (8) .... spending habits, about half of the teenagers surveyed said that they spent all their money each month. A quarter opened a bank account and saved a set amount each month and 10% set a monthly budget.

5 Now check or complete your answers by using these clues.

1 an adverb used to describe places
2 This preposition tells us who gives teenagers pocket money.
3 Which verb do we use with *housework*?
4 a pronoun which tells us who the parents buy everything for
5 a preposition often used before the infinitive form of a verb
6 a preposition used with *reason* and often followed by the gerund (-ing) form of a verb
7 This preposition is used with *such* to mean *for example*.
8 Whose spending habits did the survey ask about?

6 Work in pairs. Is what the text says about how teenagers get and manage their money true in your country as well?

Vocabulary

Collocations with *make* and *do*

1 Put the words and phrases in the box into the third column of the table.

an activity an appointment an arrangement
the bed business a change a choice
the cleaning a course a decision an effort
an excuse (an) exercise a favour friends
homework housework an impression a job
a mistake money a noise a phone call a plan
progress a promise the shopping (a) sport work

verb	definition	common collocation
make	to create or produce something	*an appointment*
do	to perform an activity or job	*an activity*

2 Students often confuse *make* and *do*. Complete the sentences with the correct form of *make* or *do*.

1 According to a recent study of teenagers, half of them do not .... housework for pocket money.
2 Many teenagers get a part-time job because they want to .... money and be financially independent.
3 If you want to .... me a favour, could you .... the shopping for tonight's dinner?
4 A few changes have been .... to the computer game and the company say they'll try to avoid .... similar mistakes in the future.
5 People who .... language courses tend to .... a lot of friends at the same time.
6 I .... a big effort to be helpful around the house last week.

3 Work in pairs. Each choose five words/phrases from the table in Exercise 1 and think about when you did or made these things. Then take turns to tell your partner about them.

I had to make a choice between going away with my family or doing a language course during the summer. Although it was a difficult choice to make, I decided to do the language course and miss my holiday.

Speaking Part 1

▶ Page 192 Speaking bank

Exam info

• In Speaking Part 1, the examiner asks you questions about yourself. These may include questions about your life or studies, your plans for the future, your family, your interests, etc.

1 Look at these two questions, which the examiner may ask you in Speaking Part 1.

Examiner: **a** Where are you from?
b What do you like about the place where you live?

1 Which question asks you to give your personal **opinion**? Which asks you for personal **information**?

2 Which question needs only a fairly short answer? Which question needs a longer answer?

2 Listen to Tania and Peter answering the questions above. Who do you think gives the best answers? Why?

03

3 In the exam, you will get higher marks if you use a range of appropriate vocabulary. Work in pairs. Which of these phrases can you use to describe the place where you live?

a a large industrial city
b a relaxed atmosphere
c lively cafés
d in the middle of some great countryside
e a pleasant residential district
f good live music venues
g plenty of sports facilities
h a lot of historic buildings
i lots of attractive buildings
j some pretty good shopping
k a busy city centre
l wonderful beaches nearby

4 Which of the phrases (a–l) can you use with these sentence openings? In one case, both are correct.

It is … *a large industrial city*
It has …

5 Pronunciation: word stress (1)

In the Speaking paper, you will get higher marks if your pronunciation is clear. In words of more than one syllable, one syllable is stressed more than the others. If you stress the wrong syllable, the word becomes difficult to understand. In dictionaries the stressed syllable is marked like this: resi'dential.

5.1 Underline the stressed syllable in each of these words and phrases.

industrial
relaxed atmosphere
wonderful
facilities
historic

5.2 Listen and check your answers. Then work in pairs and take turns to read the words aloud.

04

6 How can you extend your answers to the two questions below? Think about Tania's extended answers you heard in Exercise 2, and use the frameworks given here to help you.

Examiner: Where are you from?
Student: I'm from … It's a … which …

Examiner: What do you like about the place where you live?
Student: Well, it's …, so …, but … and … Also …

7 Work in pairs. Take turns to ask and answer the questions in Exercise 6. Use some of the vocabulary from Exercise 3.

8 Read questions 1–8. Think about how you can give extended answers. Then work in pairs and take turns to ask and answer the questions.

1 Do you come from a large family?
2 What do you like about being part of a large/small family?
3 Who does the housework in your family?
4 What things do you enjoy doing with your family?
5 Tell me about your friends.
6 What things do you enjoy doing with your friends?
7 Who are more important to you: your family or your friends?
8 Do you have similar interests to your parents?

Writing Part 1
An essay

▶ **Page 202 Writing bank**

- In Writing Part 1, you write an essay in which you discuss a question or topic. After the essay topic, there are some notes which you must use.
- You must also include an idea of your own.
- You must write between 140 and 190 words.

Exam advice

1 Read the writing task and note the points you must deal with.

In your English class, you have been talking about how teenagers manage their money.

Now your English teacher has asked you to write an essay.

Write your essay using all the notes and give reasons for your point of view.

> **'It is beneficial for teenagers to receive pocket money from their parents.'**
>
> **Do you agree?**
>
> **Notes**
> Write about:
>
> 1. reasons why receiving pocket money is beneficial for teenagers
> 2. reasons why receiving pocket money may not be good for teenagers
> 3. .... (your own idea)

2 Work in groups. Discuss the task and try to find two or three things you can say about each of the notes 1–3.

3 Read a student's answer to the task, ignoring the spaces. Which of her ideas do you agree with, and which do you disagree with?

(1) .... most teenagers can rely on their parents for the things they need, learning how to manage money is an important skill. Many adults believe that teenagers simply waste their pocket money on clothes, computer games and fast food. (2) .... , I believe that parents can teach teenagers to manage their money effectively by giving them regular pocket money.

Some parents prefer to buy their children everything they need rather than give them their own money. It is true that young people may not spend their money on sensible things, (3) .... parents may know better what they need, but in my view, young people need to be given the independence to make their own choices.

People often argue that young people will find it difficult to make their money last for a whole month. (4) .... , if parents help their children to set a budget, and are strict about not giving them extra money, they will soon learn to manage their money sensibly in my opinion. They are likely to be more financially responsible when they are adults and will be less likely to borrow money from their parents.

For all these reasons, I think that teenagers benefit more from receiving pocket money from their parents than if their parents buy them everything they need.

4 Complete this plan for the student's essay by matching the notes (a–d) to the paragraphs (1–4).

Paragraph 1: introduction: ....
Paragraph 2: ....
Paragraph 3: ....
Paragraph 4: conclusion: ....

a Who should decide what teenagers need and why?
b Parents can help children to manage their money and why this is good
c Most beneficial to give teenagers pocket money
d Common belief that teenagers waste money + my opinion

5 It is important to express your opinions in an essay. Find four phrases which the student uses to introduce her personal opinions.

6 When you write an essay, you should try to present contrasting points of view. Complete the student's essay by writing *although, however, on the other hand* or *whereas* in each of the spaces 1–4.

7 Complete the sentences with *although, however, on the other hand* or *whereas*. In some cases, more than one answer may be possible.

1 Adults tend to worry more about their health, ... young people are more concerned about money.
2 .... I am happy to do some of the cooking, I don't want to do it all.
3 My mum and dad have similar tastes. .... , mine are completely different.
4 .... my parents give me a lot of freedom, I would prefer to have even more independence.
5 Young people often spend many hours a week on their social life. .... , older people are often too busy.
6 I enjoy making beds. .... , I'm not at all keen on doing the ironing.

8 Write your own answer to the writing task in Exercise 1. Before you write, use the notes you made in Exercise 2 to write a plan. Write between 140 and 190 words.

• Use the student's essay as a model, but express your own ideas and the ideas which came up during your discussion.

2 Leisure and pleasure

Starting off

1 Which of the activities in the photos have you done?

2 Which do you think is ...

- the most enjoyable?
- the cheapest?
- the healthiest?
- the most relaxing?
- the least active?
- the best to do with friends?
- the most popular among young people?

3 Which would you like to try? Why?

Listening Part 2

- In Listening Part 2, you hear a talk or lecture by one speaker.
- You listen and complete ten sentences with a word or short phrase.
- You write the actual words you hear and you must spell them correctly. You don't change them in any way.
- You hear the recording twice.

Exam info

1 Work in groups. You are going to hear a professional footballer talking about her career. Before you listen, complete the sentences about professional sports players with words from the box.

> burn   chase   depend on
> doubt   influence   perform
> regret   share   train

1 In team sports, players need to learn to trust and .... their teammates.

2 They often .... a lot of energy playing sport, and so they must be careful about their diet.

3 Sportspeople should try not to .... missed opportunities or any bad decisions they make during matches and competitions.

4 Professional sportspeople .... every day to maintain their peak of physical fitness.

5 Players sometimes start to .... their ability and it's important that they overcome this.

6 Athletes need to prepare carefully so they are ready to .... at their best in an important competition.

7 In some sports, players need to .... both opponents and the ball for a long time and this requires high levels of fitness.

8 To win, players need to know what they can do to .... the game, especially if they are losing.

9 A lot of sportspeople say that the thing they like most is that they .... their experiences with their teammates and this makes their relationship with them stronger.

2 Could you be a professional sportsperson? Look again at the sentences above. Which would be easiest or most difficult for you to do? Why?

3 Work in pairs. Read the listening task text below. What type of information do you need to complete each sentence?

Professional Footballer

As a young girl Clare played in the **(1)** .... with her brother and some friends.

She used her **(2)** .... and skills because she wasn't very tall or strong.

At school she enjoyed playing in matches, but also liked **(3)** ....

The scout from the academy who watched her school team was hoping to **(4)** .... new players.

During the game Clare was worried that she wouldn't be **(5)** .... for the academy.

She realised she could be a **(6)** .... when she joined the academy.

People think that women's football is more **(7)** .... than men's because it isn't as fast.

Clare thinks that the lack of **(8)** .... is an issue for women's football.

Clare hopes that, with increased **(9)** .... for female players, people will see football as a game for everybody.

She says she is fortunate not to have had many **(10)** .... in her career.

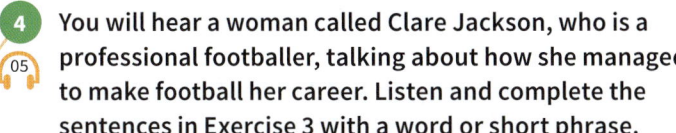

4 You will hear a woman called Clare Jackson, who is a professional footballer, talking about how she managed to make football her career. Listen and complete the sentences in Exercise 3 with a word or short phrase.

5 Work in groups. Discuss these questions.
1 Which sports do you find …
   • good for both girls and boys?
   • most complicated to learn?
2 Are there any sports you would like to try?
3 Do you have a hobby you would like to make into a career like Clare did?

Grammar
Making comparisons

▶ **Page 163 Grammar reference**

1 Students often make mistakes with comparisons. Choose the correct phrase in *italics* in these extracts from Listening Part 2.

1 At first it was difficult for me as my brother and his friends were bigger and *more strong / stronger.*
2 That probably helped me to develop into a *much better / more better* player.
3 When I played for my school team, I soon realised I was *more influential / most influential* in almost every game I played in than many of my teammates.
4 In fact my performance was *better / as good* as I could have hoped for.
5 I find it a bit irritating and confusing to be honest, but it makes me *much motivated / more motivated* to do well.
6 People say that the women's game is *more limited / the most limited* when compared to the men's game.
7 I've been *luckier / more lucky* than many female players.
8 It really is the *most amazing / amazingest* thing that's happened to me.

2 Complete the sentences with the correct form of the adjective in brackets.

1 There are lots of ways to keep fit, but I think .... (healthy) of all is zumba.
2 Playing chess is .... (cheap) than playing video games.
3 Team games are .... (sociable) than cycling because you meet and speak to a lot of people.
4 Chess is .... (hard) than most games I know.
5 For me, parachute jumping is the .... (thrilling) of all sports.
6 Speaking for myself, I find team sports the .... (not interesting).
7 Mountain biking is .... (good) for getting exercise than most sports.

3 Complete the sentences with your own ideas.

1 Learning to ride a bicycle is not as …
2 In team games, the most …
3 I'm much better at …
4 My friends are far …
5 Golf is not nearly …

Reading and Use of English Part 1

1 You are going to read an extract from a blog by a teenager about ice skating. Before you read, work in pairs. What do you think people most enjoy about ice skating?

2 Read the extract quickly to find out how the writer became interested in ice skating.

Ice skating
– my passion

I first (0) ___A___ ice skating when I was eight years old. I remember seeing a poster at my local leisure centre (1) _____ ice-skating lessons and begged my dad to (2) _____ me have a go. He agreed (3) _____ I promised not to break any bones, and the following week, I turned up at the ice rink for my first lesson. I remember feeling a bit unsteady at first, but I soon got used to the ice underneath my feet and was thrilled by the (4) _____ of sliding across the ice. Later, my instructor taught me how to do different turns and jumps. I was (5) _____ of falling at first, but I picked it up quite quickly and then it felt so exciting! I soon became much more confident about (6) _____ risks. Now I train at the ice rink twice a week and have taken part in several national contests. Next year, I am hoping to (7) _____ an international event in Switzerland. I have also kept the promise I (8) _____ to my dad – I have never fallen and injured myself while ice skating!

Exam advice

• In Reading and Use of English Part 1, you read a text of 150–160 words.

• You fill in the gaps with the best option, A, B, C or D.

3 Read the extract again and decide which answer (A, B, C or D) best fits each gap. There is an example at the beginning (0).

0 **A** took up	**B** played	**C** thought	**D** came
1 **A** taking	**B** advertising	**C** giving	**D** teaching
2 **A** allow	**B** let	**C** permit	**D** enable
3 **A** as long as	**B** as soon as	**C** as far as	**D** as much as
4 **A** emotion	**B** attention	**C** feeling	**D** touch
5 **A** worried	**B** alarmed	**C** anxious	**D** scared
6 **A** doing	**B** taking	**C** making	**D** having
7 **A** take	**B** make	**C** enter	**D** participate
8 **A** made	**B** did	**C** said	**D** told

4 Work in pairs. Choose a hobby or sport, then prepare your roles and act out the conversation.

Student A
You are a teenager. You want to take up a new hobby, but you need your parents to agree and to give you some money to have lessons. Think of reasons why you want to take up this hobby and try to persuade your mother or father to give you permission.

Student B
You are one of Student A's parents. You don't want him/her to take up this hobby. Think of reasons why he/she shouldn't do it and try to persuade him/her not to.

Vocabulary
Phrasal verbs and expressions

1 Match the phrasal verbs and expressions from the ice-skating blog (1–8) to their definitions (a–h).

1 take up (line 1)
2 have a go (line 3)
3 turn up (line 4)
4 get used to (line 5)
5 pick something up (line 7)
6 take risks (line 8)
7 take part in (line 9)
8 keep a promise (line 10)

a learn how to do something
b do what you said you would do
c be part of an event
d start doing an activity for the first time
e arrive
f try something
g do something even though something bad might happen because of it
h feel more comfortable in a new situation

2 Complete the sentences with a phrasal verb or expression from Exercise 1 in the correct form.

1 I'd never do something like sky-diving because I don't enjoy ....
2 I found playing the violin difficult at first, but my teacher says that I am .... really quickly.

3 Hans let me .... on his new bike, and now I want to get one myself!
4 I didn't like my new haircut at first, but I am starting to .... it.
5 When Diego finally .... at the gym, it was almost closing time.
6 People won't trust you unless you can .... and do what you say you're going to do.
7 I need to get more exercise, so I'm thinking of .... jogging.
8 I really enjoyed .... the school quiz even though our team didn't win.
9 I've never sung in a choir before, but I'll .... if it's just for fun.
10 You don't need to bring any special equipment for the yoga class – just .... on time.

3 Work in pairs. Take turns to answer these questions. Make a note of your partner's answers.

- What new skills have you picked up recently?
- What new activity would you most like to have a go at?
- Do you enjoy taking risks? Why? / Why not?
- Are you good at keeping promises?
- What new situations have you had to get used to in the past?

Now work with another pair and tell them about your partner.

Grammar
Adjectives with -ed and -ing

▶ **Page 164 Grammar reference**

1 Look at the sentence from the blog on page 20 and answer the questions.

> I was **scared** of falling at first, but I picked it up quite quickly and then it felt so **exciting**!

1 Which of the words in **bold** refers to how the boy *felt*?

2 Which of the words in **bold** refers to what *made him feel* like that?

2 Students often confuse adjectives with -ed and adjectives with -ing. Choose the correct adjective in *italics* in these sentences.

1 When we went to Disneyland, I think we found it more *amused / amusing* than our parents.

2 It can be very *irritated / irritating* when friends arrive late for a film.

3 You will never get *bored / boring* at night in Berlin because the nightlife is wonderful.

4 It's very *annoyed / annoying* when people eat crisps in the cinema.

5 The situation was very *embarrassed / embarrassing* for me and I felt uncomfortable.

6 I was really *excited / exciting* and wanted to see as much of the city as possible.

3 Use the word given in capitals at the end of the sentences to form a word with -ed or -ing that fits the space.

1 We were quite .... by the unfriendly attitude of the other students.
PUZZLE

2 It's very .... to be able to apply things we learn in the classroom to our free-time activities.
MOTIVATE

3 Anita looked quite .... when she left the police station.
WORRY

4 The film was not particularly ....
AMUSE

5 We were absolutely .... by the time we got to the top of the mountain.
EXHAUST

6 Everyone watches Pietro at parties because he's an .... dancer.
ASTONISH

7 My exam results were very .... I'd worked really hard and I thought I had done better.
DISAPPOINT

8 All the boys loved that .... car chase at the end of the film.
THRILL

9 Tomas sounded really .... on the phone. He's lost his place in the first team.
DEPRESS

Reading and Use of English Part 4

- In Reading and Use of English Part 4, you complete six sentences with between two and five words so that they mean the same as the sentences printed before them.
- You use the word given in CAPITALS without changing it in any way.

Exam info

1 Complete the second sentence so that it has a similar meaning to the first sentence, using the word given. Do not change the word given. You must use between two and five words, including the word given.

0 He doesn't enjoy watching TV as much as watching films.

MORE

He likes watching films *more than* watching TV.

1 It is easier to learn English than most other languages.

ONE

English is .... languages to learn.

2 Joanna finds swimming more boring than running.

NOT

For Joanna, swimming is .... running.

3 It was the strangest game I have ever seen.

SUCH

I have never seen .... game.

4 Basketball is a lot more popular than football in my country.

NEARLY

Football is .... popular as basketball in my country.

5 In general, ice skating is a lot more expensive than rollerblading.

FAR

In general, rollerblading is .... ice skating.

6 It took Marek longer to cycle home than Simone.

MORE

Simone cycled home .... Marek.

4 You will hear a girl talking about one of the experiences a–g. Listen and decide which experience she is talking about.

06

a She rode a motorbike for the first time.
b She was punished for something she didn't do.
c She had to study all weekend for an exam.
d She broke a bone.
e She was trapped in a lift.
f She won a competition.
g She did a parachute jump.

5 Listen again. Which adjectives does she use to describe these things?

06

1 the whole experience: *amazing*
2 how she felt after studying: .... and ....
3 how she felt about her best friend's suggestion: ....
4 the thought of breaking a bone: ....
5 how she felt in the plane: .... and ....
6 the jump itself: ....

6 Work in pairs. Look at the experiences a–g in Exercise 4. Have you done any of these things or have any of them happened to you? How did you feel about them? Take turns to describe your experience.

Speaking Part 2

▶ **Page 194 Speaking bank**

- In Speaking Part 2, you and the other candidate speak on your own for a minute each.
- You compare two photos which the examiner gives you.
- You answer a question connected with both photos.
- You answer a question quite briefly about your partner's photos.

Exam info

1 Work in pairs. Look at the examiner's instructions and the question and photos below. Then discuss what you can say to compare the photos.

Examiner: Here are your photographs. They show people doing different activities in their free time. I'd like you to compare the photographs, and say how you think the people can benefit from spending their free time doing these different activities.

How can the people benefit from spending their free time doing these different activities?

Photograph 1

Photograph 2

2 Listen to an examiner giving this task to a candidate called Bruno. According to Bruno, how can people benefit from each activity?

3 Listen again and tick this checklist.

Bruno	Yes	No
1 introduces the topic		
2 deals with each photo in turn		
3 describes each photo in detail		
4 refers to the first photo when talking about the second photo		
5 spends most of the time answering the printed question		
6 talks about things not connected with the question		
7 speaks until the examiner says 'Thank you'.		

4 Work in pairs. Listen again and complete the sentences from Bruno's answer which begin with these words and phrases.

1 I think they benefit from …
2 Firstly …
3 At the same time …
4 Also …
5 I think they also benefit because …

5 Which word(s) or phrase(s) (1–5) in Exercise 4 does Bruno use to:

a introduce his answer to the examiner's question?
b introduce the first point he wants to make?
c add additional points?

6 Which of these words/phrases could also be used for b and c in Exercise 5?

Besides   First of all   In addition
To start with   What is more

2

7 Pronunciation: sentence stress (1)

- We stress the words in sentences that we particularly want our listeners to hear, the words which carry the most meaning. These are usually nouns, verbs, adjectives or adverbs, not small grammar words like articles or prepositions.

7.1 Listen and underline the stressed words in these sentences.

1 Firstly, they're getting some exercise, which is always good for you.
2 It's great for your health and helps you to relax.
3 At the same time, they're having fun together …
4 … which is important because it builds up their social relationships and their friendships.
5 Also, it's good to see girls playing serious sports.
6 I think it goes against the idea that boys have better athletic ability than girls.

7.2 Work in pairs. Take turns to read the sentences aloud, paying attention to the stress.

7.3 Work in pairs. Take turns to read these extracts.

- Firstly, they're getting some exercise, which is always good for you. It's great for your health and helps you to relax.
- At the same time, they're having fun together, which is important because it builds up their social relationships and their friendships. Also, it's good to see girls playing serious sports. I think it goes against the idea that boys have better athletic ability than girls.

8 Change partners and take turns to do the Speaking Part 2 task in Exercise 1.

- Try to speak for a minute.
- Try to use some of the words and phrases from Exercise 4.
- Use your own ideas and Bruno's ideas.
- While you are listening to your partner, use the checklist in Exercise 3 and give feedback when your partner has finished.

9 Work in pairs and take turns to do this Speaking Part 2 task.

Examiner: The photographs show people doing different free-time activities. Compare the photographs, and say what you think the people enjoy about doing these different activities.

What do the people enjoy about doing these different activities?

Writing Part 2
An article

▶ **Page 206 Writing bank**

- In Writing Part 2 you do one writing task from a choice of four.
- The possible tasks are an article, a letter or email, a report, a review, or a story. The fourth task is always the set-book option.
- You must write between 140 and 190 words.

1 Look at this writing task and note the points you must write about.

> You have seen this announcement in an English-language magazine for teenagers.
>
> **A great way to spend your free time!**
>
> Tell us about a leisure-time activity you really enjoy.
> - How did you get started?
> - Why do you enjoy it so much?
>
> We will publish the most interesting articles in next month's issue.
>
> Write your **article**.

2 Work in pairs. Tell your partner about one of your free-time activities. While you are speaking, answer the questions in the writing task above.

3 Work in pairs. The article in the next column would lose marks in the exam because it is not divided into paragraphs.
1 Divide it into paragraphs.
2 Say what the main idea is in each paragraph.

Sailing
– a fun and exciting sport

I've always loved the sea, but I first experienced sailing last year. I went to stay with my aunt, who lives near the sea. She is a keen sailor and she suggested that I join the local sailing school. In the first lesson, I learnt how to steer the boat and some basic survival skills at sea. Although I found some things quite complicated at first, I soon mastered the basics. By the end of the course, I was quite a competent sailor. I really benefitted from meeting other people who were my age at the sailing club. When we became more experienced, we were allowed to take a small boat out on our own. It was really satisfying to take charge of the boat and we enjoyed being independent. It was a lot more difficult for us to sail when the weather was bad. I even fell in the water once, but it was very exciting trying to keep the boat under control in the rough sea. Despite the difficulties, I can't wait to go back there next summer. I love sailing because it's challenging and sociable.

4 You can write compound sentences by joining two sentences with *and*, *but* and *because*. Which two sentences are joined in these compound sentences?

1 I've always loved the sea, but I first experienced sailing last year.
2 She is a keen sailor and she suggested that I join the local sailing school.
3 It was really satisfying to take charge of the boat and we enjoyed being independent.
4 I even fell in the water once, but it was very exciting trying to keep the boat under control in the rough sea.
5 I love sailing because it's challenging and sociable.

5 Write compound sentences by joining these sentences with *and*, *but* and *because*. Use pronouns (*he*, *she*, *it*, etc.) to avoid repetition.

1 I'd like to learn to fly. I think learning to fly is too expensive.

   I'd like to learn to fly, but I think it's too expensive.

2 I got interested in flying when I was about 14. My father took me to an airshow.

3 My parents don't want me to fly. They think flying is dangerous.

4 One of my friends is learning to fly. My friend has asked me to come with him. My friend thinks I'd like flying.

6 You can write complex sentences by joining two sentences with words such as *when*, *who*, *which* and *that*. Write these complex sentences as two separate sentences.

1 I went to stay with my aunt, who lives near the sea.

   I went to stay with my aunt. My aunt lives near the sea.

2 I really benefitted from meeting other people who were my age at the sailing club.

3 When we became more experienced, we were allowed to take a small boat out on our own.

4 It was a lot more difficult for us to sail when the weather was bad.

7 Join these sentences using *when*, *who*, *which* and *that*.

1 I was 13. I started running seriously.

2 My uncle encouraged me. My uncle's a keen athlete.

3 I go running most days. I've finished school and done my homework.

4 Running is a sport. Running gets you really fit.

8 Join these sentences using *and*, *because*, *but*, *when*, *which* and *who*. Use pronouns (*he*, *she*, *it*, etc.) to avoid repetition.

1 I started windsurfing. I was 13. I was staying with friends by the sea.

2 One of my friends is a keen windsurfer. She encouraged me to start. She thought I would enjoy it.

3 I kept falling into the sea to start with. It was a fairly windy day. There were a lot of waves.

4 I didn't enjoy it at first. I had to concentrate quite hard. I carried on trying.

5 I started to windsurf quite fast. It was exciting. I started to find it quite enjoyable.

9 Find adjectives in the article which describe the following:

1 how the writer found learning to sail at first

2 the writer's ability to sail by the end of the sailing course

3 how the writer felt about the experience of sailing with friends

10 Complete the table with the words in the box.

> astonishing competitive delightful demanding
> depressing dreadful economical entertaining
> exhausting incredible irritating popular
> superb time-consuming tremendous unbelievable

feelings about an activity	the type of activity
astonishing	

11 You are going to write your own article to answer the writing task in Exercise 1. Before you write:

• decide on a title for your article which will encourage people to read it

• decide how many paragraphs you need, the subject of each paragraph and write a short plan

• think about some of the vocabulary you can use.

12 Write your article using between 140 and 190 words.

1 Vocabulary and grammar review

Vocabulary

1 Complete the sentences with adjectives from Exercises 1 and 2 on page 10, or their opposites. In some cases, more than one answer may be possible.

1 Hugo is very _thoughtful_ – he often helps his grandparents with the shopping.
2 My parents allow my brother to come home any time he likes because they know he is very ....
3 Pascale is very ...., so she's bound to finish her part of the project on time.
4 David is so .... that you can never trust him to do what he says he's going to do.
5 Melanie is very .... and not afraid of meeting new people.
6 I wouldn't have criticised you if I had known how .... you were!
7 Helen is very young, but she behaves in a .... and responsible way.
8 Luis is a very .... person, who is always trying new sports and activities.

2 Complete the sentences with a phrasal verb from page 9 in the correct form.

1 It's Toby's birthday next week. We need to .... some ideas for a present.
2 I can see the family resemblance. You've got your father's eyes – you really .... him, don't you?
3 Why are you standing by the window? – I'm .... the delivery person. I'm expecting an important package today.
4 I don't feel like doing much this weekend. I think that I'll just .... around the house.
5 We'll need to .... the new internet streaming service – I've heard it's much better than the others but I want to see it for myself before I pay for it.
6 I must apologise to my sister. We .... over something really small and had a massive argument. I hope she'll forgive me.

3 Complete the sentences with the correct form of *make* or *do*.

1 Could you .... me a favour and let me copy your notes from the last class?
2 Do you mind if I use your phone? I've got to .... an urgent phone call.
3 I'll .... the shopping on my way home this evening.
4 My mum's .... an English course in the evenings, and I sometimes help her with her homework.
5 I've got so much homework to .... that I can't come out with you tonight.
6 Marco has .... a big effort with his students, so I'm afraid he's a bit disappointed with their results.
7 Sarah wasn't enjoying the party, so she .... an excuse and left.
8 We phoned the police because our neighbours were .... too much noise.

Grammar

4 Complete the sentences with the present perfect simple or continuous form of the verbs in brackets. In some cases, both forms are possible.

1 I'm celebrating because my team .... (win) the league!
2 At last you .... (arrive) – we .... (expect) you for ages.
3 Of course I'm annoyed. I .... (spend) ages preparing for this party and no one .... (turn up) yet.
4 We .... (have) a really interesting time. Gavin .... (tell) us about his trip round the world. There are a few countries he still .... (not tell) us about, but I get the impression he .... (see) almost everything!
5 Kate .... (lose) weight recently because she .... (get) more exercise.
6 I wonder if Irina .... (finish) reading that book yet. I .... (wait) to read it for ages.
7 Tatiana is so greedy! She .... (eat) all the cakes and she .... (not leave) any for us.
8 Paolo .... (look) very tired recently. I think it's because he .... (study) too hard.

Vocabulary

1 Complete the sentences with a phrasal verb or expression from the Vocabulary on page 21 in the correct form.

1 If you can't .... , no one will ever trust you.
2 I just don't like ...., so I'd never get a motorbike.
3 Mario is thinking of .... jogging, as he doesn't feel he's getting enough exercise.
4 I thought learning Italian would be difficult, but when I moved to Bologna I soon .... it ....
5 We .... a 10 km run at the weekend, to raise money for the local hospital.
6 I can't work out how to solve this maths problem; would you like to .... and see if you can do it?

Grammar

2 Join the sentences to form compound and complex sentences. More than one answer may be possible.

1 Katya took up karate. She was seven years old. She was interested in karate.
2 Her father is a professional karate instructor. He taught her. She progressed quickly. She soon became junior regional champion.
3 She did karate with other children. The other children were the same age as her. None of them was as good as her. She felt dissatisfied.
4 Last year, she took part in the national championship. She didn't win. She was injured during one of the matches.
5 She hopes to become a professional karate instructor. She hopes to work in the same sports centre as her father. Her father has too many students.
6 Some of her father's students have been studying karate for several years. Her father thinks they would benefit from a different teacher. They are too familiar with his style of karate.

3 Complete the second sentence so that it has a similar meaning to the first sentence, using the word given. Do not change the word given. You must use between two and five words, including the word given.

1 This motorbike is not as noisy as my previous one.
MADE
My previous motorbike .... this one.
2 Small towns are safer than large cities.
NOT
Small towns .... as large cities.
3 No one in the team plays better than Gemma.
PLAYER
Gemma .... in the team.
4 She looks more relaxed than she did before the exam.
STRESSED
She does not look .... she did before the exam.
5 Tatiana does not speak nearly as clearly as Irina.
MUCH
Irina speaks .... Tatiana.
6 None of the other sofas in the shop are as comfortable as this one.
ANY
This sofa is .... the others in the shop.

Word formation

4 Use the word given in capitals at the end of each sentence to form a word that fits in the gap.

1 What an .... band! I never expected they'd be that good. **AMAZE**
2 They found the journey so .... that they fell asleep as soon as they arrived. **EXHAUST**
3 It's a .... problem – I don't really know what to do about it. **PUZZLE**
4 Jake felt .... that he wasn't picked to play in the match. **DISAPPOINT**
5 You can't expect children to work hard if they don't feel .... **MOTIVATE**
6 We were .... by the way the other team shouted at us. **ASTONISH**

3 Happy holidays?

Starting off

1 Work in pairs. Complete the table with the words and phrases in the box.

backpacking   a beach holiday   a camping holiday
at a campsite   a city break   in the city centre
a cruise   on a cruise ship   at a luxury hotel
meeting new people   in the mountains   relaxing
at the seaside   by the sea   seeing new places
a sightseeing tour   skiing   sunbathing
visiting monuments   walking and climbing
at a youth hostel

types of holiday	holiday locations and places to stay	holiday activities

2 Choose one or two of the photos. Discuss the different types of activities you could do on this type of holiday and say what the advantages and disadvantages of this type of holiday are.

Listening Part 3

1 You will hear five short extracts in which teenagers are talking about their best holiday ever. Before you listen, underline the main idea in each statement A–H.

A I wanted my own country to be more like this.

B I was surprised how much I liked some of the food.

C I didn't want to change our holiday plans.

D I went on my first holiday without my parents.

E I didn't know where this place was before I went there.

F I had been to this place before.

G I had no idea what this place would be like.

H I preferred this holiday because I went with my parents.

2 Now listen and choose from the list (A–H) in Exercise 1 what each speaker says about their holiday. Use the letters only once. There are three extra letters which you don't need to use.

Speaker 1 ☐
Speaker 2 ☐
Speaker 3 ☐
Speaker 4 ☐
Speaker 5 ☐

3 Work in groups. Discuss these questions.

- What was your best holiday ever?
- Why did you like it so much?

Grammar

Past simple, past continuous and *used to*

▶ **Page 165 Grammar reference**

1 Complete these extracts from Listening Part 3 with the correct form of the verbs in brackets. Then listen again to check your answers.

As we **(1)** .... (leave), they **(2)** .... (take) great delight in giving us each yet another present to take home with us.

Not many people from where I live **(3)** .... (visit) Cuba at that time, so I **(4)** .... (not know) what to expect.

I **(5)** .... (start) to doubt my decision while I **(6)** .... (wait) for my food to arrive.

As we **(7)** .... (ride) around the city, I suddenly **(8)** .... (think) to myself how much nicer it would be if more people did this back home.

While we **(9)** .... (travel) to the first island, I **(10)** .... (tell) him that we should perhaps just focus on fewer islands and spend more time on each.

2 Choose the correct option in *italics*.

1 When they *walked / were walking* home, they found a wallet with a huge amount of money in it!

2 When I was at primary school, I *was doing / used to do* about one hour's homework a day.

3 As soon as Mandy *was getting / got* Simon's text, she *was jumping / jumped* on her bike and *was riding / rode* round to his house to speak to him.

4 When I was younger, we *used to spend / were spending* our holidays in my grandparents' village.

5 Luckily, we *walked / were walking* past a shopping centre when the storm *began / was beginning*.

6 My mum *used to visit / was visiting* lots of exotic places when she *was / was being* a tour guide.

3 Students often make spelling mistakes when adding -ed to past tense verbs. Add -ed to each of these verbs.

> develop   enjoy   happen   mention
> occur   open   plan   prefer   stop
> study   travel   try

3

Vocabulary

travel, journey, trip and way

1 Students often confuse the words above. Look at these sentences from Listening Part 3 and complete the definitions below with *travel*, *journey*, *trip* or *way*.

- We did an amazing **journey** by train right through the Rocky Mountains in Canada.
- On our **way** there (to Cuba), we stopped in Toronto for a bonus day.
- I remember going on a school **trip** to Copenhagen a few years ago. We only stayed for a few days …
- I don't usually enjoy international **travel**, but this was definitely an exception.

travel, journey, trip or way?

A **(1)** .... is a journey in which you visit a place for a short time and come back again.

(2) '............................' refers only to the route that you take to get from one place to another.

The noun **(3)** '............................' is a general word which means the activity of travelling.

Use **(4)** '............................' to talk about when you travel from one place to another, usually by car, train or bus.

2 Choose the correct option in *italics*.

1 She met plenty of interesting people during her weekend *travel / trip* to Montreal.
2 We stopped at the supermarket on the *way / trip* to the beach to pick up some cold drinks.
3 My mum and dad have booked a *journey / trip* to Greece for our holidays this August.
4 My mum is away on a business *journey / trip*, so the house is really quiet at the moment.
5 People spend far more on foreign *travel / journeys* than they did 50 years ago.
6 The *travel / journey* to my village will take about three hours.
7 'Have a good *travel / trip* to Budapest!' 'Thanks! See you next week when I get back!'
8 Excuse me, I'm a bit lost. Can you tell me the best *journey / way* to the bus station?

3 Complete the sentences with an adjective from the box. More than one answer may be possible.

> a(n) homeward / outward / hard / dangerous **journey**
>
> a business / sightseeing / shopping / day / round / successful **trip**
>
> a(n) outward / pleasant / safe / extended / overnight **journey/trip**

1 I'm going on a(n) .... trip to Zurich, so I won't be back till tomorrow.
2 The .... journey wasn't nearly as hard as the homeward one.
3 They've gone on a(n) .... trip, so I guess they'll come home with lots of new clothes.
4 Have a(n) .... journey and don't drive too fast!
5 I hope you have a(n) .... trip and come back with those new boots you wanted!
6 The children have a .... journey to school, including crossing the river on a kind of rope bridge.

4 Work in groups. Imagine you are planning a trip together this weekend. Decide:

- where to go
- how to get there
- what to do when you arrive.

Reading and Use of English Part 3

1 Form adjectives from these nouns and verbs by adding a suffix.

	noun (n) or verb (v)	adjective
1	nature (n)	*natural*
2	adventure (n)	
3	friend (n)	
4	memory (n)	
5	mystery (n)	
6	risk (n + v)	
7	crowd (n + v)	
8	thrill (n + v)	
9	doubt (n + v)	
10	success (n)	
11	remark (n + v)	
12	access (n + v)	

2 Form adjectives from the nouns and verbs in the box. In some cases, more than one answer may be possible. When you have finished, use your dictionary to check your answers.

> artist   caution   colour   educate   emotion
> energy   mass   predict   reason   respond   storm
> thought   wealth

- In Reading and Use of English Part 3, you read a text of 150–160 words with eight gaps and one example.
- In each gap, you write the correct form of the word given in CAPITALS at the end of the line.
- In the test, the words will be a mix of nouns, adjectives, adverbs and verbs. Some of them might need a prefix, e.g. *un-*.

Exam advice

3 Read the text on the right. Use the word given in capitals at the end of some of the lines to form a word that fits in the gap in the same line. When you have finished, use your dictionary to check your answers.

A bus journey

Sophie was **(0)** ....*relieved*.... to get out of the airport and into Seoul. She was travelling to Pusan and had decided to go there by bus. She was very pleased to find it was fairly **(1)** .... – a lot cheaper than the train. The bus felt really **(2)** .... and the big leather seats were a lot more **(3)** .... than the ones on the buses back home. Although the train would have been **(4)** .... faster, she was looking forward to stopping at the Sunsan Services that had featured in some of her favourite films. She was therefore **(5)** .... when she could get off and buy some snacks and take some photos. She could even **(6)** .... some of the places she had seen in the films. She was glad, though, when the bus started again as she was **(7)** .... about getting to Pusan. It was 5 hours before they finally arrived, but Sophie had had a **(8)** .... time getting there!

RELIEF

EXPENSE

LUXURY

COMFORT

CONSIDER

DELIGHT

IDENTITY

ENTHUSIASM

MARVEL

4 Work in groups. Have you ever felt nervous or anxious on a journey? Why?

Grammar

at, *in* and *on* in time phrases

▶ **Page 166 Grammar reference**

1 Complete these sentences from Listening Part 3 with *at*, *in* or *on*.

1 But he said that provided we get up .... 8 am every day, even .... weekends, we could make the most of our time.

2 .... December 2015, I went on a family holiday to Cuba. .... night, there was so much lively music and laughter everywhere we went.

3 .... 14th September last year, I went to New York with my friend and his family.

4 .... our very first day, we all decided to hire bikes, as Copenhagen is supposed to be a very safe place to cycle.

2 Students often make mistakes with *at*, *in* and *on* in time phrases. Make sentences.

Lots of people go to the beach		July.
		December.
The best time to visit my country is		summer.
My mother's birthday's	at	spring.
The roads here are usually busy	on	autumn.
	in	winter.
I always do my homework		the morning.
It's a good idea to go down to the harbour early		Sunday evenings.
		night.
		the weekend.
		the afternoon.
		14 September.

Reading and Use of English Part 7

- In Reading and Use of English Part 7, you read either one long text divided into four to six sections, or four to six separate short texts. The total length is 500–600 words.

- There are ten questions which you match with the different texts or sections.

Exam advice

1 Work in groups. You are going to read about four people who had unexpected experiences while they were on holiday. Before you read, suggest some things that might happen to people on holiday which they weren't expecting.

2 Read questions 1–10 carefully and identify the key words in each question.

Which person

1 was not prepared for the weather?

2 had transport difficulties because of the time of year?

3 visited somewhere at a popular time of year?

4 had an unexpected expense?

5 had to wait a long time to arrive at his/her destination?

6 changed their travel plans while on holiday?

7 received assistance from a local person?

8 received assistance from another tourist?

9 had people waiting for him/her?

10 was unable to leave on the day they had planned?

3 Read the texts opposite. For questions 1–10, choose from the four people (A–D). The people may be chosen more than once.

4 Work in groups. Which person do you think had the biggest surprise on holiday? Take it in turns to tell each other about a memorable holiday you have had. Then decide which of you had the most interesting holiday.

HOLIDAY SURPRISES

A Anna Jones – Sicily

I travelled to Sicily and had arranged to meet my host family at the airport in Palermo at 8 pm. The flight was fine and I had nearly finished my book when the pilot announced that we would be delayed because of a storm in Palermo. I felt a bit anxious at this point, but the flight continued without any problems. Then, as we were approaching Palermo, we hit the storm and the pilot announced that the flight had been redirected to another city in Sicily. We landed there, and then an hour or so later the plane took off again for Palermo. By the time we finally landed in Palermo it was almost midnight. My host family had been worried about me. They were very kind to me and we had a delicious late-night dinner as soon as we got to their house.

B Callum McKinnon – Japan

I went on a trip to Japan to visit my uncle, who was working in Tokyo. While we were there, we all decided to visit a famous site called the Inari Shrine in Kyoto. Unfortunately, we hadn't arranged accommodation, and when we arrived, we realised that most of the hotels were fully booked because it was a national holiday. We decided to visit the shrine anyway and find accommodation later. However, as we were walking back through the woods, we realised we had got lost. We were worried that we would have to sleep in the woods, but then we met an American who had a map and helped us to get back onto the path and to find our way back to the entrance. He told us that he was staying in a guest house that might have some rooms available. We received a warm welcome there and met a lot of nice people.

C Lucy Parker – Morocco

Last winter I went on an amazing trip with my family. We spent two days in Spain before taking the ferry to Morocco to visit my aunt and uncle. We had a brilliant time exploring the markets, and tasting incredible food. We had planned to take the ferry back to Spain on Thursday evening, but we decided to stay an extra night and leave early the next morning. On our final day in Morocco, we got up early to catch the train from Fez to Tangier, where we would get the ferry back to Spain and our flight back to London. Unfortunately, because it was the New Year holiday, there was a reduced ferry service that day. We managed to catch a much later ferry, but by the time we arrived back in Spain, we had already missed our connection. There were no flights with seats available for two days, but least we got to spend longer in Spain.

D Ian Roberts – Iceland

I travelled to the USA with my family last summer, and we chose a flight that had a stopover in Iceland. We decided to stay there for three nights as we had never been there before and it was a good opportunity to visit. Because it was summer, we thought that our light waterproof jackets would be warm enough for our time there. But when we arrived in Reykjavik, it was pouring with rain and very cold. We met a local woman when we were waiting for the bus who kindly gave us her umbrella and told us where we could buy warm clothes.
We eventually found an outdoor clothing shop and bought warm coats, hats and gloves. We put our new clothes to good use by doing plenty of activities, including walking, snowmobiling and whale watching. The stopover really cost us a lot, but it was worth it.
Our warm clothes stayed in the suitcase for the rest of the trip though.

Grammar

Past perfect simple and continuous

▶ Page 166 Grammar reference

1 Look at this sentence from Reading and Use of English Part 7 and answer the questions.

I travelled to Sicily and had arranged to meet my host family at the airport in Palermo at 8 pm.

1 Which of these actions happened first?
   a She had arranged to meet her host family.
   b She travelled to Sicily.
2 Which verb form is used to indicate that something happened before something else in the past?
3 Compare the sentence above with the one below. What does the sentence below suggest about when the arrangement to meet was made?

When I arrived in Sicily, I called my host family and arranged to meet them at the airport.

2 Work in pairs. Find at least six other examples of the past perfect (*had been / had done*) in Reading and Use of English Part 7. What event or situation in the more recent past (in the past simple) makes it necessary to use the past perfect? For example:
(past perfect) I had nearly finished my book – (event in past simple) the pilot announced that we would be delayed because of a storm.

3 Complete the sentences with the past simple or past perfect form of the verbs in brackets.

1 We were feeling hungry although we .... (eat) lunch only an hour before.
2 I didn't know my way around the city because I .... (never be) there before.
3 The party, which our hosts .... (organise) before we arrived, was one of the most enjoyable parts of our trip.
4 When I .... (arrive) in Nairobi, I wasn't allowed into the country because I ....(lose) my passport.
5 I .... (recognise) her from the photograph, although I .... (never speak) to her before.
6 He helped to raise money to repair homes which the hurricane .... (damage).

4 Look at sentences A and B and answer the questions.

A Paul was tired because <u>he'd been travelling</u> all day.
B Paul went to the information office because <u>he'd never travelled</u> in the region before.

1 Which sentence focuses on the length of time spent travelling?
2 Is the underlined verb in the past perfect simple or past perfect continuous?

5 Complete the sentences with the past simple, past perfect simple or past perfect continuous form of the verbs in brackets.

1 The storm damaged the house where she .... (live) since she left school.
2 We .... (walk) up the mountain for about three hours when suddenly it .... (begin) to rain.
3 I .... (already finish) the work when she .... (offer) to help me.
4 I .... (only speak) for 30 seconds when he interrupted me with a question.
5 Carla was tired and dirty when she .... (get) home because she .... (help) her grandad in his garden all afternoon.
6 I .... (never / go) to the Camp Nou stadium, so I was thrilled when my uncle .... (give) me tickets for the Barcelona – AC Milan match last week.
7 We were really hungry when we .... (get back) from the cycling trip because we .... (forget) to take any sandwiches.
8 Cristian's tooth .... (hurt) for nearly two weeks before he finally .... (decide) to go to the dentist.

Speaking Part 3

▶ **Page 197 Speaking bank**

Exam advice

- In Speaking Part 3 you and the other candidate discuss a situation or problem together and reach a decision.
- The examiner gives you a page with a task consisting of a question and five different word prompts.
- You have 15 seconds to think about the task and then you have two minutes to discuss your ideas.
- The examiner then asks you another question (which is not written down) so that you can summarise your thoughts. You will have one minute to do this.

1 Work in pairs. Read the examiner's instructions and look at the task. Which phrases in the box below could you use to talk about each option?

Examiner: I'd like you to imagine that your school has won first prize in a competition – a trip for all the students. Here are some ideas for trips that students could do and a question for you to discuss. Talk to each other about how these different trips could benefit the students.

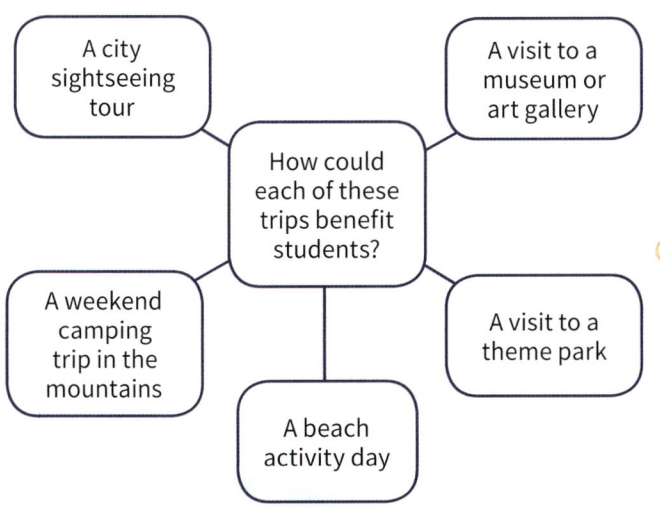

A city sightseeing tour

A visit to a museum or art gallery

How could each of these trips benefit students?

A weekend camping trip in the mountains

A visit to a theme park

A beach activity day

become more self-confident
become more independent
learn to work in a team
be educational for students
have new experiences
tough conditions

get a real thrill
learn teamwork
cope in another language
make a change from their everyday lives
appreciate other cultures
get away from their daily routine

2 Listen to two candidates, Miguel and Antonia, beginning this task. What benefits do they mention for three of the options?

3 In Speaking Part 3, it's important for candidates to react to each other's ideas and suggestions. You can do this by asking each other questions. Complete the students' questions with a word or phrase from the box. Then listen again to check your answers.

about that   don't you
shall   think   this one
what about

1 .... we start with ....?

2 How do you .... a sightseeing tour might be good for students?

3 Right. .... this sort of activity holiday in the mountains?

4 Yes, and they learn to be more independent because they're away from home and their families, ... think?

5 And the beach activity day: what ....?

3

4 **Pronunciation: intonation (1)**

You can indicate that you have finished speaking, or that you have more to say, by making your voice rise or fall. This is called intonation. A falling intonation shows that you have finished speaking, while a rising intonation often indicates that you have more to say.

The speaker's voice falls or rises most on words which are stressed.

4.1 Listen to these extracts from the conversation. Decide if the speaker's voice rises or falls on the underlined words.

1 How do you think a sightseeing tour might be good for students?

2 I think you can learn a lot about architecture and history and things like that.

3 Yes, and also you can visit somewhere very different and learn about other cultures.

4 What about this sort of activity holiday in the mountains?

5 I think it can give young people exciting experiences and adventures, things they don't get in their everyday lives.

4.2 Work in pairs. Take turns to read sentences 1–5 aloud.

4.3 Write two sentences of your own, explaining the benefits of two of the options in the speaking task. Decide which words you should stress and whether your voice should rise or fall on the stressed words.

When you are ready, work in pairs and

- take turns to read your sentences aloud
- react to what your partner says with your own ideas.

5 Work in pairs. Do the first part of the task yourselves.

- Ask each other the questions from Exercise 3.
- Talk about each of the options from the speaking task in turn. Take two minutes to do this.
- Try to use the words and phrases from the box in Exercise 1.

6 Work in pairs. Look at the examiner's instruction for the second part of the task and the list of strategies (1–6).

- Decide together which strategies would be good for this part of the task. Write Y (yes) or N (no) next to each strategy.
- Give reasons for your answers.

Examiner: Now you have a minute to decide which trip the school should choose.

1 Talk about each of the options in turn again.

2 Suggest which option you would choose, say why, and ask your partner if he/she agrees.

3 Agree with the first option your partner suggests.

4 Disagree with the first option your partner suggests, say why you disagree, then suggest another option and say why.

5 Agree with the first option your partner suggests, but then suggest an alternative and say why.

6 Disagree with everything your partner says in order to make the discussion longer.

7 Listen to two pairs of candidates, Miguel and Antonia, and Irene and Nikolai, doing this part of the task. Which of the strategies from Exercise 6 (1–6) does each speaker use?

- Miguel .... Antonia ....
- Irene .... Nikolai ....

8 Match the phrases (1–7) with their function (a–e). Some functions can be matched with more than one phrase.

1 In my opinion, the best choice is … because …

2 I think we should choose … because …

3 What do you think?

4 Yes, I think you're right, but … because …

5 You might be right, but I think we should also consider … because …

6 I think … is a better option because …

7 I think your suggestion would be fine if … , but …

a suggest an option and say why

b ask your partner if they agree

c disagree with a suggestion and say why

d suggest a different option

e agree with a suggestion, but suggest a different option and say why

9 Now work in pairs and do the second part of the task using phrases from Exercise 8.

Writing Part 2
A story

▶ **Page 208 Writing bank**

> **Exam advice**
> - In Writing Part 2, you may be asked to write a short story. This task usually gives you the words you must use to start or end your story.
> - The task tests your ability to structure your writing and to use a variety of tenses, grammatical structures and vocabulary.

1 Look at the writing task and underline:
- the words you must use to start your story
- the two elements you must include in your story
- where the story will appear, so that you know who is going to read it.

Your teacher has asked you to write a story for the English-language magazine at your school. The story must begin with this sentence:

It was a trip I'll never forget.

Your story must include:
- a group of people
- a surprise

Write your **story**.

2 Now listen to five people talking about trips and journeys they will never forget. Match each speaker to a trip or journey from the list (A–F). Use the letters only once. There is one extra letter which you do not need to use.

1 Lisa ☐   A a family excursion
2 Mark ☐   B a first flight
3 Maya ☐   C a school trip
4 Patrick ☐   D a frightening voyage
5 Sarah ☐   E a visit to a relative
            F a long car journey

3 Listen again. Which stories include a group of people and a surprise?

4 Work in pairs. Which of the stories you heard do you think would make the most interesting contribution to the school magazine?

5 Read the story and choose the correct options in *italics*.

It was a trip I'll never forget. We **(1)** *were feeling / had felt* very excited as we climbed into the rather ancient bus. With 40 noisy kids and three nervous teachers, it was very crowded. I was still at primary school and our teachers **(2)** *had decided / were deciding* to organise an excursion to a nearby wildlife park.

We found the tour round the park fascinating because we were seeing animals we **(3)** *had only read / only read* about in books before, such as zebras and elephants. It was brilliant to see them in real life. Anyway, just after we **(4)** *had entered / were entering* the part where the monkeys lived, the bus **(5)** *had / was having* a puncture. While we **(6)** *were waiting / had waited* for the driver to change the wheel, a whole group of monkeys **(7)** *approached / had approached* the bus and started climbing all over it. We **(8)** *had never seen / were never seeing* such a cool thing before and we **(9)** *started / were starting* laughing and shouting even more. I think the teachers felt relieved when the driver **(10)** *managed / had managed* to change the wheel and continue the tour. All in all, it was a very memorable trip.

6 Work in pairs. Answer these questions.
1 How many paragraphs are there and what is the subject of each paragraph?
2 What adjectives does the writer use?
3 What things do you think made the trip memorable for the writer?

7 Write your own story for the school magazine in 140–190 words.
- Before you write, think about what you want to say and make a plan of what to include in each paragraph. Your story can be true or invented.
- When you write, think what tenses you can use, and try to use a variety.
- Include adjectives to describe your feelings.
- When you have finished, check your writing for mistakes.

4 Food, glorious food

A

C

B

Starting off

1 Work in groups. Match the descriptions (1–3) of how we might prepare and eat our food in the future with the words in the box.

> 3D printed food   artificial beef
> breathable chocolate

1 It looks and feels like meat. In fact it is meat, although it's never been near a living, breathing animal. Instead, it's grown from stem cells in a laboratory. It will replace meat from farm animals in your diet.

2 You'll eat it by inhaling it. It will give you all the flavour without any of the calories. You just inhale tiny particles of chocolate as a mist. There could be other food sprays available in future too, such as aerosols containing cheese or spices.

3 You'll just select what you want to eat from the control panel of the computer. All your snacks will be printed in front of you as the ingredients are built up in layers. You'll be able to print out a chocolate biscuit or a beef burger in seconds.

2 Match the photos with the descriptions 1–3 in Exercise 1. Which foods and ways of eating in Exercise 1 would you:

- be happy to try?
- think about trying in future?
- absolutely refuse to try?

3 Work in pairs. Discuss these questions.

- What's the most unusual food you have ever eaten?
- What's the most unpleasant food you can imagine?
- If you could fill a large bowl with food that you really enjoy, what would you fill it with?

Reading and Use of English Part 6

- Read the text carefully before you look at the gaps, so you know what each paragraph is about.
- Look at the words on either side of the gap and make sure the sentence you choose makes sense with them.
- Look for words in the missing sentences that might give you a clue. For example, *Instead* in sentence A tells you that it expresses an idea that contrasts with the sentence before the gap.

Exam advice

1 Work in groups. You are going to read an article about insects as a source of food. Before you read, decide if the following sentences are true or false.

1 Some kinds of insects can be eaten.

2 Insects can provide a high level of nutrition.

3 It is difficult to farm insects on a large scale without damaging the environment.

2 Read the first three paragraphs of the article opposite as quickly as you can and check your answers to Exercise 1.

3 Read the full article and say briefly what each paragraph is about.

4 Six sentences have been removed from the article. Choose from the sentences A–G the one which fits each gap (1–6). There is one extra sentence which you do not need to use.

A Instead, it's the idea of eating one that is the cause of such upset.

B There's even a chocolate version available too.

C In fact, for every human, there are forty tonnes of them.

D Meanwhile, many other innovations are seen as the possible future of food.

E Unfortunately, the same can't be said for insects.

F So, if we want to find a way to produce more protein with fewer supplies, insects are the way to go.

G Insect burgers are likely to look like the meat ones we eat today.

5 Work in groups. Discuss these questions.

- Would you eat food containing insect flour? Why? / Why not?
- Do you think eating insects and insect-products will become an important part of people's diets in future? Why? / Why not?
- Do you think the food innovations mentioned in the final paragraph of the article will become popular in future?

Are INSECTS the future of food?

The world population is continuing to grow and in many areas of the world, the demand for animal products is rising sharply, so in the next few decades, we'll need to figure out how to produce enough food for billions more mouths.

There is one source of food that could provide at least part of the solution and they're already freely available. **1** They can be found right under our noses, as well as below our feet and all around us: insects.

You may turn your nose up at the thought, but it isn't actually such a crazy idea. Although they may not look like much, insects are a great source of food. They contain essential nutrients and can provide a nutritious meal. Insects give out such small amounts of greenhouse gas, and take up so little room on the planet compared with the animals we traditionally eat, that they are very much more environmentally friendly. Insects also require fewer food resources compared with our traditional sources of meat in order to give us the nutrition we need. They also require less water than animals or birds. **2** It seems like the obvious conclusion.

It's estimated that a third of the world's population already eat them. Boiled silkworm larvae is a popular dish across Asia, and wasps are also popular across the continent. In Africa termites can be prepared in a variety of ways to form part of a nutritious meal.

What seems to be one of the biggest barriers is convincing more people to eat insect cuisine. Some foods, like chocolate, sell themselves. **3** A lot of people in Europe and North America feel so disgusted at the idea of eating insects that they won't go anywhere near them. Psychologists tend to agree that the dislike that people have towards insects has nothing to do with them tasting disgusting. **4** There have been several experiments that have helped confirm this conclusion. In one experiment, when a sterilised insect was placed in a cup of juice and an everyday object in another, people were consistently convinced that the juice that had the insect in tasted worse, if they were willing to taste it at all. It appears to be the case that insects reliably produce negativity.

However, there is a movement to put insects on our dinner tables. Across Europe there are companies making nutrition bars that contain insects. **5** Meanwhile, in the United States, the company Chapul sells protein bars containing cricket flour.

Most of the companies selling insects and insect-based foods are only just starting up or haven't been around for very long, so we aren't sure yet how it will progress, or if the industry will be successful. Will we see an insect aisle at the supermarket? Will fast-food restaurants serve up bug burgers? **6** These range from 3-D printed food, to foods manufactured in a laboratory to resemble seafood or meat, to further developments of soy-based foods. Whether any of these will become something that the majority of us eat every day is still not certain.

4

Vocabulary

food, dish and meal

1 Students often confuse the words above. Match the definitions to the photos.

> **food** something that people and animals eat to keep them alive: *There was lots of food and drink at the party.*
>
> **dish** food prepared in a particular way as part of a meal: *a chicken/vegetarian dish.*
>
> **meal** an occasion when food is eaten, or the food which is eaten on such an occasion: *I have my main meal at midday. You must come round for a meal sometime.*

2 Complete the sentences with *food*, *dish* or *meal* in the correct form.

1 Some types of .... are connected to increased intelligence.

2 I really enjoy cooking a .... when I get home in the evening.

3 My favourite .... have always been desserts.

3 Correct the mistake in each sentence.

1 I'm quite surprised, but I'm really enjoying English meal.

2 Moussaka is one of the most delicious meals you can eat in my country.

3 This beef food is really tasty, isn't it?

4 The meal in my country is delicious.

5 When I visit you, I could cook a food that is from my country.

6 The cost of your holiday includes two dishes a day: breakfast and dinner.

4 Complete the collocations with *food*, *dish* or *meal*. In one case, more than one answer is correct.

1 a .... source / supply / shortage

2 organic / convenience ....

3 a(n) elaborate / simple .... or ....

4 a balanced / filling / light / heavy ....

5 Complete the sentences with the correct form of a collocation from Exercise 4. In some cases, more than one answer may be possible.

1 At weekends, Santos likes to spend hours in the kitchen, carefully cooking *elaborate dishes* containing many ingredients.

2 Growing populations may lead to .... in some countries.

3 I wouldn't call yoghurt and a banana a .... – it's more like a snack.

4 If we continue to overfish, we won't be able to rely on the oceans as a .... in the future.

5 Many people lead such busy lives that they tend to buy .... from supermarkets to save time.

6 My mum always tries to provide .... with fresh vegetables, pasta or potatoes and some meat or fish.

7 The severe floods are threatening the country's ....

8 There's little evidence that .... is healthier than other types of food.

6 Work in pairs. Read the future food ideas below. Which would you like to try? Can you add any more ideas? Write a list and then swap your list with another pair. Which ideas are the best?

- A skin patch – you just apply it to your skin like a plaster and it gives you all the nutrients you need to stay healthy!

- Edible cups – after you finish your drink of juice, you can eat the glass!

- Wiki balls – small balls of food covered in an edible skin, similar to the skin of soft fruit. They could contain any liquid, or solid food like ice cream. You just carry them around in your pocket and wash them before you eat them!

Grammar

so and such

▶ **Page 167 Grammar reference**

1 Complete the sentences from Reading and Use of English Part 6 with *so*, *such* or *such a*.

1 It isn't actually .... crazy idea.
2 A lot of people in Europe and North America feel .... disgusted at the idea of eating insects that they won't go anywhere near them.
3 Instead, it's the idea of eating one that is the cause of .... upset.
4 Insects give out .... small amounts of greenhouse gas, and take up .... little room on the planet compared with the animals we traditionally eat, that they are very much more environmentally friendly.

2 Complete the sentences with *so*, *such* or *such a*.

1 The idea of eating an insect is .... disgusting it's making me feel sick!
2 There was .... much food on the table that we didn't know where to start.
3 I don't think eating a pizza at your place is .... good idea if your parents have guests.
4 I ate .... a lot at lunchtime that I won't want any dinner tonight.
5 We took .... little to eat on the picnic that we were starving when we got home.
6 I like going to my friend's house because his sister makes .... delicious cakes.

3 Put the words in order to complete the sentences.

1 that / delicious / because / so / meal / remember / was / it
   I'll always
2 in / noisy / can't / restaurant / a / eat / such
   I
3 us / of / for / be / together / all / such / to / fun
   It was
4 medicine / in / such / life / disgusting / tasted / my
   I have never
5 you / long / such / time / to / after / a / see
   I'm glad
6 people / party / at / few / were / so / the / there
   What a pity

4 For questions 1–6, complete the second sentence so that it has a similar meaning to the first sentence, using the word given. Do not change the word given. You must use between two and five words, including the word given.

1 This is the best meal I've ever eaten.
   GOOD
   I have .... meal before.
2 She spoke too quickly for us to understand.
   THAT
   She spoke .... couldn't understand her.
3 We all felt hungry because the organisers didn't give us enough food.
   LITTLE
   The organisers provided us .... that everyone felt hungry.
4 It was the most enjoyable party she had ever been to.
   FUN
   She had never .... a party.
5 It's been over a month since I last had pizza.
   FOR
   I .... over a month.
6 Why aren't we allowed to eat or drink in class?
   LET
   Why .... eat or drink in class?

Listening Part 4

1 Work in pairs. You will hear an interview with a boy called Jez, who has completed a cookery course. Before you listen, discuss these questions.

- Can you cook? If yes, what kind of things do you like to make?
- Do you think it's important for young people to learn to cook? Why? / Why not?
- Is there a particular dish you would like to learn how to make?

2 Quickly read only the questions 1–7 and underline the main idea in each one. (Don't read the options A–C yet.)

1 Why did Jez decide to do the cooking course?
   A He wanted to learn some basic cooking skills.
   B His parents were keen for him to learn how to cook.
   C He was persuaded to go by a friend.

2 Jez says when he first arrived at the class he felt
   A worried by the number of students there
   B nervous about how good at cooking the other students might be
   C surprised that some of the students were quite young

3 What did Jez choose to prepare first?
   A soup
   B a curry
   C a pie

4 How did Jez feel when he made a mistake when cooking?
   A He felt like giving up completely.
   B He became more determined to get help from the teacher.
   C He accepted that it was part of learning a new skill.

5 What does Jez say about his teacher on the cooking course?
   A She made the students feel that they were all capable of achieving good results.
   B She reminded him of his teachers at school.
   C She tended to ask a lot of questions.

6 What did Jez enjoy least about the course?
   A listening to some of the talks
   B the amount of time spent outdoors
   C clearing up after cooking

7 What is Jez's immediate plan?
   A to make friends with other people who also enjoy cooking
   B to attend a cooking club
   C to try to find a special class to develop his skills

3 🎧 14 Now quickly read the options, then listen and choose the best answer (A, B or C).

4 Work in pairs. Discuss these questions.

- Do you think that Jez did an interesting cooking course? Why? / Why not?
- Would you like to do a similar course? Why? / Why not?
- Do you think it is important for young people to learn about where food comes from – how it is grown and produced? Why? / Why not?

Grammar

too and enough

▶ **Page 168 Grammar reference**

1 Complete the sentences from Listening Part 4 with *too*, *too many*, *too much* or *enough*.

1 She said she didn't feel brave .... to go along by herself.

2 I added .... water …

3 … and the pastry got .... sticky and impossible to work with.

4 There were .... talks, and they weren't always very interesting.

2 Complete the sentences with *too*, *too many*, *too much* or *enough*.

1 I really enjoyed the meal, although I thought there were .... chips and not .... fresh vegetables.

2 Few schools spend .... time teaching students about nutrition.

3 A lot of people eat .... quickly to enjoy their food properly.

4 The school canteen is .... small for everyone to eat lunch at the same time.

5 I spent .... time researching my project and not .... time writing it.

3 Students often make mistakes with *too*, *too many*, *too much* or *enough* and *very*. Choose the correct option in *italics*.

1 I liked the restaurant but *the food wasn't enough* / *there wasn't enough food*.

2 Experts say that fast food is *not very* / *not too much* good for you.

3 I don't have *money enough* / *enough money* to pay for your dinner.

4 We didn't like the bread because it wasn't *fresh enough* / *enough fresh*.

5 The food takes *too much long* / *much too long* to prepare, so customers become impatient.

6 The food was not *too much* / *very* tasty.

7 I'm afraid the meal was *too much* / *much too* expensive.

4 Complete the second sentence so that it has a similar meaning to the first sentence, using the word given. Do not change the word given. You must use between two and five words, including the word given.

1 Few people can afford to eat in that restaurant.
   TOO
   That restaurant .... most people to eat there.

2 We can't make the cake because we've just about run out of sugar.
   ENOUGH
   We haven't got .... make the cake.

3 'Sorry, we haven't got any more chocolate ice cream,' said the waiter.
   RUN
   'Sorry, we .... chocolate ice cream,' said the waiter.

4 We didn't go for a picnic because of the cold weather.
   WARM
   The weather .... us to go for a picnic.

Reading and Use of English Part 1

Exam advice

• Read the whole text before you look at the options.

• The options will be similar in meaning, but only one will fit correctly into the gap.

• Look at the words before and after the gap and check that the word you have chosen fits with them. Sometimes one of the options has the right meaning, but does not fit the grammar of the sentence.

1 You are going to read a short text about how to eat sushi. Read the text on the next page quickly. Don't worry about the gaps at the moment. Are the following sentences true or false?

1 You can use your hands to eat some kinds of sushi.

2 It is important to dip the rice into the soy sauce correctly.

3 It's a good idea to mix wasabi with soy sauce.

4 Ginger should only be eaten at the end of the meal.

2 Read the text again and decide which answer (A, B, C or D) best fits each gap. There is an example at the beginning (0).

4

Tips of the week
How to eat sushi

HOW TO EAT SUSHI

The taste and flavour of sushi is influenced not only by how it's prepared but also by how you eat it. Read the tips below to help you know what to expect and how to enjoy it!

- At most sushi restaurants, you should be able to order basic kinds of sushi such as sashimi (sliced raw fish or meat without any rice) and nigiri (a **(0)** ....A.. of pressed rice topped with a slice of fish). Use chopsticks for sashimi, but for the other **(1)** .... of sushi, it's acceptable, and even **(2)** ...., to use your hands. Hold it between your thumb and first two fingers.

- Dip nigiri into the soy sauce fish-side first and do this only **(3)** .... If you dip the rice side into the sauce, the sushi may **(4)** .... apart. Nigiri should also be eaten fish-side down.

- As a **(5)** .... rule, pieces of sushi should be eaten in a single bite – that's the traditional way. But don't attempt that with larger sushi rolls, such as California rolls.

- Sushi chefs tend to put wasabi (a green ball of paste) on the sushi when they're preparing it, but if you want to **(6)** .... more, you can simply put it onto your fish using chopsticks. Never mix it with soy sauce as the **(7)** .... flavours will overpower the sushi.

- Don't treat pickled ginger as something to put on the dish. It is **(8)** .... to be eaten between servings.

0	**A** portion	**B** share	**C** slice	**D** part
1	**A** makes	**B** groups	**C** types	**D** sets
2	**A** expected	**B** required	**C** supposed	**D** recommended
3	**A** shortly	**B** briefly	**C** directly	**D** immediately
4	**A** become	**B** fall	**C** get	**D** go
5	**A** general	**B** broad	**C** normal	**D** familiar
6	**A** spread	**B** place	**C** add	**D** lay
7	**A** gathered	**B** joined	**C** united	**D** combined
8	**A** proposed	**B** suggested	**C** instructed	**D** meant

3 Work in groups.

- Have you ever tried sushi? Did you like it? / Would you like to try it? Why? / Why not?
- Which food from your country do you enjoy? Why?
- Are there any dishes from other countries that you enjoy or that you would like to try?
- How important do you think it is for people to try food from different countries?

Speaking Part 4

▶ **Page 199 Speaking bank**

- In Speaking Part 4 the examiner asks you questions to find out your opinions on general topics related to Part 3.
- The examiner may also ask you to react to ideas and opinions which the other candidate expresses.
- This part tests your ability to express and justify opinions, agree and disagree.

Exam advice

1 Marina and Pablo are answering an examiner's question in Speaking Part 4. Read their answers, ignoring the gaps, and match the words and phrases in bold with the definitions a–g.

Examiner: Do you think fast food is bad for you?

Marina: I think it depends. I think the most important thing is to have **a balanced diet**, **(1)** .... you eat a variety of vegetables, meat, cereals and so on. I'm not sure it matters so much how long it takes to prepare, **(2)** .... I think fast food is just food which is prepared quickly. **(3)** ...., if you just **live on**, what's it called, **junk food**, for instance hamburgers and pizzas and things like that, **(4)** .... you probably need to **cut down on** those and have a more balanced diet.

Examiner: And Pablo, what do you think?

Pablo: I agree with Marina. I think it's fine to eat fast food occasionally, **(5)** .... you have to balance it with other things like fresh fruit and vegetables **(6)** .... are in season and cut down on **dairy products** and **fat**. Also, I think that **(7)** .... you eat is only one part of a healthy **lifestyle**.

a a solid or liquid substance obtained from animals or plants and used especially in cooking *fat*

b a combination of the correct types and amounts of food

c do or use less of something

d food that is unhealthy but is quick and easy to eat

e foods made from milk, such as cream, butter and cheese

f only eat a particular type of food

g someone's way of living; the things that a person or particular group of people usually do

Complete Marina's and Pablo's answers with a word or phrase from the box. Then listen to check your answers.

> because   but   in other words
>   on the other hand   then
>   what   which

Find words or phrases in Marina's and Pablo's answers where they:

1 explain what they mean using different words

2 give a reason

3 give examples

4 balance one idea or opinion with another.

4 Pronunciation: grouping words and pausing (1)

When we speak, we say words in groups which form a meaning together, almost like one word, and we pause slightly between these groups of words.

4.1 Listen to Pablo answering the examiner's next question and use a (/) to mark where he pauses.

Well, the important thing is not eating, it's spending time together so that they can talk about what they've been doing during the day. They get the chance to exchange opinions and make plans as well, because everyone can contribute and that's what makes a rich, meaningful family life.

4.2 Work in pairs. Read Pablo's answer aloud. While your partner is speaking, check where they pause and if the pause sounds natural.

5 Read the questions and think about how you might answer them. Write a few sentences for one of them and mark where you need to pause when you speak.

- What, for you, is a healthy diet?
- How are the things we eat nowadays different from the things our grandparents used to eat when they were young?
- Do you think young people should learn to cook at school? Why? / Why not?

6 Work in pairs and take turns to ask and answer the questions.

Writing Part 2
A review

▶ Page 210 Writing bank

1 Work in pairs. Read the writing task and note down the points you must deal with.

- In a review you need to show your ability to describe and give your opinion about something you have experienced, for example a restaurant or a concert.
- Think about what people will want to know when they read the review. For example: What sort of restaurant is it? What is the food like? Is it expensive?
- Make a recommendation to the reader: Is it a good place to go? Is there something you particularly enjoyed?

Exam advice

You see this announcement in your local English-language newspaper.

- Do you know a local restaurant, café or snack bar?
- If so, why not write a review for our Food section? Tell our readers what the place and the food are like, and say whether you think everyone in the family would enjoy eating there.
- All reviews published will receive vouchers for a free meal for all the family in a place of your choice.

Write your **review**.

2 Answer these questions with a partner.

1 Which features (**a–j**) do you think a review of a café or restaurant should cover?

2 Which features does the review opposite cover?

   a the type of restaurant, café or snack bar
   b the writer's general opinion of the restaurant, café or snack bar
   c a description of its design and surroundings
   d a description of the food
   e a description of the other customers
   f a description of the service
   g an explanation of how to get there
   h a recommendation
   i an indication of the price
   j the location

I visited the Cherry Blossom restaurant recently with my family to celebrate my sister's graduation from university. It is a Japanese restaurant, decorated in Japanese style, with some beautiful paintings of Japan on the walls. The style is modern and elegant, but it still felt warm and welcoming.

The service was excellent, and the waiters were very helpful. They explained the menu to us and suggested dishes that we might like. As there were eight of us, we managed to try a good variety of food. Everything was very tasty, and the seafood in particular was delicious – it was so fresh. I can personally recommend the sushi. Try the sashimi and the nigiri – the flavours are amazing!

We ended the meal with Japanese tea, which we found very refreshing. The beautiful ceramic teapots it was served in made it seem even more special. All in all it was a very satisfying experience, and we will certainly come again. It isn't the cheapest place to eat, but on the other hand we felt the cost was reasonable, and it was good value for money. We had a wonderful evening. I highly recommend it.

3 A review is a good opportunity to show your range of vocabulary. Complete the table with the adjectives in the box. You can write some adjectives in more than one row.

> delicious elegant fresh helpful modern reasonable refreshing satisfying tasty welcoming wonderful

the waiters / the service	
the interior	
the food	
the price	
the restaurant in general	

4 Now add these adjectives to the table. You can add some of them to more than one row.

> attractive colourful competitive cosy exceptional exclusive expensive limited old-fashioned original poor rude satisfactory (a bit) slow upbeat

5 Read this writing task and note down the points you must deal with.

> **You see this announcement in your school magazine.**
>
> *Have you been to a restaurant, café or snack bar in your area?*
> • If so, why not write a review for our 'Free Time' section, telling us what it is like and whether you would recommend it to our students.
> • The three best reviews will receive a prize of €50.
>
> Write your **review**.

6 Write a plan for your review and make notes on what you will put in each paragraph. Here are some things you can cover:

- introduction – the name and type of place and where it is situated
- your overall opinion of the place
- particular dishes the place serves (and your opinion of them)
- the décor, the service, etc.
- things you particularly like and/or dislike, such as the price or the atmosphere.

7 Work in pairs. Compare your plans.

8 Write your review. Write 140–190 words.

Vocabulary

1 **Choose the correct option in *italics*.**

1 The *travel / journey* wasn't as boring as I'd thought it would be.

2 Sarah came back from her shopping *trip / journey* with lots of new clothes.

3 Among Brian's many interests, he lists foreign *journeys / travel* and climbing.

4 Do you know the *way / journey* to the town centre?

5 It was a long, dangerous *trip / journey* to the South Pole.

6 I often meet my friends on my *journey / way* to school.

7 Are you all prepared for next week's *trip / travel* to Egypt?

8 Many of our students have quite a long *travel / journey* to college each morning.

Grammar

2 **Complete the second sentence so that it has a similar meaning to the first sentence, using the word given. Do not change the word given. You must use between two and five words, including the word given.**

1 During my visit to London, I took hundreds of photos.
WHILE
I took hundreds of photos .... London.

2 I didn't notice that my passport was missing until I reached the check-in desk.
LOST
When I reached the check-in desk, I realised that .... my passport.

3 I've given up using the bus to go to school because it was always late.
USED
I .... by bus, but I've given it up because it was always late.

4 She was still at school when she passed her driving test.
GOING
She passed her driving test when .... school.

5 Paola and Antonio met for the first time at yesterday's party.
NEVER
Paola and Antonio .... before yesterday's party.

6 Pablo is no longer as frightened of spiders as in the past.
USED
Pablo .... frightened of spiders than he is now.

Word formation

3 **Read this text. Use the word given in capitals at the end of some of the lines to form a word that fits in the gap in the same line. There is an example at the beginning (0).**

Paradise Hotel

We had been promised an **(0)** exceptional holiday in a four-star hotel, so we made our reservation despite the **(1)** .... expense this involved. The website said it was a **(2)** .... hotel which promised outstanding views of **(3)** .... mountain scenery. The view was indeed amazing and we could **(4)** .... many of the local landmarks in the distance from our room on the 10th floor. We were absolutely **(5)** .... to be staying there, as we are keen on climbing and were looking forward to **(6)** .... the mountain. Unfortunately, we woke up late the next morning and realised that we had forgotten our **(7)** .... Luckily, there were a lot of things to do in the hotel, so everything was to our **(8)** .... , even though we didn't manage to climb the mountain!

EXCEPT
CONSIDER
LUXURY
DRAMA
IDENTITY
DELIGHT
TACKLE
EQUIP
SATISFY

Vocabulary

1 Complete the email with the correct form of *food*, *dish* or *meal*. Sometimes more than one answer is possible.

Last week, I went out with my family for a
(1) .... in a restaurant. The
(2) .... was not very good though.
For my first course, I chose a **(3)** ....
called 'Chef's special', which turned out to be a
kind of pizza. Generally, I enjoy fast
(4) .... but this **(5)** .... was
quite disappointing because it wasn't very tasty.
The rest of my family didn't enjoy their
(6) .... very much either. Personally,
I think we would have enjoyed ourselves more if
we'd cooked a **(7)** .... at home – after
all, we always have plenty of **(8)** ....
in the fridge.

Grammar

2 Complete the second sentence so that it has a similar meaning to the first sentence, using the word given. Do not change the word given. You must use between two and five words, including the word given.

1 The food was so hot that we didn't really enjoy it.
TOO
The food was .... really enjoy.

2 The waitress spoke so quickly that we had difficulty understanding her.
ENOUGH
The waitress didn't speak ....
understand her easily.

3 We didn't get a table at the restaurant because it was too full.
SO
The restaurant .... we couldn't get a table.

4 Jack went to so much effort to make that delicious meal.
SUCH
Jack made .... to make that delicious meal.

5 Julio is not a very good cook, so he won't get a job in that restaurant.
ENOUGH
Julio doesn't .... to get a job in that restaurant.

6 We ate very late because Phil spent too much time preparing the meal.
TIME
Phil spent .... preparing the meal that we ate very late.

Word formation

3 Read this text. Use the word given in capitals at the end of some of the lines to form a word that fits in the gap in the same line. There is an example at the beginning (0).

Changing diets

Even in quite **(0)** _traditional_   **TRADITION**
societies, eating habits are
changing. In the past, people
used to prepare good filling
meals from fresh ingredients
and what was readily
available in markets, but
now **(1)** .... food is   **CONVENIENT**
becoming **(2)** ....   **INCREASE**
popular. Research shows
that eating some types of
food too often may lead to
a **(3)** .... of health   **COMBINE**
problems, so governments
and other **(4)** .... now   **ORGANISE**
offer information about diet
and nutrition in the hope that it
will make a **(5)** .... to   **CONTRIBUTE**
people eating a more
(6) .... diet.   **BALANCE**

On the other hand, some
people argue that despite
the **(7)** .... of many   **APPEAR**
traditional dishes from our
menus, in general our diets are
not as repetitive as they used
to be. There is a much wider
(8) .... of products   **CHOOSE**
available in supermarkets and
other shops than there was 20
years ago.

5 Study time

A
B
C
D

Starting off

1 Work in groups. Discuss these questions.

- What are the people doing in the photos?
- Which of the activities are the most useful?
- Which are most fun?

2 Work in pairs. Discuss these questions.

- What's your favourite subject? Why do you like it?
- Do you think you might like to study it at university in the future?
- Can you study it outside the classroom as well?
- Where could you go to learn more about it?
- Think of two or three activities a school could arrange to help you learn more about this subject.

Listening Part 1

1 You are going to hear people talking in eight different situations connected with studying. Before you listen, match these words and phrases (1–9) with their definitions (a–i).

1	tutor	**6**	pass (noun)
2	research (verb)	**7**	sit (an exam)
3	learner	**8**	course requirement
4	mark (verb)	**9**	job prospects
5	admission		

a check a piece of work or an exam, showing mistakes and giving a number or a letter to say how good it is

b someone who is learning something

c something that is needed or demanded for a course

d study something in detail in order to discover new information

e successful result in a test or course

f take a test or exam

g the possibility of being successful at finding work

h university teacher who teaches a small group of students

i permission to study at college, university, etc.

2 Read the questions and underline the main idea in each question (but not in the options A, B or C). The first one has been done for you.

1 You hear a girl complaining about a problem she has had at school.
Why was the girl upset?
  A She handed in an unfinished essay.
  B Her essay may only receive a score of 40%.
  C Her essay wasn't very good.

2 You hear a boy admitting he copied his friend's work.
Why did he do it?
  A His friend asked him to copy her work.
  B His teacher didn't know about the subject.
  C He did it because he wasn't keen on the subject.

3 You hear a girl talking about her preference for coursework over exams.
What reason does she give for her answer?
  A Exams do not always allow students to show their ability.
  B Exams are difficult for every student to do well in.
  C Exams just test how well you know a subject.

4 You hear a boy talking about learning a new language.
Why does he think that it's a good idea?
  A It's a really challenging experience.
  B There is a link between intelligence and language ability.
  C It will help with future employment opportunities.

5 You hear a girl talking to her father about choosing a future course.
What advice does her father give her?
  A just choose something she's interested in
  B find out more about the course
  C stop taking the course if she doesn't like it

6 You hear a boy talking to a friend about his favourite subject at school.
What does he like most about this subject?
  A making shapes out of paper
  B doing research
  C finding solutions

7 You hear a girl talking about why students should have to do homework.
What reason does she give?
  A Homework helps students to do better in their studies.
  B Students learn more at home than in class.
  C Teachers can tell students what they really think in the feedback.

8 You hear a boy talking about doing group projects at school.
What is his opinion about them?
  A Group projects force all members to do an equal share of the work.
  B Group projects can sometimes lead to some people doing more work than others.
  C Group projects are really annoying.

3 Listen and choose the best answer (A, B or C).

17

Vocabulary
Phrasal verbs

1 Match these phrasal verbs from Listening Part 1 with their definitions (a–j).

1 drop out
2 live up to sth
3 hand (sth) back
4 get away with sth
5 point out

6 put (sth) off
7 get through sth
8 get out of doing sth
9 take on
10 catch up with sth

a be as good as something
b delay an event or activity until a later time
c do something you didn't have time to do earlier
d manage to just pass or complete something
e succeed in avoiding punishment for something
f tell someone about some information, e.g. because they don't know it or have forgotten it
g stop going to classes before you have finished the course
h avoid doing something you don't want to do
i return something to the person who gave it to you
j accept (a challenge, job, responsibility)

2 Complete the sentences with a phrasal verb from Exercise 1 in the correct form.

1 Franz hates writing essays and tries to .... writing them till the last moment.

2 I don't know how Charo .... copying her essays from the internet, but the teacher never seems to notice.

3 Julia worked hard for the test, but when the teacher .... it .... she was disappointed that she'd got a very low mark.

4 My mum is very ambitious for me and it's difficult to .... her expectations.

5 The teacher .... that I hadn't answered the second part of the question.

6 I tried to .... tidying my room by saying I had too much homework, but Dad didn't believe me.

find out, get to know, know, learn, teach and *study; attend, join, take part* and *assist*

3 Students often confuse the words above. Choose the correct option in *italics*.

1 I'm hoping to *study / learn* geography at university.

2 I only *found out / knew* my grade just now when my teacher handed my essay back to me.

3 I know it's important to *learn / study* about lots of different things.

4 You're expected to *join / attend* all your lessons.

5 I'm *knowing / getting to know* lots of local people.

6 They also organise lots of other things for us to *assist / take part* in after school.

7 There are clubs we can *assist / join* if we're interested.

8 I'm doing a karate course *learned / taught* in Japanese.

Grammar

Zero, first and second conditionals

▶ Page 168 Grammar reference

1 Read the sentences (1–6) below. Which ...

a refer to something which the speaker thinks is possible?

b refer to something which the speaker is imagining, or thinks is improbable or impossible?

c refer to something which is generally true?

1 If you speak a bit of the language, it's much easier to make friends.

2 If I gave up football, I'd have more time to study.

3 If you're not sure when your event starts, check the programme.

4 If I could drop some subjects, I'd have more time for geography.

5 If there are any changes to the programme, the teachers will tell you straight away.

6 I won't be able to do that unless I do well in my exams at school.

2 Match the beginnings and endings of these sentences.

1 I won't mention your name
2 If I travelled round the world,
3 We don't allow people to do the course
4 I'll have to buy the book
5 I'd get another chocolate bar,
6 If I see her,
7 If I wasn't so busy,
8 If I went to study in Australia,

a I wouldn't see my family for several months.
b I'd go to the cinema with you.
c maybe I would decide to live there permanently.
d I'll tell her you called.
e unless I can find it in the library.
f unless you want me to.
g if I could afford it.
h unless they have the right qualifications.

3 Students often make mistakes with first and second conditionals. Complete the sentences with the correct form of the verbs in brackets.

1 If I .... (say) that technology does not affect the way we study, I would be lying.

2 If I .... (live) near enough, I .... (cycle) to my school, but unfortunately I live too far away to do that.

3 I agree with you about studying together. I'm sure we can! If we .... (do), we .... (be) able to test each other at the same time.

4 We can organise a class trip if we .... (have) any free time during the term.

5 If you .... (have) any problems with your homework, always .... (ask) your teacher for advice.

6 If everyone .... (stop) using plastic bags, it .... (be) good for the environment.

4 Complete the second sentence so that it has a similar meaning to the first sentence, using the word given. Do not change the word given. You must use between two and five words, including the word given.

1 We will not be able to finish the project without your help.
ASSIST
Unless .... the project, we will not be able to finish it.

2 You cannot use the swimming pool unless you become a member of the sports club.
JOIN
You can only use the swimming pool .... the sports club.

3 Stella will not participate in the concert because she is feeling ill.
PART
If Stella was not feeling ill, she .... the concert.

4 It will be necessary for us to postpone the match if the weather does not improve.
PUT
Unless the weather gets better, we .... the match.

5 My English will only improve if my teacher points out my mistakes.
UNLESS
My English .... my teacher points out my mistakes.

6 I will only play in the basketball match if I recover from my cold.
OVER
Unless .... I will not play in the basketball match.

5 Work in pairs. Discuss these questions.

• If you could study something at school that you don't learn about at the moment, what would it be?

• If you could go on holiday anywhere in the world, where would you like to go?

• How will you celebrate if you pass all your exams this year?

• If you could change one thing in your life, what would it be?

• If, one day, you became famous, what do you think you would be famous for?

5

• Before you read the sections, read the questions carefully, underlining the main ideas.

• Read the first section and find which questions it answers.

• Deal with each section in turn in this way.

• If you have any time left, go back and check what you have written and fill in any questions you missed.

Exam advice

2 Underline the main idea in each question.

Which person

1 took part in a summer course organised by their school?

2 had the summer course recommended to them by a family member?

3 decided that they would like to work in this area in the future?

4 learned a lot from another student?

5 felt better prepared for an exam after the summer course?

6 had to work harder than they thought they would?

7 studied with students of the same gender?

8 received praise for their work on the course?

9 made a good friend on their course?

10 learned about different careers they could follow?

3 For questions 1–10 above, choose from the four people (A–D) on page 57. The people may be chosen more than once.

4 Work in groups. Look at this post on a student forum. Think about the experiences of the students you have just read about, and decide what Will should do.

WILL

I'm 16 years old and would like to spend the summer doing something a bit different. I am applying to university next year and would like to do something that will look good on my application form. I would like to be a teacher in the future and am thinking of applying to study Spanish or History. Does anyone have any recommendations for summer courses which would be interesting for me and that would help me with my university application?

---

1 Work in pairs. You are going to read extracts from four reports by students about summer courses they attended. Before you read, discuss these questions.

• How do you think students benefit from attending a summer course?

• What benefits do each of the photos show?

• If you could learn something new over the summer, what would you learn?

Making the most of your summer

Have you ever attended a summer course? Four students relate their experiences ...

A *Xiao from Shanghai attended an English Language summer course in London.*

My teachers at school recommended that I study abroad during the summer to prepare for my final exams. My sister had taken an English course in the UK a few years earlier and, on her advice, I signed up for the same one. When I arrived, I found that I was the only Chinese person on the course. There were a lot of Italian and Spanish students, but as I didn't speak any of those languages, I had to try to communicate in English. I felt lonely at first, but fortunately, I met a Polish girl called Magda, who was also the only person from her country. We became close friends, and because she had a high level of English, she helped me to improve my vocabulary. Overall, it was a great

experience and I have now decided to apply to a British university.

B *James from Edinburgh went on a summer exchange with an orchestra to Bremen in Germany.*

Our school orchestra takes part in a summer exchange programme with a secondary school in Bremen. I decided to join last summer, as my older brother and several of my friends were going, and because I was taking a German exam and wanted to improve my level. I'd expected to spend a lot of time messing around, but our schedule was surprisingly tough. We had to start our rehearsals at 9.00 am every morning, and the music was more challenging than I had expected, so I had to spend a lot of time practising,

which was annoying. The German music students were a lot of fun, though, and had planned some great activities for us in the evenings. I'd hoped that we'd stay in touch, but we only chat online occasionally now. I didn't really improve my German either, as they all spoke perfect English.

C *Celine from Avignon attended a science camp in Paris.*

A university in Paris that organises summer schools for secondary school students came to our school and gave a presentation on their engineering courses. I had been considering a career in this field, so I convinced my parents to let me go. The course was specifically for girls who want to study science subjects at university. We were taught by lecturers and students from the university, who told us all about their subjects and possible jobs and professions that we could have in the future. It was a really rewarding experience, and I now feel much more confident about taking my physics exam next year.

D *Juan from Madrid attended a theatre summer school in Dublin.*

When I told my parents that I wanted to work in a theatre when I leave school, they insisted that I get some experience first. I found a summer school in Ireland which prepares young people for careers in the performing arts and I signed up for it straight away. We were trained by professionals working in different roles in the theatre. I was interested in the technical side of theatre, so I had the opportunity to work with a lighting technician for four weeks. He made me realise that lighting is a huge responsibility and that it is really hard work, but he was very encouraging and told me I was a natural technician. It was a rewarding experience, which confirmed that a theatre technician is the right job for me.

5

Reading and Use of English Part 3

1 Form nouns from these verbs.

verb	noun	
qualify	**1**	qualification
intend	**2**	
respond	**3**	
lose	**4**	
compare	**5**	
exist	**6**	
demand	**7**	
develop	**8**	
perform	**9**	
advise	**10**	
appear	**11**	
know	**12**	

2 Each of the nouns below has been formed from a verb. Write the verb next to the noun.

verb	noun
1 agree	agreement
2	assessment
3	feeling
4	involvement
5	investigation
6	confusion
7	preference
8	approval

3 Read the text below. Use the word given in capitals at the end of some of the lines to form a word that fits in the gap in the same line.

EXAM STRESS FOR TEENAGERS

Teenagers who have exams may experience **(0)** ....feelings.... of stress for a number of different reasons. Their future ambitions, such as what they will study at university, may be **(1)** .... on their exam results. They will probably feel afraid that their **(2)** .... will not be as strong as that of their friends and may feel worried about being **(3)** .... negatively to them. They may feel so overwhelmed by the amount of studying they will need to do to obtain a **(4)** .... result that they give up leisure activities which they would have previously found enjoyable and **(5)** ...., such as doing sports and listening to music. Teenagers suffering from exam stress may show a variety of symptoms, including **(6)** .... of appetite, being unable to sleep and a lack of **(7)** .... to study. It is important for teachers and parents to watch out for these signs and to be as supportive and **(8)** .... as possible.

FEEL

DEPEND

PERFORM

COMPARE

SUCCEED

RELAX

LOSE
MOTIVATE

ENCOURAGE

4 Work in groups. What can teenagers who are suffering from exam stress do to help themselves relax?

Speaking Part 1

▶ **Page 192 Speaking bank**

- In Speaking Part 1, listen carefully to the question and make sure your answers are relevant.
- Where possible, give reasons for your answer and/or add some extra information.

Exam advice

1 Work in pairs. Complete this extract of two candidates doing Speaking Part 1. Then listen to check your answers.

Examiner: Nicola, what's your favourite subject at school?

Nicola: I find physics fascinating. That's **(1)** .... I enjoy all science subjects a lot and **(2)** .... I can get high enough marks in my final exams, I'll study engineering **(3)** .... I go to university. Also, I've got three good friends in my class, **(4)** .... I enjoy doing experiments with in the lab.

Examiner: And you, Alex, how do you think you'll use English in the future?

Alex: Well, I think English is absolutely vital now, especially if you want to travel. You can get by without it, **(5)** .... it will be difficult to get a good job, even if you stay in your home country. I'm hoping to study at an American university in the future, **(6)** .... I'll definitely need to have a high level of English to do that.

Examiner: Thank you. Nicola, can you …

2 Work in pairs. Discuss these questions.

1 How many reasons does Nicola give for her answer?
2 How many situations does Alex mention for using English?
3 Why is it good to combine ideas and reasons in your answers?
4 Why is it good to sound interested and enthusiastic?

3 Think how you can answer these questions, combining your ideas and reasons for them. Then work in pairs and take turns to ask and answer the questions.

- What is/was your favourite subject at school? Why?
- How do you think you'll use English in the future?

4 Pronunciation: word stress (2)

With some related words, the stress is different depending on whether it is a noun, a verb or an adjective.

4.1 Listen to these words. Which syllable is stressed?

necessary   necessity

4.2 Decide which syllable is stressed in each of these words.

satisfying / satisfactory   educate / education
exam / examination   explain / explanation
possible / possibility   prefer / preference

4.3 Now listen to check your answers. What do you notice about where we stress words ending in -*tion* and -*ity*?

4.4 Work in pairs. Take turns to read the words aloud.

5 Think about how you can answer these questions.

- What do you particularly like about the school where you study?
- What plans and ambitions do you have for your education in the future?

6 Work in pairs. Take turns to ask and answer the questions above. While you listen to your partner, pay attention to how they stress their words. Correct them where necessary.

7 Work in pairs. Decide which of you will be Student A and which Student B and take some time to think about how you will answer your questions below. Then take turns to ask your partner their questions.

Questions for Student A

- Can you describe the school you go to?
- What would you like to study in the future if you had the chance? Why?
- How much homework do students in your country generally do?
- Can you tell me what you most enjoy about learning English?
- Tell me about the best teacher you have ever had.

Questions for Student B

- Do you prefer studying alone or with other people? Why?
- Can you remember your first day at school? Tell me about it.
- Would you like to study in a different country? Why? / Why not?
- How important are exams in your country?
- How important is learning English to you?

Writing Part 2
The set text

- The 'set text' is a book chosen by *B2 First for Schools* candidates to study with their teacher in class. The book changes every two years. In Writing Part 2, you have the option of answering a question about this set text. The question is often an essay question, but could be a review, an article or a letter instead.
- You might want to choose this question if you and your class have studied the set text together.
- You **should not** choose this question if you have not read the book or seen the film adaptation of the book.
- You **should not** write about another book instead. This is very important, because if you write about a different book, you will get a very low mark for this question, or possibly no marks at all.

Exam info

1 Read this writing task and look at the essay plan.

> Which is the most interesting character in the book you have read? What part does this character play in the story, and why is this character interesting?

Introduction: say who the character is
Paragraph 2: brief description of the character's role, giving examples from the story
Paragraph 3: reasons why the character is interesting, giving examples from the story
Conclusion: one or two sentences to sum up your essay

2 Work in groups. Read the two essays opposite.

- Which essay do you think is best? Why?
- What is wrong with the other essay?

ESSAY 1

The most interesting character in the book is definitely John Grainger. Although several other characters, such as Emma and Harry, are important to the plot, John is the one with the most energy and charm.

John is the hero of the novel, and in the very first chapter, we see how John can't help getting involved in other people's lives. For example, in the café, he tells Harry that he has spilt coffee on his jacket and this is how their unlikely friendship begins. John is always willing to help people, even in tense situations like the boat journey in the storm. As a result, people trust him and he ends up leading everyone to safety at the end of the story.

I find his character interesting because he is so unselfish. He always seems to consider other people's needs and is never afraid of putting himself in danger. This is particularly true when he jumps into the sea and rescues Emma.

John may be just a character in a book, but for all the above reasons, I would love to meet him in real life. He is the kind of person who could teach us all a great deal.

Essay 2

Although there are a number of interesting characters in this book, there is one in particular who stands out, in my opinion, and that is the main character: John Grainger.

John definitely plays one of the most important roles in the book. All the other characters can see that he is a reliable person and that is why they are happy to take his advice and follow his example. Right from the start, he stands out compared to the others, and we know he is going to be the hero.

I find him fascinating as a character because I have always been interested in unusual people. It is hard to define what makes someone stand out from the crowd. It may be a certain attitude to life, or the way the person deals with a crisis that they face. I think people can always tell when someone special walks into a room, and if John walked in, everybody would realise they were in the presence of an amazing person.

All in all, John is definitely the most interesting character in the book. The decisions he makes reflect this and engage the reader.

3 Match the teacher's comments (a and b) with the opening paragraphs of the two essays in Exercise 2.

a You start the essay well, identifying the character you have decided to focus on and mentioning other examples of characters in the book who are also central to the plot. You have justified your choice of character by briefly giving reasons why you think he is interesting. This makes your essay interesting and informative right from the start.

b You have said which character you are going to write about, which is good. You could improve your introduction by briefly giving a reason why you think the character is interesting, and possibly by mentioning one or two other main characters in the book to make a comparison.

4 Now, think of a book you have read and write your own opening paragraph for the task in Exercise 1.

5 Look at how these words and phrases were used in Essay 1 to link ideas together. Then complete the essay below with these words and phrases. In some cases, more than one answer is possible.

> although   as a result   for all the above reasons
> for example   like   such as

My favourite character in the book is Lucy, because
(1) .... at first the reader is given the impression that she is shy and a little dull, she actually turns out to be far from boring.
(2) ...., when we first see her, sitting quietly and staring out of the window at the river, Mark and Jane don't even notice that she is there.
(3) .... , she hears them talking about their plan to harm Kim, and then the reader realises that 'little' Lucy, as Gavin always calls her, is a brave and intelligent woman. Throughout the book, the reader is surprised by Lucy, **(4)** .... when she confronts Gavin about his behaviour towards his sister. Other characters in the book, **(5)** .... Kim and Mark, soon learn to respect her for her honesty and courage.
(6) ...., Lucy is the most interesting character in the book for me. I still think about her sometimes, even though she is just a fictional character and I read the book a long time ago.

6 Finish the essay you started in Exercise 4. Try to use some of the words and phrases you practised in Exercise 5.

6 My first job

Starting off

1 Work in pairs. Which of the jobs in the photos would you most like to do? Which one would you least like to do? Why?

Listening Part 3

> **Exam advice**
>
> - Before you listen, read each option carefully and think about what it means.
> - Listen for the general idea of what each speaker is saying.
> - It is important to listen for words which have the same **meaning** as the words in the options, since you will not hear those exact words on the recording.

1 Choose the correct meaning, a or b, for these sentences.

1 It is easy to do.
 a *I don't find it difficult.*
 b *I think it's hard work.*

2 It enables me to work alongside a friend.
 a *I don't have the opportunity to work with a friend.*
 b *I work closely with a mate.*

3 My parents told me I had to do it.
 a *Mum and Dad made me do it.*
 b *Mum and Dad suggested it.*

2 You will hear five short extracts in which young people are talking about their weekend job. Listen and match the speakers (1–5) with the photos (A–E).

3 Listen again. Choose from the list (A–H) the reason each speaker gives for doing their weekend job. Use the letters only once. There are three extra letters which you do not need to use.

A It is easy to do.
B It enables me to work alongside a friend.
C My parents told me I had to do it.
D It gives me the opportunity to make new friends.
E It may be useful for the career I've chosen to do.
F I'm saving up to buy something special.
G It enables me to choose exactly when I want to work.
H It is well paid.

Speaker 1 ☐   Speaker 4 ☐
Speaker 2 ☐   Speaker 5 ☐
Speaker 3 ☐

4 Work in groups.

- Would you be interested in doing any of the jobs the speakers talked about? Why? / Why not?
- What job would be 'a dream come true' for you?

Vocabulary

work and *job*; *possibility, occasion* and *opportunity*; *fun* and *funny*

1 Students often confuse the words above. Read these sentences from Listening Part 3 and choose the correct option in *italics*.

1 I've got a *work / job* in a department store on Saturdays.

2 It isn't a very well-paid *job / work*, but then lots of weekend *jobs / works* aren't.

3 I can't wait to learn to drive! It'll be great *fun / funny*.

4 I didn't really have to actively look for *job / work*.

5 We always have a good laugh together – she tells really *fun / funny* jokes.

6 It's actually hard, physical *work / job* – I didn't expect that when I started.

7 On one *possibility / occasion / opportunity* I had four dogs – I'll never do that again!

8 It's great having the *possibility / occasion / opportunity* to spend time out and about in the fresh air.

9 There's even the *possibility / occasion / opportunity* that I'll be asked to design a website soon.

2 Choose the correct option in *italics*.

1 I know he was trying to be *fun / funny*, but none of his jokes made us laugh.

2 The trip was *fun / funny* – we should do it again sometime.

3 I don't think there's much *possibility / opportunity* of him being chosen for the job.

4 I only wear these smart clothes on special *occasions / opportunities*.

5 Did you get a(n) *possibility / opportunity* to chat to Matt yesterday?

6 She's just applied online for a summer *job / work*.

7 I'm hoping to study engineering and to find *job / work* in the construction industry when I leave school.

8 One of my *jobs / works* was to teach children to swim.

3 Work in pairs. The diagram shows adjective collocations with *job* and *work*, in groups according to meaning. Complete the diagram with the words in the box. In some cases, more than one answer may be possible.

> badly-paid   challenging   demanding   fascinating   full-time   hard   holiday   manual   office   outdoor   part-time   permanent   pleasant   responsible   skilled   temporary   tiring   tough   weekend   well-paid   worthwhile

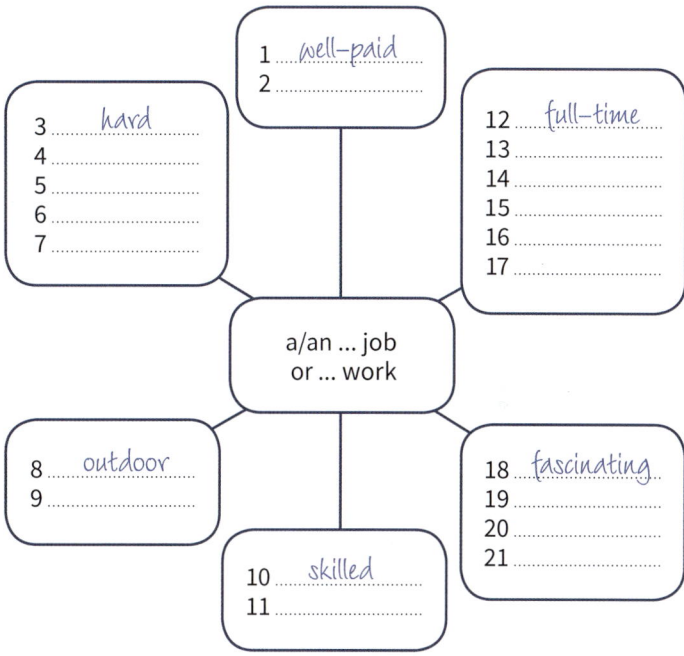

1 well-paid
2 ....

3 hard
4 ....
5 ....
6 ....
7 ....

a/an ... job or ... work

12 full-time
13 ....
14 ....
15 ....
16 ....
17 ....

8 outdoor
9 ....

18 fascinating
19 ....
20 ....
21 ....

10 skilled
11 ....

4 Work in pairs. Describe the jobs using two or three adjectives from Exercise 3. Put opinion adjectives first and adjectives that give factual information afterwards. For example:

Being a lifeguard at a swimming pool is a pleasant, outdoor, holiday job.

1 bed tester – you get paid to sleep in hotel beds around the world and report how comfortable they are

2 strawberry picker – you pick and package strawberries at a fruit farm

3 aid worker – you are sent to help in emergency situations around the world, e.g. earthquakes, floods

4 wildlife photographer – you photograph endangered species all over the world

5 Work in pairs. Which of the jobs in Exercise 4 would you most like to do? Why? Can you think of any more unusual jobs? Write a list and then swap your list with another pair. Which jobs are the best?

Reading and Use of English Part 5

1 You are going to read an extract from a blog by a student called Jenny, who is describing her very first job. Before you read, work in groups.

- What do you think are the advantages and disadvantages of working at weekends?

2 Read the first paragraph quickly and choose the correct answer.

How did Jenny get her job?

A through a friend
B through an advertisement
C through a relative

My first JOB

When I was 16, life seemed so unfair because just about everyone I knew had a weekend job and I didn't. They were lucky enough to have a 'hook up'. That's when someone like your parents, or a friend, gets one for you so you don't have to waste time reading through countless job advertisements. But then one of my mates got a Saturday job as a cleaner in a big hotel down the road from my house, so when there was an opening, I joined her. Now, I know what you're thinking. 'I'm not cleaning for anybody.' I was thinking the same. But it paid the usual hotel rate of £5 an hour and anyway, cleaning couldn't be *that* difficult, could it?

There was a lot more to the job than you might expect. First, I'd collect my cart from the storeroom and load it with all the supplies I needed – a pile of fresh sheets and towels, as well as toiletries like shampoo and soap. Then I set to work on cleaning the rooms. I made the beds, vacuumed the carpets, cleaned the baths and dusted the furniture. Such was the reality of my very first job. It wasn't particularly fun. In fact, it could be really unpleasant at times, especially at the beginning. The first time I made a bed, I didn't fold the sheets correctly and the manager made me do it all over again. But one of my colleagues showed me exactly what to do and I took notes, just like I did in school. It took ages for me to get it right but when I did, I felt happy and confident, and it wasn't long before I could make a bed in no time at all!

The guests were mostly pleasant and I even learned new words in a few different languages by speaking to some of them. However, on a few occasions, they would get annoyed because they had returned to their room to find me there cleaning it. Then there were a few guests who left stuff like empty pizza boxes and clothing on the floor, making it just about impossible for me to do any cleaning at all. But the worst thing was when we lost clothes guests had asked to be dry cleaned – occasionally I'd forget to put a ticket on an item, and it would simply disappear!

Although it wasn't well paid, the job enabled me to party with my friends and keep my mobile phone in credit. It wasn't just the money that made it all worthwhile. For the first time I was able to spend time with adults other than my parents and teachers. I had always thought that it would be difficult to get on with them, but as long as I was willing to work as hard as them, we all got on fine. They didn't have any authority over me either – we were all the same – pushing the same carts and cleaning the same number of rooms. And if I didn't want to do the work, these grown-ups wouldn't try to twist my arm. They wouldn't yell at me or punish me, it was up to me to motivate myself. That was one very important lesson for me to learn and one I never got taught in school.

My time at the hotel also taught me that you can gain new skills from any kind of work, even a job you never thought you'd do. And at the same time, it showed me where I didn't want to be in future. And I didn't want to be in a hotel cleaning baths and folding towels for the rest of my life. I was looking for something a lot more challenging.

52

- First read the text quickly to get a general idea of what it is about.
- Read the first question, find where it is answered in the text, and read that section carefully more than once before you read the options A, B, C and D.
- Read the options carefully and choose the one which matches what the text says.
- Pay attention to words like *often, never, generally.*

Exam advice

---

3 **Read the questions which you will have to answer in Exercise 4 and find the parts of the text which provide the answers.**

1 What best describes Jenny's feelings in the first paragraph?

2 What do we learn about Jenny's job in the first two paragraphs?

3 What impression does Jenny give of the hotel guests?

4 What best describes Jenny's relationship with her colleagues?

5 What does 'twist my arm' mean in line 52?

6 What conclusion does Jenny draw about her job?

4 **Choose the answer (A, B, C or D) which you think fits best according to the text.**

1 What best describes Jenny's feelings in the first paragraph?

   A She had assumed finding a job would be easy.

   B She envied people she knew who already had jobs.

   C She was unwilling to find a job.

   D She was surprised at the number of job opportunities available.

2 What do we learn about Jenny's job in the first two paragraphs?

   A It was better paid than she expected.

   B It was easy to do.

   C It took a long time to complete each task.

   D It was more challenging than she thought it would be.

3 What impression does Jenny give of the hotel guests?

   A They were generally friendly.

   B They tended to be untidy.

   C They often complained.

   D They made it difficult for her to do her job.

4 What best describes Jenny's relationship with her colleagues?

   A She felt she had little in common with them.

   B She felt that she was expected to do more work than them.

   C She felt that they treated her as an equal.

   D She felt they worked harder than she did.

5 What does 'twist my arm' mean in line 52?

   A try to prevent me from doing something

   B persuade me to do something I don't want to do

   C pretend to agree with me when they don't

   D threaten to hurt me if I don't agree to do something

6 What conclusion does Jenny draw about her job?

   A She was disappointed that she had learned so little from it.

   B She regretted all aspects of it.

   C It inspired her choice of career.

   D It was a rewarding experience but she was glad it was over.

5 **Work in pairs. Discuss these questions.**

- Would you enjoy doing a job like Jenny's? Why? / Why not?

- Which parts of her job would you enjoy more and which would you enjoy less?

- What would be your ideal weekend job? Why?

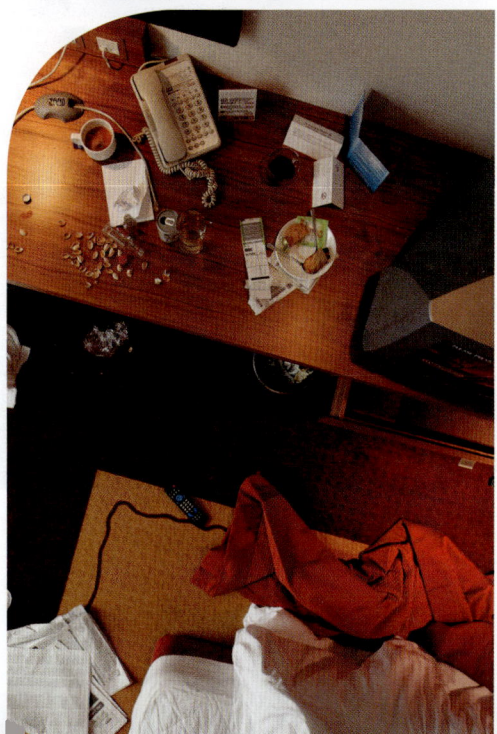

Speaking Part 2

▶ **Page 194 Speaking bank**

1 Work in pairs. When you compare photos, you can say what the photos have in common as well as what is different about them. Look at the photos and discuss how you could answer the examiner's instruction below to say:

- which things are similar
- which things are different.

Examiner: I'd like you to compare the photographs and say what you think the people are learning from doing these two types of work.

What are the people learning from doing these two types of work?

- Compare the general differences between the two photos and also spend time answering the printed question.
- You can talk about one photo first and then the other (as you saw in Unit 2), or both at the same time (as in this unit).
- Keep speaking till the examiner says 'Thank you'.

Exam advice

2 How could you use these words or phrases to talk about the photos?

a involve
b deal with
c not well paid
d coaching
e full-time
f part-time
g keep somebody in order
h work under pressure
I keep cool

3 Listen to Bruno and Sofia doing this part of the test. Which photo do they use each word or phrase with? Write 1 or 2 or B (both) by each word or phrase (a–i) in Exercise 2. 🎧 22

4 Which of these strategies (a or b) does Bruno use when doing the task?

a He describes the first photo and answers the question before moving on to the second photo and doing the same.
b He points out similarities as well as differences between the two photos and switches between them as he answers.

5 Listen again. Which of these phrases does Bruno use? Tick ✓ the ones you hear. 🎧 22

- Both photos show …
- Both the jobs in the photos involve …
- neither of them is …
- Anyway, the first photo shows …
- While the girl in the first photo …
- … whereas in the second photo …
- … whereas the boy's …
- Another thing in the second photo is …
- I think both can …
- On the other hand …
- not just … but also …

6 Pronunciation: sentence stress (2)

- We can use stress to contrast ideas or information.

6.1 Which ideas or information does Bruno contrast in this sentence?

- Anyway, the first photo shows a girl serving young people in a restaurant, whereas in the second photo a boy is working with children.

6.2 Listen to the sentence and underline the stressed words. 23

6.3 Decide which words are stressed in these sentences. Then listen to check your answers. 24

- The girl's job may be full-time, / whereas the boy's is probably part-time.
- The girl can learn how to keep customers happy, / while the boy has to keep children in order.
- He'll probably learn not just to deal with children, / but also their parents.
- I'd prefer to coach children than work in a restaurant / because really I enjoy being in the fresh air more than being indoors.

7 Write three sentences to compare the photos on page 66 and say which job you think is more difficult. Use phrases from Exercise 5.
Then work in pairs and take turns to read your sentences aloud, using stress to contrast your ideas.

8 Work in pairs.

Student A: Do the speaking task in Exercise 1 on page 66.

Student B: Time your partner and make sure they speak for one minute.

9 Work in pairs.

Student B: Follow the examiner's instructions below.

Student A: Time your partner and make sure they speak for one minute.

Examiner: Here are your photographs. They show people doing different part-time jobs. I'd like you to compare the photographs and say what you think the people might enjoy or not enjoy about doing these jobs.

What might the people enjoy or not enjoy about doing these jobs?

Grammar
Countable and uncountable nouns

▶ **Page 169 Grammar reference**

1 Choose the correct option in *italics*.

1 Could I have some more *informations / information* about the job?
2 I've done a bit of babysitting, so I can give you *an advice / some advice* if you like.
3 My brother's just found *a work / a job* as a chef.
4 On our school language exchange the *accommodation was / accommodations were* with host families.
5 The *furnitures / furniture* in the office where my dad works is so old-fashioned!
6 The football flew through the open window into the living room, but luckily it didn't do any *damages / damage*!
7 When we go on holiday, we always take too *many luggages / much luggage*.
8 Everyone loves the band, because they play such fantastic *musics / music*.

2 Students often make mistakes with countable and uncountable nouns. Find all the *uncountable* nouns in each list.

1 accommodation hotel luggage staff
2 advice information knowledge news suggestion
3 accident bus damage traffic transport
4 air conditioning bed carpet furniture
5 dish food meal music
6 homework job task work
7 equipment factory machinery tool
8 cash dollar money wealth
9 fun joke stuff

3 Complete the sentences with the words in the box. In some cases, more than one answer may be possible.

> amount bit deal
> number piece

1 Can I give you a .... of advice about shopping in this town?
2 During the storm, quite a large .... of trees were blown down.
3 Have you brought that .... of equipment I asked for? The amplifier, I mean.
4 I've just been given a great .... of news – I've passed my exams!
5 Seb put a great .... of effort into organising the party.
6 There were a large .... of guests at the party, judging by the .... of food that was eaten!

Articles

▶ **Page 170 Grammar reference**

4 Match the underlined examples from the reading text (1–6) with the rules for articles (a–f). The first one has been done for you as an example.

1 One of my mates got a Saturday job as a cleaner … *b*
2 … in a big hotel down the road from my house.
3 My time at the hotel also taught me that you can learn new skills from any kind of work.
4 There were a few guests who left things like empty pizza boxes and clothing on the floor …
5 The worst thing was when we lost clothes …
6 … the job enabled me to keep my mobile phone in credit.

a *a* and *an* are not used with uncountable nouns.
b *a* and *an* are used with singular countable nouns mentioned for the first time.
c *the* is used when it's clear who or what we are referring to from the context.
d No article is used when talking about plural and uncountable things in general.
e *the* is used with superlative adjectives and adverbs.
f *the* is used with things mentioned before.

5 Read the text as quickly as you can, ignoring the gaps. Choose the best way to end the title, A or B.

Babysitting …

A a great deal harder than it looks!

B a simple way to earn a bit of money!

B A B Y sitting …

Most people think that babysitting is one of **(1)** .... easiest jobs available to **(2)** .... young people. They imagine a teenager putting **(3)** .... well-behaved child to bed at 8 o'clock in the evening and then relaxing on the sofa until **(4)** .... parents come home. Well, they couldn't be more wrong!

I had decided that **(5)** .... good way to earn some extra cash would be to look for **(6)** .... babysitting job, and it didn't take long for me to find one.

I now work all day on a Saturday for **(7)** .... family with two young boys. I expected to look after **(8)** .... perfect children who would behave well and listen to me all **(9)** .... time. Unfortunately, I've found out that **(10)** .... kids like that don't exist at all! While **(11)** .... two boys are usually polite and calm, they are also typical kids who like to fight, scream and shout for no real reason at times! Sometimes they really test my **(12)** .... patience!

Being **(13)** .... babysitter requires **(14)** .... flexibility. I have to be a friend when I play with them, but **(15)** .... teacher when they fight with each other over **(16)** .... silly things like sharing their toys. So, every Saturday for me is like an adventure, but one I look forward to!

6 Complete the text with *a*, *an*, *the* or '–' if no article is needed.

7 Work in pairs. Discuss these questions.

- Have you ever babysat for younger brothers or sisters or someone else's children? If so, did you find it easy or difficult? Why?
- Do you think babysitting is a good job for a teenager? Why? / Why not?

Reading and Use of English Part 2

- Read the text quite quickly to get a general idea what it is about.
- Look at the words before and after the gap and decide what type of word you need (an article, pronoun, preposition, etc.).
- When you've chosen a word, read the completed sentence to make sure it makes sense.
- Words may sometimes be part of fixed phrases, e.g. *in order to, as far as I know*, etc.

Exam advice

1 Read the text below and think of the word which best fits each gap. Use only one word in each gap. There is an example at the beginning **(0)**.

You don't get paid when you do volunteering but it can be a very rewarding experience. Interested? Then read on!

Volunteering is **(0)** ....*a*........ great way to spend your free time. Whatever your interests, there will be a volunteering role **(1)** .... is ideal for you. If you like animals, why **(2)** .... take dogs for a walk at an animal rescue centre? If you are keen on sport, you **(3)** .... organise team games like football and basketball for young children in a sports hall. If you are interested in protecting the environment, then what about spending a day cleaning up a section of river? Not **(4)** .... is volunteering fun, but it can also teach you useful new skills **(5)** .... as team work and problem solving. Another benefit is that you can meet new people who might turn **(6)** .... to be good friends too! It can also develop your confidence as well as your general knowledge, and you'll always have **(7)** .... interesting to talk about. So, what are you waiting for? **(8)** .... volunteering a try!

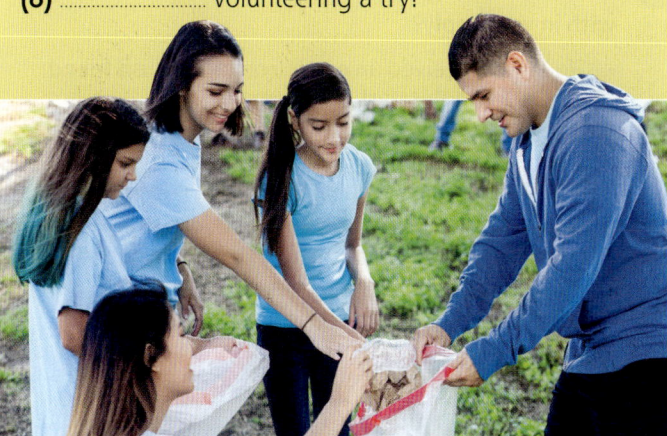

2 Check or complete your answers using these clues.

1 a relative pronoun
2 a negative
3 a modal verb
4 *not … but also*
5 a synonym of *for example*
6 part of a phrasal verb
7 a pronoun
8 part of an expression which means the same as *try something*

3 Work in groups. Discuss these questions.

1 Do you think all young people should get experience of these things? Why? / Why not?
- working in a team
- problem solving
- doing outdoor activities
- helping other people
- looking after animals

2 Which of the experiences above do you think are the most useful to have?

Writing Part 2
A letter or email

▶ Page 204 Writing bank

Exam advice

- Read the email in the task carefully and underline the points you must reply to.
- Write a plan, dealing with each point in turn, probably one in each paragraph.
- Write the email following your plan.

1 Read this writing task. Which three points must you deal with in your reply?

You have received an email from an English friend, Rosie. Read this part of the email.

I'm doing a school project on weekend jobs that teenagers in different countries do while they are still at school. Can you help me by describing the sort of weekend jobs teenagers do in your country, any problems they have and how people find part-time jobs?

Thanks,

Rosie

2 Work in pairs. Discuss what you can say to answer the three points. Note down your ideas as you speak.

3 Write a brief plan for your reply (in note form).

- How many paragraphs do you need?
- What ideas or information will you include in each paragraph?

4 Read Pablo's email to Rosie, ignoring the spelling mistakes, and answer these questions.

1 How does Pablo begin and end his email?
2 How do we know the subject of each of the three main paragraphs straight away?

Hi Rosie

It's good to hear from you.

In Spain, it's quite hard for young people to find jobs. Some teenagers have parents who run small businesses like shops or restaurans, and they often help out at the weekend. Others may do babysitting or earn extra money by washing cars for their neibours or their parents' friends.

Teenagers who work regularly at the weekend have two main problems. First, it can be quite difficult for them to combine part-time work with the large amount of homework and studing for exams wich they have to do. Second, the jobs are often not well payed. On the other hand, the money is usefull becaus they can buy little things for themselves and be a bit more independent.

Finding a weekend job isn't always straightforward, especialy if you don't live in a big city, or in an area which is visited by tourists. Teenagers in my area usually do a bit of work from time to time for family members or people they know, rather than having a regular weekend job.

I hope this helps and good luck with your project.

Cheers,

Pablo

5 Pablo's email contains eight spelling mistakes often made by students. Find and correct the mistakes.

~~restaurans~~   restaurants

6 Decide whether these words are spelled correctly or not. Where they are spelled wrongly, write the correct spelling.

accomodation
accommodation

embarrassing	opportunity
confortable	convenient
greatful	believe
environment	necessary
experience	begining
communicate	excellent
forward	preffer
received	recommend
definately	easely
course	advertisment

7 Read the writing task below and note the points you must deal with in your answer. Then write a short plan.

You have received an email from an American friend, Sam. Read this part of the email.

I'm doing a project on teenagers' part-time jobs. Can you help me by describing a part-time job you've done (or the job of someone you know well), what you or they learned from it and any problems you or they had with it?

Thanks,

Sam

8 Write your email. You should write between 140 and 190 words.

Vocabulary

1 Complete the sentences with phrasal verbs from page 53 in the correct form.

1 It's getting harder for students to .... copying essays from the internet, because there are an increasing number of ways teachers can check.

2 Tom's university course didn't .... his expectations, and he .... after the first term.

3 Dmitry doesn't like doing housework, so he .... doing it by pretending he has homework.

4 I missed a year of school, so I needed to .... my classmates, but I still managed to .... my exams without any problems.

5 When my teacher .... my essay, she .... that I hadn't answered the question exactly and that there was a lot which was irrelevant.

2 Choose the correct option in *italics*.

1 Mario is thinking of taking lessons to *know / learn* how to drive.

2 Ludmila wants to *know / study* biology at university.

3 Sven is *teaching / learning* me to ski.

4 If you *join / assist* this club, you will *know / get to know* people from all over the world.

5 You should *attend / assist* lessons every day if you want to get high marks.

6 Sayed decided to *assist / take part* in the debate on human rights.

Grammar

3 Complete the second sentence so that it has a similar meaning to the first sentence, using the word given. Do not change the word given. You must use between two and five words, including the word given.

1 He won't pass the test because he doesn't work hard enough.
HARDER
If he worked .... pass the test.

2 Cycling to school will make you more independent.
BECOME
If you cycle .... more independent.

3 Sandra only goes to dance classes because she wants to keep fit.
ATTEND
If Sandra didn't want to keep fit, ... dance classes.

4 I'll lend you my book if you take care of it.
AFTER
If you .... , you can borrow it.

5 I can't tell you the answer because I don't know.
WOULD
If I .... tell you.

6 He's not very enthusiastic because he's tired.
SO
If .... , he'd be more enthusiastic.

Word formation

4 For questions 1–8, read this text. Use the word given in capitals at the end of some of the lines to form a word that fits in the gap in the same line. There is an example at the beginning (0).

It is sometimes said that 'Your schooldays are the happiest days of your life', and people often feel that this should be a period of (0) *enjoyment* . However, exams often affect students' happiness, and many students express a **ENJOY**

(1) .... for alternative methods of assessment, where the work they do throughout the year counts towards their final mark. **PREFER**

They say that exams test short-term memory and (2) .... , which is forgotten immediately after the exam. Also, assessing coursework as part of the final mark changes students' (3) .... , making them more responsible about studying. There are some students, however, who prefer final examinations, saying that in **KNOW**

BEHAVE

(4) .... they only have to work hard for two months a year and so they have more time for their leisure (5) .... They say that some students receive **COMPARE**

ACT

(6) .... with their coursework from their parents, so it is not an accurate (7) .... of how hard they have worked or of their real (8) .... in the subject they are studying. **ASSIST**

MEASURE

ABLE

Vocabulary

1 Complete the sentences with a word from the box.

> fun funny job occasion occasion
> opportunity possibility work

1 Andrea's birthday was a great .... – I won't forget it for a long time.

2 Excuse me! I have to get to .... and I'm already late.

3 My sister did an excellent .... arranging the party for us so well!

4 My uncle has lost his temper on only one .... as far as I can remember.

5 I didn't find the gym class much .... because the other people there weren't very friendly.

6 Olga sees the school play as a great .... to show how well she can act.

7 Polly took us to see a very .... film which made us laugh a lot.

8 You have no .... of getting a better-paid job with your lack of qualifications.

Grammar

2 Complete the second sentence so that it has a similar meaning to the first sentence, using the word given. Do not change the word given. You must use between two and five words, including the word given.

1 I found my first day at work so enjoyable.
FUN
I .... my first day of work.

2 Were you able to speak to your teacher after class?
OPPORTUNITY
Did you .... to your teacher after class?

3 Our class may be able to go on an exchange trip to Canada next year.
POSSIBILITY
Our class may .... on an exchange trip to Canada next year.

4 We didn't expect the news to be nearly so good.
MUCH
The news .... we expected.

5 Patricia helped us a lot with her advice.
DEAL
Patricia provided us .... helpful advice.

6 William has only spoken to his great-uncle once during the year.
OCCASION
William has only spoken to his great-uncle .... all year.

3 Complete the sentences by writing one word in each gap. In some cases, more than one answer may be possible.

1 Careful! This laptop cost my mum a great .... of money.

2 I heard an interesting .... of news at school this morning – we're going to get a new sports hall next year.

3 You need to put in a certain .... of effort if you want to be successful.

4 That's a really useless .... of equipment – you should throw it away!

5 There are a large .... of shops in the town centre where you can buy souvenirs.

4 Complete the story with *a*, *an*, *the* or '–' if no article is needed.

I was travelling around Europe by **(1)** .... train one summer when I was about 18 years old and I arrived in **(2)** .... city (I can't remember **(3)** .... name) just as it was getting dark. I went looking for somewhere to stay, such as **(4)** .... youth hostel, but the only one I found was full, and they couldn't recommend anywhere else for **(5)** .... cheap accommodation. As usual, I had **(6)** .... problem with **(7)** .... money: I didn't have enough for **(8)** .... hotel. I wandered round **(9)** .... city looking for **(10)** .... park to sleep in. It was very dark when I came to **(11)** .... pair of **(12)** .... imposing gates leading into what looked like **(13)** .... park. I went inside, and fortunately I had **(14)** .... excellent sleeping bag, which I unrolled and climbed inside. Then I ate some bread, which was **(15)** .... only food I had. When I woke up and looked around me, I had **(16)** .... enormous surprise when I saw I had been sleeping in **(17)** .... someone's back garden!

Starting off

1 Match these activities with the photos.

> camping   hiking   mountain biking   parachuting
> rock climbing   volunteering

2 Work in groups. Discuss these questions.

1 Which of these activities looks the most fun? Why?

2 Which do you think would be the easiest / most difficult to do? Why?

3 Are there any activities you wouldn't like to do? Why not?

Listening Part 2

1 Work in pairs. You are going to hear James giving a talk about completing his Duke of Edinburgh Award as part of a school project. Read the text and discuss what type of information you need for each gap.

The Duke of Edinburgh Award

To get his Duke of Edinburgh Award, James had to complete four different tasks, including volunteering, a physical activity, skills development and going on an **(1)** ....

The award scheme began in the UK in **(2)** .... There are three different types of award. James thought that the **(3)** .... award was the most suitable for him.

For the volunteering part, James worked at a local **(4)** ....

Despite the hard physical work and the cold, James thought the work was **(5)** ....

For the physical activity, he planned a series of cycling trips with his **(6)** ....

The best part for James was taking part in an expedition with a group of friends. They spent three days **(7)** .... in Scotland and sleeping in tents.

Before they left, they were taught some simple things, such as **(8)** .... and how to cook food on a small stove.

It was a challenging experience, but James enjoyed feeling **(9)** ....

When James was volunteering, he had to be responsible and follow **(10)** .... rules.

2 Listen and complete the sentences with a word or short phrase.

3 Work in groups. Discuss these questions.
- What do you think are the advantages of taking part in an award scheme like this?
- What are the main difficulties of getting the award?

Vocabulary
Verb collocations with adventure activities

1 Complete these extracts from Listening Part 2 with the correct form of *go*, *do* or *take part*.

1 My work included planting trees and clearing the paths so that people could .... running and cycling there.
2 I had .... a bit of mountain biking before with my older brother on family holidays.
3 I wanted a bigger challenge, so I arranged to .... on a series of longer bike rides with my best friend.
4 For me, the highlight of the Duke of Edinburgh Award was .... in the expedition.
5 Me and a group of school friends planned to .... hiking and camping for three days in the highlands of Scotland.

2 Complete the sentences with a suitable verb from the table below. More than one answer may be possible.

1 I think local governments should .... competitions for schools in their area in which any student over 15 can ....
2 I would encourage people to .... swimming two or three times a week because it's an excellent way of .... exercise.
3 People who enjoy team sports often .... basketball or football, whereas people who enjoy individual sports .... athletics or .... cycling.

verb	sport
hold / organise / compete in / enter / take part in	a race / a competition / a tournament / a championship
do / take	exercise
go*	running / cycling / skiing / swimming / hiking
play**	football / golf / basketball
do***	sports / athletics / gymnastics / judo / weightlifting / mountain biking

* for sports that end in *-ing* and are usually done outdoors
** for sports which are considered games
*** for other sports which do not use *go* or *play*

3 Work in groups. Plan your own expedition.
- Where would it be?
- What activity would it involve?
- How long would it last?
- What would you have to take with you?

Tell the class about your expedition.

Which one sounds the most fun? Which one sounds the hardest?

Reading and Use of English Part 6

1 Work in pairs. You are going to read an article by a student who went on a school expedition to Romania. First, read the title and the introduction in *italics*. What do you expect to find out by reading the article?

2 Read the article on the opposite page quickly and see if your ideas were right.

> • Look for words and phrases in the sentences which you think refer to something in the article.
>
> • Look at the words on either side of the gap. What do they tell you about what the missing sentence will be about?
>
> • Read the sentences and find one that fits the meaning.
>
> • Check that it links with both the sentence before and the sentence after. Pay attention to pronouns (*we, that, it,* etc.), adverbs (*however, even so,* etc.) and other reference words in the sentences.

Exam advice

3 Six sentences have been removed from the article. Choose from the sentences A–G the one which fits each gap. There is one extra sentence which you do not need to use.

A However, we wouldn't be spending any time there until the end of the trip.

B For example, a few people suffered from sickness because we were so high up in the mountains.

C It was much more challenging than I thought it would be at times.

D Above all though, it has made me realise how easy my life is.

E This was where we met other team members and chose our destination.

F I would never have imagined that these powerful creatures could be so gentle and calm.

G This had to be raised by us to fund the trip.

4 Work in pairs. Discuss this question.

• Would you like to go on an adventure trip like this? Why? / Why not?

Grammar

Infinitive and verb + *-ing*

▶ **Page 171 Grammar reference**

1 These sentences from the article contain examples of when to use the infinitive and when to use the verb + *-ing* form. Match the sentences (a–j) with the rules (1–9) below. Some sentences match more than one rule.

a **Not having** television, internet and hot running water for three weeks was certainly a challenge.

b We decided **to plan** a three-week adventure in Romania.

c This would involve **trekking** in the mountains, **collaborating** on a project with members of the local community and **taking** part in a conservation project at a brown bear sanctuary.

d I never got tired of **watching** the sun rise every morning over the pine forests.

e We arranged a variety of events **to raise** the money.

f This meant that they were too weak **to continue walking**.

g Of course, it was not a case of simply **signing up** and paying the money.

h I didn't hesitate **to sign up** for the initial meeting.

i **Feeding** the bears in the sanctuary was also incredible.

j In fact one of the team decided **not to continue** the journey.

The infinitive is used:

1 to say why you do something   *sentence e*

2 after *too* and *enough*

3 after these verbs (there is a more complete list on page 171):

agree	appear	arrange	ask,
decide	expect	fail	help
hesitate	promise		

4 The negative is formed by placing *not* before the infinitive.

The verb + *-ing* is used:

5 after prepositions

6 as the subject or object of a verb

7 after these verbs (there is a more complete list on page 171):

admit	continue	enjoy	finish
involve	mind	postpone	risk
suggest			

8 after these expressions:

it's no good	it's not worth	it's not a case of	it's no use
it's a waste of time		spend time	can't help

9 The negative is formed by placing *not* before the verb + *-ing*.

ARE YOU READY FOR A SCHOOL CHALLENGE?

Victoria recently participated in an expedition to Romania with an organisation called School Challenge, which helps school students plan their own adventure trips to exciting destinations all over the world. Her trip included trekking in the mountains, collaborating on a project and doing conservation work at a wild animal sanctuary.

I heard about School Challenge through a friend who had travelled to South America with pupils from her school. When my school offered the opportunity to take part in a School Challenge, I didn't hesitate to sign up for the initial meeting. [1] We decided to plan a three-week adventure in Romania. This would involve trekking in the mountains, collaborating on a project with members of the local community and taking part in a conservation project at a brown bear sanctuary.

Of course, it was not a case of simply signing up and paying the money. [2] We arranged a variety of events to raise the money, including a school dance, a coffee morning for parents and a sponsored walk. We also had to organise our project in Romania. We had decided to go to a remote rural village and to work with a team of local people to improve the school buildings.

We left for Romania in July. We were going to be away for three weeks, and we had to travel light, as we would have to carry our backpacks. We packed light, waterproof clothes to keep us warm and dry while we were trekking in the mountains. We flew into Bucharest, the capital city of Romania. [3] Once we landed, we headed straight to the countryside to begin a week of trekking in the mountains.

We had been warned that our trip would not be a holiday and that things would not always go to plan. We certainly experienced our fair share of difficulties during the trip. [4] This meant that they were too weak to continue walking and we were not able to travel as far as we had intended. In fact one of the team decided not to continue the journey. On our first day working on the school project in the village, we didn't have the right materials to get started, so our work was delayed by a whole day.

Despite these setbacks, it was a truly amazing trip. I never got tired of watching the sun rise every morning over the pine forests. Feeding the bears in the sanctuary was also incredible. [5] My best memory, though, was working on the school building project. I will never forget the hospitality and kindness of the villagers. They cooked us amazing meals and did everything they could to make us feel comfortable and welcome.

My School Challenge trip influenced my life in so many ways. It gave me a taste for independence and adventure, and certainly made me want to travel more. [6] Not having television, internet and hot running water for three weeks was certainly a challenge, but in many ways
I enjoyed living a simpler life for a short time.

2 Complete the sentences with the correct form of the verb in brackets.

1 Carlos has suggested ...._starting_.... (start) a five-a-side football team. What do you think?

2 It's no good .... (run) in a marathon if you're not wearing the right shoes.

3 We've decided .... (hold) the race early in the morning before it gets too hot.

4 .... (train) is essential if you want to perform well as an athlete.

5 I've joined a gym .... (get) myself fitter.

6 If you train too hard, you risk .... (injure) yourself before the race.

7 She was disqualified from the race for .... (push) an opponent.

8 I don't think the weather is good enough .... (go) sailing this afternoon.

3 Choose the correct option in *italics*.

1 What sport would you advise someone *to do / doing* in order to make friends?

2 What sport would you choose *to learn / learning* if you had plenty of time and money?

3 If someone needed to get fit, what sport would you suggest *to do / doing*?

4 What sports do you avoid *to take part in / taking part in* and why?

4 Work in pairs. Ask and answer the questions in Exercise 3, giving your opinions.

5 Students often make mistakes with the infinitive and verb + *-ing*. Find and correct the mistakes. Some sentences are correct.

1 Students are not allowed running along school corridors.

2 Few people choose spending their time taking exercise.

3 The internet means that we spend more time sitting at home, but we cannot imagine to live without it.

4 Being fit and healthy does not mean to run 20 km a day.

5 Many students would prefer to cycle to school than go by school bus.

6 Many people only think about take exercise when they are overweight.

7 Unless they try to compete as a team, they will not succeed to win the competition.

8 Doing a sport is a good alternative if you are bored to sit and read a book.

9 It may be good to use a bicycle instead of going by public transport.

10 There are several good reasons for ride a bike.

Reading and Use of English Part 4

- Use the word given in CAPITALS without changing it.

- Count the words you use. Contractions (*isn't, don't*, etc.) count as two words.

- Read both sentences again at the end to check that they mean the same.

Exam advice

1 Work in pairs. For questions 1 and 2, choose the correct answer A–D. Why are the other answers incorrect?

Complete the second sentence so that it has a similar meaning to the first sentence, using the word given. Do not change the word given. You must use between two and five words, including the word given.

1 Why don't we start running if we want to train for the competition?

TAKING

He suggested .... in order to train for the competition.

A that they should take up running

B taking up running

C to take up running

D going running

2 She climbed the mountain without difficulty.

EASY

She found .... the mountain.

A it easy to climb

B that it was easy to climb

C she could easily climb

D it simple to climb

2 Now do these Part 4 questions. Use the clues below each question to help you.

1 Victoria prepared for the trekking trip by going walking every weekend.
READY
Victoria went walking every weekend .... for the trekking trip.

- Can you think of an expression with *ready* which means *prepare*?
- Why did Victoria go walking every weekend?
- Do you use a verb + *-ing* or an infinitive to say why she went walking every weekend?

2 I found it impossible not to feel sorry for him.
HELP
I .... sorry for him.

- You need an expression with *help* which means 'find it impossible'.
- Your answer needs to be in the same tense.

3 Cycling on this road is prohibited.
USE
Cyclists .... this road.

- What verbs go with *use* to mean it's prohibited?
- Do you use a verb + *-ing* or an infinitive with them?

3 Now do these Part 4 questions.

1 We'd like all our students to participate in the sports programme.
PART
We are keen on all our students .... the sports programme.

2 Mateo managed to win the race.
SUCCEEDED
Mateo .... the race.

3 You should have phoned her to tell her the game was cancelled.
GIVE
You were supposed .... to tell her the game was cancelled.

4 Buying the equipment for this sport is cheaper than hiring it.
MORE
It's .... the equipment for this sport than to buy it.

5 'I'll never get angry with the referee again,' said Martin.
TEMPER
Martin promised never .... the referee again.

6 Tanya found skydiving easy to learn.
DIFFICULTY
Tanya .... to skydive.

4 Check your answers by looking at these clues for each of the questions in Exercise 3.

1 Did you use a fixed phrase which means *participate*?
2 *Managed* is followed by an infinitive. Is *succeeded* also followed by an infinitive? Do you also need a preposition?
3 Did you use an expression which means *phone* (*give her a …*)?
4 Have you used an opposite of *cheap*? Did you use an infinitive or a verb + *-ing*?
5 Did you remember an expression with *temper* which means *get angry*?
6 You cannot write *didn't have any difficulty in learning* because it's seven words.

7

Listening Part 4

Exam advice

- You have one minute to read the questions before you listen.
- Read the main part of each question carefully first and underline the key words.
- If you have time, go back and read the options for each question.

1 Work in pairs. You are going to hear an interview with a girl who did a parachute jump for the first time. Before you listen, discuss these questions.

- Do you think skydiving / parachuting is a risky sport?
- Would you like to try it? Why? / Why not?

2 Read the questions and find the key words in each one.

1 What was Emily's initial opinion of extreme sports?
- **A** She was attracted to them.
- **B** She thought they were a waste of time.
- **C** She wasn't interested in trying them.

2 Why did Emily want to do a parachute jump?
- **A** She wanted to raise money for charity.
- **B** She wanted to write an article about it.
- **C** She wanted to try a new extreme sport.

3 Why did Emily decide to go to New Zealand for her jump?
- **A** The companies in New Zealand have a better reputation.
- **B** It would have been more expensive in the UK.
- **C** She had always wanted to visit the country.

4 Why did she choose Adrenaline Sky Tours?
- **A** Their jumps were cheaper.
- **B** She wanted to jump with an instructor.
- **C** All of the reviews for the company were positive.

5 What did Emily think about before jumping out of the plane?
- **A** her instructor jumping out of the plane
- **B** the door of the plane opening
- **C** a relaxing image of a beach

6 What made Emily feel most afraid during the jump?
- **A** waiting for her parachute to open
- **B** looking at the view below
- **C** landing

7 What is Emily's most important piece of advice for people wanting to do a jump for the first time?
- **A** Choose your company carefully.
- **B** Don't jump on your own.
- **C** Don't think too much about what you are doing.

3 Listen and choose the best answer (A, B or C).

Vocabulary

look, see and *watch; listen* and *hear*

1 Candidates often confuse the words above. Complete these sentences from Listening Part 4 with the correct form of *look (at), see, watch, listen* or *hear*.

1 I had .... some amazing video clips of people doing adventure sports there.
2 I .... carefully to the advice that my instructor, Dave, gave me.
3 He told me not to .... the plane door.
4 Then I .... my instructor telling me to look at the view.
5 I felt so free, ... the clouds drift past.

2 Choose the correct option in *italics*.

1 I *looked at / watched* my watch and saw that it was time to leave.
2 I really enjoy *looking at / watching* cartoons.
3 We live near a motorway and can *listen to / hear* the traffic non-stop.
4 I've been *looking at / watching* our holiday photos.
5 Did you *watch / see* Buckingham Palace when you were in London?
6 She knew the police officer was *looking / watching* what she did.
7 Ivan was in the kitchen, so he didn't *listen to / hear* the telephone ringing.
8 Marisa looks so relaxed when she's *listening to / hearing* music.

Speaking Part 3

▶ **Page 197 Speaking bank**

Exam advice

- When you discuss the first part of the task, you needn't talk about all of the options, but you should make suggestions, ask your partner's opinion and respond to your partner's ideas.

- When you discuss the second part of the task, it's not necessary to reach agreement, but you should:
  - discuss which option(s) to choose and give reasons for your choice(s)
  - listen and respond to what your partner says. Don't be afraid to disagree politely – this can lead to a good discussion.

1 Before you start this section, look at the work you did on Speaking Part 3 on pages 37–38. Work in pairs. Read the examiner's instructions and the speaking task below. Then take about two minutes to do the task in pairs.

Examiner: I'd like you to imagine that the head of your school is interested in getting students to do more sport. Here are some ideas. Talk to each other about how each of them might encourage students to do more sport.

A visit to the national athletics championships

A talk by a professional footballer

How could these activities encourage students to do more sport?

A weekend doing adventure sports

A school sports day

Free membership of a sports club

2 Look at this checklist. Which things did you do in your discussion?

		yes	no
1	Talk about all of the activities.		
2	Listen to each other and respond to what the other person says.		
3	Ask each other's opinion.		
4	Interrupt each other.		
5	One student tried to speak much more than the other.		

3 Now listen to Miguel and Irene doing the speaking task from Exercise 1. Which of the things on the checklist in Exercise 2 did they do?

4 Listen to Miguel and Irene again, and then put the phrases in the box in the correct column in the table.

How do you think …?   Well, perhaps …
Yes, and …
I imagine students would see …
Maybe, but …   What about …?
I suppose that might be …
I suppose so, but …
Yes, I see what you mean.
That's a good point, and …
Do you really think …?   That's true.
Yes, good idea.   You're right.   Yes, but …

suggesting ideas	asking your partner's opinion	agreeing	disagreeing
	How do you think…?		

5 Pronunciation: intonation (2)

You will make a good impression in the exam if you sound interested and enthusiastic about what you discuss. You can use intonation to show your interest.

5.1 Listen to how the voices rise and fall on the highlighted words.

🎧 28

Miguel: Well, perhaps this could be organised in a more adult ==way== – you know, with some ==serious== sports for people who were ==interested== and ==less serious== activities for ==other== people. That way ==everyone== could get ==involved==.

Irene: ==Yes==, good ==idea==, and people could be organised into ==teams== and it could all be made quite ==competitive== and ==enjoyable== at the same ==time==. When I think about it, it could be ==really successful==.

5.2 Now work in pairs and read the extract aloud. Take turns as Miguel and Irene.

6 Work in pairs. Follow the examiner's instructions for the second part of Speaking Part 3.

Examiner: Now you have a minute to decide which idea the head of your school should choose.

7 Work in pairs. Take about two minutes to do the first part of the speaking task below.

Examiner: I'd like you to imagine that a town wants young people to spend their free time in ways which are useful for them. Here are some ideas that they are thinking about and a question for you to discuss. Talk to each other about how these ideas would provide useful ways for young people to spend their free time.

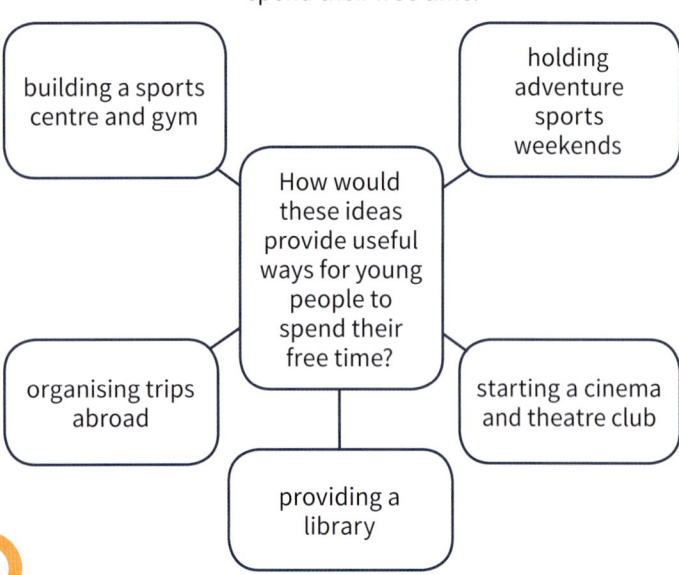

building a sports centre and gym

holding adventure sports weekends

How would these ideas provide useful ways for young people to spend their free time?

organising trips abroad

starting a cinema and theatre club

providing a library

8 Now follow the examiner's instructions for the second part of Speaking Part 3.

Examiner: Now you have a minute to decide which two facilities the town should build.

Writing Part 2
An article

▶ page 206 Writing bank

page 206 Writing bank

- Underline all the points you must deal with in your essay.

- Write a plan before you start writing and organise your ideas into paragraphs.

- Think about who is going to read your article and write in an appropriate way. Think about what they will find interesting, enjoyable or useful.

- Use linking words such as: *however, despite, in addition, for example* and *on the other hand.*

Exam advice

1 Read this writing task. Who are you writing for and what are the main points you must deal with in your answer?

You see this notice on your school noticeboard.

> The editors of the school magazine would like contributions to the magazine on the following subject:
>
> **A great way to keep fit**
>
> Describe a sporting activity or form of exercise you enjoy, how you started and why you would recommend it to other people.
>
> The writer of the best article will receive ten tickets to the local cinema.

Write your **article**.

2 Work in pairs.

- Discuss the ideas each of you could use to deal with the main points in the task.

- Which ideas would you use in your article?

3 Read the article on page 83.

- What does the writer enjoy about her way of taking exercise? Why?

CLIMBING: A GREAT WAY TO GET FIT OUTDOORS OR INDOORS

I love climbing. I joined a climbing club last year and **despite** living in the city, I now spend most of my free weekends travelling to the nearby mountains to go climbing with other members of the club. It's a great way to spend time in the countryside.

Although climbing is typically an outdoor activity, it's also possible to do it indoors on a climbing wall. This is very useful for beginners who want to learn to climb with an instructor in a safe environment. You don't need a lot of equipment, other than comfortable clothes and shoes that grip the surface of the wall. For some people climbing is a competitive sport, and there are tournaments you can take part in. **However**, many climbers do it just because they enjoy it.

I would recommend climbing to anyone who loves doing exercise either outdoors or indoors and keeping fit. I particularly recommend climbing in the mountains, as it is a great way to get out of the city. You can go climbing in all seasons and as long as you go with an experienced climber, you are unlikely to get injured. not eat the right sort of food.

5 Study how the words in **bold** in the article are used. Then complete the sentences with *although*, *however* or *despite*.

1 .... the swimming pool is quite far from where I live, I try to go there three times a week.
2 .... being given tickets to the football match, we decided to watch it on TV.
3 .... I'd love to be a professional footballer, I don't think I'm talented enough.
4 She was very easy to talk to, ... being a famous tennis star.
5 .... feeling very tired, she managed to finish the race.
6 I didn't enjoy the tournament. ...., most of the teams played very well.

6 Study how the writer used the words in the box in the article. Then use them to complete the sentences below.

> beginners   competitive   equipment
> experienced   injured   instructor   tournament

1 Although Valerie enjoys .... sports, she prefers exercising on her own.
2 It is not advisable to go climbing alone, even if you are very ....
3 If you don't train before the race, you are more likely to get ....
4 This course is suitable for all levels, including ....
5 If you want to learn to dive, you must find a qualified .... to teach you.
6 My school football team are playing in an important .... this weekend.
7 If you go skiing, you can usually hire most of the .... you will need.

7 Now write your own answer to the writing task in Exercise 1.

• Before you start writing, make a brief plan.
• Try to use structures and vocabulary you have studied in this writing section and this unit.
• Write between 140 and 190 words.
• Read through your article when you have finished to improve it and to check it for mistakes.

4 Look at the structure of the article. In which paragraph does the writer deal with these points?

1 describing an activity
2 how she started
3 why she would recommend it

8 Dream of the stars

Starting off

1 Work in groups. Match the speakers 1–4 with the correct photograph.

1 'You need to be artistic and have a good eye for colour. The ability to work under pressure, and to create a look that the actor in the chair is happy with, is very important too.'

2 'You have to be very physically fit and skilled in a range of fighting techniques. You also need to feel confident using weapons like swords as well as everyday objects such as bottles and sticks.'

3 'It's important to be able to communicate really well and be confident in your ability. Having a good memory helps too, as you need to learn a lot of lines.'

4 'You need to be able to sing and act to a very high standard and to enjoy it, too. And you also have to get on well with everyone you work with, like the musicians and the other members of the cast.'

2 If you worked in films or in the theatre, which job would you like to do?

Reading and Use of English Part 7

Exam advice

• Some of the sections may say quite similar things. You will have to read carefully to decide which section answers the question exactly.

• Underline phrases in the texts which give you the answers and check them against the questions.

1 You are going to read a magazine article about four young people who do different jobs in the film and theatre industry and answer questions about them. First take two minutes to skim read the article, then say what you have learned about the people.

2 Read the questions to see the kind of information you are looking for. Look for the key words in the questions.

Which young person

1 prefers working in the theatre to working in film?

2 is involved in the teaching of other people?

3 likes learning new things from colleagues?

4 had intended to work in a different area?

5 talks about having to turn down invitations?

6 thinks it is important to make a good first impression?

7 complains about the length of time it takes to find work?

8 believes it is important to be ready to accept negative comments?

9 enjoys the unpredictable nature of their work?

10 says that people tend to have the wrong idea about their work?

3 Read section A and look again at the questions, answering any that you can. Part of section A has been underlined to help you answer one of the questions. Do the same for sections B, C and D. Underline the relevant parts of the text as you answer the questions.

4 Work in groups. Discuss these questions.

• If you had to choose, which of the four young people would you prefer to change places with for a day? Why?

• Which person would you definitely *not* want to change places with? Why?

Careers in film and the theatre

A Jenna Bell

<u>I train actors to act out fight scenes</u> either on stage or on screen. It's my job to make sure all the actions in the scene look as realistic as possible and that actors use the correct techniques. Theatre is very different from film as you have to create something that can be performed in front of a live audience, time and time again. I started doing martial arts at school and then went on to study at drama college, where I was introduced to stage combat. I loved it from the beginning, and decided this was what I was meant to do! I work for myself, so I have to put up with the lack of financial security that goes along with it. Looking for a job takes ages, which is really frustrating. Working with actors who have had no experience of stage combat can be challenging too – especially when you have to tell them that they're doing everything wrong!

B Roland Green

I sing and act in shows and musicals on stage, accompanied by an orchestra. I joined a choir at school and that gave me a great introduction to singing as a profession. You have to put in hours of practice before each performance but it's worth it when you're on stage. The most difficult aspect of the job is being able to take criticism from the director or the conductor without question. Some of it can seem pretty harsh but that's the nature of the profession, so you just have to be prepared for it. You've got to be disciplined, too. If friends ask me to go out the evening before a performance, I have to say no but it doesn't bother me too much. I'm happy to concentrate on my singing and build a successful career.

C Chloe Desmond

I'm an actor and I spend a lot of time auditioning for roles in the theatre and film. The director isn't just looking for someone who can act, they want someone who can grab the audience's attention from the moment they walk on stage. But acting isn't as glamorous as people think it is. When I'm not auditioning, I'm often rehearsing or reading through a script at home. During filming, there's a lot of waiting around, which is really boring. That's why my heart lies in theatre acting, because it's more structured. I'm doing a play at the moment and I've got a timetable of all the performances I'll be in. I originally wanted to be a dancer, but at college I was on a course that didn't do street dance, so they told me to try the acting course. I realised then that I really wanted to pursue a career in acting and I just kept working towards achieving my ambition.

D Freddy Lee

I'm a make-up artist and work in theatre and film productions. I'm self-employed, which may sound scary, but I haven't had any problems getting work so far. I love not knowing what I'll be doing from one week to the next. So I can be creating cuts and wounds for a horror film or creating a lion face for musical theatre! Working alongside more experienced artists is great too as they can show you how to apply lipstick when there's bad lighting or no mirrors! When I started, I was happy just to work in small theatre productions. But now I want to gain as much experience as I can – whether it's doing make-up for the stage or the big screen. One thing's for sure, no matter what job I'm offered, I'm not going to turn it down!

8

Vocabulary

Verb collocations with *ambition*, *career*, *experience* and *job*

1 Complete these extracts from Reading and Use of English Part 7 with a word or phrase from the box in the correct form.

> achieve   gain   offer   pursue   turn it down

I realised then that I really wanted to **(1)** .... a career in acting and I just kept working towards **(2)** .... my ambition.

Now I want to **(3)** .... as much experience as I can.

One thing's for sure, no matter what job I'm **(4)** .... , I'm not going to **(5)** .... !

2 Complete the collocations with the words in the box.

> an ambition   a career   experience   a job

1 gain / get / have / lack ....

2 apply for / find / look for / offer / turn down ....

3 build / make / pursue / start out on ....

4 achieve / fulfil / realise ....

3 Choose the correct option in *italics* to complete Eve's story.

BLOG

I've always enjoyed performing in front of an audience, so I'd like to **(1)** *gain / build* a career as an actor. If I could **(2)** *achieve / make* my ambition of going to drama school, I'd **(3)** *lack / gain* the knowledge and experience I need if I'm going to **(4)** *pursue / find* a job in the theatre. Acting is a very competitive profession and you have to **(5)** *look for / build* your career step by step. I hopefully, one day a well-known director will notice your talent and **(6)** *offer / gain* you a job which will enable you to **(7)** *start out on / fulfil* your ambition!

4 Work in pairs. Talk about:

- the ambitions you have for your future
- a career or careers you might like to pursue

People and the theatre

5 Candidates often confuse these words: *playing*, *performance* and *acting*; *audience*, *public* and *spectators*; *scene* and *stage*. Choose the correct option in *italics* in each of these sentences.

1 Theatre is very different from film as you have to create something that can be performed in front of a live *audience / public / spectators*, time and time again.

2 You have to put in hours of practice before each *performance / acting*.

3 I sing and act in shows and musicals on *scene / stage*, accompanied by an orchestra.

4 That's why my heart lies in theatre *playing / acting*, because it's more structured.

Check your answers by looking at the texts on page 85 again.

6 Look at the photos. Then complete the sentences with a word from the box. Use each word only once.

> acting   audience   performance   play
> the public   scene   spectators   stage

1 The garden in all its glory is now open to ....

2 He wrote his latest .... in under six weeks.

3 The thing I enjoy most about .... is the chance to work in films on location.

4 She gave a superb .... in the leading role of the play.

5 The .... were clearly delighted with his performance as Hamlet.

6 In the final .... of the play, the actor forgot what he was supposed to say.

7 The show ended with all the performers singing on .... together.

8 He broke the world 400-metres record in front of over 40,000 cheering ....

audience

spectators

the public

Grammar

at, *in* and *on* to express location

▶ **Page 172 Grammar reference**

1 Candidates often confuse *at*, *in* and *on* when saying where something is located. Complete these sentences from Reading and Use of English Part 7 with the correct preposition.

1 I started doing martial arts .... school and then went on to study .... drama college.

2 I'm an actor and I spend a lot of time auditioning for roles .... the theatre and in films.

3 When I'm not auditioning, I'm often rehearsing or reading through a script .... home.

4 That's why my heart lies .... theatre acting, because it's more structured.

5 … but .... college I was .... a course that didn't do street dance.

2 Complete the sentences with *at*, *in* or *on*.

1 Every Sunday, we got up early and went for a walk .... the mountains.

2 Every year, many people are injured .... the roads because of bad driving.

3 I am studying English .... school, and a spell in your country would be a great chance for me to improve.

4 I think that your cinema is the best .... the city.

5 I was alone .... home – my parents were .... a party and my sister was .... a friend's house.

6 Despite spending two hours a day commuting, I prefer living .... the outskirts of London.

7 The seaside is the ideal place for a family holiday because children can swim .... the sea as well as play .... the beach.

8 Our next destination was Italy, where we spent a week .... the seaside.

9 The journey was a good one, and I met an old friend .... the train.

10 You can waste a lot of time .... a car .... traffic jams.

8

Listening Part 2

Exam advice

- Be careful to choose the right information from what you hear, e.g. if you need to write a type of animal in the gap, the speaker might mention other animals which are not the correct answer.
- Write exactly the word(s) you hear without changing them in any way.
- Read the completed sentences to make sure the words fit grammatically and match what the speaker said. Answer every question, even if you're not sure.

1 Work in pairs. You are going to hear a girl called Clara giving a talk to students in her year about a project she has done on unusual sports. Before you listen, read the sentences very quickly. For which question do you have to write a number only?

Read the sentences again and match the question number (1–10) with the type of word required (in the list below). There is an example to help you.

Nouns

a person ....
a material ....
a place [plural] ....
a sport ...1...
a countable noun [plural] ....
an uncountable noun ....
an adjective ....
a period of time ....
a number ....

Unusual Sports

Clara had wanted to talk about sports such as **(1)** .... at first.
Her **(2)** .... gave her the idea for her talk.

Land quidditch

It is played in more than **(3)** .... countries and is gaining in popularity. Sticks can be made of wood as well as **(4)** ....

Octopush

Competitors are required to play for **(5)** .... each half.
Clara says that it is **(6)** .... for spectators.

Land yachting

Land yachting events are held on **(7)** .... because they need strong winds. Yachts run on wheels and are powered by **(8)** .... , whereas the buggies use a large kite.
Competitors are not expected to have much **(9)** .... to race land yachts.
Clara recommends a book called *Out of the Ordinary* because of its **(10)** ....

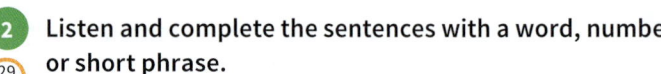

2 Listen and complete the sentences with a word, number or short phrase.

3 Work in groups. Discuss these questions.
- Which of the sports mentioned would you consider trying? Why?
- Which one or ones would you definitely refuse to try?
- What is more important – winning a sporting competition or taking part? Why?
- Which do you prefer – watching sports on TV or watching them live as a spectator?

Grammar

Reported speech

▶ **Page 174 Grammar reference**

1 Look at these three sentences which Clara said in Listening Part 2. What do you think Clara's mum and dad's exact words were, a or b?

1 … they said it would be a bit boring because most people knew all about the usual ball sports already.
  a 'It will be a bit boring because most people know all about the usual ball sports already.'
  b 'It would be a bit boring because most people knew all about the usual ball sports already.'

2 When I told Mum about it, she said that running around on grass with a stick between her legs wasn't exactly her idea of a good time.
  a 'Running around with a stick between my legs wasn't exactly my idea of a good time.'
  b 'Running around with a stick between my legs isn't exactly my idea of a good time.'

3 When I mentioned it to Mum and Dad, they told me that it didn't sound like the most interesting spectator sport in the world.
  a 'It didn't sound like the most interesting spectator sport in the world.'
  b 'It doesn't sound like the most interesting spectator sport in the world.'

2 Match the reporting verbs on the left with the sentences on the right that could be used to express the ideas. There is an example to help you.

1 persuade
2 suggest
3 agree
4 refuse
5 apologise
6 accuse
7 admit
8 promise
9 remind
10 warn

a Why don't we go to the cinema this evening?
b Go on, come to the party with us! It'll be great. 1
c I'm really sorry for not doing my homework.
d It was me who lost the tickets. It's all my fault.
e I'm afraid I'm not prepared to do that.
f I'm with you on that. You're absolutely right.
g You took my laptop without asking me first, didn't you?
h I'll definitely get there on time. You can count on it!
i That machine is very hot so be careful not to touch it!
j Don't forget to buy some milk on your way home.

3 For questions 1–6, complete the second sentence so that it has a similar meaning to the first sentence, using the word given. Do not change the word given. You must use between two and five words, including the word given.

1 'There's no way I'm going to join the hockey team,' said Mark.
INTEND
Mark told me that .... join the hockey team.

2 'I'll return quite late from the theatre tonight,' said Elena.
BACK
Elena said that .... quite late from the theatre that night.

3 'I won't be late for the match,' said Lucy.
ARRIVE
Lucy promised she .... time for the match.

4 'You can't borrow my camera, Mike,' said his father.
ALLOWED
Mike's father told him he .... his camera.

5 'I know I got several answers wrong in this exercise,' Hannah said.
MISTAKES
Hannah admitted that she .... in the exercise.

6 'I really enjoyed the show,' Katie told George.
FOUND
Katie told George that she .... very enjoyable.

4 Choose the correct form of the verb in *italics* in these sentences from Listening Part 2.

1 I asked Dad whether he fancied taking part in a race, but he refused *to even consider / even considering* it!
2 So, I don't think I'll be able to *persuade her to join / persuade her joining* a team any time soon!
3 We don't actually have that book in school, but the library has promised *to get / getting* a copy.

5 Complete the sentences with the verb in brackets in the correct form.

1 She admitted .... (steal) the watch.
2 Vera accused James of .... (lie).
3 Mark's mother agreed .... (buy) him a car.
4 The children apologised for .... (break) the window.
5 Peter has invited me .... (visit) him in Switzerland this summer.
6 Ewan persuaded his father .... (lend) him his bike.
7 Karen has promised .... (phone) me tonight.
8 I would suggest .... (install) new computers in the school.
9 Can I remind you .... (send) your grandmother a birthday card?
10 Cara warned me .... (not use) the machine.

Reading and Use of English Part 1

- Read the title and the text quickly to get a general idea of what it's about.

- Deal with the gaps one by one. Read carefully before and after each gap.

- Check that the word fits into the sentence grammatically by looking at prepositions and other grammatical structures.

- If you are not sure which option is correct, reject the options you think are wrong and choose from the others.

- When you have finished, read the whole text quickly again to check your answers.

Exam advice

1 Work in pairs. You are going to read an article about the job of a stunt performer. First, look at the photo and decide if sentences 1 and 2 are true or false.

1 Stunt people have to be good at more than one sport.

2 Stunt people spend more time filming than preparing the scene.

2 Read the article quickly and check your answers.

3 Read the article again and decide which answer (A, B, C or best fits each gap. There is an example at the beginning (C

0	A succeed	B manage	C arrive	D achieve
1	A impressive	B excellent	C impossible	D tremend
2	A exact	B original	C right	D real
3	A remove	B make	C take	D do
4	A career	B job	C work	D position
5	A recommended	B required	C crucial	D advisable
6	A truth	B matter	C event	D case
7	A offer	B lend	C provide	D recomme
8	A in	B out	C over	D on

4 Now check your answers to Exercise 3 by using these clue

1 The word *incredibly* can't be used with extreme adjectiv Which word is not an extreme adjective?

2 The word you need also means 'genuine' or 'true'.

3 This word forms part of a phrase which means 'replace'.

4 Only one option can follow the verb *pursue*. Look back to the vocabulary section in this unit.

5 Only this word can be followed by the preposition *to* – th others use *for*.

6 Only this word forms part of a phrase beginning with *It is often/usually the ____ that* …

7 Only this word can be followed by a direct object and the word *with*.

8 This word forms part of a phrasal verb which means 'to have a result that you aren't expecting'.

I want your job:

stunt person

Have you ever watched a film and wondered how the actors **(0)** .... to perform incredibly **(1)** .... things like jumping from tall buildings or driving at high speed? Well, in fact, they don't do these things at all! The **(2)** .... performers are stunt men or women who **(3)** .... the place of the film star.

In order to pursue a **(4)** .... as a stunt person, you have to be good at several sports including skiing, swimming and horse riding. Preparation is **(5)** .... to the success of a scene, so every single action is planned very carefully. In fact, it is often the **(6)** .... that it takes longer to prepare for the scene than to film it!

If you want to find out more about this exciting job, there are plenty of websites that can **(7)** .... you with all the information you need. And who knows? It might just turn **(8)** .... to be the perfect job for you!

5 Discuss these questions in groups.

- Can you do any of the sporting activities mentioned in the text? If so, how well can you do them?

- Would you like to be a stunt person? Why? / Why not?

Speaking Part 4

▶ **Page 199 Speaking bank**

- The questions here will be general questions of opinion. Give your opinion and support it with reasons and/or examples.
- Listen carefully to what your partner says: you may be asked if you agree.

Exam advice

1 In Speaking Part 4, the examiner will ask you questions which encourage you to give your opinions on topics related to Part 3. Read and listen to Tania and Peter answering the examiner's question. Which words or phrases do they use to speak in general?

Examiner: Do you think schools should teach subjects such as dance, drama or music?

Tania: Well, I think, generally speaking, schools should teach these subjects to small children so that they can find out if they like them. I think these subjects help children to learn how to express themselves. But I don't think generally it's so important for older children or teenagers to do these subjects because they tend to have lots of other things to study. So, on the whole, I guess these subjects should be voluntary, not compulsory, as children get older.

Examiner: Peter, do you agree with Tania?

Peter: Generally, yes, but I feel it's a pity when students don't have time for the subjects they enjoy.

2 Read Tania and Peter's conversation again and answer the questions.

1 How does Tania give a balanced answer?
2 What reasons does she give?
3 Which of these things does Peter do?
 a He just says he agrees.
 b He says he agrees, but adds his own opinion.
 c He says he agrees and gives a reason.

3 Think of general things you can say to give a balanced answer to this question. Then, in pairs, take turns to ask and answer this question.

Do you think that schools should teach subjects such as painting and photography? Why? / Why not?

4 Pronunciation: grouping words and pausing (2)

We tend to pause between groups of words which form a meaning together, for example: The family had a small shop / just round the corner from where we live, / and one day my aunt was working there on her own.

4.1 Use a (/) to mark where you think Tania pauses in her answer in Exercise 1.

4.2 Now listen again and check your answers.

4.3 Work in pairs. Take turns to take the part of Tania and read her answer aloud.

5 Read these questions. Then decide which phrases in the box you could use in your answer to each question. Some phrases can be used for more than one answer.

1 Do you think that all young people should learn to play a musical instrument? Why? / Why not?

2 What things do young people learn from acting in plays?

3 What are the advantages of seeing a film in the cinema instead of on television?

4 Should newspapers and magazines pay so much attention to singers' and actors' lives and relationships? Why? / Why not?

5 What do you think is the purpose of television: to entertain or to educate people? Why?

a celebrity
avoid/cause a scandal
help society develop
the media
a tabloid (newspaper)
work in a team
a compulsory/voluntary activity
develop their acting/musical abilities
develop their artistic expression
develop their musical knowledge
disturb/protect someone's privacy
interrupt a film with advertisements
make people aware of problems
when the film is released

6 Think how you can give balanced, general answers to each question in Exercise 5. Then, in pairs, take turns to ask and answer the questions.

Writing Part 1
An essay

▶ **Page 202 Writing bank**

- To make your argument easy to follow, you can start paragraphs with a short sentence which says what the paragraph is about.

- If you decide to write a 'balanced essay', try to have the same number of points in favour as against, or advantages as disadvantages.

- In order to complete the writing task successfully, you must express your personal opinion clearly.

Exam advice

1 Read this writing task. What are the key points you must deal with?

In your English class, you have been talking about the advantages of being famous as a film star.

Now your English teacher has asked you to write an essay.

Write your essay using all the notes and give reasons for your point of view.

> **'Being famous as a film star has both advantages and disadvantages.'**
>
> **Do you agree?**
>
> **Notes**
> Write about:
>
> 1. media attention
> 2. lifestyle
> 3. .... (your own idea)

2 Work in groups. Discuss the advantages and disadvantages of being famous as an actor or film star. While you discuss, you should:

- note down the main points of your discussion
- cover all three points in the essay task in Exercise 1.

3 Work alone and write a brief plan for your essay. In your plan, you should have:

- the number of paragraphs
- the main idea of each paragraph.

4 Write an opening paragraph for your essay. When you have finished, work in pairs and compare your paragraphs.

5 Work in pairs. Read this opening paragraph. How does it compare with yours?

> Many young people dream of achieving fame as actors or film stars. However, it is a life which has both advantages and disadvantages.

6 Javier wrote a balanced essay to answer the question in the writing task. Read the essay. Then, in pairs, answer questions 1–7 opposite.

a Many young people dream of achieving fame as film stars. However, it is a life which has both advantages and disadvantages.

b There are three main advantages. Firstly, if actors are well known, people will want to watch their films, and if their films are popular, they will be offered more jobs in the future. Also, they live exciting and glamorous lives with plenty of foreign travel and luxury. There is no doubt that most actors find this very enjoyable. Finally, fame and success go together.

c On the other hand, fame brings disadvantages for actors too. First, many film stars have little privacy or time to themselves because they are always being followed by reporters and photographers. Next, people with glamorous lifestyles meet other glamorous people and this can sometimes cause problems with, for example, their family relationships. Finally, they have to work very hard to be successful and this may lead to considerable stress.

d To conclude, I think for film stars the advantages of being famous outweigh the disadvantages because being well known is a result of their professional success. However, they need common sense to deal with the disadvantages.

1 Are Javier's ideas about being famous similar to yours?

2 How does he balance his arguments in the essay?

3 What is the purpose of the underlined phrases in the essay?

4 What do the highlighted phrases show?

5 Note down the words and phrases he uses to link ideas together throughout the essay.

6 In which paragraph (a–d) does Javier give his own opinion?

7 Why is it important to make your opinion clear?

7 Work alone.

- Write a second paragraph where you outline the advantages you discussed in Exercise 2. Start it using an introductory sentence.
- Write a third paragraph where you balance the advantages of the second paragraph with the disadvantages. Start it with an introductory sentence as well.

8 Write your answer to the task below.

- Follow the stages that you have practised: identifying the key points in the question, thinking of ideas and planning your essay.
- Use Javier's answer in Exercise 6 as a model.
- You should write between 140 and 190 words.

In your English class, you have been talking about the advantages and disadvantages of a career in music or acting. Now your English teacher has asked you to write an essay.

Write your essay using all the notes and give reasons for your point of view.

'There are both advantages and disadvantages to a career as a musician or an actor.'

Do you agree?

Notes
Write about:

1. doing something you enjoy
2. becoming well known
3. .... (your own idea)

7 Vocabulary and grammar review

Word formation

1 Read this text. Use the word given in capitals at the end of some of the lines to form a word that fits in the gap in the same line. There is an example at the beginning (0).

Adventure RACING

The teams that come first are the ones who race **(0)** ..intelligently.. and adapt to the sort of **(1)** .... situations which arise in these races. The teams who do well show both flexibility and **(2)** .... Unfortunately, our **(3)** .... for the race in Australia weren't methodical in any way. In fact, as a beginner, I was so **(4)** .... that the training I actually did was **(5)** .... to run and cycle as much and as hard as I could. When we actually did the race, one of my team-mates became just too tired to continue. We had been going really fast without taking any rests, and he had been **(6)** .... to ask us to take a break. I knew that our team had not been **(7)** .... about the pace we could keep. Not finishing that race was the most **(8)** .... lesson I could have learned.

INTELLIGENT

PREDICT

PATIENT
PREPARE

EXPERIENCE
SIMPLE

WILL

REAL

VALUE

2 Complete the sentences with the infinitive or -ing form of the verb in brackets.

1 Can I suggest .... (take) a break in about ten minutes?
2 Did you manage .... (get) in touch with her?
3 Do you want me .... (invite) her?
4 My cousin's considering .... (change) his car.
5 He absolutely refuses .... (wear) any other make of trainers.
6 He admitted .... (finish) all the cake.
7 He persuaded them .... (finish) the job.
8 I expect .... (become) very rich one day.

9 I really don't mind .... (help) my little sister with her homework.
10 It's no good .... (ask) him anything. He's really unhelpful.
11 My brother enjoys .... (work) in a coffee shop.
12 You know it's not worth .... (spend) so much money on one computer game.

Grammar

3 Complete the second sentence so that it has a similar meaning to the first sentence, using the word given. Do not change the word given. You must use between two and five words, including the word given.

1 You can't go skydiving until you're 18 years old.
   ALLOWED
   People under 18 .... skydiving.

2 He didn't want to get sunburnt, so he stayed in the shade.
   AVOID
   He stayed in the shade .... sunburnt.

3 Paola hates windsurfing when the weather is cold.
   BEAR
   Paola .... when the weather is cold.

4 Could you please turn your mobile phone off?
   MIND
   Would .... your mobile phone off?

5 You might have an accident if you don't take all the safety precautions.
   RISK
   If you don't take all the safety precautions, ... an accident.

6 The weather is so wet that it's not worth going for a walk today.
   POINT
   The weather is so wet that there's .... for a walk today.

Vocabulary

1 Decide which answer (A, B, C or D) best fits each gap.

1 The flying display attracted about 50,000 .... despite the rain.

A public B assistants C spectators D audience

2 As a police officer, I get a lot of questions from members of the .... asking how to get to one place or another.

A people B public C audience D spectators

3 During the musical, the .... clapped at the end of every single song.

A audience B spectators C public D attendants

4 The children really did put on a good .... in the school play.

A play B act C performance D acting

5 I'd love to have a career in .... one day!

A acting B playing C performance D stage

6 That play is much better on the .... than it is in the film version.

A theatre B play C scene D stage

7 My sister is thinking of pursuing a .... in the music industry.

A work B job C career D position

8 My uncle always says it's more important to do a job you enjoy than one where you .... a lot of money.

A win B earn C gain D pay

Grammar

2 Complete the sentences with *at*, *in* or *on*.

1 She arrived for the audition .... a taxi.

2 The new cinema will be built .... the outskirts of the town.

3 They have band practice .... the basement of his grandmother's house.

4 We had to wait for ages .... the queue to get the tickets for the performance.

5 I wish I had joined my friends .... the festival this weekend.

6 She was really nervous when she first went .... the stage.

7 He has posters of all his favourite stars .... the walls of his bedroom.

8 He was .... the phone to his agent hoping she could get him a part .... the new film.

9 They met each other .... the party after the premiere of the film.

10 The person .... the back door is looking for the theatre manager.

3 Complete the second sentence so that it has a similar meaning to the first sentence, using the word given. Do not change the word given. You must use between two and five words, including the word given.

1 'I won't lend you my new bike, Sue,' said Sam.

REFUSED

Sam .... Sue his new bike.

2 'I am really sorry that I was late for the rehearsal,' said Michelle.

APOLOGISED

Michelle .... for the rehearsal.

3 Sarah said, 'He forgot to bring the camera on purpose.'

ACCUSED

Sarah .... the camera on purpose.

4 'I will definitely be at the cinema on time,' said Lewis.

ARRIVE

Lewis promised .... on time.

5 'Don't forget your money for the theatre trip,' said our teacher.

BRING

Our teacher reminded .... for the theatre trip.

6 'OK, we can all go in my car to the concert,' said Steve.

DRIVE

Steve agreed .... to the concert.

9 Secrets of the mind

Starting off

1 Work in pairs. Match the words and phrases to find eight things which might make people happy.

1	being admired	**a**	a loving family
2	being part of	**b**	in your studies or work
3	doing really well	**c**	friends
4	having enough money to	**d**	work too hard
5	having lots of	**e**	by the people around you
6	having lots of time to spend	**f**	in a nice neighbourhood
7	living	**g**	on the things you enjoy doing
8	not having to	**h**	live well

2 Which of the things in Exercise 1 do you think are essential for happiness? Which do you think are not so important?

What other things make people happy?

3 Work in pairs. Take turns to do the task below.

- Student A should look at photos A and B.
- Student B should look at photos C and D.

The photos show people who are happy. Compare the photos and say why you think the people might be happy.

Reading and Use of English Part 5

- Read the title of the text, as it will tell you what the text will be about.
- When a question asks what a word or phrase refers to, read carefully what is said in the sentence and make sure you understand it before you read the options.

Exam advice

1 You are going to read an article about the Green family, who experimented with banning the use of electronic devices in their home for one month. Read the article opposite quickly to find out why they decided to do this.

2 For questions 1 and 2, the sentences in the article which give you the answers have been underlined. Read the questions and the underlined sentences. Then choose the answer (A, B, C or D) which you think fits best according to the underlined sentences.

1 What does the first paragraph suggest about the Green family?
- **A** They don't normally have dinner together.
- **B** They prefer to be quiet during mealtimes.
- **C** They often complain about their food.
- **D** They normally use their phones during mealtimes.

2 Why was Susan Green worried about her children's use of electronic devices?
- **A** They were going to bed later than usual.
- **B** They had stopped spending time with their friends.
- **C** Their relationships with other people had changed.
- **D** They were not spending enough time outside.

Our month in a tech-free house

1 It's dinner time in the Green household, a family of four from Melbourne, Australia. Susan Green sets the table, as her husband Michael and two children emerge from the kitchen with dishes of food. As the family take their
5 seats at the table, an awkward silence descends. 14-year-old Carolyn plays restlessly with a fork, while 16-year-old Billy frowns at the dish of broccoli in front of him. Meanwhile, Michael reaches absently for an object that isn't there, an unmistakable look of disappointment
10 on his face. In this typical family scene, one thing is missing. There is not a single mobile phone on the table or anywhere in the room. The Greens are experiencing their first evening without electronic devices, as part of a month-long experiment to see if going without
15 technology will make them a happier family.

The use of electronic devices has increased dramatically over the past 10 years, and recent studies suggest that they may be responsible for decreased levels of happiness. Susan Green had noticed these worrying
20 tendencies in her own family. 'I was aware of the obvious dangers to teenagers who spend too much time online,' she says. 'I was regularly telling Billy to turn off his game and go and get some fresh air, or Carolyn to stop chatting with her friends and get some sleep. That's
25 just a normal part of family life today. What worried me more is that their constant mobile phone use was affecting their social interactions. Even when they invited their friends over, I would find them all sitting together looking at their phones and not talking.'

30 Susan's concerns prompted her to carry out her own research into the issue. When she came across an article in a weekend newspaper about people who gave up using electronic devices for a month, she was keen to try it with her own family. However, she realised that it was
35 going to take more than reading an article to persuade them. 'I found some of the research mentioned in the

article very worrying, particularly the increased risks of anxiety and depression in young people, but I doubted that my family would be convinced,' she says. 'But I
40 wanted to avoid financial rewards, as they felt a bit too individualistic.' In the end, the promise of a fun family day out at a theme park persuaded the Greens to go tech-free for a whole month.

It wasn't easy at first. 'I felt completely lost without my
45 phone,' Carolyn recalls. 'I felt isolated because I couldn't chat with my friends online. But after two weeks, things got easier. I started to meet up with my friends more and it was much nicer to catch up face to face. I already knew that online chat is not always an ideal use of time
50 and often delays more important tasks like studying, but I just couldn't resist. I was also aware that teenagers are often bullied online and that this can make them anxious and depressed. Fortunately, this hasn't happened to me personally, but it's certainly true that people can
55 be much meaner online than they would be face-to-face. What I hadn't noticed was that it was making me less happy in general.'

The Green family's experiment is now over, but they have made a commitment to try and stick to some of the
60 principles that they established during their tech-free month. 'Mobile phones and tablets are strictly banned during mealtimes,' says Michael. 'And we have agreed to have a tech-free weekend activity each week, where we all leave our phones at home.' Susan feels delighted
65 with the results of the experiment and is certain that it helped her to achieve her aim of improving her family's happiness. 'We now devote more time to one another than we did when we used to spend every waking hour glued to our screens,' she says. 'It just goes to show
70 that it is possible to enjoy the convenience of modern technology without having to compromise our family relationships and general happiness.'

Now, for questions 3–6, choose the answer (A, B, C or D) which you think fits best according to the text.

3 How did Susan convince her family to go 'tech-free' for a month?
A by getting them to read an article on the subject
B by giving them money
C by trying to scare them
D by arranging an activity for them

4 What did Carolyn realise about chatting online after her family's experiment?
A It can waste a lot of time.
B It is more enjoyable to chat face to face.
C Young people are more often unkind to each other online.
D It made her feel anxious.

5 What does *it* refer to in line 56?
A chatting online
B online bullying
C being mean
D delaying important tasks

6 Which of the following is true about the Green family after the experiment?
A They no longer use mobile phones at home.
B They are very happy to have their phones back.
C They regularly do some activities without their phones.
D They always leave their phones at home when they go out.

9

4 **Work in groups. Discuss these questions.**

- Do you think that electronic devices such as mobile phones can make people less happy? Why? / Why not?
- Do you think that it is a good idea to ban mobile phones during family mealtimes and activities? Why? / Why not?

Vocabulary

achieve, carry out and devote

1 **Complete these sentences from Reading and Use of English Part 5 with the correct form of *achieve*, *carry out* or *devote*.**

1 Susan's concerns prompted her to .... her own research into the issue.
2 Susan feels delighted with the results of the experiment and is certain that it helped her to .... her aim of improving her family's happiness.
3 'We now .... more time to one another than we did when we used to spend every waking hour glued to our screens,' she says.

2 **Complete the collocations with the correct form of *achieve*, *carry out* or *devote*.**

1 Last year, my uncle .... a lifelong **ambition** to visit New York.
2 Scientists have been .... **research** to discover the cause of the disease.
3 The project is quite easy, so you won't need to .... very much **time** to doing it.
4 Igor felt very tired because he had .... a lot of time and **energy** to the project.
5 My mum said she'd stop my pocket money if I was home late, but I don't think she'll .... her **threat**.
6 In the army, you have to be obedient and .... **instructions** immediately.

stay, spend and pass; make, cause and have

3 **Students often confuse the words above. Choose the correct option in *italics*.**

1 Remember, your behaviour will *have / cause* an effect on other people.
2 I'm very sorry if I've *made / caused* you any problems.
3 I have *passed / spent* my life studying happiness.
4 Yesterday, I *spent / stayed* two hours listening to the radio.
5 I really enjoy late-night films on TV when I can *stay / be* awake.

4 **Complete the sentences with the correct form of *stay*, *spend*, *pass*, *make*, *cause* or *have*.**

1 I decided to .... the afternoon in the park.
2 Colin played a game on his phone to .... the time while he was waiting for the train.
3 They say the weather is going to .... like this for the rest of the week.
4 How did you .... the weekend? Did you enjoy yourself?
5 I .... two hours today trying to finish my homework.
6 The bus strike has been .... problems for students trying to get to school.
7 The bad sound quality .... the film very difficult to understand.
8 Using up-to-date materials can .... a dramatic effect on the amount students learn.
9 The news that his sister had had a baby .... him very happy.

5 **Which verb, *make*, *cause* or *have*, forms a collocation with each of these nouns? In some cases, more than one verb–noun collocation is possible.**

> an accident   a change   an effect   an impact
> the impression   a problem   trouble

6 **Complete the sentences with a collocation from Exercise 5. More than one answer may be possible.**

1 A dog ran onto the road and would have .... if the driver hadn't reacted quickly.
2 Amalia obviously .... a good .... on the examiners because they gave her a Grade A.
3 I hope I haven't .... you any .... by coming to stay unexpectedly.
4 I .... that she's not very organised. Otherwise, she'd hand her work in on time.
5 Living in the country .... a nice .... after spending the last three years living in a city.
6 Your choice of subjects at university will .... a big .... on your future career.

Listening Part 1

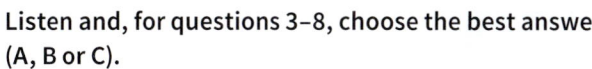

32

> **Exam advice**
>
> • Listen to the whole piece before you choose: the answer may depend on the general idea rather than a few words.
>
> • Pay attention to words like *most likely* and *the most*.
>
> • If you are not sure about the answer after listening the first time, try to decide which answers you think are wrong before you listen the second time.

1 You are going to hear people talking in eight different situations. Before you listen, work in groups. Discuss whether you agree with these statements or not.

• What people do in life is influenced by their personality.
• Twins typically have very similar personalities and interests.
• Young people nowadays are generally under more pressure than their parents were.
• Many people find it difficult to motivate themselves to do exercise.
• Everyone sometimes has a dream where they're flying, falling or running.

2 Work in pairs. Read questions 1 and 2 and find the key words in each question that will help you listen for the correct answer.

1 You hear an expert talking about why we buy certain products. Which factor is most likely to determine whether we choose to buy a product in a supermarket?

   A cost
   B appearance
   C location

2 You hear a girl talking about her relationship with her twin sister. What difference between them surprises people the most?

   A their interests
   B their personalities
   C their looks

3 Now listen, and for questions 1 and 2, choose the best answer (A, B or C).

31

4 Listen and, for questions 3–8, choose the best answer (A, B or C).

3 You hear a psychologist talking about stress. What is her main concern about young people?

   A They work too hard at school.
   B They grow up too fast.
   C They feel pressure from adults.

4 You hear two friends talking about a classmate. Why are they talking about him?

   A They want to arrange a meeting with him.
   B They are both annoyed with him.
   C They are interested in his test results.

5 You hear a psychologist talking about personality types. What aspect of people's lives do these personality types influence?

   A their academic performance
   B their future job
   C their future husband or wife

6 You hear a girl talking to a boy about a dream. What does she think that the dream means for her?

   A She's worried about lack of success.
   B Her life is in danger.
   C She's feeling stressed about something.

7 You hear a girl talking about things which motivate people. What motivates her to do exercise?

   A setting goals
   B meeting new people
   C feeling better

8 You hear a boy talking to a friend on his phone. Why is he calling his friend?

   A to apologise for his behaviour
   B to discuss a problem
   C to cancel a plan

5 Work in pairs.

• When you feel stressed, what do you do to relax?
• Talk about someone in your family. What do you think their free-time activities might show about their personality?

Grammar

Modal verbs to express certainty and possibility

▶ **Page 176 Grammar reference**

1 Read these extracts from Listening Part 1 and look at the underlined modal verbs. Then answer the questions below.

1 People assume that because Louisa and I are twins, we <u>must</u> be very similar.
2 The first interpretation <u>can't</u> be true but the second one <u>may</u> be, as I'm feeling under a lot of pressure to fit in at my new school.
3 I suppose he <u>might</u> have been disappointed with his result.
4 I guess he <u>could</u> have found this test more difficult.

1 Which of the underlined verbs do we use:
   a when we are certain something is true?
   b when we are certain something is not true?
   c when we think something is possibly true? (3 verbs)
2 Which of the sentences refer(s) to:
   a the present?
   b the past?

2 Students often make mistakes with modal verbs. Four of these sentences contain mistakes. Find and correct the mistakes.

1 I think the school play was lovely. You may have really enjoyed acting in it!
2 He's had a really good sleep, so he mustn't be tired any more.
3 The road is very busy, so cross it carefully or you can have an accident.
4 She lives in a really nice house, so her mum and dad can be earning a lot of money.
5 I have a lot of homework to do, so I may go to bed late.

3 Complete the sentences with a modal verb and the correct form of the verb in brackets. In some cases, more than one answer may be possible.

1 Everyone in the class .... (work) incredibly hard because you have all passed the exam!
2 I think she .... (be) a really happy person because she's always smiling and laughing.
3 Jamie woke up in the night screaming. He .... (have) a nightmare.
4 I don't know why Irina hasn't arrived yet. She .... (have to) stay on late at school, or she .... (stop) on the way home to see some friends.
5 I don't know how old the teacher is, but he looks quite young, so he .... (be) more than 25.
6 They say it .... (rain) at the weekend. I hope football training won't be cancelled.

4 Work in pairs. Look at these two photos and answer the questions using *may*, *might*, *must*, *could* and *can't*.

What do you think has happened or is happening in each picture?
How are the people feeling and why?

Reading and Use of English Part 4

1 Work in pairs. Choose the correct answer, A, B or C. Why are the other answers incorrect?

Complete the second sentence so that it has a similar meaning to the first sentence, using the word given. Do not change the word given. You must use between two and five words, including the word given.

1 Paola went to bed late after watching a film.

STAYED

Paola .... a film.

  A stayed up late because she was watching

  B stayed up late to watch

  C stayed up late after watching

2 I can't go on holiday during the school term.

FINISHES

I can't go on holiday.. .

  A until the school term has finished.

  B when the school term finishes.

  C until the school term finishes.

3 My father usually collects me from school in the car.

UP

My father usually .... school in the car.

  A takes up me from

  B picks me up from

  C gets me up from

4 Juan didn't study enough for his exam.

SHOULD

Juan .... his exam.

  A should have studied more for

  B should have spent longer studying for

  C should study more for

5 This dress was a present from my sister.

WAS

This dress .... my sister.

  A was gave to me by

  B had been given to me by

  C was given to me by

6 'Eva wasn't at the party last night.'

SEE

James said that .... Eva at the party last night.

  A he hadn't seen

  B he wasn't seeing

  C he hasn't seen

2 Now do these Part 4 questions.

1 My dad hates it when people leave a mess in the kitchen.

STAND

My dad can't .... in the kitchen.

2 'You must try the new Italian café,' said Karl to his friend.

ADVISED

Karl .... the new Italian café.

3 I couldn't run as fast as Sven in the race.

KEEP

I couldn't .... in the race.

4 I'm sure Annabel was not in school yesterday.

HAVE

Annabel .... in school yesterday.

5 How long did it take you to read the book?

SPEND

How long .... the book?

6 It's possible that my brother has discovered that I have broken his computer.

MAY

My brother .... out that I have broken his computer.

Speaking Part 2

▶ **Page 194 Speaking bank**

▶ **Page 194 Speaking bank**

> **Exam advice**
>
> • When you're not sure how to answer the question in the task, use phrases which allow you to speculate.
> • Spend about half the time comparing the photos and half the time answering the question.

1 Look at this speaking task. Then complete Bruno's answer with words or phrases from the box which he uses to compare or speculate about what he can see.

Examiner: Here are your photographs. They show young people doing difficult activities. I'd like you to compare the photographs and say why you think the people have decided to do these activities. All right?

Why have the people decided to do these activities?

could be   different   exactly what   looks as if
may have decided   must   perhaps
seems   unlike   who appears

Bruno: The first photo shows a girl **(1)** .... to be painting a city scene. I think she **(2)** .... in Italy. She **(3)** .... to be quite far away from the buildings she's painting and she **(4)** .... she's happy with her painting so far. She may be doing a school art project or **(5)** .... she's going to give it to somebody as a present.

The second photo shows another girl skateboarding. I'm not sure **(6)** .... she's going to do, but it **(7)** .... be a jump or a trick because she seems to be concentrating very hard. She could be practising for some kind of competition. Skateboarding is quite an unusual sport for girls and I think this girl enjoys being a bit **(8)** ....

The girl in the first photograph **(9)** .... to paint this scene because she finds it peaceful and relaxing. She looks quite calm, **(10)** .... the girl in the second photograph, who looks confident, but a bit tense.

2 Now listen to check your answers. 🎧 33

3 Work in pairs. Read the examiner's instructions and look at the photos on the page opposite. Then complete the sentences with your own ideas.

Examiner: Here are your photographs. They show people celebrating at different events. I'd like you to compare the photographs and say what you think the people are enjoying about the different situations.

1 In the first photo, the children look as if …
2 They seem to be …
3 They are probably going to …
4 In the second photo, the girls appear to be …
5 They could be …
6 Unlike the first photo, …
7 In both photos, the people seem …

What are the people enjoying about the different situations?

4 Pronunciation: sentence stress (3)

- We can use sentence stress to emphasise certain words in a sentence.

4.1 Listen to two versions of the same answer. How does the different emphasis change the meaning of what the speaker says?

The second photo shows another girl skateboarding. I'm not sure exactly what she's going to do, but it must be a jump or a trick because she seems to be concentrating very hard. She could be practising for some kind of competition.

4.2 Work in pairs. Take turns to read the answer above to your partner. Your partner should listen and say if you sound like version 1 or version 2.

4.3 Listen to Bruno and notice which words he emphasises. Then, with a partner, take turns to read Bruno's answer using the same emphasis.

The girl in the first photograph may have decided to paint this scene because she finds it peaceful and relaxing. She looks quite calm, unlike the girl in the second photograph who looks confident, but a bit tense. She could be practising for some kind of competition.

5 Look again at the extract in Pronunciation Exercise 4.3. How many words or phrases can you find which mean *a little*?

6 Look at the sentences you completed for Exercise 3 and decide which words you would like to emphasise when you speak. Then work in pairs and take turns to read your sentences aloud.

7 Now take turns to do the task in Exercise 2. When talking about people's feelings, use words or phrases which mean *a little* where appropriate.

8 Work in pairs. Take turns to do the speaking tasks on page 104.

- While you listen to your partner doing the speaking task, think about the things he/she is doing well and the things he/she could do better.
- When he/she has finished, give feedback and suggestions. If necessary, look at the checklist in Exercise 3 on page 24 to give you ideas.

Task 1

Examiner: Here are your photographs. They show people who have just done something special. I'd like you to compare the two photographs and say how you think the people feel about what they have just done.

How are the people feeling about what they have just done?

Task 2

Examiner: Here are your photographs. They show people in frightening situations. I'd like you to compare the two photographs and say why you think the people are frightened in these situations.

Why are the people frightened in these situations?

Writing Part 2

A story

▶ **Page 208 Writing bank**

1 Look at the writing task on the right and think about a special day in your life. What made it special? Here are some suggestions:

- You met someone interesting.
- You were successful at something (passing an important exam, winning a competition, etc.).
- You spent the day somewhere unusual.
- You did something really enjoyable.

You see the following announcement on an English-language website for teenagers.

Short story competition

Write a story for our short story competition for teenagers!

Your story must begin with this sentence:

When David read the email, he realised it was going to be a very special day.

Your story must include:
- some tickets
- a friend

Write your **story**.

2 Work in pairs. Decide what happened to David that day. Think about:

- what the email was about and why it meant the day was going to be special
- events before the email
- what the tickets were for and who the friend was
- what happened on the day.

3 Read the following answer to the writing task. It should be divided into three paragraphs. Where do you think each new paragraph should begin?

When David read the email, he realised it was going to be a very special day. It said, 'Congratulations, you have won two tickets to tonight's concert!' A month ago, he **(1)** *'d entered / was entering* a competition to win tickets to a concert, but **(2)** *didn't hear / hadn't heard* anything since then. His favourite band was going to play in his town, but the tickets **(3)** *had been selling out / had sold out* immediately and he'd been unable to get one. He **(4)** *'d been listening / was listening* to the musicians and downloading all their songs for two years, so he'd felt very disappointed. Now, however, he **(5)** *'d received / been receiving* this incredibly exciting email. He called his best friend Marco straight away. Marco **(6)** *listened / was listening* to one of the band's songs when David called and at first he couldn't believe it. 'That's just so incredible!' he exclaimed. The tickets were VIP tickets, which **(7)** *had included / included* a meeting with the band before the concert started. David and Marco **(8)** *were walking / walked* straight through security at the concert hall and then **(9)** *spent / had been spending* an hour sitting on comfortable sofas chatting to the band. They also got to watch the concert from right in front of the stage, which **(10)** *made / was making* it the best concert ever!

4 You can make a story more interesting for your reader by using a variety of tenses. Read the sample answer again and choose the correct verb tenses.

5 Read the writing task below and think about what you can write about.

- Why was Barbara smiling?
- What or who was in the photograph?
- Who went on a journey and where did they go?

You see this announcement in an English-language magazine for teenagers.

> ### Stories wanted!
> Write a short story for our magazine. The best story will win a prize!
> Your story must begin with this sentence:
> *Barbara just couldn't stop smiling.*
> **Your story must include:**
> - a photograph
> - a journey

Write your **story**.

6 Work in pairs. Take turns to make up a story. When you tell your story:

- describe the photograph
- say why Barbara was smiling
- say what happened on the journey.

7 Do the writing task following the steps below. Write between 140 and 190 words.

- Think about what you will say and make notes.
- Plan your story: how many paragraphs do you need and what will you put in each paragraph?
- Write your story following your plan.
- Check what you have written for mistakes.

- When you have finished writing, read your story again and make sure it follows on from the prompt sentence.
- Check your work carefully for mistakes. If you often make certain spelling mistakes, check that you haven't made them again. Have you used the right verb tenses?

Exam advice

10 On the money

Starting off

1 Which of these things do you enjoy buying? Where would you buy each of them? Would you buy any of them online?

2 Work in pairs. Discuss these questions.

- Are you given a regular amount of money by people in your family to spend on whatever you like?
- Do you think children should have to help their parents around the house if they want a bit of 'pocket money'?
- Have you ever saved up to buy something? If so, what was it? How long did it take you to save up the money you needed?

Reading and Use of English Part 2

1 Work in groups. You are going to read a text by a teenager about her shopping habits. Before you read, discuss these questions.

- What are the advantages and disadvantages of shopping online?
- Which do you prefer: online shopping or going to shops? Why?

- Answer the questions you find easy first.

- Pay careful attention to the meaning of the text to help you think of the right word.

- Answer all the questions. If you can't decide, think what type of word you need (preposition, pronoun, etc.) and guess.

- Check your answers by reading the completed text again. Make sure the words you have chosen go with the prepositions, verbs, etc. in the text.

Exam advice

2 Read the text in one minute, ignoring the gaps. Choose TWO letters that answer the question.

What does the writer buy on the internet?

A   stationery

B   clothes

C   interactive games

How I like to shop

Some adults think that because teenagers spend so **(0)** ...much............. time online, they probably also shop that way. That isn't actually true, at **(1)** .... not for me and my friends. I buy some things online though, such as pens and notebooks, and I get computer games that way too. It's very convenient, as I can order exactly **(2)** .... I want. There are no huge crowds of people to put **(3)** .... with either. And online stores don't have closing times, so it's perfect for me as a teenager who has **(4)** .... of hobbies at the weekend. However, I never buy T-shirts and stuff like that online, as you can't try anything **(5)** .... before you buy. Sometimes things look quite different **(6)** .... real life. A blue jumper might turn **(7)** .... to be green! I like the social aspect of going shopping for clothes. I'd much **(8)** .... spend time with friends in a shopping centre than sit at home in front of my computer.

3 Work alone. Think of the word which best fits each gap. When you have finished, compare your ideas with other students.

4 Work in pairs. Discuss these questions.

*   Are there any things you would never buy online?
*   What are your favourite shops to visit in town? What do you like about them?
*   Do you think that we will still go to shops in the future?

▶ **Page 177 Grammar reference**

Grammar

as and *like*

1 Look at sentences a–d and answer the questions below.

a   It's very convenient, as I can order exactly what I want.

b   ... so it's perfect for me as a teenager …

c   I never buy T-shirts and stuff like that online …

d   She is 33, but she acts like a teenager!

1   In which sentence(s) is *as* or *like* followed by a clause?

2   In which sentence(s) is *as* or *like* followed by a noun or pronoun?

3   What does *as* mean in sentence b? How is it different from *like* in sentence d?

2 Complete the sentences with *as* or *like*.

1   He has a weekend job .... a shop assistant.

2   He was regarded by his teachers .... one of the most brilliant students they had ever taught.

3   How embarrassing! Donna came to the party wearing exactly the same clothes .... me!

4   I find subjects .... physics and chemistry very difficult.

5   I'll be on holiday next week, ... you know.

6   I'm afraid I don't study .... much .... I should.

7   I'm speaking to you .... a friend.

8   My English teacher is lovely. She's .... a mother to me!

9   Some Swiss cities, such .... Zurich and Berne, have earned a reputation .... excellent places to live.

10 Tanya's father gave her a car for her 18th birthday .... she'd done so well in her exams.

1 Work in groups. You are going to read a true story written by a young woman called Eva. Look at the title of the text and choose the answer you think is correct: A, B or C.

Eva …

A sold all her belongings to her relatives and friends.

B gave away most of her possessions to people she knew.

C gave away some personal items to complete strangers.

2 Read the text quickly and check your answer.

I GOT RID OF NEARLY EVERYTHING I OWNED!

1 When the people first came round they were all sitting around drinking tea nervously and occasionally glancing at the cupboards. I didn't like the atmosphere and found the whole situation
5 unsettling. I was beginning to wonder why I had asked these people round to go through my stuff and take what they wanted. Then my sister Louise arrived at the door. Without putting down her bag or saying hello, she headed for the bedroom, determination
10 on her face. She couldn't get there quick enough. 'I knew she'd be the competition!' cried my friend Rosa, jumping off the sofa and heading in the same direction. This is what happens when you open your home to friends, family and
15 neighbours, telling them they can help themselves to everything within it. Moments later, Rosa and Louise reappeared with armfuls of clothes and pot plants. I was surprised that they hadn't taken the whole lot.

Last month, I moved abroad for two years to study,
20 taking just a single suitcase with me. I couldn't afford to keep my flat, so when it came to my possessions, extreme measures were called for. Some of my stuff, like old novels and pairs of jeans, I could cope with giving away. But there was a list of things like
25 precious paintings and my childhood teddy bear that I couldn't bring myself to let go. I just wasn't up to that. So, I decided to offer these things up for long-term loan. It's not recycling, or even freecycling: I'm calling it 'sharecycling'. It was my beloved tent
30 that formed the premise of it. I made the decision as I thought about the pointlessness of putting stuff into storage for two years. Instead, I imagined someone I loved putting my tent onto their back and setting off into the countryside in the summer sunshine. I was
35 moving to the other side of the world, but this made it feel as though I would still, in some small way, be with my friends. And once I'd come up with the idea, it just grew and grew. I decided to give away everything – the plants on the balcony, the
40 computer games, the chairs, even the towels in the bathroom.

To get rid of it all, I had an open house, inviting everyone I knew to take my belongings. 'This is just like supervised stealing!' said one friend, as
45 she loaded books by the handful into a carrier bag. I became like a sales assistant. I recommended novels, waved toys at babies, and brought out coats and jeans for people to try on.

Now I am sitting in a flat on the other side of the
50 world as the last of the monsoon rains pour down outside, turning the pavements into mud and sending the street sellers sheltering under doorways and umbrellas. I feel very far from my home, and from my stuff. That list I made of the things I want back?
55 I'm not sure how much I'll need it. So far, I haven't missed any of my pictures, or that strange purse shaped like a mouse which I've had since I was seven years old. Instead, I've missed my family, my friends, and my city.

60 And my 'sharecycling' plan ties me back to them. A friend took my tent to a music festival. And my favourite picture ended up on the wall of my best friend's flat back home. This is what gives me a real buzz: the thought of all my bits and pieces in
65 my friends' lives, a physical reminder of our ties. It's like I've pressed 'pause' on my city life rather than 'stop', making the move easier. It shows I'm not ready to travel around the world forever with just a laptop.

- The answers to the questions come in the same order in the text, so, for example, you will locate the answer to question 2 after question 1.
- The final question may refer to the whole passage: in this case, consider the general message, but also skim the text for words which support your choice.

Exam advice

3 Choose the answer (A, B, C or D) which you think fits best according to the text.

1 What best describes Eva's feelings in the first paragraph?
A She felt happy that her guests were enjoying themselves.
B She felt uncomfortable at first.
C She wanted her guests to leave as quickly as possible.
D She felt she was expected to do too much for her guests.

2 What does 'unsettling' mean in line 5 in the first paragraph?
A worrying
B comforting
C exciting
D surprising

3 What do we learn about Eva's attitude to her possessions in the second paragraph?
A She was sad that she couldn't afford to keep all of her things.
B She felt a strong emotional attachment to all of them.
C She was keen to share them with other people.
D She wanted to put some of the items in storage.

4 What does 'this' refer to in line 35 in the second paragraph?
A the idea of sharecycling
B the world
C the idea of camping
D the summer sunshine

5 What is meant by 'a real buzz' in line 64 in the final paragraph?
A an interesting topic of conversation
B a low, continuous sound
C a sudden memory from a long time ago
D a strong feeling of excitement

6 What best describes Eva's experience of giving away her things?
A It was enjoyable but she will be glad to get them back.
B It was a lot harder to do than she expected.
C It made her value people more than things.
D She was surprised at how strange it felt.

4 To understand a text, you often need to understand exactly what the writer is referring to at different points in the text. Which noun phrase (a or b) does each of these words/phrases refer to?

1 'the whole lot' (line 18) paragraph 1
a cupboards
b everything

2 'these things' (line 27) paragraph 2
a books and clothing
b valued possessions

3 'it' (line 30) paragraph 2
a offering things for loan
b a special tent

4 'it' (line 42) paragraph 3
a her house
b her possessions

5 'it' (line 55) paragraph 4
a the stuff
b the list

6 'them' (line 60) paragraph 5
a special places
b important people

7 'This' (line' 63) paragraph 5
a a thought
b a picture

5 Work in groups. Discuss these questions.
- Do you think you have many things you could easily live without? If so, what are they?
- Do you have a possession that you couldn't live without? If so, what is it and why is it so special?
- Why do you think some people buy things that they don't really use?
- How can we reduce the amount of things we buy?
- Are there any benefits in having less stuff? If so, what are they?

Vocabulary

arrive, get and *reach*

1 Students often confuse the words above. Choose the correct option in *italics*.

1 Then my sister Louise *arrived / got / reached* at the door.

2 She couldn't *arrive / get / reach* there quickly enough!

3 I'll certainly tell you when I *arrive / get / reach* my destination.

2 Complete the sentences with the correct form of *arrive*, *get* or *reach*. In some cases, more than one answer may be possible.

1 After an hour's discussion we finally .... a decision.

2 The traffic was so bad that they didn't .... to the concert till after it had started.

3 She's driving home and she'll phone me when she ....

4 What time do you normally .... to school in the morning?

5 When they .... at the hotel, they went straight to their rooms.

6 When you .... the end of the road, turn left.

3 Complete the sentences with the adverbs and adverbial phrases in the box.

> finally   in time   on time   safe and sound
> shortly   unannounced

1 Mum was worried that we might have an accident because of the snow, but we arrived home ...., much to her relief.

2 Sandy was late for the refreshments, but he arrived .... to hear the speeches.

3 The airline has a great reputation for punctuality, with 90% of flights arriving ....

4 The Orient Express from Paris will be arriving .... at Platform 13.

5 Uncle Kamal arrived .... in the middle of lunch, so we had to set an extra place for him at the table.

6 We were very late because of the traffic, and when we .... arrived, the match had nearly finished.

Listening Part 4

- You will hear options A, B and C referred to in some way, but only one of them is the correct answer to the question.

- Listen for the same *idea* to be expressed, not the same words.

Exam advice

1 Work in pairs. You are going to hear an interview with a student called Martin, who helped to organise an event for 'Buy Nothing Day'. What do you think this is? Choose TWO answers.

'Buy Nothing Day'

A takes place on an annual basis.

B encourages people to give away things they don't need.

C is always held on a Sunday.

D is held to try to make people realise they don't need everything that they buy.

2 Listen to the first part of the interview and check your guesses.

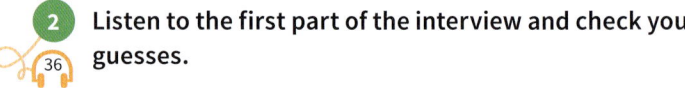

3 Read questions 1–7 and underline the key words.

1 Martin first became interested in Buy Nothing Day when

A he was told about it by his parents.

B he read about it online.

C he heard about it through another pupil.

2 How did Martin feel about the different activities suggested on the Buy Nothing Day website?

A He felt there were a lot to choose from.

B He thought most of them were dull.

C He was surprised at how few there were.

3 Where was the location for the Buy Nothing Day zombie walk?

A a shopping mall

B a supermarket

C a shopping street

4 Martin and his friends agreed to have identical

A masks.

B clothes.

C plastic bags.

5 What aspect of moving like a zombie did Martin find most challenging?

A walking in a straight line

B holding his arms out

C avoiding keeping his head up

6 How did Martin feel during the zombie walk?

A He felt proud that the spectators were so impressed.

B He felt very embarrassed.

C He was too busy concentrating to notice people's reaction.

7 What does Martin say about participating in the walk next year?

A He thinks he will be too busy to attend.

B He thinks it would be fun to be a zombie again.

C He plans to do something more serious next time.

4 Now listen to the full interview, and for questions 1–7, choose the best answer (A, B or C).

37

5 Work in groups. Discuss these questions.

- Do you think Buy Nothing Day is a good idea?
- Can Buy Nothing Day help people think more about how much they buy?
- Would you enjoy taking part in a zombie walk like Martin and his friends? Why? / Why not?

Vocabulary
Phrasal verbs

1 Match the phrasal verbs (1–9) from the reading text with their definitions (a–i). Look back at the reading text to help you do this.

1	head for	a	give (something) free of charge
2	give away	b	throw (something) away
3	set off	c	begin a journey
4	come up with	d	go in the direction of
5	get rid of	e	take (something) for yourself
6	try on	f	think of (a plan / an idea)
7	turn into	g	put on (clothes) to see if they fit or look right
8	end up	h	finish by (being / becoming / doing)
9	help yourself to	i	change something into something different

2 Complete the sentences with the correct form of the phrasal verbs in Exercise 1.

1 Chantal .... the brilliant idea of selling her old clothes in the market on Saturday.
2 I never buy jeans without .... them .... first to make sure they're the right size.
3 .... a biscuit if you'd like one – I just made them this morning.
4 Our flight leaves early tomorrow morning, so we'll need to make sure we .... for the airport in plenty of time.
5 Are you .... the station? I'm going in that direction too, so jump in and I'll give you a lift.
6 My jumper has got two big holes in it, so I think I .... it.
7 I don't want to sell the books or throw them away. I'd like to .... them .... to someone who enjoys reading.
8 I entered the competition for fun. I never thought I'd .... winning first prize!
9 Do you remember that old shop on the corner? They've .... it .... a café.

3 Choose the correct option in *italics*.

1 Do you usually *head for* / *set off* the same shops when you go shopping?
2 Have you ever spent a long time in a shop and *come up with* / *ended up* buying nothing?
3 Some people buy clothes and shoes without *trying them on* / *trying on them*. When is this a good idea?
4 When was the last time you *got rid of* / *came up with* some clothes?
5 How common is it for people to *set off* / *give away* items of clothing in your country?

4 Work in pairs. Ask and answer the questions in Exercise 3.

Grammar
Modal verbs to express ability

▶ **Page 177 Grammar reference**

1 Read these sentences and answer the question below.

a When my mate suggested that we organise our own Buy Nothing Day event, I thought it <u>could</u> be a lot of fun.

b It wasn't exactly easy persuading other people to take part. But in the end we <u>managed to</u> get just about everyone in our class to join in.

c So, you <u>can</u> choose a big shopping centre or a supermarket to walk in.

d I <u>can</u> spread my arms out like a zombie pretty well now!

e Most of us <u>were able to</u> do that without too much practice.

f The zombie walk <u>could have</u> gone badly, but actually it went well.

Which of the underlined modal verbs in sentences a–f refer to the following? The first one is done as an example.

1 general ability in the past .... *e*
2 ability on one difficult occasion in the past ....
3 possibility in the present or future .... and ....
4 ability in the present ....
5 something that was possible but actually did not happen ....

2 Choose the correct form of the verb in *italics*. There may be more than one correct form in some sentences.

1 We walked all day, and at five o'clock we finally *could / were able to / managed to* reach the top of the mountain.

2 I *couldn't / can't / wasn't able to* get to sleep, so I ended up staying awake all night.

3 When I was a small child, I *could / was able to / can* sing beautifully, but my voice isn't so good now.

4 *Can you / Are you able to / Could* you hear the neighbours' television? It's far too loud!

5 I *could play / could have played / can play* tennis with Luis yesterday, but I wasn't feeling well, so I stayed at home.

6 Although the shop was very crowded, we *could / were able to / managed to* get the shopping done quite quickly.

3 Write some sentences about yourself, your family or a friend. Use each word or phrase in the box twice.

> could   was/were able to   could have   can

4 Complete the second sentence so that it has a similar meaning to the first sentence, using the word given. Do not change the word given. You must use between two and five words, including the word given.

1 Manon wasn't able to think of any good ideas for a present.
COME
Manon .... with any good ideas for a present.

2 You were lucky that you didn't have an accident – you were driving so fast.
COULD
You were lucky because .... an accident – you were driving so fast.

3 Nobody wanted these old toys, so I'll keep them.
RID
I .... these old toys, so I'll keep them.

4 Is it possible for me to take one of these apples?
HELP
.... to one of these apples?

Speaking Part 1

▶ **Page 192 Speaking bank**

- Practise by working in small groups, asking and answering questions about your personal life and interests. Make sure you choose topics that involve using a range of phrases.

- Don't go to the exam with memorised answers, as you will lose marks for not responding naturally. However, you can prepare by thinking about the vocabulary to describe your life, your studies or work, the neighbourhood where you live, etc.

- Look at the examiner while you're speaking and try to sound confident.

Exam advice

1 Read these Speaking Part 1 questions and note down a few ideas you could use to answer each of them. (Do not write complete sentences.)

1 Are you ever given money by people in your family? (If so, are you given money regularly, or on special occasions?)

2 What do teenagers in your country typically spend their money on?

3 Do you have a favourite shop? (Can you describe it to us?)

4 Is there anything you'd like to buy but can't afford?

2  Read the descriptions of how some candidates answer Part 1 questions. Then listen to Pablo and Marina answering the questions in Exercise 1 and match the candidates with these descriptions. Write P (Pablo), M (Marina) or B (both).

1 This person is not sure how to answer at first, but then gives quite a long, complete answer. ☐

2 This person gives lots of other information about themselves while they give reasons for their answer. ☐

3 This person gives two alternative answers as well as a combined answer. ☐

3 Choose three questions from Exercise 1 and think how you will answer them. Think about the types of answer in Exercise 2.

- When you are ready, work with a partner and take turns to ask and answer the questions you have chosen.

- While you are listening to your partner, for each answer, decide how they are answering the question and how successful they are at answering it.

4 Pronunciation: linking (1)

To speak fluently, speakers often

- do not pronounce the last consonant of a word. This often happens if the word ends in two consonants, e.g. ne**xt** Monday or if it is a short word ending in 't'.

- do not pronounce the final 't' of negatives such as *didn't*, *couldn't*, etc. when the main verb begins with a consonant

- link the last consonant of the word to the word which follows when it begins with a vowel

- do not pronounce the 't' in *often*.

4.1 Listen to these example sentences.

I saw them last week.

I couldn't find my trainers.

I like eating and talking.

I don't often buy clothes and shoes.

4.2 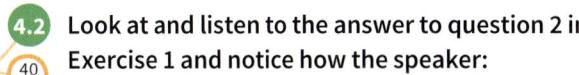 Look at and listen to the answer to question 2 in Exercise 1 and notice how the speaker:

- does not pronounce the crossed-out letters

- joins the words indicated with ‿.

I think it really depends, because teenagers are all different and so they spend their money in all sorts of ways. I guess some people spend more money on clothes and magazines, while others spend more on music and things like sports equipment. In general though, I think most teenagers spend money on things like going out to cafés or cinema tickets.

4.3 Work in pairs. Take turns to read the answer in 4.2 aloud, in the same way.

4.4 Look at the answer to question 3 in Exercise 1 below and:

- cross out the final consonants you think the speaker won't pronounce

- mark with a ‿ the words you think the speaker will link.

Then listen to check your answers.

Hmm, I'm not sure, because I don't go shopping much really. Umm, but there is one shop I really like. It's one of a chain of sports shops and what's cool about it is I can just wander round and see all the clothes and equipment and stuff they sell. I look at clothes and equipment I'd like to buy – when I can afford it, I mean.

5 Listen to Marina and Pablo answering the examiner's question below. Which type of answer (1–3) from Exercise 2 do they each give?

Examiner: What sort of shops do you go to regularly?

6 Work in pairs. Look at the words in the box and the questions below. Which words could you use to help you answer the questions?

> a bargain   a brand   competitive   a consumer
> to purchase   the sales
> in stock / out of stock   unavailable

- What sort of shops do you go to regularly?
- Tell us about a shop you've visited recently. Why did you go there?
- Which shops in your area are the most attractive? Why?
- What's the best time of year to go shopping in your town?
- Tell us about something you really enjoyed buying.
- If you won a lot of money in a competition, how would you spend it?

7 Now take turns to ask and answer the questions.

Writing Part 2
A review

▶ **Page 210 Writing bank**

- Think about who will read your review and what information they want to know.
- Write a plan thinking about each of the things you want to describe and in what order.
- Decide what recommendation you are going to make and include it in your answer.

Exam advice

1 Look at this writing task. What are the key points you must deal with?

> You've seen this announcement on an English-language website for teenagers.
>
> **Reviews wanted!**
> We are looking for reviews of something our readers have been given or bought recently. It could be a gadget, a piece of clothing, or something else.
>
> Write a review describing your purchase. Tell us whether you like it and why, and if you would recommend it to other people.
>
> Write your **review**.

2 Work in groups. Discuss what you could review and what information and ideas you could use to deal with the points you have identified in Exercise 1.

3 Write a plan for your review. Then compare your plan with a partner's.

4 Read Matt's answer on the opposite page and write notes to complete his plan below.

Plan

Paragraph 1:

what the thing is: a bike; do I like it — yes

Paragraphs 2 and 3:

....

Paragraph 4:

....

THE CRUISER – the perfect bike for me

I was recently given a new bicycle for my birthday – an AbacusCruiser, costing £500. All the other bicycles I've ever had were second-hand, **so** I love how shiny and amazing it looks. **Apart from** looking cool, this bike is also a joy to ride.

It's a road bike, and **although** it isn't as high-tech as the ones in the Tour de France, it **still** goes pretty fast. I love the fact that it's very light and extremely comfortable to ride. In fact, the saddle is the most comfortable I've ever had, as it is made of leather. **What's more**, it's good in the rain as the tyres are made of good thick rubber that doesn't slip on wet roads.

My Cruiser has three gears, **which** are all I need **because** I live in **such** a flat part of the country **that** I wouldn't use more if I had them. However, if you live somewhere hilly, I would advise you to go for the 11-gear models, which are not very expensive either.

If you want a good-quality bicycle at a fairly inexpensive price, I would definitely recommend the Abacus Cruiser. Go to your local shop or have a look online and see if you can find it!

5 Study how Matt uses the **highlighted** words or phrases. Then join these sentences using the words in brackets and making any other changes which are necessary.

1 I've always wanted a new camera. This was the perfect present. (so)

I've always wanted a new camera, so this was the perfect present.

2 This camera is very easy to use. It takes excellent pictures. (apart from)

3 It's blue, which isn't my favourite colour. The camera looks very smart. (although, still)

4 It has a strong case. This is very important. I am a clumsy person. I would soon damage it while carrying it around. (which, because, such, that)

5 It has a good instruction manual. It also comes with a DVD. The DVD is very helpful. (and what's more, which)

6 Write your own answer to the writing task in Exercise 1. Before you write, think how you can use some of the highlighted words in Matt's answer in your own review.

Write between 140 and 190 words.

Vocabulary

1 Choose the correct option in *italics*.

1 Sheila *spent / passed* most of her holiday at her cousins' house.

2 I think the bad weather might *cause / have* an impact on the plans for the class trip.

3 Air travel *causes / makes* a lot of pollution.

4 People play with their mobile phones to *spend / pass* the time when there's nothing more interesting to do.

5 Patricia studied really hard all weekend, but it *had / caused* no effect on her final result in the exam.

6 Hearing my brother's good news *caused / made* me very happy.

7 I *stayed / spent* six hours doing homework for my English class last weekend.

Grammar

2 Look at the photos and question for Speaking Part 2. Then complete the candidate's answer with the words and phrases in the box.

What do the people enjoy about these free-time activities?

---

appear to   both   could just   look   look as if   may be   might be doing it   perhaps   very different

---

The first photo shows two young people doing archery. They **(1)** .... taking part in a competition, or they **(2)** .... be practising, I'm not sure. They **(3)** .... as part of a traditional activity in their country or because they enjoy the sport.

The second photo shows a **(4)** .... situation. In this photo, there are two elderly people playing the piano together. They **(5)** .... very happy and relaxed.

The teenagers in the first photo **(6)** .... be enjoying themselves because they're having to concentrate hard in order to hit the target or win the competition.

On the other hand, in the second photo, the people **(7)** .... they're just enjoying each other's company and **(8)** .... they're not taking the music too seriously. In **(9)** .... photos, the people are enjoying doing things which need a lot of practice.

---

3 Complete the conversation with the correct form of the verbs in brackets.

Andy: Why won't Stephen answer his mobile phone?

Nigel: He **(1)** .... (must / switch) it off while he was playing football and forgotten to turn it back on again.

Andy: He **(2)** .... (can't / turn) it off for that reason because he didn't have football training today – it was cancelled.

Nigel: Well, he **(3)** .... (may not / hear) it, or he **(4)** .... (could / leave) it at home. Try ringing again. He **(5)** .... (might / answer) this time. Anyway, why do you want to call him?

Andy: I want to remind him that he's coming round to my house today after school. He **(6)** .... (might / forget) – you know what he's like.

Nigel: He **(7)** .... (can't / forget) – he was talking about it yesterday and he was looking forward to it.

Vocabulary

1 Read the text and decide which answer (A, B, C or D) best fits each gap.

I think that we, as teenage shoppers, are naturally very **(0)** _____B_____ to price. We're always hunting for **(1)** _____ and many of us plan our shopping and do not just **(2)** _____ into shops and buy on impulse.

Funnily enough, many of my friends say their parents have a lot of **(3)** _____ both on how much they spend on clothes and on what they buy, even if they have **(4)** _____ the money themselves from a part-time job. In short, despite what many older people might think, we worry about our parents' reaction to the clothes we **(5)** _____. The shops in my area operate in a highly **(6)** _____ environment, so they have to make sure they **(7)** _____ for young people's tastes by having a wide range of fashion clothes in **(8)** _____ at any one time.

	A	B	C	D
0	A sensible	B sensitive	C affected	D considerate
1	A values	B cheapness	C bargains	D decreases
2	A jump	B pop	C enter	D pass
3	A impact	B importance	C pressure	D influence
4	A earned	B won	C gained	D acquired
5	A invest	B achieve	C purchase	D obtain
6	A competent	B competitive	C contested	D combative
7	A offer	B cater	C sell	D supply
8	A stock	B shelf	C place	D existence

Grammar

2 Complete the second sentence so that it has a similar meaning to the first sentence, using the word given. Do not change the word given. You must use between two and five words, including the word given.

1 Manu didn't succeed in completing the crossword.
ABLE
Manu .... off the crossword.

2 It's important that we start our journey early tomorrow.
SET
We need .... early tomorrow.

3 Carl couldn't go towards the beach because the road was closed.
HEAD
Carl wasn't .... the beach because the road was closed.

4 Pierre was unable to suggest an answer to the problem.
COME
Pierre .... an answer to the problem.

5 James never believed that he would finally become a doctor.
END
James didn't think ....
a doctor.

6 John couldn't throw away his old things.
RID
John wasn't .... his old things.

3 Complete the text with *as* or *like*.

When my grandfather left school at the age of 14, he got his first job **(1)** _____ an office assistant. In those days, he was extremely thin, **(2)** _____ he wasn't paid very much and couldn't afford to eat a lot. But he was in the same situation **(3)** _____ a lot of boys at that time, **(4)** _____ most children left school at that age and had to look for a job. I have one or two photos of him from that time, and he looks just **(5)** _____ me, but thinner! When he was older, he worked at all sorts of things, such **(6)** _____ reporting for a local newspaper and working **(7)** _____ a part-time mechanic. **(8)** _____ many people of his generation, he worked hard all his life, but he always found time for the things he enjoyed, **(9)** _____ walking in the country or spending time with his grandchildren.

I hope I'll be **(10)** _____ him when I'm an old man!

11 Medical matters

1 Here I am, in my 80s, still quite .... – I mean, I go shopping, visit my friends and go to the cinema when I want to. What more can you ask for?

3 I do .... the occasional cold or other .... I'm a doctor, so I can't really avoid them, but I .... them pretty quickly and they don't usually stop me going to work.

2 I do an hour's .... in the morning before school, and in the evening I usually have time for a couple of hours' football, so I really think I'm very fit.

4 I visit the doctor regularly once a year for a .... Once or twice I've needed .... for something she's found, but it's never been anything very serious.

5 I never go to the doctor and in fact I don't even know my doctor's name. I'm lucky. I've never had a day's .... in my life.

Starting off

1 Work in pairs. Complete what each of the people says about their health with the words and phrases in the box.

> active   balanced diet   catch
> check-up   get over   illness   infection
> putting on   treatment   workout

- Do you ever think about your health?
- Do you think you and your friends have a healthy lifestyle?

2 Work in pairs. Listen to the first part of what each speaker (A–F) says about their health and, when you hear the 'beep', predict which extract (1–6) from Exercise 1 comes next.

Example: A2

3 Now listen to the complete extracts to check your answers to Exercises 1 and 2.

4 Work in pairs. Discuss these questions.

- How important is it to get regular exercise? What do you do to get exercise?
- What does the phrase 'everything in moderation' mean? Are there some things you think people should avoid even in moderation?

6 I'm very careful to eat a .... – only a little meat and plenty of fresh fruit and vegetables – and I'm careful about not .... weight, so I do a reasonable amount of exercise as well.

Listening Part 3

Exam advice

- Before you listen, you should read and think about the meaning of each option.
- Wait until each speaker finishes before you choose an answer.
- Remember that the speakers may talk about something connected with other sentences, but there is only one correct option for each speaker.

1 You are going to hear five people talking about a visit to the doctor. First, match the words (1–10) with their definitions (a–j).

1	cure	6	prescription
2	bruise	7	surgery
3	symptom	8	treat
4	examination	9	scar
5	dose	10	injury

a a piece of paper on which a doctor writes the details of medicine that someone needs

b the amount of medicine someone is told to take

c to make someone with an illness healthy again

d a specific characteristic of a disease or problem

e a dark mark on a person's skin after they have been hurt

f to give medical care to someone

g a mark, often permanent, on a person's skin, after it has been cut

h an operation

i damage to a person's body, often through sport or an accident

j a thorough check by a doctor to discover a patient's problem

2 Now listen and tick (✓) the words and phrases from Exercise 1 as you hear them.

45

3 Listen again. For speakers 1–5, choose from the list (A–H) what each speaker says about their visit. Use the letters only once. There are three extra letters which you do not need to use.

A I needed to wait for a long time to be seen.

B I agreed with the diagnosis.

C I asked to increase the dose.

D I was surprised at the effectiveness of the treatment.

E I was worried that I would not fully recover.

F I am going to get the opinion of a specialist.

G I missed my appointment.

H I decided not to take the medicine.

Speaker 1 ☐
Speaker 2 ☐
Speaker 3 ☐
Speaker 4 ☐
Speaker 5 ☐

4 Work in pairs. Answer these questions.

- How often do you go to the doctor?
- Do you feel nervous before you go to the doctor? Why? / Why not?

Vocabulary
Idiomatic expressions

1 It's important to be able to guess the meaning of idiomatic expressions from the context. Match the ==highlighted== expressions (1–6) in these extracts from Listening Part 3 with their definitions (a–f) below.

I was booked in for surgery the next day. But the next morning, it was cancelled – I was (1) ==taken aback==.

Six months later, I was (2) ==over the moon== to find that I'd made a full recovery.

I arrived late as I'd (3) ==lost track of time== and I was afraid that I'd missed my appointment.

I'm often ill and am always (4) ==coming down with something==.

I've just requested an appointment with another doctor who's an expert in these sorts of mysterious illnesses, and hopefully he'll be able to (5) ==get to the bottom of it==.

As a child, I had terrible problems with my skin. It looked like I had scars. I often (6) ==felt a bit off-colour== too.

a starting to suffer from an illness
b delighted
c felt slightly ill
d discover the real reason for something
e surprised or shocked so that you don't know what to say
f wasn't aware of the time

Reading and Use of English Part 4

1 Read the email from Sophie to her friend Mumtaz. What does Sophie have to do for her school science project?

Hi Mumtaz

How are you doing? Do you remember me telling you about my school science project on a famous person in medicine? I need to decide on my topic now, but **(1)** I'm finding it almost impossible to make up my mind. Everyone else in my class seems to know what they're doing, so it seems as if **(2)** I'm the only person who hasn't decided. I'll need to spend a lot of time researching this person so that I can write about them and give a presentation. I've never had to do such a long piece of writing before and I'm not sure how I'll **(3)** manage to complete it. **(4)** I didn't expect it to be nearly so hard when our teacher first told us about it.

I **(5)** initially considered doing my project on Dr Edward Jenner, who introduced the first vaccination in the 18th century. Vaccination certainly **(6)** marked a major advance in medicine because it has eradicated serious diseases in many countries. However, I'm also thinking of researching Sir Alexander Fleming, who discovered the first antibiotic, penicillin, in the early 20th century. Antibiotics were another key breakthrough in medicine and led to many lives being saved.

I'll **(7)** keep thinking about my topic and when I've finally **(8)** managed to make up my mind, I'll let you know! In the meantime, I'd love to hear what you think. I know that you love science and medicine.

All the best,

Sophie

2 Read the text in Exercise 1 carefully and replace the underlined words with one of the options below. There are five options you do not need to use.

a   everyone apart from me has

b   got ready to make

c   represented an important development

d   it's far harder than I'd thought

e   it's extremely hard for me

f   continue to consider

g   first thought about

h   thought it was impossible

i   succeed in finishing

j   much progress is likely to be made

k   major advances are being made

l   it was almost as hard as I'd expected

m   succeeded in making

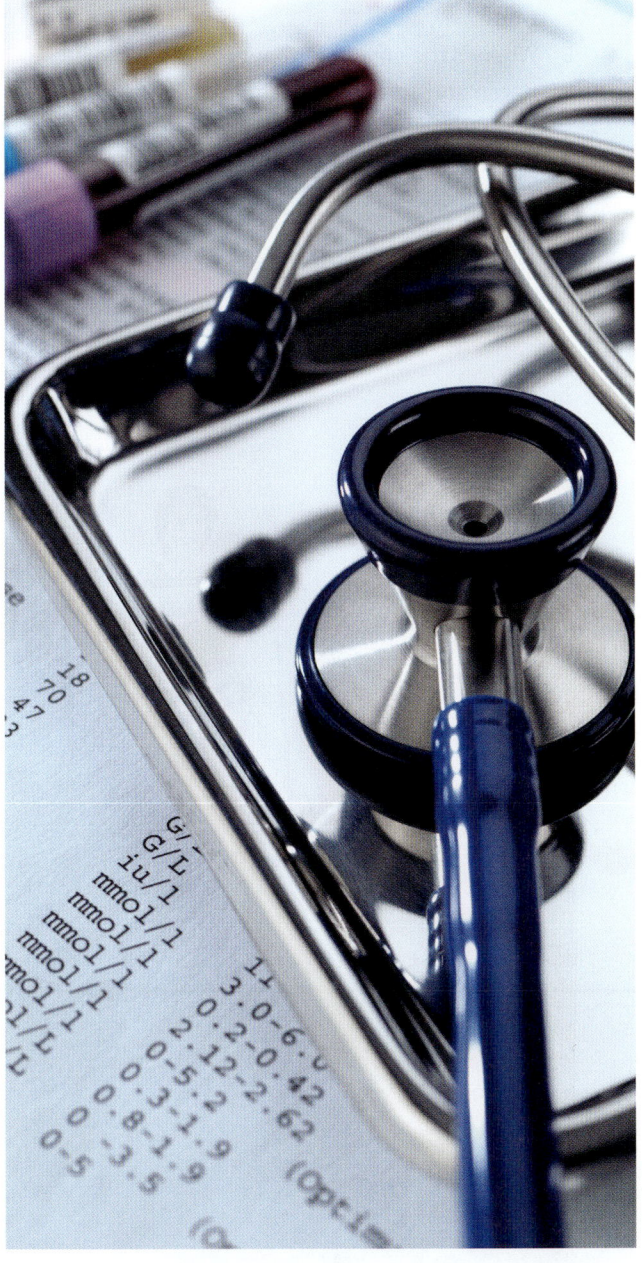

3 For questions 1–6, complete the second sentence so that it has a similar meaning to the first sentence, using the word given. Do not change the word given. You must use between two and five words, including the word given.

1 If I continue to follow a healthy diet, I will stay healthy.

KEEP

If I .... a healthy diet, I will stay healthy.

2 I hadn't expected the injection to hurt so much.

FAR

The injection .... I'd expected.

3 I finally managed to make an appointment to see the doctor.

SUCCEEDED

I finally .... an appointment to see the doctor.

4 The doctors don't think that my father will need an operation.

UNLIKELY

The doctors say that .... my father will need an operation.

5 As a result of the doctor's mistake, the patient was wrongly treated.

LED

The mistake by the doctor .... wrongly treated.

6 My sister is the only person in my family who doesn't wear glasses.

APART

Everybody in my family .... my sister.

4 Write sentences about yourself and your friends using the words and phrases in the box.

> apart from   as long as   far ... than   led to
> succeeded   unlikely

Grammar
Relative pronouns and relative clauses

▶ **Page 178 Grammar reference**

1 Complete the extracts from Listening Part 3 with a relative pronoun. In some cases, more than one answer may be possible.

1 The doctor .... I saw at the hospital told me she had seen this type of injury many times.
2 I just took the painkillers .... I was given.
3 I knew that these diseases had really serious symptoms and could be difficult to cure, ... meant I needed to be seen.
4 I was treated using some strange herbs, ... I wasn't too keen on as the taste was pretty bad.

2 Read these sentences. Which contain defining relative clauses? Which contain non-defining relative clauses? Write D for defining or ND for non-defining after each sentence.

1 The village where I go for my holidays has a very healthy climate.
2 Mrs Altmeyer, who you met on the train, is a nurse.
3 The children who you've been talking to all go to the same school.
4 Have you still got the book which I lent you?
5 My physical education teacher, who was an Olympic champion, says that exercise is essential for good health.
6 Students who eat a good breakfast often do better at school.
7 The people whose house we are staying in are working abroad for a few months.

3 In which of sentences 1–6 in Exercise 2 could you use *that* instead of *which* or *who*?

4 In which sentences in Exercise 2 could you omit *who* or *which*? Why?

5 Join the sentences using a relative clause. In some cases, more than one answer may be possible.

1 Did you see the film? They broadcast it on television last night.

Did you see the film (that/which) they broadcast on television last night?

2 He studied hard for his maths exam. He found it quite easy.
3 The man is a taxi driver. They sold the car to him.
4 Could you give me the newspaper? You were reading it earlier.
5 That white house over there is the house. I was born there.
6 Where's the envelope? I put the money in it.
7 Karen and Teresa are on holiday in the Caribbean at the moment. We're looking after their dog.
8 Every morning, I go running in the park with Andy. You know his sister.

Reading and Use of English Part 3

1 Read this sentence and answer the question below.

As a result of the doctor's mistake, the symptoms of the illness were misunderstood.

What does *misunderstood* mean?

a understood badly or wrongly

b not understood at all

2 Now read these two sentences and answer the questions.

In the past, the cause of this disease was unknown, so it couldn't be prevented.

1 What does *unknown* mean?

    a known badly

    b not known at all

Many dentists disapprove of fruit juices because they contain a lot of sugar.

2 What does *disapprove* mean?

    a not approve of

    b approve of wrongly

3 Which prefix, *mis-*, *un-* or *dis-*, has a different meaning from the other two?

4 Complete the sentences with the negative form of the verb in capitals. Remember to use the correct form of the verb.

1 You must not .... your seatbelt until the plane has landed. **FASTEN**

2 I'm sorry to .... you, but you haven't passed the test. **APPOINT**

3 You must be very careful with the saw. If you .... it, you could injure yourself. **USE**

4 I couldn't .... my shoelaces because the knots were too tight. **TIE**

5 My surname is very unusual, which means that many people .... it. **SPELL**

6 I saw George at the party an hour ago, but now he seems to have .... **APPEAR**

7 I was so tired that I fell asleep on my bed without getting .... **DRESS**

8 We were told that the test was today, but we must have been .... as we had a normal lesson. **INFORM**

5 Add a prefix *un-*, *dis-*, *in-*, *im-* or *mis-* to form opposites of these words. In some cases, more than one answer may be possible.

> ability   agreement   appear   experienced   formal
> happiness   helpful   honest   like   likely   patient
> predictable   prepared   reliable   satisfied
> understand

• Check:
 – what type of word you need, e.g. noun, verb, etc.
 – whether nouns need to be singular or plural
 – whether a prefix or suffix is needed
 – what form verbs should be in
• You must spell your answers correctly.

Exam advice

6 Read the text below. Use the word given in capitals at the end of some of the lines to form a word that fits in the gap in the same line. Before you decide on the word, think about what type of word you need (adjective, noun, etc.), and whether you need a negative or plural form or a correct verb form.

Afraid of the dentist?

You're sitting in the waiting room looking nervously through a magazine. The receptionist calls your name and you walk slowly into the surgery. You lie back in the chair and open your mouth so that the dentist can give your teeth a thorough

(1) .... Many people feel   **EXAMINE**

some **(2)** .... related to   **ANXIOUS**

visiting the dentist. However, for a

small **(3)** .... , the fear is   **MINOR**

so great that they avoid making an

(4) .... to see their   **APPOINT**

dentist for many years. This can have

serious consequences for those who

are affected. They are likely to suffer

from dental problems and may feel self-

conscious about the **(5)** ....   **APPEAR**

of their teeth as a result.

People may **(6)** .... going to the   **LIKE**

dentist for a variety of reasons. Fear of pain

is the most common one, and many people

also hate feeling **(7)** .... in the   **HELP**

hands of the dentist. However, dentists

can help to make their patients feel more

relaxed by talking to them and perhaps

playing soothing music to make them feel

less **(8)** ....   **EASY**

Speaking Part 2

▶ Page 194 Speaking bank

Exam advice

• If you can't think of a word, explain what the thing is used for or what it looks like.

1 Complete the table below with these phrases, which can help you in the Speaking paper.

> **Phrases for getting out of difficulties**
> I can't think of the word, but it's a type of …
> I'm not sure how to say it, but it's used for …
> I'm sorry, what I meant was …
> Let me think …
> No, I mean …
> What I want to say is that …
> What's the word? Um …
> Sorry, I mean …

when you need time to think	when you can't think of the word	when you've made a mistake

2 Work in pairs. Look at the photos and listen to Nicola doing Speaking Part 2 and then complete the checklist above right.

Nicola...		Yes	No
1	spoke for the complete minute or until the examiner said, 'Thank you'.		
2	compared the photos and spent roughly equal time on each.		
3	answered the examiner's question clearly with her opinion.		
4	gave (a) reason(s) for her opinion.		
5	found ways of explaining things when she didn't know a word.		
6	corrected her mistakes.		
7	sounded interested and enthusiastic about what she was saying.		

3 Work in pairs. Read the examiner's follow-up question an different candidates' answers. Then answer the question:

Examiner: Now, which activity would you prefer to do?

Miguel: I'd prefer to go cycling, because I'm not very good at cooking and I really enjoy making – I mean, *doing* – physical exercise. I find cycling in the city quite exciting, but if I can, I'd rather cycle in the country because it's less polluted.

Peter: Making salad is better because the other is dangerous.

Nikolai: Oh, I think cycling is very good for the health, even in the city, and also it's important to have a healthy diet because you know what they say we are what we eat!

1 Who do you think gave the best answer, Miguel, Peter or Nikolai? Why?

2 Match what the examiner might be thinking with each candidate's answer (a–c).

a 'Did he listen to my question? He isn't answering it at all!

b 'This is a good answer: two or three sentences, he corrects himself and he uses a variety of vocabulary.'

c 'Too short! He hasn't used much language and he's not really answering the question!'

How important is each activity for staying healthy?

4 Pronunciation: intonation (3)

We tend to use more intonation on stressed words than on unstressed words.

4.1 **47** Work in pairs. Look at this extract from Nicola's answer. Underline the words you think she stresses. Then listen to check your answers.

OK, so both photographs show people doing things which might be good for their sanity, sorry, I mean their health. In the first photo, I can see someone who looks as if he's … um, what's the word? … he's commuting by bicycle in busy traffic.

4.2 **48** Listen to the extract with two different intonations.

- In which version, **a** or **b**, does the speaker sound more certain and confident?
- Does the voice rise or fall on the final stressed word in each sentence? What does this show?

4.3 **49** Decide which words will be stressed in this extract. Then listen to check your answers.

On the other hand, if you live in the city, it's a good way of getting exercise. In the second photo, the kids should remember that they need to eat a mixed, sorry, a balanced diet, not just salad and fruit.

4.4 Take turns to read the extract aloud.

5 **50** Work in pairs. Student A should listen to the examiner's instructions and do the task in Exercise 2. Student B should complete the checklist in Exercise 2 and give feedback at the end.

6 **51** Now, Student B should listen to the examiner's follow-up question and answer it.

7 **52** Work in pairs. Student B should listen to the examiner's instructions and do this task. Student A should complete the checklist in Exercise 2 and give feedback at the end.

8 **53** Now, Student A should listen to the examiner's follow-up question and answer it.

Why is it important for these people to deal with their illness or injury?

Writing Part 1
An essay

▶ **Page 202 Writing bank**

1 Work in groups. Look at the discussion question below. Note down at least three healthy or unhealthy aspects for each discussion point (a–e). When you have finished, change groups and report what your group decided.

Do you think modern lifestyles are healthy or not? Talk about:

a the environment and health
b diet
c work activities
d information, e.g. about exercise, diet
e free-time activities.

2 Work in pairs. Read the writing task below.

- Underline the main ideas in the task.
- Decide which points from your discussion you would include in your answer and write a plan.

In your English class, you have been talking about whether modern lifestyles are healthy or not.

Now your English teacher has asked you to write an essay.

Write your essay using **all** the notes and giving reasons for your point of view.

> **'Modern lifestyles can seriously endanger our health.'**
>
> **Do you agree?**
>
> **Notes**
> Write about:
>
> 1. food
> 2. physical activity
> 3. .... (your own idea)

3 Work in pairs. Discuss what the strong points and weak points of this essay are. Then say what comments you would write at the end if you were this student's teacher.

It seems strange that although we know a lot about how to live healthily, many people continue to do things which may be harmful to their health.

The modern world offers us plenty of opportunities to live healthily. For instance, we all know about the importance of eating a balanced diet and taking regular exercise. Moreover, in rich countries we have easy access to good-quality fresh food and suitable sports facilities, so it should be easy to adopt healthy living habits.

However, there are things which prevent people from having a healthy lifestyle. For example, industry and traffic have led to serious environmental pollution. What is more, we spend a lot of time sitting down, and this often means we have less time for activities which keep us fit. For example, there are many people who spend many hours sitting in front of computers working, studying, or playing computer games. In addition, many people do not eat the right sort of food.

Exam advice

- Your concluding paragraph should summarise your opinion and the reasons for it.
- Don't include new ideas in your final sentence because you won't be able to support them with reasons or examples.
- Be careful not to spend too long on Part 1, or you won't have time to do Part 2 well.

4 Work in pairs. Read these concluding paragraphs and decide which one is most suitable for the essay in Exercise 3. Why?

1 All in all, I believe that we have to find ways of living which are as healthy as possible. Also, I think people should try to drive more carefully.

2 In conclusion, I would agree with the statement because although we have plenty of opportunities to follow a healthy lifestyle, in practice we often choose a less healthy alternative.

3 To summarise, modern lifestyles have good and bad aspects, but the lifestyle we choose depends on us. However, often our health depends on factors which we cannot control.

5 Match each of these teacher's comments (a–c) to one of the concluding paragraphs in Exercise 4.

a A good brief final paragraph where your opinion is clearly stated and you summarise the main arguments of your essay.

b This concluding paragraph doesn't seem to sum up the arguments you expressed in the main part of the essay, but it sums up other arguments. What a pity, because it's well written!

c You're giving an opinion which is not exactly connected with the essay question. Also, your final sentence introduces a new argument which hasn't been dealt with in the main part of the essay, so it's not really a conclusion.

6 If you're not sure how to begin a paragraph, you can begin with a sentence which:

- says what the paragraph will contain
- relates the paragraph to the previous paragraph.

Look at the opening sentences (a and b) from paragraphs 2 and 3 of the sample answer in Exercise 3 and answer the questions below.

a The modern world offers us plenty of opportunities to live healthily.

b However, there are things which prevent people from having a healthy lifestyle.

1 What will each paragraph contain?

2 Which word relates one of the paragraphs to the previous paragraph?

7 Write opening sentences for paragraphs which will contain:

1 three advantages of living in the country

2 some disadvantages of living in the country

3 reasons exercise is important

4 dangers of taking too much exercise

8 Work in groups. Discuss whether you agree or disagree with the statement in the essay question in Exercise 9 below. You can talk about:

- diet
- sport and exercise
- free-time activities.

9 Do this writing task. Write between 140 and 190 words. Before you write, make a plan. When you write, you can use the essay in Exercise 3 as a model.

In your English class, you have been talking about how interested young people are in health and fitness.

Now your English teacher has asked you to write an essay.

Write your essay using **all** the notes and giving reasons for your point of view.

'Young people generally don't pay enough attention to their health and fitness.'

Do you agree?

Notes
Write about:

1. physical exercise
2. other habits which affect health
3. .... (your own idea)

12 Animal kingdom

A

B

C

D

E

F

Starting off

1. Work in pairs. Discuss these questions.

- What is the relationship between the people and the animals in each photograph?
- Are animals important in your life? If so, why are they important?

  Here are some words and phrases to help you.

> pet   owner   farming   leisure
> a member of the family   competitive sport
> develop a strong bond   depend on
> take part in competitive sports
> used for farming purposes   a working animal

Listening Part 1

- You will hear what the topic is, but you won't hear the question before the extract. Underline the main idea in the question before you listen.
- Don't decide on your answer until you have heard the whole of the extract.
- Check your answer the second time you hear the extract.

Exam advice

1. In pairs, decide what is the main idea in the questions in Exercise 2.

2 You will hear people talking in eight different situations. For questions 1–8, choose the best answer (A, B or C).

54

1 You hear a man and a woman talking about a wildlife documentary.

What did the woman find most surprising?

A the number of different animals that were in the programme

B the fact that one country has such a wide variety of animals

C how dangerous the animals from this country are

2 You hear a boy and his sister talking about a safari trip they went on.

What does the boy say he liked best about the trip?

A watching the lions feeding

B being out in the warm weather

C going out early in the morning

3 You hear part of a lecture on animal conservation.

What does the speaker say is the most important thing people should do?

A reduce use of plastic bottles

B support a ban on single-use products

C give money to wildlife charities

4 You hear two friends discussing zoos.

What is the main reason that the boy feels we should keep zoos?

A They give the opportunity to see animals you would not usually see.

B They help to stop animals disappearing from the planet.

C They supply animals with their basic needs.

5 You hear a conversation between a volunteer at an animal shelter and her friend.

The volunteer says that her shelter's policy is to …

A keep all related puppies together when they rehome them.

B see if the new homes are appropriate.

C keep the larger dogs at the shelter for longer.

6 You hear a man talking about being a vegan.

What does he think is the biggest reason why more people are becoming vegan?

A They are worried about their health.

B They are concerned about conditions for animals.

C They can get enough vitamins without meat.

7 You hear a woman talking to her friend about working with lions.

When did the woman first realise she wanted to work with lions?

A at school

B at university

C during her second job

8 You hear a woman and her husband discussing whether to let their cats outside.

What does the husband say about the idea?

A He's worried about letting them out.

B He agrees with his friend that it's a good idea.

C The vet recommended letting them out.

Vocabulary

avoid, prevent and protect; check, control, keep an eye on and supervise

1 Students often confuse the words above. Choose the correct option in *italics* in these extracts from Listening Part 1.

1 I want to talk about how we can *avoid / prevent / protect* harming the endangered species that live in our oceans, seas and rivers.

2 Zoos *avoid / prevent / protect* animals and help them to breed and increase their populations.

3 It's important that we're sure that the person will look after the dog and be able to *check / control / supervise* it.

4 I still need to be *checked / controlled / supervised* by a more experienced keeper, but I'm getting there.

5 I've put up a special fence in the garden to *avoid / prevent / protect* them from getting out.

6 I think we should let the cats out, but we'll have to *check / keep an eye on / supervise* them.

2 Complete the sentences with a word or phrase from Exercise 1 in the correct form. In one case, more than one answer is possible.

1 This cream is perfect for .... you from insect bites.

2 The new law .... people from building houses in the National Park.

3 There was a man who was .... the tickets as people walked into the stadium.

4 I think we should set out early to .... the worst of the traffic.

5 You ought to be wearing a hat to .... your head from the sun.

6 It's the chemistry teacher's responsibility to .... students when they're doing experiments, to make sure nothing explodes!

7 Make sure you .... your essay for mistakes before you hand it in.

8 We should always respect the forces of nature because we will never be able to .... them.

3 Complete the sentences with an adverb–verb collocation from the box in the correct form.

> avoid … at all costs   check … carefully
> closely supervise   heavily protect   narrowly avoid
> properly protect   strictly control   successfully prevent

1 Ben .... the bear from attacking them by making a lot of noise.
2 Juan .... an accident when a dog ran in front of his car.
3 The camp is .... with a high fence and an alarm to prevent dangerous animals from getting in.
4 The number of visitors to the game reserve is .... to avoid upsetting the animals.
5 Tourists visiting the wildlife park need to be .... to make sure they don't go too near the wild animals.
6 When it rains heavily, you should .... crossing the river ...., as the current can be very strong.
7 You need to .... your route .... on the map before you start your journey, as you could easily get lost.
8 Rhinos are an endangered species and need to be .... by game wardens.

Grammar

Third conditional and mixed conditionals

▶ **Page 179 Grammar reference**

1 Look at this sentence from Listening Part 1 and then decide whether the statements (1–3) are true (T) or false (F).

If we hadn't opened zoos, many animals would have become extinct.

1 They opened zoos.
2 Many animals became extinct.
3 The speaker is talking about the past.

2 Now look at these sentences and answer the questions below.

a If I had seen that big cat in the wild, I would have been scared to death.
b If I saw that big cat in the wild, I would be scared to death.

Which sentence (**a** or **b**) …

1 means: *It's not likely that I will see that big cat in the wild*?
2 describes an imaginary situation in the past?
3 has this form: *if* + past simple, *would* (or a modal e.g. *could, might*) + infinitive?
4 has this form: *if* + past perfect, *would have* + past participle?
5 is known as a second conditional? (see pages 54–55)
6 is known as a third conditional?
7 has the same form as *If we hadn't opened zoos, many animals would have become extinct* in Exercise 1?

3 Students often make mistakes with tenses in third conditional sentences. Complete the sentences with the correct form of the verb in brackets.

1 If Martin had concentrated on his work, he .... (finish) it earlier.

2 If I .... (know) that the train was going to be so late, I would have caught an earlier one.

3 If there had been a swimming pool in the garden, I .... (go) for a swim.

4 John would have spoken to Emma if his phone .... (not be) broken.

5 If you had been there, you .... (enjoy) yourself, too!

6 Sorry! I .... (not make) so much noise if I'd known you were asleep.

7 We wouldn't have heard the burglar downstairs if the dog .... (not bark).

4 Work in pairs. Answer these questions in any way you like.

• What would have happened if you'd got up an hour later this morning?

• Where was the last place you went on holiday? What would you have done if you hadn't gone on holiday there?

• What was the last exam you passed? What would have happened if you'd failed the exam?

5 If you want to talk about past and present time in the same conditional sentence, you can combine the second conditional with the third conditional. Look at the two extracts from Listening Part 1. Which part of each sentence (a or b) …

• refers to the present time, and which refers to the past?

• is a second conditional, and which part is a third conditional?

1 If we hadn't thrown so much rubbish away, (**a**) they wouldn't face such a crisis. (**b**)

2 If people weren't aware of how some animals are treated, (**a**) they would never have become vegans. (**b**)

6 Complete the sentences with the verb in brackets. Use a second conditional and a third conditional in each.

1 My dad doesn't have a car, so he didn't drive me to my dancing lesson yesterday.
If my dad .... (have) a car, he .... (drive) me to my dancing lesson yesterday.

2 Katie feels nervous about the test because she didn't study last weekend.
If she .... (study), she .... (not feel) nervous about the test.

3 Our dog barks too much, so we didn't take him on holiday with us.
If our dog .... (not bark) so much, we .... (take) him on holiday with us.

4 Karl was very rude to me, so we are no longer friends.
If Karl .... (not be) so rude to me, we .... (still be) friends.

Reading and Use of English Part 1

1 Work in pairs. You are going to read a short article by a girl whose parents train puppies to become guide dogs to help blind people. First, look at the photo and discuss the questions.

- What kind of dog is the dog in the photo? What might it do?
- Do you have this type of dog in your country?

- Read the words before and after the gap carefully.
- Try all the options in the gap before deciding. Make sure the word you choose goes with any prepositions etc. after the gap.
- Read the text again carefully when you have finished.
- Make sure you choose an answer for all the questions.

Exam advice

2 Read the article quickly without paying attention to the gaps. What do the writer's parents do in their free time?

NOT JUST A HOBBY

My mother and father **(0)** ...*have*... an unusual hobby, which involves the whole family. They train puppies to **(1)** .... guide dogs for blind people. Of course it's my parents' responsibility to **(2)** .... the puppies. My sister and I just keep **(3)** .... on them when they are out. We all **(4)** .... the puppies for regular walks and my parents teach them how to **(5)** .... to different situations, such as crossing a busy road. They also teach the puppies how to behave when they **(6)** .... people and other dogs. It is very important for a guide dog to stay calm and focused and not to get **(7)** .... from its work. After one year, the puppies continue their **(8)** .... at a special school. I often wish that it had been possible to keep one of our puppies.

3 For questions 1–8, read the text again and decide which answer (A, B, C or D) best fits each gap. There is an example at the beginning (0).

	A	B	C	D
0	make	play	have	take
1	convert to	become	begin	turn into
2	respond	run	control	supervise
3	a look	an eye	a view	a control
4	take	go	have	give
5	reply	respond	answer	return
6	encounter	experience	visit	undergo
7	entertained	confused	distracted	disturbed
8	schooling	training	coaching	exercising

4 Work in pairs. Discuss the questions.

- Would you like to keep a pet for only one year? Why? / Why not?
- What kind of pet *wouldn't* you like?
- What pets do you think would be difficult to keep?
- At what age should children be allowed to have a pet?
- Apart from dogs, what other animals can be trained to help people?
- Do you think animals enjoy working with people?

Grammar

wish, if only and hope

▶ **Page 180 Grammar reference**

1 Read sentences a–f and answer the questions below.

a I wish we had seen the new panda cubs at the zoo.
b I wish the dog next door wouldn't bark, especially at night.
c My aunt has a white cat, and I wish I had one too.
d If only I was still living in Italy!
e I hope this dress doesn't look old-fashioned.
f I hope you enjoy your holiday and have good weather!

1 In which sentences is the speaker talking about something in the present?
2 In which three sentences is the speaker saying he/she would like the present situation to be different?
3 In which sentence is the speaker complaining about an activity which is annoying?
4 What tenses are possible after *wish* and *if only* when referring to present time?
5 In which sentence is the speaker talking about something which happened in the past?
6 What tense is used after *wish* (and *if only*) when referring to past time?
7 In which sentence is the speaker talking about something in the future?
8 What tense can be used with the verb after *hope* when we talk about the future?

2 Students often confuse *wish* and *hope*. Read these sentences and decide when *wish* is used correctly and when you should use *hope*.

1 It was lovely seeing you and I wish to see you again very soon in my house.
2 Going to the theme park together was great and I wish you enjoyed the experience.
3 I wish I'd visited you last summer when I had the chance.
4 I'm looking forward to having news from you soon and I wish you have a good time in New York.
5 My neighbour's children are always shouting; I wish they wouldn't be so noisy.

6 The performance was really good but I wish more people will come next time.
7 I don't get many letters from you and I wish you'd write to me more often.
8 We wish you enjoy your stay at our hotel while you're here in Tokyo.

3 For questions 1–5, complete the second sentence so that it has a similar meaning to the first sentence, using the word given. Do not change the word given. You must use between two and five words, including the word given.

1 I regret not studying harder when I was at school.
   STUDIED
   If only .... when I was at school.

2 I want the neighbours to stop making so much noise.
   MAKE
   I wish the neighbours .... noise.

3 What a pity that they cancelled the match!
   CALLED
   If only they .... the match!

4 I'm sorry you didn't meet my brother.
   WISH
   I .... my brother.

5 It's a pity I can't cook well.
   BETTER
   I wish I .... cook.

Reading and Use of English Part 7

- If you have unanswered questions after you have read all the texts, scan them again to find the information you need, rather than trying to read them in detail again.
- If you see a word you don't understand, and you think you need to understand it to answer a question, try to guess what it means by reading the text around the word.

1 Work in groups. You are going to read a newspaper article about people who have been involved in rescuing animals. Before you read, discuss these questions.

- Do you think people in your country are good at taking care of animals?
- What would you do if you saw an animal that needed help?

2 Read questions 1–10 and underline the main idea in each.

Which person

1 was injured by the animal?
2 found an animal that had escaped?
3 accidentally scared the animal?
4 looked after the animal straight after it had been rescued?
5 was able to keep the animal?
6 decided to change their behaviour after rescuing an animal?
7 noticed something unusual about the animal's behaviour?
8 was delighted to see the animal again?
9 helped to release the animal?
10 could only keep the animal for a short time?

3 Now read the article and, for questions 1–10, choose from the people (A–D). Each person may be chosen more than once.

4 Work in pairs. What would you have done in each of the situations described in the text?

ANIMAL RESCUE

What would you do if you came across an animal that needed help? Four people share their animal rescue stories.

A Anita Perez

I was taking the rubbish out, when I heard a mewing sound behind the bins. I looked down and a tiny kitten peered out. It looked very thin, so I brought it into the house and gave it a dish of water and some food. I begged my mum to let me keep it, but as we already had two cats, she was worried that it wouldn't be a welcome addition to our home! We took it to the vet, who called the local cat rescue charity. They didn't have space for the kitten and asked us if we could keep it until they were able to find it a new home. We enjoyed taking care of it for two weeks until it eventually went to live with an elderly couple.

B Jane O'Neill

I was volunteering in a conservation area in Costa Rica. There were a lot of sea turtles on the beach, as it was the time of year when they lay their eggs. One afternoon I noticed a turtle which hadn't moved for a long time. I approached it quietly, trying not to frighten it. That's when I saw that it had a ring of plastic stuck around its neck and was having difficulty breathing. I lifted it gently into a box and rushed it to the animal rescue centre. They cut the plastic off and treated its injuries, which fortunately weren't too serious. After a few days, I went with them to return the turtle to the sea. It felt amazing to see it swimming away, and at that moment I made a promise to stop buying products with plastic packaging.

C Jack Smith

One summer, my cousins and I were picking apples on my uncle's farm when we heard a distressed cry. We saw that a goat had got its front legs caught in the fence. It was quite badly injured, so my cousin rushed back to the house to tell my uncle. I stayed with the goat and tried to untangle the barbed wire around his legs. Unfortunately, he didn't realise that I was trying to help and started kicking his back legs in fright. If I hadn't moved away so quickly, I could have been badly hurt. Luckily, at that point, my uncle arrived with the vet, who was able to cut the goat free and treat his injured legs. My uncle told us that this goat would often jump over the fence. After a few days, the goat returned to his field, but he never tried to run away again!

D David da Silva

I was walking home from school one day when I heard a loud howling sound coming from under a tree. I saw a small dog sitting there looking sad. I wondered whether it had escaped from the dog rescue home, but when I saw the bag of dog toys next to it, I realised it had been abandoned. When I put out my hand to touch the dog, it bit me. I decided that it probably wasn't a good idea to handle it myself, so I called the rescue home. A few days later, I went with my mum to check on the dog. He came running up to me. One of the volunteers said to me, 'I think that dog has chosen you!' I was absolutely thrilled that he had remembered me. My mum wasn't sure at first, because of the bite, but eventually she gave in and we took him home that afternoon.

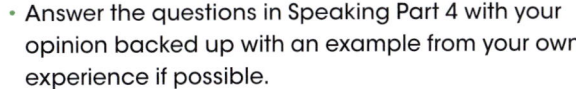

Speaking Parts 3 and 4

▶ **Page 197-199 Speaking bank**

- Answer the questions in Speaking Part 4 with your opinion backed up with an example from your own experience if possible.
- Be prepared to discuss with your partner – you will gain marks if you have a conversation rather than just speaking one at a time.

Exam advice

1 Work in pairs. Look at the speaking task below and listen to Pablo and Marina doing the task. *55*

1 What is going wrong?
2 What can Marina do to put things right?

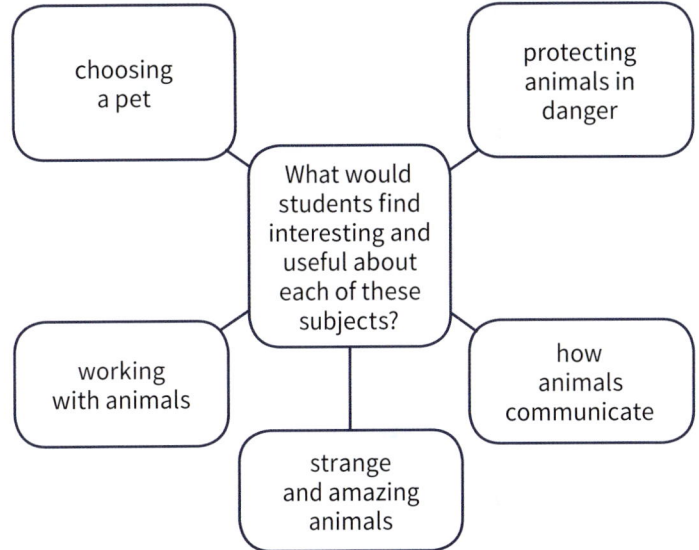

choosing a pet

protecting animals in danger

What would students find interesting and useful about each of these subjects?

working with animals

how animals communicate

strange and amazing animals

2 Now listen to Pablo and Marina doing the task again. What phrases does Marina use to interrupt? *56*

3 Work in pairs. Do the speaking task in Exercise 1, but take turns playing the role of a very talkative student and a student who wants to interrupt.

4 Now listen to the examiner and do the second part of Speaking Part 3. *57*

Animal kingdom 135

5 Part 4 questions are on topics related to Part 3. Listen to Marina answering two Part 4 questions. How does she answer the questions?

58

A She just gives her opinion.

B She expresses a range of ideas, but doesn't say which she agrees with.

C She summarises other people's opinions, then gives her own.

6 Put these phrases from Marina's answer in the correct column of the table.

I'm not sure that I agree   People often suggest that
Some people say that   That's a difficult question.
I think that's true   That's quite interesting.

comment on the question	introduce other people's opinions	say whether you agree or disagree with the other people's opinions
		I think that's true

Work in pairs. Think of two more phrases you can add to each column of the table.

8 Work in pairs and take turns to ask and answer these Part 4 questions.

1 What pet do you think is most suitable for young children? Why?

2 How can children benefit from having an animal to look after?

3 Why is it important to protect animals and other wildlife?

4 Do you think animals should be kept in zoos? Why? / Why not?

7 Pronunciation: word stress (3)

We sometimes pronounce individual words differently, depending on whether we stress them or not.

7.1 Listen to these phrases from Marina's answers again and underline the highlighted words which are stressed.

59

That's a difficult question. Some people say that it's cruel to keep animals in zoos, where they don't have the freedom that they'd have in their natural habitat.

They say that animals get stressed and can't relax, but I'm not sure that I agree. I think they can. If animals have some space, they can have a nice relaxed life in a zoo.

That's quite interesting. People often suggest that children learn to be responsible because they have to look after the animal.

I think that's true and also, from my experience, I think that it's an extra relationship which develops children's ability to love and care about the animals and the people around them.

7.2 Listen again and notice how the pronunciation of the highlighted words changes depending on whether they are stressed or not.

59

7.3 Work in pairs. Take turns to read the sentences in 7.1 aloud.

Writing Part 2
A letter or email

▶ **Page 204 Writing bank**

1 Work in pairs. Read this exam task and discuss the questions below.

You have received a letter from your British friend, Leo. Read this part of the letter.

> My family is thinking of visiting your country this summer. We'd be interested in seeing some beautiful scenery. Also, we'd like to see some wildlife. Can you advise me on where to go, what to see and the best way of getting around?
>
> Best wishes,
> Leo

Write your **letter**.

1 What three things must you deal with in your letter?
2 What advice would you give Leo about your country?
3 What style would you use: formal or informal? Why?

2 Work in pairs. Write a plan for your letter.

3 Read Manolo's reply to Leo's letter and answer these questions.

1 How does Manolo show that he has read Leo's letter?
2 Has he answered all three points in the question? What advice does he give about each?
3 Does he give reasons for his advice?
4 What style does he use: formal or informal?

4 Find these ways of giving advice in Manolo's letter.

1 *I'd advise you* + *to* infinitive
2 *You should* + infinitive (without *to*)
3 *If I were you, I'd / I would ...*
4 *The best idea would be* + *to* infinitive
5 *Make sure that ...*

5 Write five similar sentences using each of the five phrases in Exercise 4 once to give advice to Leo about visiting your country.

6 Write your own answer to the question.

- Use Manolo's letter as a model.
- Write between 140 and 190 words.

Dear Leo,

I'm very glad to hear that you're thinking of visiting my country this summer. You can see beautiful countryside and scenery all over the country, although it varies a lot, depending on the region.

If you want somewhere that's not usually too hot in summer, I'd advise you to go to Asturias, in the north of Spain. It's a region which has some fantastic mountains as well as green countryside and beautiful rivers. You should visit the 'Picos de Europa', which are really spectacular mountains and canyons. All the paths are clearly marked, which makes walking quite safe, and you're sure to see a lot of wildlife while you're there. You may even see bears and wolves if you're lucky!

If I were you, I'd hire a car to get around. The best idea would be to hire it online before you leave home. Make sure that you take warm clothes and a raincoat, as we can have heavy rain, even in summer.

I hope you enjoy your holiday and have good weather!

Best wishes,

Manolo

11 Vocabulary and grammar review

Vocabulary

1 Complete the sentences with a word from the box in the correct form.

> bruise   cure   dose   examination   injury
> prescription   scar   surgery   symptoms   treat

1 Although the accident happened a long time ago, you can see a .... on his face from where he was badly cut.

2 Harry has a big dark .... on his leg from where he got kicked playing football.

3 The main .... of the illness are feeling tired and thirsty all of the time.

4 The doctor insisted on give me a medical .... to check I was alright, and fortunately I was.

5 The label on the medicine says you should take a .... three times a day.

6 My grandfather is making a good recovery after they had to perform .... on his heart.

7 Rana's doctor has given her a .... for antibiotics to treat her illness.

8 Take this medicine. It should .... you in a few days.

9 Unfortunately the illness is serious and he will need to be .... for it in a special clinic over a long period.

10 There was a train crash last night, but fortunately none of the passengers suffered any ....

Word formation

2 Use the word given in capitals at the end of each sentence to form a word that fits in the gap.

1 I'm sorry about the mistake. The trouble is I .... the instructions. **UNDERSTAND**

2 My mum and dad .... of some of my friends because they make a lot of noise when they come round to our house. **APPROVE**

3 My dad said he felt very .... with the quality of the food at that restaurant and he complained to the waiter, which was rather embarrassing. **SATISFY**

4 My friend's joined our hockey team, and although she's a little ...., she's very keen and tries hard. **EXPERIENCE**

5 Luis goes to school even when he's feeling ill because he .... missing lessons. **LIKE**

6 Even though Sandra offered to lend her favourite book to her brother, he was .... to help her with her essay. **WILL**

7 It would feel a bit strange and .... to chat with my teachers online. **NATURE**

8 We got the answers wrong because we were given .... information by the teacher. **LEAD**

9 I am wearing .... clothes because I don't want to ruin my good ones while I'm fixing my bike. **FASHION**

10 My friend was told that his behaviour was totally .... in the classroom. **ACCEPT**

11 Teresa is quite ...., so I'm not sure if she'll turn up to dance practice every week. **RELY**

12 I want to know the truth, so don't dare be .... with me. **HONEST**

Grammar

3 Complete the second sentence so that it has a similar meaning to the first sentence, using the word given. Do not change the word given. You must use between two and five words, including the word given.

1 The boy with the broken arm is still in hospital.
WHOSE
The boy .... not left hospital yet.

2 Did the doctor treat this injury?
ONE
Is this .... doctor treated?

3 Everyone who lives in the town Paola comes from is very friendly.
INHABITANTS
Paola comes from a town .... very friendly.

4 The teacher liked how Jan answered the questions.
WAY
Jan answered the questions .... the teacher liked.

5 His email left us in no doubt about his opinion.
WHAT
It was clear to us .... his opinion was.

6 No one finds Chiaro's jokes amusing.
TELLS
The jokes .... amuse anyone.

Vocabulary

1 Read the text and decide which answer (A, B, C or D) best fits each gap.

Due to the destruction of their natural habitat, more and more animals need to be **(1)** .... by creating nature reserves and passing laws. The laws are often designed to **(2)** .... farmers from using land where rare species live. The idea is that humans and animals **(3)** .... coming into conflict by not competing for the same land. Sometimes local people complain about losing farmland to nature reserves. However, jobs are often created for wardens, whose job is to **(4)** .... the nature reserves to make sure everything functions correctly. Other people get jobs selling tickets to visitors, and there are also jobs for people to **(5)** .... the tickets as the visitors pass the entrance. In nature reserves containing dangerous animals, it may only be possible to visit them by car, and wardens need to **(6)** .... the number of cars entering the reserve to make sure they keep within reasonable limits.

1	**A** prevented	**B** protected	**C** avoided	**D** defended
2	**A** avoid	**B** end	**C** prevent	**D** disallow
3	**A** avoid	**B** prevent	**C** miss	**D** fail
4	**A** check	**B** control	**C** prevent	**D** supervise
5	**A** check	**B** control	**C** look	**D** supervise
6	**A** look	**B** control	**C** prevent	**D** supervise

Grammar

2 Complete the sentences with the correct form of the verb in brackets. In some sentences more than one answer is possible.

1 The lions wouldn't have attacked us if they .... (not be) so hungry.

2 I wish it .... (be) summer – then we could go to the beach!

3 If my maths teacher .... (be) ill at the moment, we .... (have) a maths test yesterday.

4 If only you .... (not make) so much noise! I can't concentrate on my studies, and it's really annoying me!

5 I wish I .... (live) near the city centre. It's such a long bus ride from here.

6 Where's Candice? I hope she .... (not miss) the train.

7 I wish you .... (speak) more clearly so I could understand you better.

8 I think this soup .... (be) nicer if I'd used a bit less salt, don't you?

9 I hope you .... (change) your shirt before we go out to the restaurant.

10 I know my mother wishes she .... (study) harder when she was my age.

11 We .... (get) to the cinema in time if there hadn't been so much traffic.

12 If you .... (eat) more breakfast this morning, you wouldn't be feeling hungry now.

3 Complete the second sentence so that it has a similar meaning to the first sentence, using the word given. Do not change the word given. You must use between two and five words, including the word given.

1 We are lost because we didn't bring the map with us.
LEFT
If we .... the map behind, we would not be lost now.

2 My sister only did the work in our neighbour's garden because they gave her some money for helping them.
PAID
My sister would not have done the work in our neighbour's garden unless they .... for helping them.

3 Even if he had worked harder, the result would have been the same.
DIFFERENCE
It would not .... if he had worked harder.

4 It's a pity I don't get on better with my brother.
RELATIONSHIP
I wish I .... my brother.

5 Sasha would like Irina to help him from time to time.
ONCE
Sasha wishes Irina .... a while.

6 Sergei is disappointed because the youth orchestra rejected him.
TURNED
If the youth orchestra .... , Sergei would not be disappointed.

13 House space

A

B

C

D

E

F

Starting off

1 Work in pairs. Match the descriptions 1–6 with the photos A–F.

1 Motorhome for sale: suitable for sleeping and cooking. Comes with TV, cooker and fridge! Tyres in excellent condition.

2 Luxury villa on two floors with amazing views from the large balcony. Beautiful garden and swimming pool. Reasonable rent.

3 Second-floor flat for rent in modern block. Two bedrooms, kitchen, living room and bathroom.

4 Traditional chalet with timber roof, balcony and wooden shutters for sale in beautiful hillside area. Two bedrooms.

5 Houseboat available for let July and August. Situated on a quiet river. Enjoy beautiful views from the deck. Sleeps two people.

6 House for rent in coastal village. Ideal family holiday home with several beaches a short walk away.

2 Look at the photos again. If you had to choose, which of the places would you prefer to stay in for a month? Why?

Reading and Use of English Part 5

1 Work in pairs. You are going to read an extract about life in a yurt. Before you read, look at the photo and discuss the questions.

- What is a yurt?
- What do you think would be the good and bad things about living in one?

- Think carefully about what the text is actually saying, as incorrect options will not reflect the true meaning of the text, although they may sound similar.

- If you aren't sure of the answer, have a guess. You won't lose marks for a wrong answer.

Exam advice

2 Read the first paragraph of the extract quickly and choose the correct answer.

The extract is taken from a

A blog

B newspaper article

C novel

D review

LiViNG iN A YURT

Today I want to talk about what living in a yurt is actually like. It's been a while since my last 'building our house' post, but it took us quite a while to get things organised. We didn't have time to settle into our new round space slowly. When we moved in, winter was around the corner and we had lots of rain and wind, and then two solid weeks of snow. The roof leaked, so we had to secure it as best we could. I was afraid that was only the start of worse things to come. But fortunately we haven't had any problems since, so I can't complain!

So, let me answer the first question people ask us: 'Aren't you cold?' Well, the answer is no. I know it looks like a tent, but the thick sheep's wool insulation does a fine job of keeping the heat in, and our little stove warms up pretty quickly too. I can't argue with the fact that the mornings are [22]cold – they are. But the way we deal with *it* is to get up early and start doing things. Mark gets the fire going and I put away the convertible bed to create extra space, and then I go for a walk with the dog. On my way back, I get wood from the shed so we have enough for the day. By the time we return, the yurt is nice and warm and we sit down to have breakfast.

The list of things that need fixing or building is long and ever growing. But we're trying to change the way we look at these things. After all, living the way we do, it's part of the deal. So for us things don't go wrong – they happen.

And we're usually capable of fixing whatever needs fixing. But what we would really like is to have a sink put in. It would be much easier for cooking and doing the dishes. We store water in cans, so we can manage without one, but it's the first on the list of things to get done. What we don't have, but won't build, is a bath. It doesn't make sense to have one inside as it takes up too much room. For a shower, we need to build one that uses solar heating or electricity. But since we live a few metres from Mark's parents' house, that isn't a priority.

A yurt is very different from a typical house. For a start, it's just not as solid. And I don't mean in construction (it can stand wind speeds up to 100km/h), but in the way it shields you from the world outside. We're so much more aware of the weather. The rain on the roof is noisy, just like in a tent. We can hear the wind and feel it pushing against the walls. We can hear the cows in the field by day and the foxes and the owls by night. We hear our neighbours too, when they're outside, but we're lucky to live in such a quiet location.

We'd been living in a truck and in other people's homes for a year before we moved here. The yurt was actually what we *aspired* to – a step up for us, a place for ourselves. And one[54] that we built ourselves and which was already becoming our home while we were constructing it. We didn't have to move in and find traces of other people, to fill the space up with our belongings to erase these. The empty yurt already felt like a part of us in a way that I've never experienced with a house. We still say to each other how happy we are to be living here, almost every day. And yet, we're already making plans for our next adventure – finding a piece of land and building our next home.

---

3 **Choose the answer (A, B, C or D) which you think fits best according to the text.**

1 How did the writer initially feel about the leak in the roof?
A disappointed that she didn't know how to repair it
B surprised at how successful she was in repairing it
C concerned that other problems might develop
D angry that the yurt couldn't cope with the weather conditions

2 What does 'it' refer to in line 22?
A the cold
B the stove
C the fact
D the heat

3 In the immediate future, the writer is keen to install
A solar heating.
B a shower.
C electricity.
D a sink.

4 What does the writer say makes a yurt different from typical houses?
A It is more dangerous than living in a normal house.
B You can feel the wind from the inside.
C It is not waterproof.
D Foxes and owls can get in at night.

5 What does 'aspired' mean in line 54?
A expected other people
B felt unable to do
C had the ambition
D were afraid

6 What best sums up the writer's feelings about her yurt?
A She resents the difficulties and challenges it presents.
B She would prefer to live in a conventional house.
C She feels frustrated at the lack of space it has.
D She is proud of what she has created.

4 Work in pairs. Discuss the questions.

- Would you like to live in a yurt? Why? / Why not?
- Can you think of any other unusual places to live?
- What would you miss most if you lived in a yurt or one of the unusual places that you mentioned?

Vocabulary

space, place, room, area, location and *square*

1 Students often confuse the words above. Choose the correct option in *italics* in these sentences from Reading and Use of English Part 5.

1 We didn't have time to settle into our new round *space / location* slowly.
2 It doesn't make sense to have one inside as it takes up too much *room / area*.
3 We're lucky to live in such a quiet *location / square*.
4 The yurt was actually a step up for us – a *room / place* for ourselves.
5 We didn't have to fill the *space / square* up with our belongings.

2 Choose the correct option in *italics*.

1 We don't have enough *area / space* in our garden to hold the party.
2 I hope I'll have enough *place / room* for all the things I've bought.
3 I'm enclosing a map which shows the *location / place* of my school.
4 It's dangerous to go walking in a mountainous *area / place* without the correct equipment.
5 The animals in this zoo have a lot of *area / space* to move around in.
6 The concert will take place in the main *square / place* in front of the cathedral.
7 There isn't enough *place / space* to build more houses in this neighbourhood.
8 It's fine for you to stay at our *location / place*, as we've got loads of *room / area*.

3 Work in pairs. Write *area, place, room* or *space* in the gaps to form collocations, e.g. *hiding place*. Then discuss what each of them means, e.g. *A hiding place is a place to hide or in which to hide something.*

1 hiding / market / meeting   *place*
2 floor / green / office / parking / personal / public

   ....
3 head / leg / standing ....
4 residential / picnic / play / reception ....

4 Complete the sentences with a collocation from Exercise 3.

1 If someone makes you feel uncomfortable by standing too close to you, we say that they are invading your ....
2 I love my school. It's surrounded by .... with lots of trees and lawns.
3 I'm tall, and the seats on the plane didn't have enough ....
4 There are lots of stalls in the .... selling fresh fruit and vegetables.
5 On the edge of the park there's a lovely .... where you can sit and eat a sandwich.
6 My little cousin found a good .... in the trees.

Listening Part 2

1 You are going to hear a student called Kit giving a talk to his classmates about a house he built. First, read the sentences and think about the kind of word required to complete them – noun, verb, etc.

The house that Kit built

Kit usually spends his free time building small planes and (1) ....

He found it very useful that the website informed you where to purchase (2) ....

He raised money for the things he needed by doing small tasks such as clearing (3) ....

He was pleased to be given a (4) .... by a neighbour for his house.

Thanks to Kit's father's friend, the house has got (5) .... but there isn't any running water.

He was unsuccessful in making a (6) .... in the kitchen area.

In the lounge area he uses a (7) .... containing reading material as a seat.

He spends the night there at (8) .... and during the holidays.

Kit thinks that his friends (9) .... him having a house of his own.

Kit is now going to help his (10) .... to build a house.

2 Listen and complete the sentences with a word or short phrase.

60

3 Work in pairs. Discuss these questions.

- Which would you prefer to do: build your own house or get someone to build one for you?
- What would your ideal house look like?
- How would you furnish and decorate it?

Grammar

Causative *have* and *get*

▶ Page 181 Grammar reference

1 In Listening Part 2, Kit describes the work that was done on the house. What work does he mention? Listen again if necessary.

2 Look at these pairs of sentences and answer the questions.

a I wired the house.
b I got the house wired.

a I painted all the doors and window frames.
b I had the glass in the window frames fitted professionally.

1 Which sentences (**a** or **b**) did you hear on the recording?

2 Which sentences (**a** or **b**) mean ...
Kit did it himself?
he asked someone else to do it for him?

3 In the **b** sentences, who do you think did these things?

3 Complete the sentences with the correct form of *have* or *get* and a verb from the box.

> cut down   deliver   extend
> paint   pull out   renew

1 My parents are planning to .... the house .... Then I'll get a room of my own!

2 She went to the dentist yesterday and .... a tooth .... , so she's not feeling too well today.

3 We're thinking of .... the house .... blue. What do you think?

4 I love the old tree in the park near my house, so I'm sorry the council have decided to .... it ....

5 You'll need to .... your passport .... before we go to America next autumn.

6 When my parents go out for the evening, they arrange for us to .... pizzas .... from a local restaurant.

4 Complete the second sentence so that it has a similar meaning to the first sentence, using the word given. Do not change the word given. You must use between two and five words, including the word given.

1 Someone stole my bag during the bus journey.
HAD
I .... I was on the bus.

2 A professional photographer is taking a photo of Stephan.
PICTURE
Stephan .... by a professional photographer.

3 Marianne wants the hairdresser to change the colour of her hair.
DYED
Marianne wants to .... at the hairdresser's.

4 The college rejected Pascual's application.
TURNED
Pascual had .... the college.

5 Someone is building a pool at my friend's house at the moment.
BUILT
My friend .... at her house at the moment.

Reading and Use of English Part 2

Reading and Use of English Part 2

1 Work in pairs. Look at the photo. Would you like to live in the red house? Why? / Why not?

2 Read the text quickly, ignoring the gaps.

Cover the text and answer the questions.
Use ONE WORD ONLY.

1 Where is the house situated?
2 What colour is it?
3 Was the house constructed in 1900?
4 Who was Robert Jones?
5 Did he like living in the house?
6 Is it possible to prepare food in the house?

3 Now read the text again and think of the word which best fits each gap. Use only one word in each gap.

4 Now compare your answers with the types of grammatical words listed in the Exam advice. The words you need follow the same order as those listed.

> • The words you need are mainly grammatical, for example verbs or parts of verbs, articles, prepositions, relative pronouns, phrasal verbs, linking words, negative forms and possessive adjectives.
>
> • You must spell the words correctly.
>
> **Exam advice**

5 Work in pairs. Discuss these questions.

• Would there be any advantages in living in a very small house like Quay House?

• Do you think it's important for a house to have plenty of space? Why? / Why not?

• What things would you like to have room for in your house? Why?

• Would you like to live in a different type of home, or a different place? If so, where? If not, why not?

• The smallest house in Britain •

The smallest house in Britain **(0)** .... is located in the town of Conwy in Wales. It is **(1)** .... as Quay House and is a popular tourist attraction. This tiny house has **(2)** .... floor area of 3.05 metres by 1.8 metres and it is painted bright red, so you can't really miss it! It was built in the 16th century and remained **(3)** .... use until 1900. The last person to live there was a local fisherman called Robert Jones, **(4)** .... happened to be very tall. The rooms were so small that he couldn't stand up in them fully.

Eventually, he **(5)** .... up moving out because it was so uncomfortable. However, **(6)** .... the house is very small, it's still extremely practical. There's a living area with cooking facilities and there's enough room for a bed too. So, if you're ever in Conwy, why **(7)** .... pop in and see it for yourself? It's well worth a visit! And, it certainly won't take up too much of **(8)** .... time!

Grammar

Expressing obligation and permission

▶ **Page 181 Grammar reference**

1 Work in pairs. You will hear five English teenagers who are staying with host families while on a school exchange visit to Germany. Before you listen, make a list of things students who stay with a host family in your country should and shouldn't do, e.g. *You should keep your room tidy. You shouldn't stay up too late.*

2 Look at these sentences and then answer the questions below.

A *I can* use their phone to call my parents.
B *I have to* help with the housework.
C *I can't* take food from the fridge.
D *I'm supposed to* go to bed quite early.
E *They let me* invite a friend round.
F *They won't let me* do any cooking.

1 Which phrases in *italics* have a similar meaning to
　　a I must?
　　b I'm not allowed to?
　　c I'm allowed to?
2 Which phrase has a similar meaning to *I'm supposed to* in D?
　　a I must be.
　　b I should, but sometimes I don't.

3 Listen and choose which sentence (A–F) in Exercise 2 best summarises what each student says. There is one extra letter which you do not need to use.

61

1 Matt 　　◯
2 Gaia 　　◯
3 Megan 　◯
4 Luke 　　◯
5 Lauren 　◯

4 Which speaker said each of these sentences? If necessary, listen again to check.

1 *I don't have to* do anything around the house.
2 *I had to* make conversation in German.
3 *They don't allow me to* spend much time online talking to my English friends.
4 Apparently, *I was supposed to* phone to say I was going to be late back.
5 … *they didn't let me* go to a party in the evening the other day.

5 Work in pairs. Complete the table with the phrases in Exercises 2 and 4.

	present	past
obligation		
prohibition		
permission		
no obligation		

13

Speaking Part 2

▶ **Page 194 Speaking bank**

Exam advice

- It is alright to take a few seconds to think about what you are going to say before you start speaking.
- Remember you will be asked a question about your partner's photos, so pay attention while your partner is speaking.

1 Work in pairs. Read the examiner's instructions and look at the photos. Then brainstorm words and phrases you could use to talk about each photo.

Examiner: Here are your photographs. They show two different places to live. I'd like you to compare the photographs and say what you think it is like for the people to live in each of these places.

2 Look at these words and phrases. Which could you use with the first photo, which with the second photo, and which with both?

close to nature	environment
fresh air	hi-tech
maintain a lifestyle	occupants
organic food	a rural setting
spend quality time	social life
pollution	sophisticated entertainment

3 Work in pairs. Take turns to speak for a minute about the photographs following the examiner's instructions.

What is it like for the people to live in each of these places?

146

4 Work in pairs. Listen to Peter and Tania doing the task, then say whether the statements on this checklist are true (T) or false (F).

Checklist		T	F
1	Peter spends a lot of time describing what he sees in each photo.		
2	He outlines the main idea of each photo.		
3	He concentrates on answering the question more than comparing the details of the photos.		
4	He compares what it would be like to live in each place.		
5	He mentions things which he thinks are similar about the people in both photos.		
6	He uses language which shows he is imagining the lifestyle in each photo.		
7	He uses a good range of vocabulary to express his ideas.		
8	He uses short, simple sentences.		
9	Tania gives a long, detailed answer to her question.		

5 In the Speaking exam it is important to be able to use a wide range of words which go beyond basic vocabulary. Look at the sentences taken from Peter and Tania speaking and choose the best way to complete them. Then listen again and check.

1 The first photo shows a *traditional / old country house / cottage* with the *people who live there / occupants*.
2 I guess that both photos show a *lifestyle / life* which the people have chosen.
3 Living in the country cottage must be very *peaceful / quiet* with very little stress …
4 … and plenty of physical work, healthy *natural / organic* food and fresh air.
5 … living in the city flat … you're at the centre of things, with *entertainment / cinemas and theatres* and friends close by.
6 The family in the second photo must need to earn quite a lot of money to *take care of / maintain* their lifestyle.
7 I can only *achieve / reach* my ambitions in a city.

6 Work in pairs. Choose either Task A or Task B on the next page. Then discuss what you can say to do the task in a similar way to Peter. (Use the checklist above.)

7 Change partners and work with someone who chose the other task.

- Take turns to do your tasks.
- While you are listening to your partner, use the checklist in Exercise 4.
- When your partner has finished, use all the points in the checklist to give him/her feedback.

Task A

Examiner: Here are your photographs. They show people on holiday in different places. I'd like you to compare the photographs and say what you think the people are enjoying about having a holiday in these places.

What are the people enjoying about having a holiday in these places?

Task B

Examiner: Here are your photographs. They show old people living in two different types of place. I'd like you to compare the photographs and say which place you think is better for old people to live in.

Which place is better for old people to live?

Writing Part 2

An article

▶ Page 206 Writing bank

- Note who you are writing the article for and make the article suitable and appealing for them. Remember that an article is written in a less formal style than an essay.
- Think carefully about which verb tenses to choose.
- Use a wide range of language to demonstrate your ability.
- Check your answer, looking for mistakes you know you often make.

Exam advice

1 Work in groups of three. Read this writing task and discuss the questions below.

You see this announcement in your school magazine.

My ideal home

If you could choose the type of house you would like to live in and its location, where would you live, what sort of house would it be and what features would it have?

The best articles will be published in the next issue of our magazine.

Write your **article**.

1 What would be the ideal location for your house?
2 What sort of house would you choose?
3 What features would your ideal house have?

2 Work in pairs with someone from another group.

- Take turns to give a short talk describing your ideal house.
- When your partner finishes speaking, ask a few questions to find out more details.

3 Look at the writing task again and discuss these questions.

1 Who will read your article?
2 What style would be suitable for this article?
3 Which of these should your article particularly use: present simple, *going to / will*, conditional with *would*? Why?
4 What information must it contain?
5 How can you make the article interesting for your readers?

4 Read the sample answer to the writing task opposite, ignoring the gaps.

1 How does this ideal home compare with your own?
2 Has the writer answered the question completely?

5 Complete this plan for the sample answer by writing the notes in *italics* beside the correct paragraphs.

Advantages of ideal flat
Characteristics of flat
Conclusion: room for my friends
My present accommodation
Type of flat and location

Para. 1: ....
Para. 2: ....
Para. 3: ....

6 Complete the sample answer. Write one word in each gap.

7 Work in pairs. Discuss whether these statements are true (T) or false (F).

		T	F
1	The article uses plenty of adjectives.		
2	It uses a conditional.		
3	The writer mentions all the furniture she would need.		
4	You can tell something about the writer's personality and tastes from the article.		
5	There are plenty of relative clauses.		
6	The writer doesn't say where she lives now.		

8 Write your own article.

• Before you write, decide what features of the sample answer you could also use. Then write a plan.
• When you write, follow your plan.
• Write 140–190 words.

My space, my place

I dream of living in a small, stylish modern flat in a historic old building near the centre of a large city **(0)** ....._such_..... as Barcelona, where my aunt lives. What a change that would be **(1)** .... the ordinary suburban house **(2)** .... I live now! I could enjoy all the things a big city has to offer, going to cool shops, trendy cafés, seeing the latest films at modern cinemas or going bowling with my friends – who would naturally all live nearby!

What would the flat be like? Well, for a start, I'd live on my **(3)** .... , so I'd be able to do **(4)** .... I wanted whenever I wanted. The flat would be hi-tech, with the heating and lighting controlled automatically. There would be a light, airy sitting room with an enormous comfortable sofa in it, a huge TV screen and all the latest gadgets, of course. Ideally, it would **(5)** .... big windows in all the rooms.

I wouldn't need much space, as **(6)** .... as I had room to have a **(7)** .... friends round too. **(8)** .... I had all these things, I'd be happy for years.

14 Fiesta!

Starting off

1 Work in pairs. Complete the descriptions of festivals and celebrations with the verbs in the box.

> celebrate   commemorate   dress up   gather round
> hold   let off   march   perform   play   wearing

1 We hold a festival every March to .... the arrival of spring.
2 People in our region .... in **traditional costumes** and then they .... one of our traditional dances.
3 People .... through the town in a spectacular **parade** to .... a famous battle.
4 In many parts of the town, residents .... **street parties**.
5 **Bands** .... dance music all night long.
6 Crowds .... **street performers**.
7 During the festival, we .... **fireworks**.
8 People from the town go out in the streets .... **disguises**.

2 Which words and phrases in bold in Exercise 1 are illustrated in the photos?

3 Look at the photos again. They show different events which take place during festivals.

1 Why do people do these different things at festivals?
2 Which type of activity is most enjoyable for people to watch?
3 Which country do you think each of the photos was taken in?

4 Work in pairs. Tell each other about a festival you have been to, or one you have seen on TV.

- What kind of festival was it?
- Did you enjoy it? / Would you like to go to this festival? Why? / Why not?
- Would you recommend it to other teenagers? Why? / Why not?

Listening Part 4

1 Work in pairs. You are going to hear an interview with a man who has spent the last year travelling around Britain visiting festivals. Before you listen, discuss these questions.

- What different types of festivals around the world have you heard about?
- Is there any festival you have heard about that you would particularly like to visit?
- What are the advantages and disadvantages of having festivals in your home town?

- As you read the questions and options, try to predict what you might hear on the recording.
- When you are listening, wait until the speaker has finished talking about an idea before you choose your answer.

Exam advice

2 Now listen, and for each question, choose the best answer (A, B or C).

1 Why did Nick first decide to go travelling to British festivals?
- **A** He had lots of free time after he retired.
- **B** He wanted to know how good British festivals were.
- **C** He loved a Spanish festival he once went to.

2 Nick now thinks that the Hay-on-Wye Festival was
- **A** not particularly interesting.
- **B** his favourite festival.
- **C** better than he expected.

3 Nick says that the WOMAD festival
- **A** is as famous as Glastonbury.
- **B** features music from different countries.
- **C** is relatively unheard of.

4 Why did Nick go to the festival at Sidmouth?
- **A** He wanted the same experience as he had at Hay and WOMAD.
- **B** He wanted to participate more and not just watch.
- **C** He wanted to go to a festival by the sea.

5 What happened after Nick lost his bag at Sidmouth?
- **A** He stuck with his original plans.
- **B** He thought about stopping his festival tour.
- **C** He decided he would only go to Edinburgh and Notting Hill.

6 What did Nick say about the Diwali festival he went to?
- **A** It was the best festival.
- **B** It was very memorable.
- **C** It had the best food.

7 What does Nick say about the idea of doing another festival tour?
- **A** He may do one but will make a decision later.
- **B** He is going to do one in Spain.
- **C** He doesn't have the energy to do another one.

3 Work in pairs and discuss these questions.

- Which festival from the recording sounded most/least interesting? Give reasons.
- Would you like to do a tour of festivals in the UK or your country? Why? / Why not?

14

Grammar
The passive

▶ **Page 182 Grammar reference**

1 The passive is formed by the verbs *be* + a past participle (*eaten*, *done*, *played*, etc.). Find the passive verbs in these extracts from the recording.

a It was recommended to me by my wife, as it's her favourite festival.

b Here, the lyrics of songs, plots of films and verses of poems are all celebrated.

c I went to … WOMAD in western England, which is held every July.

d Spectators gathering around the many stages are definitely very well entertained.

e Unfortunately, my bag with all my non-dancing clothes was taken – I think by mistake.

f Lots of fireworks were let off – it's called the Festival of Light for a good reason.

2 Work in pairs. In which extracts in Exercise 1 does the speaker do the following? (You can use the extracts for more than one answer.)

1 He tells us who or what does/did the action.

In extract a (my wife)

2 He uses the passive because he doesn't need to say who or what does/did something because it's obvious from the situation or context.

3 He uses the passive because what happens is more important than who does it.

4 He uses the passive because he doesn't know who or what does/did something.

3 Rewrite the sentences in the passive, starting with the words given.

1 They founded our school in 1904.
Our school ....

2 Someone has stolen my wallet!
My wallet .... !

3 You won't be able to email me while they are repairing my laptop.
You won't be able to email me while my laptop ....

4 Have you heard? They've awarded me second prize!
Have you heard? I .... !

5 If you hadn't done the work, your teacher would have told you off.
If you hadn't done the work, you ....

4 Read this text quickly to find out what happens at the Sapporo Snow Festival in Japan.

SAPPORO SNOW FESTIVAL, JAPAN

The Sapporo Snow Festival is a huge snow and ice sculpture festival, which (1) .... held every year in early February in the city of Sapporo, Japan. It is said to be one of Japan's most popular events. Every year, huge sculptures (2) .... built from ice and snow, which often has to (3) .... transported from the nearby mountains. The sculptures, which (4) .... created by teams from all over Japan, feature subjects such as cartoon characters and famous buildings. They (5) .... typically built life-size and include a great deal of detail. The first festival (6) .... held in 1950, when six high school students were said to have competed to build the most impressive snow sculpture. It has since (7) .... transformed into a huge commercialised event. In 2007 over 2 million people were reported to have attended. The 1972 snow festival is thought (8) .... have been an important turning point for the success of the festival as it coincided with the Sapporo Winter Olympic Games. The festival now includes seasonal activities, such as ice skating and snow slides, and traditional local seafood (9) .... served from food stalls. At night, the sculptures (10) .... lit up and look spectacular against the snowy backdrop of the city.

5 Read the text again and think of the word which best fits each gap. Use only one word in each gap.

6 Look at this sentence from the text about the Sapporo Snow Festival and answer the questions below.

The 1972 snow festival is thought to have been an important turning point for the success of the festival as it coincided with the Sapporo Winter Olympic Games.

1 What does the sentence mean, **a** or **b**?

a People think that 1972 was an important turning point for the success of the festival.

b People used to think that 1972 was an important turning point for the success of the festival.

2 It follows the pattern 'subject + passive verb + infinitive'. Other verbs which can be used in this way include: *believe, report, say, consider, expect.*

Which other three sentences in the text follow the same pattern?

3 The sentence above could also be expressed as follows: *It is thought that 1972 was an important turning point for the success of the festival.*

How would the other three sentences be expressed using this pattern instead?

7 Rewrite the following sentences beginning with the words given.

1 The Sapporo Snow Festival is thought to be the most famous winter festival in South East-Asia.

It is thought …

2 2,500 people are known to have built snow sculptures in 1959.

It is known …

3 It is reported that last year's festival attracted record numbers of visitors.

Last year's festival is reported …

4 It is said that our festival has the best snow sculptures in the world.

Our festival is said …

8 Complete the second sentence so that it has a similar meaning to the first sentence, using the word given. Do not change the word given. You must use between two and five words, including the word given.

1 People believe that the festival originated in the 18th century.

HAVE

The festival .... in the 18th century.

2 People expect that she will be chosen as carnival queen.

BE

She is .... as carnival queen.

3 The festival is said to be more popular than ever.

THAT

It is .... more popular than ever.

4 They think Channel 4 is the only channel which will broadcast the opening ceremony.

THOUGHT

Channel 4 .... the only channel which will broadcast the opening ceremony.

5 People think that Carnival is the best festival of the year.

CONSIDERED

Carnival .... the best festival of the year.

6 They haven't arranged a date for the festival next year.

BEEN

A date for the festival .... for next year.

Reading and Use of English Part 6

1 Work in groups. You are going to read an article about a Dutch festival. Before you read, look at the festival in the photos.

- What do you think is happening?
- Would you enjoy a festival like this? Why? / Why not?

KONINGSDAG: Europe's most lively festival

When we arrived in the city centre, I barely recognised the place that I had visited two years earlier. Every street was crowded with people dressed from head to toe in <u>orange - orange dresses, trousers, shoes, face paint</u> and wigs. **[1]** My aunt, uncle and cousin Marc had invited me to visit them in Amsterdam to celebrate the weekend of Koningsdag, which is Dutch for 'King's Day'. Of course, we have royal celebrations back home in the UK, but I had never seen anything quite like this before!

King's Day is a traditional celebration of the Dutch monarch's birthday. On this day, everybody in the Netherlands is given a day off work or school and a huge carnival is held in Amsterdam. It is celebrated by people of all ages, and many tourists travel from different countries to be part of the festivities. **[2]** It certainly felt more crowded than usual as we made our way through the lively, bustling streets wearing the orange clothes that Marc had told me to bring with me.

We passed street parties with people dancing, and stalls selling a variety of food. Marc insisted that we stopped for a tompouce, which turned out to be layers of pastry filled with a lot of cream and topped with orange icing. I'm not a big fan of very sweet things, but it didn't seem right not to try one. Round every corner we found ourselves in what looked like a street market. **[3]** People had brought any unwanted items that they owned and were trading and selling them on the street. Even children were trading their old books and toys.

We stopped on a bridge to watch the canal boats. **[4]** This time, all the boats were decorated with colourful flags and were filled with dancers. Loud music was pumping out of different boats on the canal, and it was a proper party atmosphere. We stood on the bridge and watched them roll past, and it was almost impossible not to dance along with the people on the boats.

Tired out from all the dancing, we decided to go for a walk around the city. We passed the Rijksmuseum, one of the most famous museums in Amsterdam, and I was surprised when Marc asked me if I wanted to go in. **[5]** However, when we got inside, I saw that it was packed with people dressed in orange. Apparently, many museums are open during the King's Day celebrations, and people enjoy visiting them when they want a break from the celebrations. It was certainly a lot more interesting than visiting museums back home.

We stayed out until around 10 pm and then made our way back to my aunt and uncle's house with the celebrations still going on around us. **[6]** I would have to say that King's Day is one of the most unusual festivals that I have ever been to, and one that I will never forget.

2 Six sentences have been removed from the article. Read the article (but not the missing sentences) quite carefully. As you read:

- think about the subject of each paragraph
- underline any words and phrases before and after the gaps which may refer to the missing sentences (one has been done for you as an example).

3 Now choose from the sentences A–G the one which fits each gap (1–6) in the text. There is one extra sentence which you do not need to use.

A Marc told me that this was one of the traditional events on King's Day.

B In fact, it is estimated that between 600,000 and a million people visit Amsterdam for King's Day.

C It seemed like a strange thing to do in the middle of a huge carnival.

D Of course, I had done this often on my last visit, but today the scene looked completely different.

E Marc told me that they continued all night, and that maybe if I came next year, we could stay out a bit later.

F We were really hungry by now and decided to get something to eat.

G These colourfully dressed people were dancing, singing, eating and having an amazing time.

4 Work in pairs. Discuss these questions.

- What would you like about visiting this festival?
- Do you think festivals in your country are more for tourists or more for local people?

Reading and Use of English Part 3

- Don't forget to check if you need a negative prefix or a plural form.
- Remember to write your answer in capital letters.

Exam advice

1 Look at these extracts from the text on page 154 and use the word given in capitals to form a word that fits in the gap. Then check your answer by looking at the text again.

1 … many .... travel from different countries to be part of the festivities. **TOUR**

2 … all the boats were decorated with colourful flags and were filled with .... **DANCE**

2 Complete the table with the correct nouns for people.

noun/verb	person	noun/verb	person
1 design		7 guitar	
2 novel		8 comedy	
3 research		9 sales	
4 collect		10 special	
5 survive		11 refuge	
6 consult		12 assist	

3 Read the text below. Use the word given in capitals at the end of some of the lines to form a word that fits in the gap in the same line.

The week my town goes back in time

My home town in Wales was a **(0)** ...*fashionable*... holiday resort in the 19th century. A Victorian Festival is now held every summer, so that people can experience life in the town during this period of history. If you visit my town during the festival, you'll notice that local people are dressed **(1)** .... Men walk around the town in suits, waistcoats and tall hats, and women in long skirts and high-necked blouses. The **(2)** .... for the festival begin in spring. A committee of volunteers makes the necessary **(3)** .... for the festival. Typical activities include an old-fashioned funfair, stalls selling tea and cakes, and performances by street **(4)** .... The highlight of the festival is a procession of **(5)** .... people who walk through the town carrying flaming torches, followed by an **(6)** .... firework display at the lake in the town centre. Most of the **(7)** .... are people from the town, but many people from the **(8)** .... area also visit at this time.

FASHION

USUAL

PREPARE

ARRANGE

MUSIC

ENERGY

IMPRESS

PARTICIPATE

SURROUND

Speaking Parts 3 and 4

▶ Pages 197-199 Speaking bank

- You needn't discuss all five prompts – it's better to discuss a few in more detail.
- Remember to allow your partner to express his/her ideas.
- Try to reach a decision together, but don't worry if you can't agree.
- In Part 4, give your opinion plus an explanation, reason or example.
- Listen carefully to what your partner says and be ready to say something about it or comment on it.

Exam advice

1 Work in pairs. Listen to the examiner's instructions and then spend two minutes doing the first part of this Part 3 task.

64

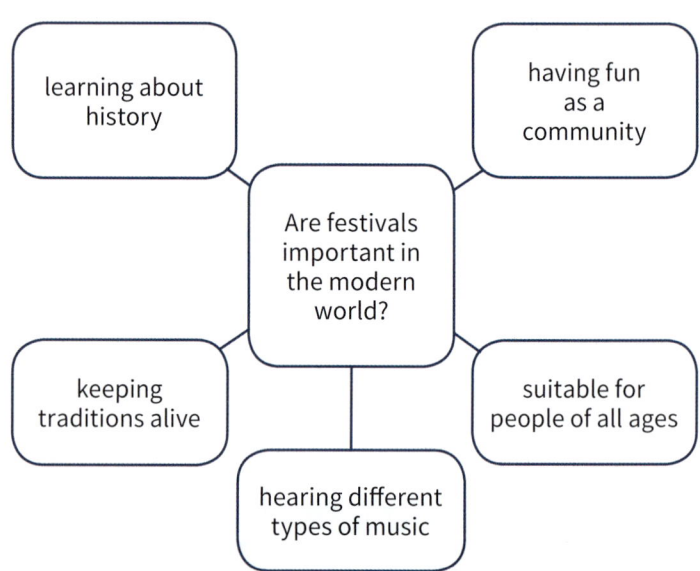

learning about history

having fun as a community

Are festivals important in the modern world?

keeping traditions alive

suitable for people of all ages

hearing different types of music

2 Listen to the examiner's next instruction and spend a minute doing the second part of the Speaking Part 3 task.

65

3 Now listen to Nicola and Alex doing the first part of Speaking Part 3. Were their ideas different from yours?

66

4 Listen again. Nicola and Alex help each other to do this part of the exam.

66

1 How is it clear that they are listening carefully to each other, and why is this important?

2 What phrases do they use:

a to encourage each other?

b to help their partner to express an idea?

c to take over when their partner gets into trouble?

5 Work in pairs. Listen to the examiner's instructions and do the first part of this Part 3 task. Try to use phrases you noted down in Exercise 4 to help the discussion along.

67

a new baby in the family

passing exams

How should we celebrate each of these occasions?

a first car

moving into a new home

winning at a sport

6 Listen to the examiner's instructions and do the second part of the Part 3 task.

68

7 Work in pairs. Listen to Sofia and Bruno answering this Part 4 question. Who do you agree with more? Why?

69

Examiner: How do towns and cities benefit from having festivals and other celebrations?

8 Pronunciation: improving fluency

8.1 Work in pairs. Read and listen to Sofia's answer and underline the words she stresses.

70

Hmm, that's a good question. Some people say that it's good for, what's it called, community spirit, but I think the main benefit is for local businesses because tourists and visitors are attracted to the town to spend their money in shops and restaurants.

8.2 Listen again and mark with a ↗ or ↘ a to show where her voice rises or falls on stressed words.

70

8.3 Use a (/) to mark where you think she pauses. Then listen again to check your answers.

70

8.4 Now read and listen to Bruno's answer and follow steps 1–3 above.

71

Yes, I partly agree with her. I think in many places people spend a lot of time during the year preparing for their festival and I think it really encourages a feeling of cooperation and a community feeling.

8.5 Take turns to read both answers aloud.

8.6 Think for a moment how you will answer this question. Then take turns to answer it, using suitable stress, intonation and pauses.

Do you think festivals should be organised more for tourists or more for local people?

9 Work in groups of three. One student should take the role of the examiner and ask these questions to the others. When you have finished, change roles and ask and answer the questions again.

1 What can tourists learn from visiting a festival in another country?

2 Do you think that some towns and cities spend too much time and money on organising festivals?

3 How important is it for people to remember their traditions?

4 Do you think there should be a limit to noise at festivals or other celebrations?

14

Writing Part 1
An essay

▶ **Page 202 Writing bank**

- Write a plan before you start writing your answer.
- Make sure your plan includes all the things you must write about.
- Check your answer for any careless spelling or grammar mistakes.

Exam advice

1 Work in pairs. Read the writing task below.

- Make a note of the key points in the task.
- Make a list of the advantages and disadvantages of going to music festivals and concerts to listen to live music instead of listening to recorded music.
- Discuss: Which do you prefer? Why?

In your English class, you have been talking about the advantages and disadvantages of going to music festivals and concerts to listen to live music instead of listening to recorded music.

Now your English teacher has asked you to write an essay.

Write your essay using all the notes and give reasons for your point of view.

'Is it better to listen to live music or recorded music?'

Notes
Write about:

1. quality
2. convenience
3. .... (your own idea)

2 Decide which of the ideas you discussed you can use in the essay and write a brief plan.

When you have finished, work in pairs and compare your plans.

3 Read Ulli's essay and answer these questions.

1 Which of her ideas are the same as yours?
2 Which is her own idea?
3 Do you agree with her opinion?

Although people can listen to recorded music on their music players when [1]they are travelling working or studying music festivals and concerts are becoming more and more popular. [2]This is I believe because [3]they offer two main advantages.

The first advantage is that the quality of the sound is much better at live concerts where the music and voices come directly from the performers. [4]This makes [5]it a much more emotional experience because you have direct contact with the musicians and you react to [6]them and they react to you.

The second advantage is the atmosphere. Instead of listening to a recording alone on your personal music player you are listening with a huge crowd of people and enjoying the music together. [7]This means it is a social as well as an artistic experience.

The main disadvantage is that you can't listen to live music whenever you want like you can on a personal device. In addition to [8]that the noise from the audience sometimes spoils the quality of the sound.

In my opinion however the best way to enjoy music is the spontaneous atmosphere of a live concert. [9]It is more exciting because you are surrounded by other enthusiastic fans.

4 Candidates often make mistakes with punctuation. Ulli's answer in Exercise 3 is missing ten commas. Punctuate it correctly by adding the ten commas.

5 Work in pairs. Ulli connects her ideas by using words which refer to other parts of her essay. What does each of the underlined words in her essay refer to?

1 *'they' refers to people.*

6 Students often make mistakes with *it*, *this*, *that* and *they* when referring to other parts of their writing. Complete the sentences with *it*, *this*, *that* or *they*. In some cases, more than one answer may be possible.

1 In my opinion, going to live concerts is better. .... gives you the chance to really connect with the band.

2 Listening to live music is better, but on the other hand .... is more expensive.

3 A further disadvantage is that when young people want to go to a concert, ... cannot always afford the ticket price.

4 During the tour, the band performed in Paris and Berlin, but .... had played in Amsterdam before ....

5 The band's tour had various problems: the coach broke down and some of their equipment was stolen. On top of all ...., there was a storm on the night of the concert.

6 Many live concerts are held late at night. .... leads to complaints from people living nearby who cannot sleep.

7 The sound quality of the recording is not very good, and in addition to ...., it is quite expensive.

8 I am not very keen on being in large crowds. In spite of ...., I would never miss a concert by my favourite band.

7 Now do this writing task.

In your English class, you have been talking about the advantages and disadvantages of going to the cinema rather than streaming films or watching them on television.

Now your English teacher has asked you to write an essay.

Write your essay using all the notes and give reasons for your point of view.

'Is it better to watch films at the cinema or at home?'
_____

Notes
Write about:
_____

1. quality
2. cost
3. .... (your own idea)

Vocabulary

1 Choose the correct option in *italics*.

1 I never seem to have enough *space / place* for everything on my desk!

2 Bring your family to stay with us! We've got plenty of *room / place* for all of you.

3 He loves travelling and the first thing he does when he arrives in a new *location / place* is take a photo.

4 The teacher said he'd found an excellent *location / space* for our class picnic this year.

5 There aren't really many sports facilities in this *area / location*.

6 There's an empty *place / room* at that table if you want to sit there.

7 We may have to take two taxis because I don't think there's *space / place* in one for all of us.

8 You can buy international newspapers at the newsagent's in the main *square / place*, just behind the station.

9 I found the flight uncomfortable because there wasn't enough leg *place / room*.

10 She's got a good hiding *place / room* for the money she keeps in her bedroom.

Grammar

2 Read the text and think of the word which best fits each gap. Use only one word in each gap.

LIVING IN CAVES

Wherever people live, they need to protect themselves **(0)** ....*from*.... the weather, and ever **(1)** .... humans started to walk the Earth, they have lived in caves. To start with, they **(2)** .... use of natural caves, but they soon ran **(3)** .... of these. It was then simpler for them to create their own caves **(4)** .... to build shelters using other materials or techniques. On volcanic islands, for example, people found the rock was soft **(5)** .... to dig into, and **(6)** .... are places in the world where these artificial caves are still inhabited. Modern-day caves have some unexpected advantages. For anyone who has ever visited **(7)** .... , the benefits are immediately apparent: they will have found that the cave is insulated from noise and has a generally pleasant temperature. It is not too hot in the summer, while it stays warm in the winter. **(8)** .... is more, a modern cave is likely to contain all the modern household gadgets that make life comfortable.

3 Complete the second sentence so that it has a similar meaning to the first sentence, using the word given. Do not change the word given. You must use between two and five words, including the word given.

1 My grandparents are hoping to employ someone to paint their house soon.

HAVE

My grandparents are hoping to .... soon.

2 Make sure that someone checks the bike for you before your parents buy it.

HAVE

Make sure that .... before your parents buy it.

3 Magda must tidy her room each morning.

CLEAR

Magda has .... her room each morning.

4 They make us do three hours of homework a day in this school.

HAVE

We .... three hours of homework a day in this school.

5 In this restaurant, you should pay for your food when you order it.

SUPPOSED

In this restaurant, you .... for your food when you order it.

6 Speaking is forbidden during the exam.

ALLOWED

You .... during the exam.

Word formation

1 Read the text. Use the word given in capitals at the end of some of the lines to form a word that fits in the gap in the same line. There is an example at the beginning (0).

Getting work experience is a good way for young people who are still at school to see whether they would enjoy a particular career. Future **(0)** _employers_ like to **EMPLOY** see work experience on CVs and it can be a good way to see whether, for example, someone will enjoy being a **(1)** .... **LAW** before they start on a law degree. They get the chance to consider various **(2)** .... for **POSSIBLE** a future career with working professionals whose advice they will find **(3)** .... **SPECIAL** helpful when thinking about the different choices they will have to make. Work experience often involves uncomfortable situations but people who do it learn how to behave **(4)** .... in **APPROPRIATE** front of clients and how to take **(5)** .... for things in **RESPOND** the workplace. Appearance is important and they need to dress **(6)** .... whether they are **SUIT** going for a job as an air-traffic controller or an IT specialist or a job which is perhaps less technical but equally **(7)** .... , such as a sales **DEMAND** **(8)** .... or a teacher. **REPRESENT**

2 Use the word given in capitals at the end of each sentence to form a word that fits in the gap.

1 Tanya has a .... as a very hard-working student. **REPUTE**

2 In this airline, we make sure that we follow all the .... procedures in order to avoid accidents. **SAFE**

3 My teacher just looked at me in .... when I answered all the questions perfectly. **AMAZE**

4 My mother expressed her .... with the work, which was very badly done. **SATISFY**

5 Visitors are often confused to find the .... of two streets with similar names in the town. **EXIST**

6 If only Maria would tell us the .... instead of trying to deceive us with obvious lies! **TRUE**

7 Pierre swam the .... of the river in five minutes. **WIDE**

8 The .... of a swimming pool has made the hotel much more popular. **ADD**

9 Can you tell the .... between this fake Rolex and the original one made in Switzerland? **DIFFER**

10 I have several other .... in July, so I won't be able to go on holiday then. **OBLIGE**

Grammar

3 Complete the second sentence so that it has a similar meaning to the first sentence, using the word given. Do not change the word given. You must use between two and five words, including the word given.

1 It is almost certain that the flight will arrive on time.
EXPECTED
The flight .... on time.

2 Thieves entered our school at the weekend.
BROKEN
Our school .... thieves at the weekend.

3 According to reports, seven firefighters were injured in the fire.
REPORTED
Seven firefighters .... been injured in the fire.

4 It's two months since I last tidied my room!
BEEN
My room .... two months!

5 According to many people, elephants' memories are excellent.
SAID
Elephants' memories .... excellent.

6 There were very few cakes left by the end of yesterday's party.
EATEN
Almost every .... by the end of yesterday's party.

Grammar reference

PRESENT PERFECT SIMPLE AND CONTINUOUS

Present perfect simple: *have* + past participle

positive	negative	question
I've read the article in a newspaper.	She hasn't had lunch.	Have they arrived yet?

Present perfect continuous: *have been* + present participle

positive	negative	question
I've been watching the match.	She hasn't been waiting long.	Have they been working with you?

Both the **present perfect simple** and **present perfect continuous** talk about something which started in the past.

- The present perfect simple is a completed action which has a result in the present:
She's passed her driving test, so now she can take the children to the day care centre herself.
- The present perfect continuous is an action which is still happening now:
They've been working hard on their presentation, but it isn't finished yet.

The two tenses are often very similar in their usage. However:

present perfect simple	present perfect continuous
- emphasises the result: *They've worked on the environmental project all week and they're going to present the final version tomorrow.* - focuses on how much of an activity is complete: *I've listened to all of the audio novels you recommended.* - may give the idea that something is permanent (and may be accompanied by a time expression which shows this): *She's been a lecturer in the science department for well over twenty years and she is still actively involved in research.*	- emphasises the action: *They've been working on the environmental project all week, but they've still got some way to go.* - focuses on how long an activity has been in progress: *I've been listening to the audio novels you recommended and I've still got two left.* - may give the idea that something is temporary (and may be accompanied by a time expression which shows this): *She's been working here part-time this week, but she goes back to her normal job on Monday.*

- focuses on how many times an action has been repeated:
We've watched that programme about celebrities several times.
- focuses on the process of change over a period of time and that the changes are not finished:
My use of grammar has been getting more accurate since I started testing myself.

Note:
Some verbs are not used in the continuous form, e.g. *know, hate, understand, want.*
I've known Guy for a long time. (NOT: ~~I've been knowing~~ Guy for a long time.)
I've understood everything you've outlined. (NOT: ~~I've been understanding~~ everything you've outlined.)

PRACTICE

1 Complete the sentences with either the present perfect simple or continuous form of the verbs in brackets.

1 I .... (prepare) my presentation on mammals all week, but I .... (not finish) it yet.

2 What .... (you do)? Your hands are covered in dirt.

3 Your parents .... (look) exhausted recently. Have they .... (work) too much?

4 I .... (not complete) my essay yet, because I .... (chill out) in the garden for over an hour.

5 Have you got a plaster? I .... (do) some work around the house and I .... (damage) the nail on my thumb quite badly.

6 I .... (be) to Spain several times this year. Every visit was really outstanding.

7 Recently the government .... (become) more aware of the need to promote music education.

8 I .... (change) a wheel on my car, so I'm not really in the mood to go out.

2 Tick the correct sentences. Correct the sentences with mistakes.

1 The surgeon has just finished a nine-hour operation, so he's exhausted.

2 We have lived in Berlin for two years and before that we lived in London for five years.

3 I have finally been learning how to use the passive in English. I feel over the moon that I can do it at last.

4 I can see that he has eaten too much recently. He's gained a lot of weight.

5 The rain has been pouring down all day, so I chose to stay indoors.

6 They haven't mastered Chinese, but they can communicate at a basic level. That's an incredible achievement!

7 They have browsed for jobs in sport management for over four hours and still haven't found anything.

8 I have gone to the weight lifting session every weekend for years.

3 Make sentences with either the present perfect simple or continuous.

1 Scientists / discover / vaccines / to cure / many fatal illnesses.

2 He / not put / his recent qualifications on his CV / yet.

3 Wake up! You / sleep for / over two hours now.

4 We all feel thirsty, / because / as usual / not / drink enough / during training.

5 She / know him / since / he was a small child.

6 It snow / heavily / all morning / and as a result / the roads / are slippery now.

2

MAKING COMPARISONS

The form of comparatives and superlatives depends on the number of syllables in the original adjective or adverb.

One-syllable adjectives

adjective	comparative	superlative
high	high**er**	high**est**
small	small**er**	small**est**

Adjectives ending in a single consonant

adjective	comparative	superlative
fa**t**	fat**ter**	fat**test**
sa**d**	sad**der**	sad**dest**

Adjectives with two syllables

adjective	comparative	superlative
clever	cleverer / more clever	cleverest / most clever
narrow	narrower / more narrow	narrowest / most narrow

Adjectives with three or more syllables

adjective	comparative	superlative
experienced	more experienced	most experienced
inconvenient	more inconvenient	most inconvenient

Note:

Adjectives with two syllables, ending in -y, replace the y with i:

| easy | easier | easiest |
| happy | happier | happiest |

These very common adjectives have irregular comparative and superlative forms.

adjective	comparative	superlative
good	better	best
bad	worse	worst
little	less	least
much	more	most
far	further / farther	furthest / farthest

Use:

- Comparative adjectives compare differences between two nouns. Sentences have the following structure:
  noun (subject) + verb + comparative adjective + *than* + noun (object)
  My SUV   is   more reliable   than   your jeep.

- Superlative adjectives compare one noun to a group of nouns.
  noun (subject) + verb + *the* + superlative adjective + noun (object)
  His flat   is   the   most luxurious   home on the estate.

- To say two things are the same, use:
  as + **adjective** + *as*
  She finds doing physics as challenging as solving maths equations.
  (= She finds doing physics and solving equations in maths equally challenging.)

- To say that one thing is less than another, use:
  not so/as + **adjective** + *as*
  The party's majority in Parliament is not so/as substantial as before.

- To say that one thing is more or less than another, use:
  less/least + **adjective**
  This coat is less expensive than the other one.
  This is the least expensive coat in the shop.

- These adverbs form irregular comparisons:
  well – better – best   badly – worse – worst

- To say that we do one thing the same as another, use:
  as + **adverb** + *as*
  She dresses as elegantly as a fashion model.

- To say that we do one thing differently from another, use:
  not so/as + **adverb** + *as*
  He doesn't adapt to new situations as rapidly as his peers.

- We can use words and phrases with comparative forms to express large and small differences. These are some ways of expressing a large difference:

much | far | a lot | considerably + adjective/adverb + **-er | more** + adjective/adverb

Acts of kindness in that century were much rarer than nowadays.

not nearly as + adjective/adverb + **as**

The study of genetics is not nearly as well developed as we would wish.

by far + superlative

Surprisingly, the common pizza is by far the most authentic dish in Italy.

one of the most + superlative + infinitive

Amazingly, one of the filthiest parts of the human body is the mouth, which has 600 different types of bacteria living in it.

- These are some ways of expressing a small difference:

slightly | a bit | a little + adjective/adverb + **-er | more** + adjective/adverb

Because of the new gambling law people spend slightly less time in casinos than they did in the past.

not quite as + adjective/adverb + **as**

The launch of the new product was not quite as successful as anticipated.

PRACTICE

1 Complete the sentences with the correct comparative or superlative form of the word in brackets.

1 Today is the .... (bad) day I've had this year.

2 You call in sick .... (often) than anyone else in the class.

3 This questionnaire about energy use is the .... (complicated) I've ever completed.

4 The conference on tropical diseases was the .... (memorable) I've ever attended.

5 The ferry from Staten Island to Manhattan is the .... (cheap) in the world. It's free!

6 This shape is much .... (irregular) than the other one.

2 Tick the correct sentences. Correct the sentences with mistakes.

1 He's the more hard-working student in the class.

2 I think that this natural medicine is most effective than those tablets.

3 Generally the inhabitants of that part of town are not as affluent as we are.

4 This curry is hotter and more exotic than the one we had yesterday.

5 The climate in certain parts of Spain is considerably harsh than many people realise.

6 At the weekend he wears casual clothes than during the week.

7 Her use of English grammar is the more accurate in the class.

8 By far efficient way of mastering a foreign language is to live in the country where the target language is spoken.

3 Put the words in order to make sentences with the comparative or superlative.

1 His ambition / than / has always / his brother's. / greater / been /

2 was as accurate / the report / Her analysis / the financial situation / as / in the magazine. / of /

3 The lecturer is / since she started / less / work on her / available to her students / thesis.

4 His skills / are not / as fast / as people predicted. / developing /

5 My interest in / considerably / than / the project is / greater now / it was / at the beginning.

6 ideally want. / high / My motivation is / as / not quite / as I would /

7 than / There are slightly / living in / fewer people / ten years ago. / the town /

8 more / than by train. / It's / to travel by car / considerably / exhausting /

ADJECTIVES WITH -ED AND -ING

People often confuse adjectives that end in -ed, like **bored** or **excited**, with adjectives that end in -ing, for example **boring** or **exciting**.

The difference is that:

- adjectives that end in -ed describe emotions – they tell us how people feel about something.
*Did you see that video about spiders? Yes, I was **terrified** by it.*
- adjectives that end in -ing describe the thing that produces the feeling.
*I watched a **terrifying** video about spiders on YouTube.*

Spelling changes when adding -ed and -ing

-ed

If the base word ends in an 'e', just add 'd':

surpris**e** ➜ surprise**d**   amus**e** ➜ amuse**d**

-ing

If the base word ends in an 'e', remove the 'e' and add 'ing':

surpris**e** ➜ surpris**ing**   amus**e** ➜ amus**ing**

PRACTICE

1 Choose the correct adjective.

1 I was *fascinated / fascinating* by the presentation.

2 He was *irritated / irritating* to meet Milly in town after they had had an argument.

164

3 She talks a lot about the time she worked in a circus. She's so *amused / amusing*.

4 You look *exhausted / exhausting*. Why don't you lie down for a bit?

5 Feeling *tired / tiring* and *depressed / depressing*, she phoned her best friend for a chat.

6 I really can't eat this! It smells *disgusting / disgusted*! What is it?

2 Complete the sentences with the correct form of the adjectives.

1 The plot of the story was really interesting and the characters were very .... (appeal).

2 I could listen to her all night. She's one of the most .... (fascinate) people I know.

3 Although some people are not directly .... (involve) in education, they can still be very influential.

4 Put your notebook down and listen. I've got some .... (astonish) news for you.

5 His parents were very .... (dissatisfy) by his result in the test.

6 She's got the .... (irritate) habit of speaking with her mouth full.

7 Children! Your behaviour is .... (disgust)! Don't eat without washing your hands!

8 The new Professor of Politics is very .... (prejudice). Very few students attend his lectures.

PAST SIMPLE, PAST CONTINUOUS AND *USED TO*

Past simple

positive	negative	question
subject + verb + *ed* + object	subject + *didn't* + verb + object	*Did* + subject + verb + object?
They **adopted** a baby girl.	He **didn't succeed** in the exam.	**Did** she **identify** all the errors?

Past continuous

positive	negative	question
subject + *be* + verb + *-ing* + object	subject + *not be* + verb + *-ing* + object	*Be* + subject + verb + *-ing* + object?
He **was** criticis**ing** his employees in his speech.	He **wasn't** emphasis**ing** the main points sufficiently.	**Were** they enquir**ing** about the vacancies at the hotel?

Used to

positive	negative	question
subject + *used to* + verb + object	subject + *didn't use to* + verb + object	*Did* + subject + *use to* + verb + object?
She **used to** be a fighter pilot.	He **didn't use to** impress people at interviews.	**Did** they **use to** offend people by their actions?

Past simple

We use the past simple to describe:

- actions or events in the past:
  He outlined his proposal to the audience.
- actions or events which happened one after another:
  The author participated in the workshop, then she gave a presentation on her latest novel and finally she signed copies of it.
- things which happened over a long period in the past:
  All the time he was at school, he rebelled against the rules.

Past continuous

We use the past continuous to describe:

- an activity which started before and continued until an event in the past:
  The mayor was opening the ceremony when the lightning struck and the lights went out.
  He scratched his car when he was driving into a multi-storey car park.

Used to

We use *used to* to describe:

- situations in the past which are no longer true:
  I used to go running every evening in the summer.
- repeated activities or habits in the past which no longer happen:
  She used to go to school by bus every day, but now she walks.

PRACTICE

1 Choose the correct option in *italics*.

1 I always *used to worry / was worrying* if I made grammatical mistakes in English, but I couldn't care less now.

2 During her five years at university, she seldom *socialised / was socialising* with other students.

3 She *used to scuba dive / was scuba diving*, when a shark suddenly appeared.

4 She impatiently unwrapped the parcel, quickly examined the contents and then *used to discard / discarded* it.

5 She regularly used to participate in races until her health *was deteriorating / deteriorated*.

6 She was gazing out of the window, when the postman *rang / used to ring* the bell.

2 Complete the sentences with the past simple or continuous form of the verbs.

1 We .... (put) the finishing touches to supper, when the guests .... (ring) to say they were not coming.

2 I .... (win) the tennis match, when my opponent .... (claim) the light was too dark to continue.

3 He .... (serve) behind the counter in a fast food restaurant, when I first .... (notice) him.

4 I .... (stroll) home, whistling cheerfully, when a man in a mask .... (run) out of the post office.

5 It was total chaos when we .... (enter) the sitting room – the children .... (draw) on the walls and .... (jump) up and down on the sofa.

6 The detective .... (ask) me where I .... (head) in such a hurry on the night of the burglary.

AT, IN AND ON IN TIME PHRASES

We use *at* with:

- specific times:
  In fairy tales the witches always emerge at night, at midnight to be precise.
- mealtimes:
  Let's discuss it tomorrow at breakfast.
- weekend and holiday periods:
  Did you say you had plans to go to Italy at Easter?

We use *in* with:

- periods of time (years, months, seasons and centuries):
  She graduated in 2017.
  He launched his new campaign in April.
- parts of the day:
  They always hold their progress meetings in the morning.
- periods of time before something happens:
  The next election will take place in two months' time.
- how long something takes:
  She figured out how to do the calculation in about two minutes.

We use *on*:

- for particular dates, days, parts of days or types of days:
  The American Declaration of Independence was on the 4th of July 1776.
  I'll confirm my decision on Monday morning.
  He disappeared on a freezing cold night in December.

PRACTICE

1 Match the beginnings and endings of these sentences.

1 My appointment with the eye specialist is at

2 I'm not going to miss spending the festive period with my relatives at

3 The company relocated to southern Asia on

4 In Russia, certain museums and art galleries are closed to the public on

5 The gardens of that mansion are full of beautiful flowers in

6 The population of that industrial town is predicted to double in the

a Mondays.

b early spring.

c 25 July 2018.

d New Year.

e next few years.

f five o'clock.

2 Tick the correct sentences. Correct the sentences with mistakes.

1 I'll send an email and attach a copy of the agenda of the meeting in Tuesday morning.

2 We usually go backpacking in southern Europe at August.

3 This castle was demolished in 1542 during the reign of Henry VIII.

4 We never take a vacation at Easter in order to avoid the overcrowded airport lounges and the frequent flight delays.

5 It isn't true that Einstein's famous theory got its name because he developed it at a relatively short period of time.

6 It's highly risky to be on your own on night in that part of town.

PAST PERFECT SIMPLE AND CONTINUOUS

Past perfect simple: *had* + past participle

positive	negative	question
I'd read her dissertation in a professional journal.	*She hadn't eaten her packed lunch.*	*Had they arrived at the ice rink?*

Past perfect continuous: *had been* + present participle

positive	negative	question
I'd been considering all the possibilities.	She hadn't been looking after herself properly.	Had they been working with you?

Past perfect simple

We use the past perfect simple to describe something which happened before a single event in the past:
The police arrested him, even though he had not done anything illegal.
When he opened the safe, the top-secret documents had already disappeared.
The trainee pilot in the light aircraft took off before everybody had fastened their seatbelts.

Note: We often use the past perfect simple with *already, just* and *never*.

Past perfect continuous

We also use the past perfect continuous to describe something which happened before a single event in the past, but the continuous tense focuses on the length of time:
She needed to start to do some very gentle exercise, because she'd been lying in bed for nearly a month after the operation on her spine.
It was nearly a year before his boss realised that he had been leaving the office early every Friday afternoon.

PRACTICE

1 Complete the sentences with the past perfect simple or continuous form of the verbs in brackets.

1 We were furious, because we .... (wait) for over five hours before the plane got permission to take off.

2 He .... (cheat) for over a year in all his exams before one of the teachers finally found evidence to prove it.

3 The hurricane completely destroyed the cottage that they .... (build) only a year ago.

4 I must have dropped the confidential documents that he .... (hand) to me.

5 When they got home, they discovered that their babysitter............................... (already put) their toddler to bed.

6 When I finally reached the end of the queue, I found out that my colleague............................... (pick up) the tickets an hour earlier.

2 Complete the sentences with the past perfect simple or continuous form of the verbs in brackets.

1 The waiter, who was under a lot of pressure, brought a fruit drink that I .... (not order).

2 I had enormous difficulty recalling the complex password I .... (commit) to memory the previous night.

3 The children excitedly collected the nuts that .... (fall) from the trees.

4 She .... (ride) her pony all afternoon when we glimpsed her briefly as she went into the wood.

5 I .... (watch) the programme every week for nearly two months, but to my horror I had to miss the last episode.

6 She .... (live) in London all her life and was reluctant to move, even when she got married.

SO AND SUCH

So and *such* (*a/an*) are intensifiers meaning 'very' or 'extremely'.
I'm so pleased to hear that you passed your exam!
That child's behaviour was so unacceptable!
We had such a fabulous holiday.
He is such a splendid public speaker.

We use *so* and *such* (*a/an*) to talk about cause and effect:

cause	effect
so + adjective or adverb (+ *that*)	
He was so down when he failed his driving test	that he wouldn't speak to anybody.
She performed so well in the audition	that she got the lead role in the film.
such + adjective or adverb + noun (+ *that*)	
He's such a talented salesperson	that his company has just promoted him.
She's such a gifted musician	that she plays in the National Youth Orchestra.
such + adjective + uncountable noun / plural noun (+ *that*)	
They committed such terrible crimes	that they both spent a long time in prison.
France cooks such exceptional food	that we always put on weight when we are there on holiday.
so + much/many/few/little + noun (+ *that*)	
He had so many belongings in his luggage	that he had to pay an excess baggage charge.
She makes so many grammatical mistakes	that she is unlikely to pass either the written exam or the oral test.
such a/an + adjective + singular countable noun (+ *that*); such a lot of	
The restaurant served such dreadful food	that we refused to pay the bill.
She's got such a lot of friends on social media	that she's constantly getting messages.

Note:

- We also use *such* (+ noun) to mean 'of a similar type':
  When the owners of vicious dogs take them out without a lead, parents of small children are often alarmed, but fortunately such behaviour is not widespread.

TOO AND ENOUGH

- **too** means 'more than is needed or wanted':
  She's too qualified for that unchallenging office job.
- **enough** means 'as much as is necessary or needed':
  I don't think the company has enough staff with the necessary technical skills.

PRACTICE

1 Choose the correct option in *italics*.

1 So *much / many* acid rain fell that the leaves on the trees became damaged.

2 He made so *few / little* mistakes when he spoke German that he did very well in the oral exam.

3 He's *so / such* an imaginative artist that his paintings are in very big demand.

4 He had *such a lot of / so many* success with his latest invention that he has made a fortune.

5 Most of the dishes were *such / so* spicy that the children wouldn't even try them.

6 He ran *so / too* quickly in the marathon that he beat some of the elite runners.

2 Tick the correct sentences. Correct the sentences with mistakes.

1 They were such thrilled that he had graduated with a very good degree.

2 The neighbours' music was so loud that she reported them to the police.

3 He's to exhausted to row in that boat race.

4 She hadn't got enough stamina to complete the last circuit of the track.

5 At the end of the exam, she had much little time left that she didn't tackle the last question.

6 She designed so fabulous clothes that she was offered permanent employment with one of the well-known fashion houses in Paris.

3 Choose a sentence from the box to match each sentence 1–6.

1 The dark chocolate filling in the cream cake tasted too bitter for most guests at the wedding celebration.

2 The beef stew smelled good, but the meat was tough.

3 She couldn't bite into the pear because it was too firm.

4 The curry was meant to be hot, but I found it too mild.

5 The hot chocolate drink from the machine looked good at first sight, but it was just too weak.

6 The salad bowl had stood on the counter for several hours and the lettuce, in particular, was a bit off.

A It was not fresh enough.

B It was not strong enough.

C It was not tender enough.

D It was not spicy enough.

E It was not ripe enough.

F It was not sweet enough.

5

ZERO, FIRST AND SECOND CONDITIONALS

Conditionals

Conditional sentences express a condition (*If ...*) and the consequence of the condition. The consequence can be expressed before or after the condition:
If you win a sport scholarship, you can study at that American university.
You can study at that American university if you win a sport scholarship.

Note: If the condition comes first, a comma is used.

Zero conditional

We use the zero conditional to express things that are generally or always true (e.g. scientific facts):
If you heat water to 100 degrees centigrade, it boils.
Most people tend to be extremely aggressive if you accuse them of lying.

Note: In zero conditionals, *when* and *if* are often interchangeable. The present simple is used in both clauses.

First conditional

We use the first conditional to express a future situation which we think is real or possible:
I'll research that topic today, if I remember to take my laptop with me.
If it's not raining, we will go to the beach.
If there isn't a sandstorm again tomorrow, we'll go hiking in the desert.
Unless my local team loses their next match, they'll be top of the championship league.

Note: In first conditional sentences, it's not important which clause comes first.

The structure is usually *if* + present simple and *will* + infinitive.

We can often use *unless* instead of *if not*:
I won't be able to go snowboarding unless I get all my gear sorted out.
(If I don't get all my gear sorted out, I won't be able to go snowboarding.)

Second conditional

We use the second conditional to express things which are imaginary, contrary to the facts, impossible or improbable:
If I won something like an international golf tournament, I'd probably spend my winnings on buying a luxury yacht.
If you reduced your calorie intake and joined a gym, you would easily lose all your excess weight.

Note: In second conditional sentences, it's not important which clause comes first.

The structure is *if* + past simple and *would* + infinitive.

Although many conditional sentences use *if* + *will/would*, conditional sentences can also use other words instead of *if*, for example *when*, *as soon as*, and *in case*. Other modal verbs can be used instead of *will/would*, for example *can/could*, *may* and *might*.

Provided

Provided can sometimes be used instead of *if*:
Provided *the weather is fine, you could take a tour around the city.*

PRACTICE

1 Choose the correct option in *italics*.

1 The sun's very strong today, so if you don't sit in the shade, you *get / will get* badly burnt.

2 If you mix oxygen and hydrogen together, you *get / will get* water.

3 A lot of wild animals tend to attack if they *are / will be* scared.

4 When the manager is out of the office, her personal assistant *takes / will take* all her calls.

5 *If / Unless* the weather doesn't improve significantly, we'll have to postpone the barbecue.

6 You *won't win / will win* a fortune in the lottery unless you buy a ticket.

2 Complete the sentences with the first or second conditional form of the verbs.

1 If he .... (be) late, we .... (have to) leave without him.

2 If I .... (be) you, I .... (buy) that computer.

3 If you .... (come) this way, the doctor .... (see) you now.

4 If I .... (have) more money, I .... (not be) here now.

5 Provided you .... (study) hard, you .... (pass) the exam.

6 I .... (buy) a new Ferrari, if I .... (win) the lottery.

3 Tick the correct sentences. Correct the sentences with mistakes.

1 I would sleep more peacefully if the neighbours stop having parties late at night.

2 We take a taxi to get to the hotel from the airport if our flight arrives late.

3 Babies usually only cry when they are hungry, thirsty or wet.

4 If she doesn't go on the excursion, I will either.

5 We definitely will cancel the beach party unless it pours with rain.

6 If you weren't so stubborn, we wouldn't have so many massive rows.

COUNTABLE AND UNCOUNTABLE NOUNS

Nouns can be either **countable** [C] or **uncountable** [U]. However, some nouns can be both countable [C] and uncountable [U], but with a difference in meaning.

Most people claim that it's healthy to drink tea regularly.
(uncountable, because it's tea in general)

She ordered a tea with a slice of lemon.
(countable, because it's a cup of tea)

Preparing for a major exam is an enormous amount of work.
(uncountable, because it's work in general)

That sculpture is a famous work of art.
(countable, because it's a particular work)

The grammar for countable nouns is different from the grammar for uncountable nouns.

Countable nouns

- use *a* or *an* in the singular: *a firefighter, an accountant*
- can be made plural: *platform – platforms, portrait – portraits*
- use *some* and *any* in the plural: *some ponds, any replies*
- use *few* and *many* in the plural: *few mayors, many manufacturers*

Uncountable nouns

- do not use *a* or *an*
- cannot be made plural:
pollution, behaviour
- use verbs in the singular:
The BBC news is independent.
- use *some* and *any* in the singular:
Some student accommodation is available.
He wasn't seeking any help or advice.
- use *little* and *much* in the singular:
There was little information available on the website.
- use other words to refer to a quantity:
*I gave her **a piece of** advice about getting a bank loan.*
*He wanted to borrow **a small amount of** money.*

Some common uncountable nouns in English

accommodation, advice, behaviour, cardboard, countryside, damage, equipment, experience, food, furniture, homework, housework, information, knowledge, luggage, media, music, newspaper, pollution, research, scenery, smoke, software, stuff, transport, work

PRACTICE

1 Tick the correct sentences. Correct the sentences with mistakes.

1 The students finally found some suitable accommodations at a reasonable rent.

2 We were astonished to discover that the airline charged us extra for our luggages.

3 A pollution caused by plastic in the ocean is responsible for the death of marine life.

4 I usually reject an advice from my doctor.

5 The company's brochure contained little information about prices and delivery dates.

6 All of the paintings in the art gallery are extremely valuable work of art.

2 Choose the correct option in *italics*.

1 Many experts argue that it is not wise to drink *coffee / coffees* just before going to bed.

2 He considered going to the citizen's advice centre, but finally decided he didn't need to ask for *some / any* help.

3 There's a container for recycling *cardboards / cardboard* and waste *papers / paper* behind our block of flats.

4 Some of the news about the political situation *were / was* very upsetting.

5 The cost of the *equipment / equipments* needed to play golf *is / are* beyond the reach of most people.

6 The engineers were desperately struggling to repair the *damages / damage* caused to the bridge by the explosion.

ARTICLES

The indefinite article

We use **a** or **an**:

• with singular, countable nouns mentioned for the first time:
***A** new car loses ten percent of its value as soon as you drive it out of the showroom.*

• to talk about jobs:
*My ambition is to become **a** surgeon.*

We do not use **a** or **an** with uncountable nouns or plural countable nouns:
If you have knowledge and experience you have power.
More women than men gain top university degrees.

We use **an** before words beginning with a vowel sound (including words with a silent 'h'):
*I've just downloaded **an** app, but I'm worried now about the security of my data.*
*Let's meet up in **an** hour.*

Note:
We don't use **an** when the letters 'u' or 'e' are pronounced with a 'y' sound:
That Swiss army knife is a useful tool.

The definite article

The is used:

• with things we have mentioned before, or when it's clear who or what we are referring to from the context:
*Two experienced trainers – one for tennis and one for martial arts – have just joined **the** club.*
***The** tennis coach is from Spain and **the** judo black belt is from Japan.*
*Could you get me some detergent and some flour from **the** shop, please? (i.e. the shop we always go to)*

• when referring to particular things:
*I love most sci-fi, but I don't like **the** science fiction written by that new, best-selling, American author.*

• with things which are unique:
*Since I bought a telescope, I spend hours studying **the** sky at night. **The** moon and **the** stars fascinate me.*

• with adjectives to express groups:
*In Europe, **the** wealthy are investing heavily in property, especially in second homes in coastal areas.*

• with nationalities:
***The** French tend to spend their summer holidays in their own country rather than travelling abroad.*

• with superlative adjectives:
*The ferry from Staten Island to New York provides **the** cheapest service for commuters in the world. It's free!*

PRACTICE

1 Complete the sentences with definite or indefinite articles.

1 I heard .... loud noise in .... basement.

2 I think that .... woman riding .... bicycle is .... member of .... Dutch royal family.

3 We are looking for .... apartment in .... centre of .... town.

4 What's .... longest bridge in Europe?

5 .... poor in many towns are having to feed themselves from food banks.

6 He's .... university student in one of .... most historic towns in Europe.

170

2 Choose the correct option in *italics*.

1 Could you go to *the / a* chemist's and get my prescription?

2 The company has bought two new vehicles for its car fleet. *The / A* luxury, three-litre car is for *the / a* CEO and *the / a* Mini is for her assistant.

3 *The / A* French and *the / a* Welsh are very protective of their national languages.

4 *The / A* window in *the / a* sitting room is *the / a* largest in *the / a* whole house.

5 She's just been awarded *a / an* university degree in modern foreign languages.

6 *The / an / –* accommodation can be quite cheap in some parts of *the / an / –* Ireland.

INFINITIVE AND VERB + -ING

Infinitive

We use the infinitive:

*   to say why we do something:
    *She put a tick **to accept** the terms and conditions.*
    *He's taken up long-distance running **to improve** his health.*

*   to say why something exists:
    *They've erected the metal barrier on that sharp bend **to reduce** accidents.*

*   after *too* and *enough*:
    *It was too late **to express** my opinion because the professor had already moved on to another topic.*
    *The image wasn't clear enough **to illustrate** what it was supposed to depict.*

We use the infinitive in the following verb patterns:

verb + *to* infinitive	agree, appear, bother, decide, demand, fail, hope, learn, manage, offer, plan, refuse, seem, be supposed, threaten	They agreed to vote on the new reform.
verb + (somebody/ something) + *to* infinitive	ask, choose, expect, help, intend, promise, want	He expected to do well in the test. I expect you to do well in the test.
verb + somebody/ something + *to* infinitive	advise, allow, enable, encourage, forbid, force, invite, order, permit, persuade, recommend, remind, teach, tell, warn	My parents forbade me to boast about my academic achievements.

We use the verbs in the lists above to report speech.

Verb + -ing

We use a verb + *-ing*, e.g. *I can't stop **yawning**:*

*   after prepositions:
    *He's improved his English **by reading** extensively.*
    Note: We also use a verb + *-ing* after *to* when *to* is a preposition:
    *I'm looking forward to **receiving** a detailed reply to my letter of complaint.*

*   as the subject or object of a sentence:
    ***Correcting** mistakes is a crucial part of the learning process.*
    *When he was fully recovered after the operation, he decided to take up **wrestling**.*

*   after the verbs *admit, appreciate, avoid, celebrate, consider, delay, deny, dislike, enjoy, finish, imagine, involve, keep, mind, miss, postpone, practise, regret, risk, stop, suggest:*
    *I considered **swapping** this task for another one.*
    *She celebrated **passing** all her exams by going on a trip to Thailand.*
    *I now regret **borrowing** money from my grandparents.*

*   after the expressions *it's no good, it's not worth, it's no use, it's a waste of time, can't stand, can't bear, can't help:*
    *It's a waste of time **trying** to increase the bee population.*
    *It's not worth **buying** expensive ski gear – you can hire it.*
    *I can't bear **seeing** my best friend making such a fool of herself.*

Verbs followed by either an infinitive or a verb + -ing with almost the same meaning

I hate criticising people. I hate to criticise people.
It continued being foggy all morning. It continued to be foggy all morning.

Note: When *love, hate, prefer* and *like* are used with *would*, they are always followed by the infinitive:
We would like to devote more time to our exam preparation.

Verbs followed by either an infinitive or a verb + -ing with a difference in meaning

	verb + infinitive	verb + -ing
remember	Did you remember to bring your running shoes? (an action you have to do)	I remember wondering if I would ever get down off the summit of the mountain. (a memory of something in the past)
forget	Don't forget to complete your physics presentation. (an action you have to do)	I'll never forget seeing my wife for the first time at my best friend's wedding. (a memory of something in the past)
regret	I regret to tell you that the room you booked is no longer available. (I'm sorry to give you this information.)	I regret not arriving at the hotel at the agreed time. (I'm sorry I didn't do this.)

try	I'm mailing my CV every day to IT companies to try and get a job. (My objective is to get a job in IT.)	If you want to get a job in IT, why don't you try phoning the companies? (Phoning is a method to reach your objective.)
mean	Martin means to get a scholarship to cover some of the costs of his college course. (This is his intention.)	He wanted to get a scholarship to cover some of the costs of his college course, but it meant getting top grades in all his subjects. (it involved)
stop	She stopped playing the game of chess to phone her mother. (in order to phone her mother)	When her opponent made a winning move, she stopped playing the game of chess. (She didn't continue.)

Note: The form *forget* + verb + *-ing* is unusual. It is more normal to use *(not) remember*: *I don't remember being three years old.* (NOT ~~I forget being three years~~ old.)

PRACTICE

1 **Tick the correct sentences. Correct the sentences with mistakes.**

1 He decided make a high offer to be sure he could buy the second-hand car.

2 I intend to continue to improve my level of spoken English.

3 They persuaded me applying for the position of assistant manager.

4 It's recommended to book a table in advance.

5 Can I remind you not driving without having your licence on you.

6 The lawyers advised him say he was guilty of the crime.

2 **Choose the correct option in *italics*.**

1 I can't stop *to speak / speaking*. I'm in a hurry.

2 He's completed the design on time by closely *follow / following* the brief he was given.

3 I'm looking forward to *joining / join* the expedition to the North Pole.

4 I admit to foolishly *celebrate / celebrating* victory before the game was over.

5 I regret not *taking up / take up* the place I was offered at university.

6 I can't bear *watching / watch* politicians being dishonest.

7 If you forget *to do / doing* the homework, you will have problems with the teacher.

3 **Match the beginnings and endings of these sentences.**

1	It's not	**a**	not taking driving lessons.
2	It's a waste of	**b**	people talking about money all the time.
3	It's no use	**c**	time learning foreign languages.
4	I can't stand	**d**	worth complaining to the manager.
5	She prefers to	**e**	eat fish rather than seafood.
6	I very much regret	**f**	buying property. It's better to rent.

4 **Complete the sentences with the correct form of the verb in brackets. In which sentence are two answers possible?**

1 I meant .... (buy) my grandfather a birthday present, but I forgot.

2 I remember .... (carry) the painting I bought you all round Mexico!

3 She's stopped .... (take) sandwiches to work. She eats in the canteen now.

4 Camping isn't for me. I prefer .... (stay) in a comfortable hotel.

5 .... (analyse) the problem is not enough – what we need is a solution.

6 Tom doesn't believe in .... (pay) for anything if he can get it for free.

 8

AT, IN AND *ON* TO EXPRESS LOCATION

at

We use *at*:

- when we think of a place as a point, not an area (including *at home, at school, at work, at university*):
  The delivery man is at the back door.
  The cars were waiting at the barrier.

- to talk about an event with a number of people:
  We'll both be at the reception this evening.
  The students were at the seminar about virtual reality.

in

We use *in*:

- when we think of a place as an area or space:
  He had his workshop in the basement of his house.
  The headquarters of the company are located in Silicon Valley.
  Many British criminals try to escape the law by living in villas in the south of Spain.

- for cars and taxis:
  He spent two hours in a taxi because of the rush hour.
  I keep up to date with the news by listening to the radio in the car.

- normally with *in class, in hospital, in prison, in court*:
  My partner is still in hospital after the accident in the warehouse at work.
  He defended his client in court.

- with people or things which form lines:
  She was prepared to wait in a queue for hours for a bargain.

- with *the world*:
  There's a lot of competition between Dubai and Saudi Arabia to construct the tallest building in the world.

on

We use *on*:

- to talk about a position in contact with a surface:
  They posted announcements on the walls of the building.
  The frying pan is on the cooker.
  She was relaxing on the terrace all afternoon.

- with *border, coast, road to, the outskirts of, the edge of, the way to/from,* etc:
  On the border between France and Germany, there was a bakery selling bread and pastries.

- with means of transport apart from cars and taxis:
  The wind demolished the sail on our yacht.

- for technology:
  He denies that he spends hours on the phone.
  I rediscovered a friend from school on Facebook.

- with *left* and *right:*
  There was a sharp bend in the road on the left.
  Can you see the man in shorts leaning against the door over there on your right?

at	in	on
at your/my house	in the world	on the beach
at the festival	in the city/town	on the/a train
at the party	in the mountains	on the island
at the theatre	in the country	on the/a farm
at the/your hotel	in the sky	on the outskirts
at the concert	in the hotel	on the floor
at my school	in a car	on the stage
at the camp	in this area	on the bus
at the university	in the street	on the road(s)
at the beach	in the sea	on the plane
at the airport	in traffic jams	on the bridge

PRACTICE

1 Complete the sentences with the correct preposition.

1 In old spy films they often exchanged prisoners .... the border.

2 Over two hundred guests were .... the wedding reception.

3 He kept all his rubbish .... his attic rather than getting rid of it.

4 Their head office is .... a prestigious part of the capital.

5 The criminals who burgled my flat will be .... court tomorrow.

6 We played football all day .... the new pitch.

2 Tick the correct sentences. Correct the sentences with mistakes.

1 They waited patiently on the back door for him to come back.

2 They had to wait all afternoon at the queue for the opera tickets.

3 That snake is reputed to be the most poisonous on the world.

4 All the cutlery is on the tray ready to be carried into the dining room.

5 She used to own a luxury villa on the outskirts of a medieval town.

6 The facilities in that cruise ship are incredible.

3 Choose the correct preposition in *italics*.

1 There are lots of fortified castles *on / in / at* the border between Spain and Portugal.

2 A lot of children are failing to achieve at school because they are spending too much time *on / in / at* their phones.

3 He damaged his car quite badly because he didn't see the vehicle parked *on / in / at* the left until too late.

4 I saw several old friends and acquaintances *on / in / at* the festival.

5 I didn't set out early enough and got stuck *on / in / at* a traffic jam *on / in / at* the M25 ring road.

6 The last time I saw that talented young actor was on the stage *on / in / at* the Royal Shakespeare Theatre.

REPORTED SPEECH

We change tenses in reported speech. If the reporting verb (*said*, *told*, *admitted*, *warned*, etc.) is in the past, we tend to change the original verb to a past form as well. Here are some changes we make:

	speech	reported
present simple ➜ past simple	*'I am a sales representative for a steel company.'*	She said she was a sales representative for a steel company.
present continuous ➜ past continuous	*'I'm filing this correspondence.'*	He said he was filing the correspondence.
present perfect ➜ past perfect	*'I've tried eating insects in Asia.'*	She said she had tried eating insects in Asia.
past simple ➜ past perfect	*'I missed the last flight.'*	He told me he had missed the last flight.
will ➜ would	*'I'll reply to your email tomorrow.'*	She promised she would reply to my email tomorrow.

Modal verbs change in the following way:

can ➜ could	*'I can gently jog for long periods, but I can't run fast.'*	She said she could gently jog for long periods, but she couldn't run fast.
may ➜ might	*'I may let you use the calculators to solve the problems later.'*	The teacher suggested he might let us use the calculators to solve the problems later.
must ➜ had to	*'I must sort out my financial difficulty.'*	She said she had to sort out her financial difficulty.

We do not change:

- modal verbs *could, would, should, might, ought to* and *used to* in reported speech:
  'I would prefer to have two starters rather than a main course.'
  ➜ She said she would prefer to have two starters rather than a main course.

- *must* when it's negative:
  'You mustn't open the files relating to the new product launch.'
  ➜ Her boss told her she mustn't open the files relating to the new product launch.

- *must* when it expresses a deduction:
  'The candidates must still be waiting in reception.' ➜ She said that the candidates must still be waiting in reception.

Note: If the reporting verb is in a present tense, no tense changes are necessary:
'I'll help you when you move into your new flat.' ➜ She says she'll help me when I move into my new flat.

Questions in reported speech

- We change the word order in the question to the same as a normal sentence.

- We make the same tense changes as in reported speech (see opposite).

- We use the same question words (*when, how*, etc.).

- We use a full stop (.), not a question mark (?):
  'How long have you been working in the marketing department?'
  ➜ She asked me how long I had been working in the marketing department.
  'When can I interview you?'
  ➜ The researcher asked the students when he could interview them.

- We do not use the auxiliary verbs *do, does* and *did*; the question has the same form as a normal sentence:
  'What time do you take a coffee break?'
  ➜ The new employee asked what time we took a coffee break.

- We use *if* or *whether* with Yes/No questions:
  'Can I wear casual clothes at the presentation tomorrow?'
  ➜ He wanted to know whether he could wear casual clothes at the presentation the following day.

- We often use these verbs and phrases to introduce reported questions: *ask, wonder, want to know, enquire*.

Pronoun, adjective and adverb changes in reported speech

We usually make the following changes:

you ➜ he/she/they	*'I warned **you** earlier.'*	He said he had warned **her** earlier.
your ➜ his/her/their our ➜ their	*'I noticed **your** grammar mistake earlier.'*	He mentioned that he had noticed **her** grammar mistake earlier.
this/that (as pronouns) ➜ it	*'You should erase **this** from your memory.'*	She told him he should erase **it** from his memory.
this/that/these/those + noun ➜ the + noun	*'**This** report is very detailed.'*	She told him **the** report was very detailed.

Remember that references to times also need to change in reported speech:

'I delivered the package this morning.'
➜ She said she had delivered the package that morning.

Other changes include:

present reference	today this week/month/year	that day that week/month/year
future reference	tomorrow next week/month/year	the next / the following day the next / the following week/month/year
past reference	yesterday last week/month/year	the day before OR the previous day the previous week/month/year OR the week/month/year before

Descriptions of place also frequently change:
'Did the courier service deliver the package here?' ➜ He asked if the courier service had delivered the package there.

PRACTICE

1 Complete the reported speech with the verbs in the correct tense and any other words necessary.

1 'I work in the human resources department.' ➜ She said she .... in the human resources department.

2 'I'm having a late breakfast.' ➜ He phoned to say that he .... a late breakfast.

3 'I've never done anything adventurous or dangerous.' ➜ He admitted that he .... anything adventurous or dangerous.

4 'I think I got food poisoning from the fish I ate.' ➜ She suspected that she .... food poisoning from the fish she ....

5 'I'll ring as soon as I wake up.' ➜ She promised that she .... as soon as she ....

6 'I can speak and understand Chinese but I can't write it.' ➜ He told me that he .... speak and understand Chinese but that he .... write it.

2 Choose the correct option, A or B.

1 She shouted that she .... into the river from the top of the cliff.

   A could jump   B can jump

2 The waiter said that he .... an extra portion of cheesecake, if we wanted it.

   A could bring   B can bring

3 She whispered that she .... pay the bill.

   A can't   B couldn't

4 She told them that they .... better in the tests this year.

   A must do   B had to do

5 She stated that she .... to travel by ferry rather than by plane.

   A would prefer   B will prefer

6 The lecturer told the students they .... at the exam questions until ten o'clock exactly.

   A mustn't look   B had not to look

3 Tick the correct sentences. Correct the sentences with mistakes.

1 She said that the passengers must still be going through customs and immigration.

2 He promises he would help me to put the winter tyres on my car.

3 He asked me how long had I been employed as a receptionist?

4 They asked her when would she be available for interview?

5 She wanted to know what time did we finish work?

6 She wondered whether she could express herself freely in the meeting without first getting permission from the manager.

4 Complete the sentences in reported speech. Pay particular attention to the correct pronouns, adjectives and adverbs.

1 'Martin, I gave you clear instructions about what to do yesterday.'

   She told Martin that she had
   ....

2 'Cynthia, we discovered your missing sports gear in the washing machine this morning.'

   They told Cynthia that ....

3 'What project are you working on tomorrow, Jack?'

   I asked Jack what project ....

4 'Tom, your essay is extremely confusing.'

   The lecturer told Tom that ....

5 'What did you do yesterday, Maria?'

   He asked Maria what ....

6 'Have you noticed any of my belongings here?'

   He asked if she ....

9 MODAL VERBS TO EXPRESS CERTAINTY AND POSSIBILITY

We use:

- **must** to express certainty about the present:
He's won four Olympic gold medals, so he must be highly talented.
Note: We usually have a good reason for expressing this certainty, e.g. *He's won four Olympic gold medals.*

- **can't** or **couldn't** in negative sentences (not *mustn't*):
You can't be hungry, you just had dinner.

- **must have** + past participle to express certainty about the past:
She must have calmed down before starting the talk, because her delivery was perfect.

- **can't have** and **couldn't have** + past participle in negative sentences:
She couldn't have fought harder to defend her point of view.
He can't have lost his wallet – I saw him holding it at the supermarket checkout.

- **may**, **might** or **could** to express possibility about the present or future:
They could challenge you over this topic.
I might comment later.
I may ask you to lend me some money.
We might go on holiday after all, if we save enough money in time.
We'd better leave now because the traffic could be very heavy later.

- **may not** and **might not** (or **mightn't**) in negative sentences (not *can't* or *couldn't*):
Don't wait up for me because I might not be back until after midnight.

- **may have**, **might have**, **could have**, **may not have**, **might not have** + past participle to express possibility about the past:
His case felt very heavy. I think he may have picked up the wrong one at the airport and might not have noticed.
I'm astonished that she isn't here yet. She's usually so punctual. I think she may have missed her train or she might not have bought the right ticket.

PRACTICE

1 Choose the best modal verb in *italics*.

1 You *must / might / may* be tired – you haven't been to bed for two days!

2 He's just been successful in getting a place on a postgraduate course, so he *might / could / must* be very academic.

3 It *can't / mustn't / might* be John over there; he's already moved to Canada.

4 She *must / will / may* have revised very well, because her exam results were outstanding.

5 He *can't / mustn't / didn't* have been to Moscow, because he doesn't have a Russian visa in his passport.

6 I was amazed by her performance. She *couldn't / can't / mustn't* have spoken more convincingly in the debate.

2 Match the beginnings and endings of these sentences.

1 I think she might not have noticed that she

2 I think she may

3 Sometimes it can be

4 We could be late if we don't

5 She might not have

6 Somebody could be

a remembered she was supposed to meet us at the airport.

b difficult to understand her.

c be delayed at the office.

d dropped her scarf when she got out of the taxi.

e in danger – I just heard a scream outside.

f hurry up a bit.

3 Complete the sentences with a suitable modal verb. More than one answer may be possible.

1 Mum says we .... be able to afford those mountain bikes after all, even though they are quite expensive.

2 I absolutely love these earrings! You .... chosen a better present for me.

3 He would never have said that to you. You .... have heard him properly.

4 You'd better book, otherwise you .... be sure to get a seat.

5 My phone isn't in my bag. I .... left it at school. That's the only place it could be.

6 Let's eat out tonight. I .... have time to go to the supermarket today.

10

AS AND *LIKE*

As

We use *as*:

- to say someone or something is that thing, or has that function:
  He is employed part-time as a lorry driver.
  She uses social media mainly as a means of communication.
  The role of a financial adviser is to act as a critical friend.

- to express the same as was predicted, expected, imagined, promised, etc:
  He did exactly as he had promised.
  As expected, the driving test was very stressful.

- to mean 'because':
  As this is an official written examination, I must warn all candidates that no talking is allowed.
  As he exceeded the speed limit, he has to pay a fine.

- after certain verbs, e.g. *describe* and *regard*:
  The police regard this man as potentially very dangerous.
  The staff at the zoo are describing the escaped monkey as a risk to the public.

- with adjectives and adverbs to make comparisons:
  The waltz is nowhere near as dramatic as the tango.

- to mean 'for example' in the phrase *such as*:
  We have been trying out lots of different activities at the gym, such as aerobics, yoga and cycling.

- with *the same ... as*:
  *There's a Russian joke about two men who met each other after fifty years. One said to the other: 'How did you recognise me after all this time?' The other replied: 'It was easy, you're still wearing **the same** jacket **as** when we last met.'*

- in the following phrases:
  as far as I know (I think it's true but I don't know all the facts):
  As far as I know, my wife's grandparents came from Poland.
  as far as I'm concerned (this is my personal opinion):
  As far as I'm concerned, you can continue wasting your time trying to finish that 5000-piece jigsaw puzzle.
  as far as I can see/tell (this is what I've noticed or understood):
  As far as I can see, he'll be lucky to pass his exams if he doesn't study more.

Like

We use *like*:

- to mean 'similar to' (especially after the verbs *be, seem, feel, look, sound, smell* and *taste*):
  When he plays the violin, it sounds like a cat in pain.

- to mean 'for example':
  He takes part in a wide range of cultural activities like singing in a choir, modern dance and classical ballet.

PRACTICE

① **Tick the correct sentences. Correct the sentences with mistakes.**

1 He works full time like a dental receptionist.

2 When he serves in badminton, he looks as a professional player.

3 By far as I can tell, she has probably twisted her ankle.

4 They've added a lot of traditional dishes, such like onion soup and Irish stew, to the restaurant's menu.

5 The customs officers at the airport regard men on their own with large suitcases as highly suspicious.

6 Like she stole a bottle of expensive perfume from the duty-free shop, she was arrested and missed her flight.

② **Complete the sentences with *as* or *like*.**

1 There's really no point in learning to bake pastry .... far .... I'm concerned.

2 She's actively involved in lots of extreme sports, ... rock climbing and white-water rafting.

3 She gave her husband a sports car for their wedding anniversary, ... promised.

4 He uses his Swiss army knife .... a bottle and can opener.

5 That teenager's bedroom looks .... the inside of a recording studio.

6 The new Professor of History is not .... entertaining .... the person who held the post before her.

MODAL VERBS TO EXPRESS ABILITY

To say someone has an ability, we use *can, can't, could, couldn't,* and *be able to*.

In the **present**, we use:

- *can* or *am/is/are able to* to express ability:
  That athlete can run at a steady pace over long distances, but she can't sprint on the last lap.

- *can't* or *am not / isn't / aren't able to* for things which are not possible:
  The bank manager isn't able to discuss your loan today, but is able to see you tomorrow morning.

Note: We usually use *can* and *can't* when speaking because they are shorter and less formal than *able to*.

In the **past**, we use:

- *could*, but only when speaking in general:
  When she was at primary school , she could recite several lengthy poems off by heart. (NOT ~~was able to recite~~ several lengthy poems off by heart.)

- **was/were able to** when speaking about one particular occasion when someone succeeded in doing something:
When the waiter brought the bill, I realised that I didn't have enough cash on me to pay, but I was able to ring a friend who came and paid it. (NOT I could ring a friend who came and paid it.)

- **couldn't** and **wasn't/weren't able to** when speaking in general and also when speaking about one particular occasion:
I wasn't able to / couldn't calculate the exact dimensions of the store room from the office plan.
He couldn't / wasn't able to understand many of the formulas in chemistry until he started to revise seriously for his exam.

- When talking about ability, we use *can* only in the present and *could* only in the past. For perfect and future tenses, we use *able to*:
He's been under a lot of pressure at work, so he hasn't been able to go out much recently. (present perfect)
When you finally get the job, you'll be able to organise your daily routine as you wish. (future simple)

We use *be able to*:

- after an infinitive:
She hopes to be able to study tropical medicine when she goes to university.

- after modal verbs (*might, should, may,* etc.):
I've got some free time at the weekend, so I might be able to help you fix the dent in your car.
When you've completed this assignment, you should be able to start the advanced course.

- We usually use *can* and *could* with *see, hear, smell, feel* and *taste*:
From upstairs we could smell the eggs burning in the frying pan on the stove in the kitchen.
I can hear a strange, scratching noise coming from inside the chimney.

However, we use *manage* when we succeed in doing something which is quite difficult to do:
Did you manage to run the marathon in less than two and a half hours?
She managed to get the top grade in the chemistry exam, although she hadn't attended sessions in the lab for some time.

Note: *could* is not possible in this example:
He could get the top grade in the chemistry exam, although he had not been to the lab to do experiments for some time.

Note: We do not use *be able to* in continuous forms.

1 **Complete the sentences with a modal verb from the box.**

can	can't x2	could	couldn't
	was able to		

1 .... you understand basic economics when you were eight?

2 He .... get to the meeting on time yesterday, because his car broke down.

3 She's absolutely amazing – she's only seven and she .... speak five languages, including Japanese.

4 He was delighted, because he .... find a taxi and get to the party on time.

5 I've searched everywhere for my car keys, but I .... find them anywhere.

6 I .... lift this armchair – it's so heavy! Could you help me, please?

2 **Tick the correct sentences. Correct the sentences with mistakes.**

1 I wasn't able translate the text into French, because it contained too many unfamiliar expressions.

2 When the garage mechanic showed me the bill for the repair, I didn't have enough money on me to pay for it, but fortunately I could use my credit card this time.

3 Thank you for your job offer, but I am afraid I couldn't accept it.

4 When you finally move into your new flat, you'll be able to decorate it as you wish.

5 I could taste and smell the garlic for hours after the meal.

6 He could run the marathon in less than three hours, although he hadn't been training regularly for ten days.

 11

RELATIVE PRONOUNS AND RELATIVE CLAUSES

A clause is a group of words containing a subject and a verb in a tense which form a sentence or part of a sentence. Relative clauses start with these relative pronouns:
who, which, that, whose, where, when and *why*.

Defining relative clauses

- Relative clauses which tell us which particular person or thing the speaker is talking about are called defining relative clauses. They give essential information:
The optician who tested my eyes is my cousin.
The relative clause tells us which optician we are talking about.

Non-defining relative clauses

- Relative clauses which give us extra information are called non-defining relative clauses:
My cousin is an optician, who is a member of your golf club. We already know which optician (it's my cousin); *who is a member of your golf club* does not tell us which optician we are talking about; it just adds extra information.

There are differences in grammar:

defining relative clauses ...	non-defining relative clauses ...
don't have commas	use commas (or pauses in spoken English)
use the following relative pronouns: *who, which, whose, where, when* and *why*	use the following relative pronouns: *who, which, whose, where* and *when*
can use *that* instead of *who* or *which*	don't use *that*
Who, which or *that* can be omitted when they are the object of the clause: *The eye drops (–/which/that) the optician gave me should be used twice a day.*	The relative pronoun cannot be omitted.

PRACTICE

1 Choose the correct relative pronoun.

1 Vienna, *which / where / whose* is the capital of Austria, is a city famous for its history and culture.

2 Melanie, *who / whose / which* mother is from Kyoto, speaks English and Japanese fluently.

3 This phone, *who / which / where* I bought on holiday, takes absolutely superb photos.

4 Buckingham Palace, *which / where / whose* members of the British royal family live, is located in the centre of London.

5 Ms Wilde, *who / which / where* is my physics teacher, is going to retire in the near future.

6 The film star Russell Crowe, *which / who / whose* has starred in numerous successful films, was born in New Zealand.

2 Complete the sentences with a relative pronoun.

1 The abstract painting .... was damaged by yesterday's fire is being repaired.

2 The place .... the lorry had been abandoned was a pedestrian precinct.

3 The reason .... I came here early this morning is not of any significance.

4 The doctor .... I was hoping to see wasn't on duty when I arrived at the medical centre.

5 The woman .... spoke at the meeting was very knowledgeable.

6 That's the owner .... vicious dog ferociously attacked the postman.

THIRD CONDITIONAL

We use a third conditional to talk about:

- something which did not happen in the past and its results, which are imaginary:
If you had texted me yesterday, I would not have forgotten that I had an appointment at the hospital. (You didn't text me yesterday and I forgot I had an appointment at the hospital.)
If he hadn't jumped out of the way of the speeding car, it would have run him over. (He jumped out of the way of the speeding car, so it didn't run him over.)

Notes

- We can contract the third conditional as follows:
If you'd texted me yesterday, I wouldn't have forgotten that I had an appointment at the hospital.
- We can use *could* and *might* instead of *would*:
If I had revised better for the exam, I could have passed it. (I had the ability to pass the exam, but I didn't pass it, because I didn't revise well enough.)
If the temperature had been slightly higher, we might have had a picnic in the countryside. (The picnic was a possibility.)
If the temperature had been slightly higher, we would have had a picnic in the countryside. (The picnic was a certainty.)

MIXED CONDITIONALS

- When we want to use a conditional sentence to talk about both the past and the present, we can use the second conditional in one part of the sentence and third conditional in the other:
If the cost of even the cheapest seats wasn't so high (2nd conditional, present time), *we'd have gone to see the opera* (3rd conditional, past time).
The cost of even the cheapest seats is high and that is why the speaker didn't go to see the opera.
If the runner hadn't collapsed fifty metres from the finishing line (3rd conditional, past time), *she would be the winner* (2nd conditional, present time).
The runner collapsed fifty metres from the finishing line and that is why she isn't the winner this year.
Note: You cannot use zero or first conditionals in mixed conditional sentences.

Wish or hope?

Optimistic about something? Use *hope*.	*I hope everybody arrives on time, so that our departure isn't delayed.*
Pessimistic about something happening, or sure it won't happen? Use *wish*.	
Talking about a present situation? Use *wish* + past simple.	*I wish I had an American work permit.* *She wishes she had more time to complete the project.*
Talking about something you would like to happen or something you would like someone to do? Use *wish* + *would*.	*I wish you would be more considerate towards the others in the group.* *He wishes his children would make a greater effort at school.*
Talking about past time? Use *wish* + past perfect.	*I wish I hadn't taken your advice about accepting that position in the sales department.* *She wished she hadn't set out on the journey.*

PRACTICE

1 **Choose the correct verb tense.**

1 If the bank .... to give me a loan, I wouldn't have bought that expensive motorbike.

   A didn't agree **B** doesn't agree **C** hadn't agreed

2 I wouldn't have stayed at that luxury resort, if you .... it to me.

   A didn't recommend **B** don't recommend
   C hadn't recommended

3 She would have been seriously injured in that multiple car crash if she .... her seat belt.

   A wouldn't wear **B** didn't wear **C** hadn't worn

4 If you .... for my support, I would have willingly helped you in any way I could.

   A had asked **B** asked **C** ask

5 I would have been extremely disappointed, if you .... with us on holiday.

   A don't come **B** hadn't come **C** wouldn't have come

6 If he .... rushing to take his pregnant wife to the maternity clinic, he wouldn't have driven through the traffic light on red.

   A wasn't **B** hadn't been **C** wouldn't be

2 **Complete the third conditional sentences with the verb in brackets.**

1 If you .... (not / arrive) late at the check-in desk, we .... (not / miss) our international flight.

2 If they .... (go) to bed at a reasonable time, they .... (not / wake up) so late.

3 If she .... (enrol) in the advanced course at art school, she .... (might get) that fabulous job as a fashion designer.

4 If you .... (be) born in that part of Switzerland, you probably .... (learn) to speak three languages.

5 If Ben .... (not go) on that motorbike trip round South America, he .... (never meet) his future wife.

6 She .... (take) a taxi from the railway station, if she .... (have) enough money.

WISH, IF ONLY AND HOPE

Wish, if only

- We use *wish* / *if only* + past simple to say we would like a present situation to be different:
  I wish I lived in a villa overlooking the sea. (I don't live in a villa overlooking the sea now.)
  If only it was the end of the summer term! (But it isn't – it's the middle of the summer term.)
  Note: This use of *wish* / *if only* is similar to the second conditional, as it uses a past tense to refer to something which is contrary to the facts in the present.

- We use *wish* / *if only* + *would* to say if we want:
  - something to happen:
    I wish that terrible noise would stop. (I can't make it stop and I want it to stop.)
  - someone to start doing something they don't do:
    If only you'd do the washing up occasionally!
  - someone to stop doing something which annoys us:
    If only friends wouldn't keep asking me to go out when I'm trying to revise!

- We use *wish* / *if only* + past perfect to talk about things which we are unhappy about which happened in the past:
  He wishes he had completed the project by the deadline. (He didn't complete the project by the deadline – perhaps if he had completed it, he would have been promoted.)
  Note: This use of *wish* / *if only* is similar to the third conditional, i.e. it uses a past perfect tense to refer to something which is contrary to the facts in the past.

- *If only* means 'I wish'. When talking about other people, we use *he wishes*, *they wish*, etc. We use *if only* when we feel something very strongly. Otherwise we use *I wish*.

Hope

- We use *hope* when we want something to happen or to be true, and usually have a good reason to think that it might:
  I hope you make lots of friends when you are abroad.
  She hopes her parents will enjoy themselves on their world cruise.
  Note: We use *hope* + present/future tense with a future meaning, especially when the subject of the two clauses is different, i.e. *I* and *you* in **I** hope **you** make lots of friends when **you** are abroad.

- We often use *hope* + infinitive when there is only one subject to the sentence:
  She hopes to work in the field of entertainment after college.

- We can use *hope* when we want something to be true about the past, but we don't know if it is true:
  I hope you had a brilliant honeymoon. (But I don't know if you had a brilliant honeymoon.) –

PRACTICE

1 Complete the sentences with the verb in the simple past or with *would*.

1 I wish I .... (had) a really well-paid job.

2 If only I .... (can) meet some people who are more motivating.

3 I wish that tap in the kitchen .... (stop) dripping. It's driving me crazy!

4 If only he .... (start) being more responsible.

5 I wish I .... (weigh) a little bit less.

6 If only my mother .... (not keep) texting me asking if I'm all right.

2 Tick the correct sentences. Correct the sentences with mistakes.

1 He wishes he has chosen a different course at college.

2 I hope you made lots of money when you start your new business.

3 We really hope the children will behave well at school next term.

4 He hopes get a job in engineering after college.

5 We all hope you had managed to get a visa for your trip to the USA.

6 He hopes he will have success with his job application.

13

CAUSATIVE *HAVE* AND *GET*

- We use **have/get** + **something** + **past participle** (*cleaned/fixed/made/repaired*, etc.), when we ask someone else to do something for us:
  I've just had my car serviced. (i.e. Someone has serviced my car.)

- *get* is less formal than *have*:
  I usually get my car washed at the weekend.
  We have just got the week's shopping delivered from the supermarket.

- It's not usually necessary to say who did it for us, but it is possible:
  I'm going to get the light fixed by an electrician.

- *have/get* + something + *done* can be used in any tense or form:
  I'm going to get the trouser bottoms of my new suit shortened for the interview.

- We can also use this structure with *have* to say we have been the victim of something:
  I had my passport and driving licence stolen while I was travelling on the underground.

PRACTICE

1 Complete the sentences with the correct form of *have* or *get* and a verb from the box.

cut	deliver	dry clean	service	steal

1 I .... my hair .... at that new salon near the station tomorrow.

2 We .... a supply of logs .... for the wood burner yesterday.

3 You should .... your suit .... for the wedding.

4 She .... her handbag .... while she was on the bus.

5 .... your car .... at the garage on the high street?

EXPRESSING OBLIGATION AND PERMISSION

Obligation – *must* and *have to*

- We can often use *must* and *have to* without any difference in meaning:
  Surgeons have to / must carry out their operations conscientiously and professionally to ensure their patients make a swift recovery.

- We use *must* + infinitive without *to* in the present tense. For other tenses, we use *have to* + infinitive:
  I'd love to go on an adventure holiday, but I'll have to save up enough money first.

In order to get a tourist visa for the USA, I had to fill in an online application form and make an online payment.

- We use *have to* more often in questions:
  Do we have to complete all sections in the survey?

- We use *must* for a goal (or an obligation) that we give ourselves:
  I must make a bigger effort to meet the targets I set myself.

- We use *have to* when the obligation comes from someone else:
  My manager has just handed me a list of jobs that I have to complete by Friday at the latest.

- We use *must* for strong advice:
  You must be extremely attentive when you start learning how to handle birds of prey.

Other ways of expressing obligation

- We use *be supposed to* + infinitive to talk about an obligation which is different from what really happens:
  We're supposed to do circuit training for two hours a day. (But most people do much less.)
  Aren't you supposed to be doing group work now? (i.e. not chatting with friends over coffee)
- We use *should* + infinitive without *to* to talk about the right thing to do, but which is different from what really happens:
  You should always use your own words when you write an essay, not copy texts you have found on the internet.
- The past of *should* is *should have* + past participle:
  You shouldn't have answered that question in only 150 words!
- We can use *ought to* to mean 'should':
  In some cultures, young people are taught that they ought to be especially respectful towards older people.

Permission

- To express permission, we use *can* (past *could*), *let*, *allowed to* and *may* (past *was/were allowed to*):
  You can drive to college, but you must park your vehicles in the spaces allocated to students.
  Am I allowed to use my student identity card to get reduced fares on public transport?
  She let him copy her notes before the exam.

- We use *may* in formal situations:
  You may go and wait outside the interview room when you have completed the questionnaire.

- To say that there is no obligation, or it's not necessary, we use *don't have to*, *don't need to* and *needn't*:
  You don't have to take your shoes off, if you don't want to, but it is expected when you are invited into most homes in Sweden.
  You needn't wear a suit and tie for this job, but it's important to dress smartly.

- *I didn't need to* means 'It wasn't necessary and I didn't do it'; *I needn't have* means 'It wasn't necessary but I did it':
  I didn't need to read the novel to find out about the plot of the story because I'd already seen the film.
  You needn't have bothered to bring a present, but thanks very much anyway. It's much appreciated.

PRACTICE

1 Choose the correct verb in *italics*.

1 Do we *have to / must* leave now?

2 I *must / have* try to modify my behaviour and be more punctual.

3 The police warned me that I *might / must* never drive without insurance again.

4 We're *supposed to / should* follow all of the club rules.

5 You *should / supposed to* never cheat in an exam or copy other students' homework.

6 In my country, men accept that they *may / ought to* offer their seat to women on public transport.

7 You *can / must* buy lunch in the canteen or bring a sandwich if you prefer.

2 Tick the correct sentences. Correct the sentences with mistakes.

1 You are not let to park in front of the entrance.

2 The teacher allowed them to use calculators in the maths test.

3 You may leave the room when you have finished the exam.

4 I wish I hadn't put a coat on. I didn't need to do as now I'm too hot.

5 You needn't wear casual clothes on 'dress-down Friday', but most people do.

6 I needn't have bothered to buy a return ticket because my friend offered me a lift home.

7 The film star was hoping to have a quiet night, but he got recognised at the restaurant.

14

THE PASSIVE

The passive is formed from the verb *to be* + past participle (*done/eaten/cleaned*, etc.).

active	passive
They washed all the dirty plates by hand.	All the dirty plates were washed by hand.
It's helpful when people keep you well informed.	It's helpful when you're kept well informed.
The bedroom walls are not soundproof, so you can hear the neighbour's alarm in the morning.	The neighbour's alarm can be heard in the morning, as the bedroom walls are not soundproof.
We've packed all our cases ready for the move.	Our cases have all been packed ready for the move.

We use the passive when:

- what happens is more important than who does it:
  The roof on our holiday cottage has been replaced, so we can stay there in the spring now.

- we don't know who or what does/did something:
  My passport and my driving licence have been removed from the safe in my hotel room.

- we don't need to say who or what does/did something because it's obvious from the situation or context:
  Finally, the new international fishing regulations were accepted. (obviously by a government or by the fishing industry)

- when writing in an official style:
  A double room has been reserved for you for two nights on the 14th and 15th of May. We respectfully inform you that the room must be vacated at 11 am on the day of departure.

THE PASSIVE WITH *GET*

In informal English we can sometimes use *get* instead of *be* to form the passive, especially when we want to say that something bad happened to someone or something:
Our fridge-freezer got damaged during the move. (Formal: *Our fridge-freezer was damaged*)
She got seriously injured while climbing in the Alps. (*She was seriously injured*)
He got fined £100 for speeding.

The passive with *get* is not possible with state verbs: ~~*The chalet in the Swiss Alps got owned by a famous footballer.*~~ *The chalet is owned by a famous footballer.*

THE PASSIVE WITH REPORTING VERBS

We often use the passive to report what people say or think, especially when we don't know who said it or thought it, or it's not important:
Some of the younger members of the royal family are reported to be skiing in Scotland.
Charlie Chaplin is considered to be one of the most creative film stars ever.

This use of the passive is common in news reports:

He/She is *said/thought/considered* + infinitive:
Edward is thought to be one of our star pupils.
Pickpockets are known to operate in gangs near the station.

Verbs that we can use with this pattern are:
consider, expect, feel, know, say, suppose, think, understand
To talk about the past, we can use:

- the perfect infinitive, e.g. *He/She is said to have played/ eaten/been*, etc:
  The head teacher is understood to have spoken to Martin's parents about his appalling behaviour on the school trip.

- It is *said/thought/considered*, etc. + *that*:
  It is said that this breed of dog is very good for hunting.
  It is known that criminals operate in this area.

Verbs that we can use with this pattern are:
agree, consider, decide, expect, feel, find, know, propose, recommend, say, suggest, suppose, think, understand

- It is *agreed/planned* + infinitive:
  It has been agreed to alter the dates for moving into the new apartment without extra charge.

Verbs that we can use with this pattern are:
agree, decide, forbid, hope, plan, propose

PRACTICE

1 Make the sentences passive.

1 A member of the hotel staff opened the safe for me.
2 You can find lots of bargains at the market.
3 You can buy tickets for the event online.
4 People thought that children were to blame for the damage to the trees.
5 Someone took my phone out of my jacket pocket.
6 They've replaced the winter tyres on my car.

2 Choose the correct option.

1 Our antique chairs and sofa .... using high-quality materials.
   A were restored   B was restored   C been restored
2 My bag with all my money and cards .... at the station.
   A been stolen   B were stolen   C was stolen
3 The man in the picture .... for questioning by the police.
   A had wanted   B gets wanted   C is wanted
4 Your train tickets .... and you can collect them from a ticket machine at any mainline station.
   A had been reserved   B have been reserved
   C have reserved
5 Their car .... badly damaged in the collision.
   A been   B had   C got
6 They .... for theft.
   A were arrested   B been arrested   C arrested

3 Tick the correct sentences. Correct the sentences with mistakes.

1 Some football supporters been reported to be engaging in antisocial behaviour.
2 Pele considered to have been the best footballer of all time.
3 Homeless people are know to sleep in cardboard boxes under that bridge.
4 The manager is understood have praised the technicians for their outstanding commitment to their work.
5 It is planned to shut down the factory for a month in the summer.
6 It has been decided to buy new uniforms for the airline ground staff.

USED TO, GET/BE USED TO

positive	negative	question
used to + infinitive	*did not / didn't use to* + infinitive	*Did … use to* + infinitive?

- We use *used to* when we refer to things in the past which are no longer true. It refers to:
  - repeated actions:
    I used to eat in the college cafeteria, but now I bring a packed lunch.
  - a state or situation:
    That mountain bike used to belong to my best friend. (It belonged to my best friend in the past, but not any more.)

- In **positive** statements, the form *used to* does not change. We do not use the verb *be* before it and it always refers to the past:
  *They **used to** go to the sports club three times a week when they lived in London.*
  Not: ~~They are used to go …~~ or ~~They use to go …~~

- In **negative** statements we use *didn't use to*:
  *I **didn't use to** get very good marks in exams, but this term I'm really pleased with my results.*

- If we want to be very formal, we can use the negative form *used not to*:
  She used not to be as wealthy as she is now.

Emphatic *did*

We can use *did* with *use to* to emphasise a point.
I never used to be on friendly terms with people at the gym, but I did use to say hi to them when I arrived. (Don't use this form in written exams.)

Questions

In questions we use *did + use to*:
You look familiar. Did you use to be in the same class as me in primary school?

Tags

We normally use *did* to make tags after *used to*:
So, she used to teach you English literature, did she?
When we first started going out, we used to love eating in nice restaurants, didn't we?

Used to or *would*?

We can use both *used to* and *would* to talk about people's habits in the past. When we use them both together, *used to* generally comes first, because it sets the scene for what follows:
When I was about twelve, I used to create amazing models. I would make steam engines that really worked and I would fold ordinary paper to produce boomerangs that actually flew back to you.

However, you CAN'T use *would* to describe a state or situation, which is no longer true:
We used to work in Chicago. Not: ~~We would work in Chicago.~~

Be used to

Be used to can refer to the past, present or future. It means 'be accustomed to' or 'be familiar with'.

- *be used to* + noun or noun phrase:
  I work in a fast food restaurant, so I'm used to lots of customers.
- *be used to* + pronoun:
  She was brought up in the countryside and hates pollution. She's not used to it.
- *be used to* + the *-ing* form of a verb:
  He was a surgeon until he retired, so he was used to working in demanding situations.

Get/become used to

College life can be very stressful, but don't worry. You'll soon get used to it. (Or, more formally, *You'll soon become used to it.*)

PRACTICE

1 **Complete the sentences with the positive, negative or question form of *used to* and the verb in brackets.**

1 I .... eating olives when I was a child, but I can't resist them now. (– / enjoy)

2 Her friends .... online shopping, but now they think it's great. (– / do)

3 They .... hours playing an addictive video game. (+ / spend)

4 My father .... a vintage Italian sports car. (+ / own)

5 .... he .... in touch with his relatives after they emigrated to Australia? (? / keep)

6 I .... being alone in the dark when I was young. (– / like)

2 **Tick the correct sentences. Correct the sentences with mistakes.**

1 My dad would tour with a circus as an acrobat before he got married.

2 I would work in a steel factory when I was in my twenties.

3 When she was younger, she would enjoy riding horses and would visit the stables every day.

4 I would live in New York State near the Great Lakes until I left to go to university in Washington.

5 When I was a kid I would play outside with my friends until it was quite dark and my mother called me to go in.

6 I didn't use to enjoy the taste of caviar until I spent a few months in Russia last year.

3 Complete the sentences with the correct form of *be/get used to*.

1 Having lived in Alaska all of her life, she .... the extremely low temperatures during the winter months.

2 He has just started work on a construction site. It's taken him a long time .... the noise and dust.

3 I'm completely exhausted. I .... working such long hours.

4 We've just started our university course. It's hard for us .... writing a 5,000-word essay every week.

5 I've just started a new job and everything is new and pretty confusing, but I .... the systems and routines.

6 Living on your own for the first time can be very demanding, but just relax. You'll soon .... coping with everything.

4 Complete the second sentence so that it has a similar meaning to the first sentence, using the word given.

1 Living in such overcrowded conditions appeared unusual to her.

NOT

She .... in such overcrowded conditions.

2 She is adjusting to her new lifestyle.

GETTING

She .... her new lifestyle.

3 In his home country, Dima was a trainee accountant.

USED

In his home country, Dima .... employed as a trainee accountant.

4 When we were on holiday, my friends relaxed by the pool after lunch.

WOULD

When we were on holiday, my friends .... by the pool after lunch.

THE POSITION OF ADVERBS AND ADVERB PHRASES

type of adverb	position	example
manner (how)	They usually go in the end position. They sometimes go in the mid position if the adverb is not the most important part of the clause or if the predicate is very long.	*He drank hurriedly.* *She hurriedly drank her coffee and left without speaking.*
place (where)	They usually go in the end position. They can occasionally go in the front position, especially in writing.	*Could you please move over there?* *We'll be sitting on the sofa over there.* *Inside, there was a lot of antique furniture.*
time (when)	They usually go in the end position. They occasionally go in the front position, especially if we want to emphasise the adverb.	*I'm leaving for the Antarctic next week.* *Tonight, I'm going to complete my project! I promise!*
duration (how long)	They usually go in the end position.	*I can assure you that the meeting won't last long.*
frequency (how often)	They can usually go in mid, front and end position. But *always*, *ever* and *never* do not usually go in the front position.	*We often eat out at the weekend.* *I usually have a late breakfast at the weekend.* *Sometimes, we went deep-sea fishing on holiday.* *We don't hear the neighbours very often now.* *I could never type very fast.* Not: ~~Never could I type~~ *very fast.*
degree (how much)	*Really*, *very* and *quite* usually go in the mid position. *A lot* and *a bit* usually go in the end position.	*I really admire his ability to speak in public with such confidence.* *We go skiing in Scotland a lot.* *I must admit that I'd like to change the recipe a bit.*
viewpoint (opinion)	They usually go outside the clause, often at the beginning.	*Personally, I'd rather not go out this evening.*
evaluative	They usually go outside the clause, often at the beginning.	*Unfortunately, I forgot my sports gear, so I had to sit on the side and watch the match.*

PRACTICE

1 Choose the best place, A or B, for the adverb in each sentence.

1 _[A]_ she _[B]_ left the meeting before the chairperson started marking her closing remarks. (quickly)

2 Can you arrive for the interview _[A]_ at _[B]_ eight o'clock? We want to make a prompt start with the selection process. (exactly)

3 _[A]_ what his role as a careers adviser is all about, is making sure that his clients receive up-to-date information to _[B]_ match their specific needs. (basically)

4 There is an expectation that effective managers should _[A]_ speak _[B]_ to their staff about their strengths and weaknesses and offer sound advice on how to improve. (frankly)

5 _[A]_ I can't support your application _[B]_ for the post of assistant manager. (personally)

6 _[A]_ all the documents relating to the purchase of the property _[B]_ were destroyed in a fire. (apparently)

7 Everybody else has had their test results, but I haven't heard anything yet, so _[A]_ I haven't _[B]_ passed. (presumably)

8 It was _[A]_ made clear in the letter to all staff that bonuses would _[B]_ be suspended for the rest of the year because of the company's weak financial position. (regrettably)

2 Tick the correct sentences. Correct the sentences with mistakes.

1 Seriously he spoke about the problem.

2 Surprisingly, he is one of the country's leading experts in criminal investigation.

3 Frankly, she discussed her personal problems with her counsellor.

4 They will be arriving shortly on the hopefully delayed flight from Berlin.

5 The explanation was not clearly sufficient to satisfy everybody's curiosity.

6 Sadly, I have to inform you that your application for the post has been unsuccessful.

FUTURE PERFECT SIMPLE AND FUTURE PERFECT CONTINUOUS

Future perfect simple: *will have* + past participle

positive	negative	question
I will have left by the time you read this note.	*She won't have finished the project* by next week, in my opinion.	*Will you have had* breakfast by the time I arrive?

Future perfect continuous: *will have been* + present participle

positive	negative	question
I will have been working here for ten years by 2022.	*She won't have been waiting* for more than ten minutes, by the time we get there.	*Will they really have been learning* English for five years, when they take the exam?

We use both the future perfect simple and the future perfect continuous to project ourselves forward in time and to look back. The future perfect simple tense refers to a completed action in the future and the future perfect continuous refers to events or actions that are currently unfinished, but will be finished at some future time. Both tenses are usually used with time expressions.

future perfect simple	future perfect continuous
refers to a completed action in the future: *Hurry up, or the concert will have started by the time we get there.* *She will have eaten all her sandwiches by the time she gets to the top of the hill.* *They will have finished the new road by this time next month.*	refers to actions that are currently unfinished but will be finished in the future: *At six o'clock, we will have been waiting for the bus for half an hour.* *She will be exhausted when she gets home because she will have been running for over two hours.* *They will have been building that road for over a year by the time it's finished.*

Note: Some non-action verbs, or state verbs, e.g. *be, know, seem, like, hate* are not used in the continuous form: *On Thursday, I will have known you for over two years.* (Not: ~~On Thursday, I will have been knowing you for over two years.~~) *I will have eaten fifty mince pies by the end of the Christmas holiday.* (Not: ~~I will have been eating fifty mince pies by the end of the Christmas holiday.~~)

PRACTICE

1 Complete the sentences with the future perfect simple or continuous form of the verb in brackets.

1 By the end of the next decade, most people in America .... (drive) hybrid cars for several years.

2 Next week my best friends .... (be) married for a year.

3 I .... (live) in London for nearly two years when I finish my training course.

4 Next month Sylvia .... (work) in the hospital for 20 years, so she can answer all your questions.

5 I think they .... (reach) their hotel by now.

6 My grandfather .... (retire) by the end of the year at the age of 75!

7 I bet there will be some great food at the party. My mum .... (cook) all day.

8 How long .... (study) when you finally get your Master's degree?

9 Next week we .... (know) each other for exactly ten years. We should celebrate!

10 How much do you think you .... (earn) by the end of the year?

2 **Tick the correct sentences. Correct the sentences with mistakes.**

1 By the end of the day, I will have been learning all the new words on that list.

2 This time tomorrow we will have been working here for exactly a month.

3 Sorry I'm late. How long have you waited for me?

4 I think she will have been playing tennis all morning, so she'll be pretty tired.

5 By the time we get home, we will have been walking 20 miles. That's quite impressive!

6 They will have travelled all day so they'll want to go to bed early.

Phrasal verbs

Phrasal verbs consist of a verb with a preposition or adverb or both. The meaning of the phrasal verb is different from the meaning of its separate parts. The following are all phrasal verbs:

phrasal verb	definition
to be into sth	to be interested in something
to book sb into	to reserve a place for somebody at a hotel/event
to break up	to finish school/college at end of the term/year
to bring up	to introduce (a topic in a discussion)
to burst out	to suddenly start doing something (laughing/crying)
to calm sb down	to stop somebody feeling angry, upset or excited
to check in	to arrive and register at a hotel or airport
to check out	to leave a hotel after paying and returning your room key
to cheer up	to become happy
to copy out	to write a written text again on a piece of paper
to devote sth to sth	to use time, energy, etc. for a particular purpose
to drop out	to fail to complete something (a university course / a race)
to fall behind	to not make progress
to get away	to leave or escape from a person or place
to get back	to return
to get on	to board a plane/train/ferry/bus
to get through	to complete successfully
to go away	to go on holiday
to go over	to examine or look at something in a careful or detailed way
to hand in	to give something (homework) to a teacher
to hand out	to give something (worksheet) to each of a number of people
to keep up with	to progress or travel at the same rate/speed as others
to listen up	to pay attention
to look through	to quickly read
to make up	to invent
to pick out	to identify (details)

phrasal verb	definition
to point out	to direct someone's attention to someone or something
to pull out	to drive from the side of the road onto a different part of the road
to pull over	to drive to the side of the road and stop
to pull up	to stop in a vehicle
to read out	to read words aloud so that other people can hear
to read up on sth	to spend time reading in order to find out information about something
to refer to sb or sth	to talk or write about somebody or something, especially briefly
to rub out	to erase
to run into sb	to meet someone you know when you are not expecting to
to run into sth	to crash into something (in a vehicle or on a bike)
to set out	to start a journey
to shut up	to stop talking or making a noise, or to make somebody stop doing this
to speak up	to speak loudly and distinctly OR to express an opinion freely
to stand for	to mean
to stand up for	to defend
to stay over	to sleep overnight (often at someone's house)
to stop over	to stay somewhere for one night or more when you are travelling to somewhere else
to take off	to leave the ground and fly (of an aircraft)
to take up	to become interested or engaged in a sport or hobby
to talk sb into sth	to persuade someone to do something
to talk sth over	to discuss a problem or situation with someone, often to find out their opinion or to get advice before making a decision about it
to tell sb off	to express disapproval to someone for doing something bad
to turn up	to arrive or appear somewhere, usually unexpectedly

PHRASAL VERBS USED IN THREE THEMES (COMMUNICATION, EDUCATION AND TRAVEL)

Communication

1 Choose the correct option in *italics*.

1 We had been discussing animal habitats, but then he suddenly brought *up / in / over* the topic of illegal hunting.

2 She burst *out / up / over* laughing when she heard my suggestion about the debate.

3 They were very upset when they heard the news, so I tried to calm them *under / over / down*.

4 She speaks about her daughter all the time, but hardly ever refers *on / with / to* her son.

5 The topic of flat rentals came *over / up / in* several times during the discussion.

6 She cheered *over / up / out* when she heard that her essay had been re-marked and that her grade had improved.

2 Complete the sentences with the correct form of a verb from the box.

> deal   get   give   look   note   shut

1 I wish they would stop shouting. I think I'll tell them to .... up.

2 The speaker .... with all the questions after his presentation without difficulty.

3 She .... her point of view across very skilfully.

4 In spite of her promise, she .... away all their secrets.

5 They .... down everything the speaker said yesterday.

6 She .... forward to her skydiving lesson tomorrow.

3 Tick the correct sentences. Correct the sentences with mistakes.

1 VIP stands to 'Very Important Person'.

2 He talked his best friend in applying for a job in sales.

3 She read out an extract from her essay to the class.

4 My parents taught me to stand in for my beliefs in all arguments.

5 He pointed over all the mistakes I had made in my email.

6 They talked the problem over and finally found a solution.

Education

1 Choose the correct preposition.

> off   out x 2   through   up x 2

1 He rubbed .... the mistakes in his homework before he handed it in.

2 He picked .... the key words in the text.

3 She looked .... the chapter again.

4 She made .... a very interesting ending to her story.

5 They spoke .... clearly and confidently in the debate.

6 The teacher told him .... for being impolite.

2 Match the beginnings and endings of these sentences.

1 They broke up

2 He didn't get through

3 I handed in

4 He devotes a lot of time to

5 She's started falling behind

6 Going over

a the course and will have to redo it next year.

b for the summer holidays on the 20th of July.

c the sciences, as he is hoping to be a physicist.

d in some classes and may need to have extra coaching.

e your notes the night before the exam isn't the best revision technique.

f my homework early, so I'd be free at the weekend.

3 Tick the correct sentences. Correct the sentences with mistakes.

1 He dropped out university after the first year.

2 The teacher told her that she needed to read up in her British history.

3 Could you copy out this list exactly as it is in the textbook?

4 Could you hand the exam papers out, please?

5 They have taken over drama as one of their optional subjects.

6 Can you all listen on, please? I've got an important announcement to make.

Travel

1 **Complete the sentences with a phrasal verb from the box.**

> booked into   check into   get away
> set out   stop over   took off

1 I think it's important to .... from everything and have a proper holiday.

2 I'm afraid you'll have to wait to .... your room, as it isn't quite ready.

3 We .... our friends .... the same hotel as us, but couldn't get them the same rate.

4 They .... on the last leg of their journey up the Amazon in the early hours.

5 The plane .... several hours late because of dreadful weather conditions.

6 We're going to .... in Hong Kong on our way to Australia.

2 **Match the beginnings and endings of these sentences.**

1 He pulled his car

2 They ran into the castle to get

3 The slow old coach could not keep

4 The police car signalled for her to stop, so she

5 They decided to check

6 They didn't get

a out early and just have a light continental breakfast.

b back from their weekend break until after midnight.

c up with the other vehicles on the motorway.

d pulled up immediately.

e away from the large group of tourists.

f over to the side of the road when he heard a knocking noise.

3 **Choose the correct option in *italics*.**

1 He was driving over the speed limit on a narrow country lane when he ran *in / into / up* a tree.

2 It was raining heavily and they had no protective clothing, so they stayed *over / down / up* in the remote village.

3 He turned *up / over / on* an hour late, but he had a good reason and was very apologetic.

4 We got *on / at / over* the ferry and then just relaxed and enjoyed the crossing.

5 He pulled *out / on / at* without looking in his rear mirror and collided with a van.

6 We went *over / away / out* on holiday to a tropical island.

Speaking bank

SPEAKING PART 1

1 Read about Part 1 of the Speaking paper.

In Part 1 of the Speaking paper, an examiner asks you personal questions about familiar topics. In Part 1:

- you are with another candidate, but you only speak to the examiner, not the other candidate
- an examiner asks you questions about yourself, and you answer
- the questions are about everyday topics such as your family, your home town, likes and dislikes, your work or studies, free time, travel, celebrations and your future plans.

2 Read the tips.

> To get a good mark in Part 1 of the Speaking paper:
> - you should listen to the questions carefully and make sure you answer the exact questions the examiner asks you
> - you should use full sentences to answer the questions
> - you should add reasons, examples or extra information to support your answers
> - you should express your own opinions
> - if you don't understand a question, you should ask the examiner to repeat it
> - you should try to relax and answer the questions in a natural way.

3 Read some typical Part 1 questions. Match each question with a topic (a–e).

1 What do you like about your home town?
2 What kind of job would you like to do in the future?
3 How do people usually celebrate New Year in your country?
4 When do you usually spend time with your family?
5 What do you normally do at the weekend?
6 Tell us about an enjoyable trip that you went on.
7 Which country would you most like to visit?
8 Which subject did you most enjoy when you were at school?
9 What's the most important festival in your country?
10 What do you enjoy doing in your free time?

a Personal and family life
b Hobbies and free time
c Work and studies
d Travel
e Celebrations

4 Read and listen to Sofia's answers to four of the questions in Exercise 3. Does she add more information in every answer?

Examiner: What do you like about your home town?

Sofia: [1]Well, I'm from Milan, in the north of Italy. It's a big city, and I enjoy living there because there's always lots to do, like going to the cinema or music concerts. There are also a lot of young people there, [2]so I like that as well.

Examiner: What do you enjoy doing in your free time?

Sofia: Well, I'm quite a sporty person, so I do a lot of exercise. [3]For example, I go to the gym two or three times a week, and I play tennis. I also enjoy spending time with my friends.

Examiner: Which country would you most like to visit?

Sofia: I would love to go to Australia. [4]The reason for this is that I like hot weather and I love going to the beach. The beaches in Australia look amazing. I also think the way of life in Australia is quite relaxed, having barbecues and things like that, so I think I'd enjoy that.

Examiner: Which subject did you most enjoy when you were at school?

Sofia: [5]Could you repeat that, please?

Examiner: Yes. Which subject did you most enjoy when you were at school?

Sofia: That was definitely geography, because I'm really interested in different countries, and I love learning about how people live in other parts of the world. [6]I had a very good geography teacher at school too, and I think he made the subject very interesting.

[1] Use full sentences in your answer.
[2] Give your own opinions.
[3] Add examples to support your answers.
[4] Add reasons to support your answers.
[5] Ask the examiner to repeat a question if necessary.
[6] Add extra information to make your answer longer.

5 Look at Sofia's answers again. Does she use full verb forms, e.g. *I am, I will*, or contracted forms, e.g. *I'm, I'll*?

6 Read the tip.

> - You will sound more fluent and relaxed if you use contracted verb forms like *I'm, I'll, I've, it's*.

7 The questions the examiner asks may be about the past, present or future, and it is important to listen carefully and answer correctly. Read six more questions. What do they ask about? Write *past*, *present* or *future*.

1 Tell us about your last holiday or trip. ....

2 How often do you watch TV? ....

3 Which sport would you like to try? ....

4 What things do you usually buy online? ....

5 Which famous person would you most like to meet?
....

6 What kinds of food did you dislike when you were younger? ....

8 Choose the most suitable verb form to complete the answers to the questions in Exercise 7.

1 I .... to Spain last month with some friends.
  A 've been   B would love to go   C went

2 I .... TV very often.
  A don't watch   B didn't watch
  C 'm not going to watch

3 I .... skiing because I think it's really good fun.
  A once tried   B 'd like to try   C love

4 I usually .... clothes online.
  A bought some   B buy my   C didn't buy many

5 I .... Ariana Grande because I think she's an amazing singer.
  A 've never met   B meet   C 'd love to meet

6 I .... ice cream!
  A hated   B hate   C 'd hate

9 Write the words and expressions in the box next to the correct function.

> also   as well   because   for example
> for instance   like   plus   such as   too
> the reason for this is that

1 adding extra information ....

2 giving a reason ....

3 giving an example ....

10 Choose the correct options in *italics* to complete Bruno's answers to three more questions. Listen and check.

Examiner: In what ways do you think you will use English in the future?

Bruno: I think I'll use English for my job in the future. **(1)** *The reason for this is that / Such as* I want to work for an international company, so probably everyone will speak English to each other. I'll probably use it for travelling **(2)** *too / also*, because I'd like to travel and visit lots of different countries.

Examiner: What do you usually do on your birthday?

Bruno: I usually see my family on my birthday **(3)** *also / because* they like to wish me a happy birthday and they might have presents for me. Then in the evening I usually get together with some friends and do something, **(4)** *as well / like* go for a meal together.

Examiner: What kind of music do you enjoy listening to?

Bruno: I really enjoy R&B music. **(5)** *For instance / Too* I like American singers like Rihanna. I'm **(6)** *as well / also* keen on classical music because I find it very relaxing.

11 Practise answering some of the Part 1 questions in this section. Try to relax and talk about yourself in a natural way.

SPEAKING PART 2

1 **Read about Part 2 of the Speaking paper.**

In Part 2 of the Speaking paper, you are given a one-minute 'long turn'. In Part 2:

- the examiner will give you two photographs on a similar topic and ask you to compare them and answer a question
- the question you have to answer is written above the photographs
- you speak on your own for around one minute, and no one will interrupt you
- your partner will talk about a different set of photographs
- when your partner has finished speaking, the examiner will ask you a question about your partner's photographs. You will have around 30 seconds to answer this question.

2 **Read the tips.**

To get a good mark in Part 2 of the Speaking paper:

- you should compare the two photographs and say what is similar and different about them, rather than just describing them
- you should always make it clear which photograph you are talking about
- you should focus equally on both photographs, rather than just talking about one of them
- you should speculate about what is happening in the photographs and how the people are feeling
- you should make sure you allow enough time to answer the question after you have finished comparing the photographs
- you should listen carefully while your partner is answering, so you can answer the question the examiner will ask you.

3 **Read the exam task and look at the photographs. What topic connects the two photographs? What question do you have to answer?**

Examiner: In this part of the test I'm going to give each of you two photographs. I'd like you to talk about your photographs on your own for about a minute, and also to answer a question about your partner's photographs. Tania, it's your turn first. Here are your photographs. They show people on holiday. I'd like you to compare the photographs and say why you think the people chose these holidays.

4 Read and listen to the model answer. Does the student say why the people have chosen the holidays?

MODEL ANSWER

[1]Both pictures show people on holiday, but they're different kinds of holidays. [2]The people in the first photo are in the countryside, [3]whereas the second photo shows a big city. [4]It looks as if the people in the first photo are on a walking holiday, because they've got backpacks and a map. [3]On the other hand, the other people are probably doing some sightseeing. They seem to be up in a tower, and they're taking a selfie. Another difference is that the people in the city [5]look happy and relaxed, whereas the people in the countryside look worried. I think they might be lost. They don't look as happy as the people on the city break. I think the people in the first photo must enjoy walking. [6]Maybe they chose this holiday because they enjoy being in the countryside. I think the people in the second photo enjoy city life, so [6]I guess they probably chose to visit this city because there are lots of interesting things to see.

[1] Say what is similar about two photos.
[2] Make it clear which photo you are talking about.
[3] Use linking words to compare the photos and say what is different about them.
[4] Speculate about what the people are doing.
[5] Say how you think the people are feeling.
[6] Answer the question when you have finished comparing the photos.

5 Complete the sentences for comparing and contrasting photographs with a word from the box. Listen and check.

as	both	difference	different	other	whereas

1 .... pictures show people on holiday.

2 They're .... kinds of holidays.

3 The people in the first photo are in the countryside, ... the second photo shows a big city.

4 On the .... hand, the other people are probably doing some sightseeing.

5 Another .... is that the people in the city look happy and relaxed.

6 They don't look .... happy as the people on the city break.

6 Match the beginnings and endings of these sentences for speculating about photos. Listen and check.

1 It looks as   **a** be up in a tower.

2 They're probably doing   **b** think they might be lost.

3 They seem to   **c** if they're on a walking holiday.

4 They look   **d** walking.

5 I   **e** some sightseeing.

6 They must enjoy   **f** happy and relaxed.

7 Maybe they   **g** they probably chose to visit this city because there are lots of interesting things to see.

8 I guess   **h** chose this holiday because they enjoy being in the countryside.

7 Read the task and look at the photographs. Then listen to three students making mistakes when they complete the task. Match each speaker (1–3) with the mistake that they make (A–D). There is one answer you don't need.

A describes what they can see in both photos, but doesn't compare and contrast them

B focuses too much on one photo

C doesn't give any personal opinions about the photos

D compares and contrasts the photos but doesn't answer the question

Examiner: Here are your photographs. They show people preparing food. I'd like you to compare the photographs and say how the people might be feeling about the food they are preparing.

How might the people be feeling about the food they are preparing?

8 Read the task and look at the photographs. Complete the task, then listen to the model answer and compare your answers.

Examiner: Here are your photographs. They show people working. I'd like you to compare the photographs and say what you think might be difficult about the people's jobs.

What might be difficult about the people's jobs?

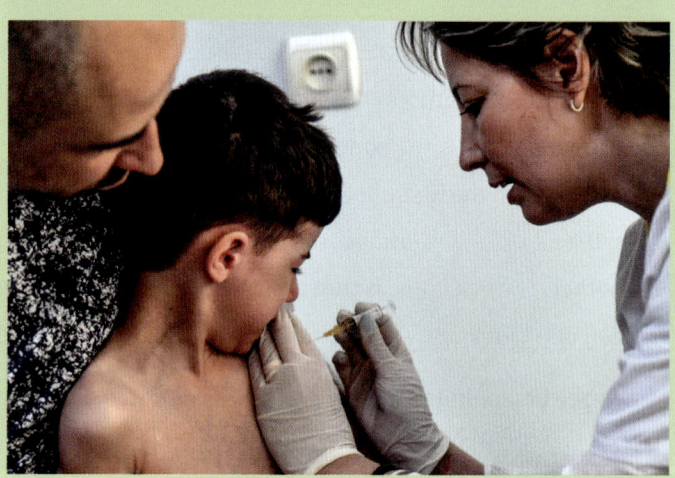

SPEAKING PART 3

1 **Read about Part 3 of the Speaking paper.**

Part 3 of the Speaking paper lasts for about three minutes, and you work with a partner. In Part 3:

- the examiner will explain an imaginary situation to you, then give you a piece of paper with written prompts that show different ideas or possibilities
- you must talk with your partner and discuss the prompts, giving your opinions about the different prompts
- you do not have to discuss all the prompts, but you should discuss most of them
- there is no right or wrong answer to the task
- the examiner will then ask you to try to reach agreement about something, and you do this with your partner
- you do not *have* to reach agreement with your partner, but you should try.

2 **Read the tips.**

To get a good mark in Part 3 of the Speaking paper:

- you should talk to your partner and listen to your partner – it is important to have a conversation with your partner, rather than just expressing your own ideas
- you should make suggestions and respond to suggestions that your partner makes
- you should express your own opinions on the different prompts and respond to your partner's opinions
- you should give reasons for your opinions
- you should try to reach agreement with your partner when the examiner asks you to.

3 **Read the exam task and read how the examiner will introduce it. What question do you have to discuss? How many prompts are there for you to discuss?**

Examiner: I'd like you to imagine that a hotel wants to attract more guests. Here are some ideas they're thinking about. Talk to each other about why these ideas would attract more guests to the hotel.

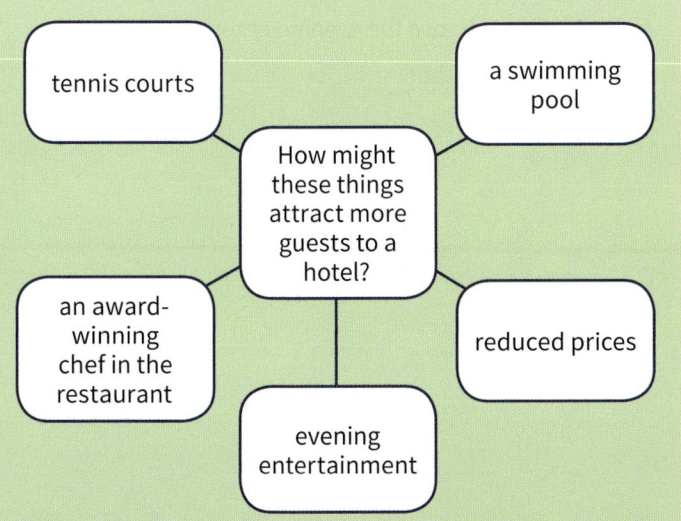

4 **Read and listen to Pablo and Marina completing the task. How many of the prompts do they discuss? Do they both express their opinions?**

Pablo: ¹Shall we start with tennis courts? This sounds like a good idea. A lot of people like playing tennis.

Marina: ²I can see what you mean, but not everyone likes tennis, and a lot of people go on holiday to relax, so they perhaps don't want to do sport. ³I think a swimming pool might be a better idea, because people of all ages can use a swimming pool. Do you agree?

Pablo: Yes, you're right. I hadn't thought about that. I agree that a swimming pool's a good idea because people like to sit by it even if they don't swim. ⁴What do you think about the idea of reduced prices? I think that would make a difference.

Marina: ⁵Yes, that's true. There are so many hotels to choose from, and people usually look at the price and try to find a bargain. But I'm not sure that price is enough on its own because people are often happy to pay a bit more money for a hotel with better facilities.

Pablo: ⁵Yes, I agree. I think evening entertainment might be a good idea, though. That's a bit different, too, because not many hotels offer it.

Marina: Yes, and it would be good if they offered entertainment for children too, not just adults.

Pablo: Yes, I completely agree with you. ⁴Do you think that having an award-winning chef would attract customers?

Marina: Yes, I do. Everyone loves good food, but a lot of hotels don't have very good restaurants. They could also open the restaurant to everyone, but offer cheaper prices for guests.

Pablo: That's a good idea. I think that would definitely encourage more people to stay at the hotel.

¹ Make suggestions to move the discussion to the different prompts.
² Use polite expressions if you disagree with your partner.
³ Give your own opinion, and give reasons to support it.
⁴ Ask for your partner's opinion.
⁵ Use a range of different expressions to agree with your partner.

5 Read the second task that the examiner gives the students, then read and listen to the students completing the task. Do they reach agreement?

Examiner: Now you have about a minute to decide which idea would be best for the hotel.

Marina: So, what do you think would be best for the hotel?

Pablo: I'd suggest either the swimming pool or the evening entertainment. Both those things are easy for people to see when they look on the website, and I think they would both be popular with guests.

Marina: Well, I think everyone enjoys a swimming pool, especially children and young people. But on the other hand, most people only use a swimming pool in the summer, whereas evening entertainment can continue all year, and, like we said, they could offer different entertainment for different ages.

Pablo: That's true, so shall we choose the evening entertainment?

Marina: Yes, let's go for that.

6 Listen to extracts from three more pairs of students completing the task in Exercise 3. What mistakes do the students make? Match each pair (1–3) with a common mistake (A–D). There is one mistake you don't need.

A The students talk about one prompt for too long, so don't have enough time to talk about the other prompts.

B The students talk for too long individually, don't listen to each other, and don't ask for each other's opinions.

C The students interrupt each other.

D The students talk about things that are not relevant to the task.

- Using expressions to make suggestions and asking for your partner's opinion is a good way of engaging your partner, and making sure that you have a conversation, rather than talking on your own for too long.

7 Match the beginnings and endings of the sentences to make suggestions. Listen and check.

1 It might be a good	**a** like a good idea.
2 Perhaps they	**b** idea to offer reduced prices.
3 Tennis courts sound	**c** offer entertainment for children, too.
4 They could	**d** an award-winning chef would be a good idea.
5 I would say that	**e** should have a swimming pool.

8 Choose the correct words to complete the questions you can use to ask your partner's opinion. Listen and check.

1 *Do / Are* you agree?

2 What *are / do* you think about the idea of a swimming pool?

3 *Will / Would* you agree with that?

4 *Do / May* you think that's true?

9 Complete the expressions for agreeing and disagreeing with a word from the box. Listen and check.

agree	better	but	mean
right	sure	that's	think

1 I .... so too.

2 Yes, ... true.

3 Yes, you're ....

4 I .... with you.

5 I can see what you .... but I think a swimming pool might be a .... idea.

6 I'm not .... about that.

7 Yes, that's true, ... on the other hand, entertainment would also be popular.

- It is important to use a polite expression like the ones in Exercise 9 when you disagree with your partner. It can seem rude to just say *No* or *I don't agree*.

10 Read and listen to the expressions for reaching agreement. (a) Which two expressions can you use to encourage your partner to reach agreement with you? (b) Which expression shows that you have reached an agreement?

1 I'd suggest either the swimming pool or the evening entertainment.

2 Are you OK with that?

3 My choice would be the reduced prices.

4 So, shall we choose the evening entertainment?

5 Yes, let's go for that.

11 Read an exam task and practise answering it with a
86 partner. Listen and compare your ideas.

Examiner: I'd like you to imagine that some people are
discussing modern technology. Here are things
that some people say it would be difficult to live
without. Talk to each other about why it would
be difficult to live without these things.

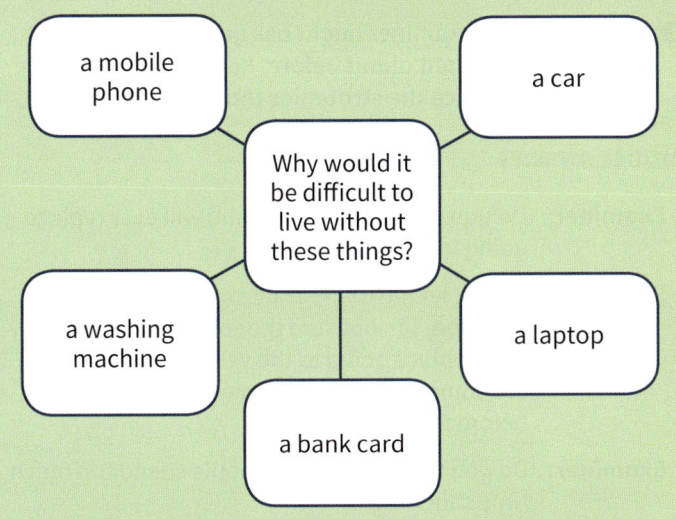

12 Read the second part of the exam task and practise
87 answering it with a partner. Listen and compare your
ideas.

> Now you have about a minute to decide which thing people
> would find it the most difficult to live without.

SPEAKING PART 4

1 Read about Part 4 of the Speaking paper.

Part 4 of the Speaking paper lasts for about four minutes,
and you work with a partner. In Part 4:

* the examiner will ask you questions on the general topic
  that you have talked about in Part 3
* the questions ask you to express your opinion rather
  than give information
* the examiner will ask you questions individually, but they
  may also bring your partner into the discussion after you
  have answered a question
* the examiner may also ask you to reply to your partner's
  opinions.

2 Read the tips.

> To get a good mark in Part 4 of the Speaking paper:
> * you should express your opinions and give reasons and
>   examples to support your opinions
> * you should avoid giving short answers and should
>   always give more information to expand your answers
> * you should listen carefully when your partner is
>   speaking, so that you can give your opinion on what
>   they have said if you are asked.

3 Read some typical Part 4 questions on the topic of travel
and holidays. Do all the questions ask about opinions?

1 What is the advantage of going on holiday with friends,
rather than with family?

2 Some people say that tourism is bad for an area. What do
you think?

3 What places are popular for holidays in your country?

4 Some people say travel is bad for the environment. Do
you agree?

5 What do you think young people can learn by going
travelling?

4 Read and listen to Alex and Nicola discussing two of
88 the questions in Exercise 3. Choose the sentence which
describes how they answer.

A They each give their own opinions, but don't listen to
each other.

B They listen to each other and respond to what the other
says.

Examiner: Alex, some people say that travel is bad for the
environment. Do you agree?

Alex: Yes, I do, because [1]I think that when people
travel they use fuel, for example in a plane or
a car, and that's very bad for the environment.
[2]They also create a lot of rubbish, for example if
they have a picnic on the beach, and that's bad
for the environment too.

Examiner: What do you think, Nicola?

Nicola: Well, I agree with Alex that travel can be bad for the environment, but on the other hand, I'd say that you can be a responsible tourist. [3]For example, I prefer to travel by train because it's better for the environment, and I never leave rubbish. So I think it's possible to travel in a way that isn't bad for the environment.

Examiner: OK. Alex, what do you think young people can learn by going travelling?

Alex: Oh, I think they can learn a lot. For example, they can learn about other cultures and ways of life, and they can also see some of the problems that exist in other parts of the world. I think that travelling is very good for young people.

Examiner: What do you think about this, Nicola?

Nicola: [4]I completely agree with Alex, and I also think that young people can benefit personally by becoming more independent when they go travelling. For example, when you're travelling you might have to deal with some difficult situations, and if you do this successfully, it can give you a lot of confidence.

[1] Express your own opinions.

[2] Give reasons and examples to support your opinions.

[3] Talk about your own likes, dislikes and preferences.

[4] Agree and disagree with your partner, and respond to what they say.

> Remember:
> - to listen carefully when your partner is answering their questions because you might be asked to give your opinion on the same question
> - to use polite expressions if you want to disagree with your partner
> - there are no right and wrong answers to the questions in Part 4. You will be marked on how well you express your opinions, not on the opinions themselves.

5 Listen to three more pairs of students answering Part 4 questions. What mistakes do the students make? Match each pair (1–3) with a common mistake (A–D). There is one mistake you don't need.

A The students' answers are too short, and they don't add more information.

B The students don't listen to each other, so they can't respond to what the other says.

C The students talk about things that are not relevant to the task.

D The students interrupt each other.

6 Read the tip. Then listen to three students answering Part 4 questions on the topic of food. What extra question does each student have in their mind?

> - Sometimes it can be difficult to think of things to say in answer to a Part 4 question. To help, it can be useful to keep question words in your mind: *Why? How? When? Where?* Asking these questions to yourself can help you think of extra things to say.

7 Sometimes the examiner might ask you a question that you haven't thought about before. Look at the model answers and notice the strategies that the students use.

MODEL ANSWER

Examiner: Do you think online shopping will ever replace going to shops?

Student: [1]Hmm, let me think. That's an interesting question. I'm not sure that online shopping will ever replace going to the shops because there are some things that people like to see or try before they buy them.

Examiner: Do you think that some people spend too much time shopping?

Student: [2]Well, it's true that some people spend quite a lot of time shopping. I guess for some people shopping is almost like a hobby. But I think that if they've got plenty of money to spend, then it isn't a problem for them to spend a lot of time in the shops. But I think it's a problem for people who don't have much money, because they might spend too much if they spend a lot of time shopping.

Examiner: Is it better to go shopping alone or with friends?

Student: [3]I think that there are some advantages to shopping alone, for example you can find things more quickly and you probably don't spend as much money. On the other hand, shopping with friends is more fun because you can chat about things and go for a coffee together. So I think I would probably say that shopping with friends is better for this reason.

[1] Use expressions to give yourself time to think about your ideas, then give your opinion.

[2] Start with a general statement about the topic of the question, then develop the idea and give your opinion.

[3] Give one point of view and then the opposite point of view, then give your own opinion.

8 Listen to three students answering Part 4 questions about health and fitness. Match each student with the strategy (1–3) from Exercise 7 that they use.

9 Practise answering these Part 4 questions. Listen and compare your answers.

1 Some people say that there will be no shops in 20 years because people will buy everything online. Do you agree?

2 Are there advantages to living in the countryside rather than a big city?

3 Why do you think that so many people dream of becoming a celebrity?

4 How do you think people benefit from going on holiday?

Writing bank

1 Read about Part 1 of the Writing paper.

In Part 1 of the Writing paper, you have to write an essay for your teacher. This task is compulsory. The topic of the essay is in the form of either a question that you have to answer, or a statement that you have to agree or disagree with.

In your essay, you can either just give arguments in favour of your own opinion or you can give arguments for and against the idea and end by giving your opinion.

You must include the two ideas that are given in the notes with the task, and you must add a third idea of your own. You should write between 140 and 190 words.

2 Read the exam task. What question should you answer? What ideas should you include?

In your English class you have been talking about the environment. Now, your English teacher has asked you to write an essay.

Write your essay using all the notes and giving reasons for your point of view.

'Will environmental problems be worse in 20 years?'

Notes

Write about:

1. pollution
2. climate change
3. ………………… (your own idea)

---

3 Study the model answer. What extra idea does it include?

MODEL ANSWER

[1]In my opinion, [2]it is possible that environmental problems will be worse in 20 years. We already face a large number of serious environmental problems, and if steps are not taken to tackle them, they will become even more serious.

[3]Firstly, there is already a huge amount of pollution in the world, for example from cars, lorries and planes. There is also a big problem with the amount of rubbish that we produce, which often ends up in the sea.

Secondly, [4]our modern way of life produces harmful gases which are causing the planet to become warmer. This is a very serious problem for animals such as polar bears, [5]which may die out if the ice that they live on melts.

Finally, the world's population is growing rapidly and this will put even more pressure on the Earth's resources. More people means more food production, more pollution and more waste.

[6]In conclusion, the world faces some very serious environmental problems which will definitely be worse in 20 years if nothing is done to solve them. [7]However, I am optimistic that scientists and politicians will find ways to improve the situation.

[1] Use phrases to express your own opinion.

[2] Start with a general introduction to the topic.

[3] Use words and phrases to organise your essay and make it clear when you are introducing a new topic.

[4] Give information which is relevant to the topic.

[5] Give reasons to support your arguments and opinions.

[6] End with a clear conclusion.

[7] Use linking words to add similar or contrasting ideas.

4 Read the tips.

Remember, to get a good mark for your essay:

- you must include the two ideas in the notes and your own idea
- all the ideas you include should be relevant to the topic
- your ideas should be organised into clear paragraphs
- there should be a clear introduction and conclusion
- you should use linking words to link your ideas and structure your essay
- you should use a wide range of grammar and vocabulary
- you should avoid informal language.

5 Read the essay question. Then decide which ideas would be relevant to include in the essay.

We shouldn't spend so much money on exploring space. Do you agree?

1 It costs a huge amount of money to send rockets into space.

2 Rockets have extremely powerful engines.

3 There are more important problems in the world that we should spend money on.

4 We can learn a lot about our own planet and solar system.

5 People first landed on the moon in 1969.

6 A lot of people in the world don't have food or shelter.

7 I would love to go into space.

8 Important scientific experiments can be carried out in space.

6 Look at the plan for a student's essay on the question in Exercise 5. Decide which paragraph the correct sentences from Exercise 5 could go in.

> Introduction
> 1 .... Is it worth the money?
> Arguments against exploring space
> 2 .... , ...
> Arguments for exploring space
> 3 .... , ...
> Conclusion
> We can learn things from exploring space, but it's probably a luxury the world can't afford.

7 Read the essay question. Then choose the best introduction and conclusion. Why is it the best one?

Do you think it is better to watch films in the cinema or at home?

1 Introductions

A There are loads of amazing films nowadays. Personally, I love science fiction films and I often watch them with my friends.

B Watching a film on the big screen at the cinema is certainly very impressive. But in my opinion, there are also advantages to watching films at home, with friends.

C Going to the cinema is quite expensive, and some people can't afford it. Also, some small towns don't have a cinema.

2 Conclusions

A To sum up, I hardly ever go to the cinema because there isn't one very close to where I live. But I often watch movies with my friends at the weekend.

B On balance, some people prefer going to the cinema to watch films, and some people prefer to watch films at home. There are lots of different reasons for this, for example some people can't afford to go to the cinema.

C In conclusion, I would say that for most films, it is more enjoyable to watch at home, with a few friends. However, for films with a lot of special effects, it is worth the trip to a cinema to see these on the big screen.

8 Study the words and expressions in the *Key language* box.

KEY LANGUAGE FOR ESSAYS

Ordering your ideas:
firstly, secondly, finally

Expressing your opinion:
in my opinion, in my view, I would say that, Personally, I think

Giving reasons:
because, as, since

Giving results or consequences:
consequently, as a result, therefore, for this reason

Giving examples:
for example, for instance, such as, one example of this is

Linking similar ideas:
in addition to this, furthermore, moreover

Linking contrasting ideas:
however, on the one hand / on the other hand, in contrast, although, whereas

Giving a conclusion:
in conclusion, to sum up, on balance

9 Choose the correct words and phrases in *italics*.

1 In my opinion, computers are essential in schools *as / for this reason* students need them to find information on the internet.

2 It is clearly necessary to test new medicines, but *in my opinion / therefore* this doesn't justify causing animals to suffer.

3 Cars create a lot of pollution in city centres. *In addition to this / Consequently*, they can cause accidents and injure or kill pedestrians.

4 There are several reasons why I am against exams. *Finally / Firstly*, they only test what someone can remember on one particular day.

5 Sports *such as / furthermore* tennis and football are more sociable than running.

6 The climate is becoming warmer and *in contrast / as a result* a lot of animals are now in danger of dying out.

10 Read the exam task and plan your essay.

In your English class you have been talking about city life. Now, your English teacher has asked you to write an essay.

Write your essay using all the notes and giving reasons for your point of view.

> **'Some people believe that cycling is the best way to travel around cities. '**
>   **Do you agree?**
> _____
> **Notes**
> Write about:
> _____
> 1. health
> 2. safety
> 3. .... (your own idea)

11 Write your essay in 140–190 words. Use the checklist on page 213.

EMAIL / LETTER

1 **Read about the email / letter in Part 2 of the Writing paper.**

In Part 2 of the Writing paper, you choose a task from three possible ones. One of the tasks might be an email / letter. It might be an informal email / letter to a friend, or a formal email / letter, for example to apply for a job. The input to the task might be an email / letter that you have to answer, or a job advertisement or notice that you reply to.

The task will give details about what points you should write about, or it will have questions for you to answer. You should make sure you cover all the points in the task and you should write 140–190 words.

2 **Read the exam task. Who should you write an email to? What should you write about in your email? What questions should you answer?**

> You have received this email from your English-speaking friend, Jo.
>
> > I guess you've been in your new home for about a month now. All your old friends are really keen to know how you're getting on. What's your new home like? And are there lots of exciting things to do in the city? Also, have you made plenty of new friends?
> >
> > Write and tell me all about it!
> >
> > Jo
>
> Write your **email** in 140–190 words.

3 **Study the model answer. Does it answer all the questions in Jo's email? Is the tone formal or informal?**

MODEL ANSWER

¹Hi Jo,

²It was great to hear from you! I miss all my old friends, but I'm getting used to living here in Manchester now.

³My new flat is amazing! It's modern and quite big, and it's got a lovely balcony which looks out over a park. There's also a large living room with comfortable sofas and our new huge TV! My room's quite small, but I don't mind that because I'm out during the day, so I only use it for sleeping.

⁴Manchester's a really lively city. Did you know it's the biggest university city in Britain, so there are loads of young people here? There's always something new and exciting to do. I've discovered some amazing music venues where there are live bands.

⁵I've been lucky with friends and I've met some really nice people here. I'm seeing some of them this evening, to go to the cinema, and I know ⁶you'll get on with them when you meet them. When are you going to come and visit me? Let me know when you're free and we can ⁶fix a date.

⁷See you soon,

Ali

¹ uses a suitable greeting

² gives a reason for writing

³ answers the first question

⁴ answers the second question

⁵ answers the third question

⁶ as it is an informal email/letter, uses informal words and phrases

⁷ uses a suitable ending phrase

4 **Read the tips.**

> Remember, to get a good mark for your email or letter:
> - you must answer the questions or provide the information mentioned in the input text
> - your email/letter should be organised into clear paragraphs
> - you should use a suitable formal or informal tone, depending on who the email/letter is to
> - you should use a wide range of grammar and vocabulary.
>
> **Tip:** Vary the expressions you use. For example, if you need to make more than one suggestion, use a different expression to make the second suggestion.
>
> **Tip:** It is important to use the same formal or informal tone right through the email/letter. For example, in a formal email/letter, don't use any informal expressions, and remember to choose a suitable formal beginning and ending.

5 **Read this task. Then decide if the sentences below are true or false.**

> You see this notice in your college.
>
> > Our college wants to organise an event this summer to raise money for schools in developing countries. Below are some of our ideas. Please email me to let me know which you think is the best idea and why. Please also tell us how we should organise the event, to make sure it is a success.
> >
> > 1 a fun sports day
> > 2 a quiz evening
> > 3 a concert
> >
> > Thank you for your help.
> >
> > Anna Bradley, Principal
>
> Write your **email**.

1 You need to write a notice about the event.

2 You have to choose one idea.

3 You should explain your reasons for choosing this.

4 You should suggest a date for the event.

5 Your email is to the college principal.

6 You should use an informal tone.

6 **Choose the four sentences that are suitable to include in your email in Exercise 5. Why are they suitable?**

1 I think it's a great idea to raise money for schools in developing countries.
2 I would suggest that a fun sport day would be the best option.
3 I think a quiz evening would be amazing!
4 Loads of people enjoy listening to live music.
5 Concerts are extremely popular with lots of people of different ages.
6 I think it would be a good idea to keep the ticket price fairly low.
7 Why don't you serve food during the event, too?
8 I'm sure that the event will be a huge success and hopefully it will raise a large amount of money.

7 **Choose the correct option in *italics* in this formal email.**

(1) *Dear Ms Copeland,* / *Hi Anne,*

I am writing (2) *because of / in response to* your advertisement for staff to work in your hotel this summer. I am (3) *currently / at the moment* studying hotel management at college and (4) *would love to work / would be interested in working* in your hotel.

I have (5) *learned all about / studied different aspects of* hotel work as part of my course, and I also have some experience of hotel work as I (6) *was employed / had a job* in a large international hotel in Spain for six weeks last summer. I worked mainly as a waiter, but also (7) *gained some experience as / had a go as* a receptionist when the regular receptionist was ill.

I am friendly and hardworking, and work well as part of a team. I also understand that in a hotel, (8) *keeping the customer happy / customer satisfaction* is vital.

(9) *I would be grateful if you would / Please will you* consider me for a position in your hotel.

(10) *I look forward to hearing from you. / Write soon!*

Joseph Brown

8 **Read the exam task. Then read the relevant Key language box and plan your letter.**

You see this advertisement in your local newspaper.

Staff wanted for summer work

We require staff to work with our English-speaking guests in our busy hotel this summer.

We are looking for people for the following roles:
– Waiter
– Coffee bar assistant
– Receptionist

Write to Maria Simpson at Top Beach Hotel saying which job interests you and why, and explain why you would be suitable for the job.

Write your **letter**.

9 **Write your letter in 140–190 words. Use the checklist on page 213.**

KEY LANGUAGE FOR INFORMAL EMAILS AND LETTERS

Opening an informal email/letter:
Hi, Hi there, Hi (Jack), Dear (Jo)

Giving reasons for writing:
Thanks for your letter/email. It was great to hear from you.

Referring to something mentioned in the email/letter:
You said in your email/letter that …, You mentioned that … You asked whether …

Making suggestions / giving advice:
Why don't you …? You could always … I think you should … It might be an idea to …

Offering to do something:
I can … if you like. I could always …

Making requests:
Can you …? Could you …?

Asking for information:
Let me know … Can you tell me …?

Apologising:
I'm sorry about …

Closing an informal email:
See you soon. Write soon. Hope to hear from you soon.

KEY LANGUAGE FOR FORMAL EMAILS AND LETTERS

Opening a formal email/letter:
Dear (Mr/Mrs/Ms Edwards), Dear Sir/Madam,
Only use Mrs if you are sure that the woman you are writing to is married. Otherwise, use Ms.

Giving reasons for writing:
I am writing in response to … I saw your notice/advert in …

Referring to something mentioned in the letter/notice/advert:
Your letter/notice/advert mentioned that … Your letter/notice/advert asked for …

Making suggestions / giving advice:
It would be a good idea to … It might be sensible to … You might like to consider …

Offering to do something:
I would be able/willing to … if necessary.

Making requests:
Would it be possible for you to …?

Asking for information:
Could you give me some information on …? Could you let me have more details about …?

Apologising:
I would like to apologise for …

Closing an informal email:
Yours sincerely (after Dear Mr Edwards), Yours faithfully (after Dear Sir/Madam), I look forward to hearing from you, Kind regards

ARTICLE

1 **Read about the article in Part 2 of the Writing paper.**

In Part 2 of the Writing paper, you choose a task from three possible ones. One of the tasks might be an article. The task will give details about what you should write an article about and what information you should include.

You might be asked to write a description, give examples or give your opinions about something. The task will also say where people will read your article, e.g. on a website or in a magazine or newspaper.

You should make sure you cover all the points in the task, and you should structure your article in a suitable way. You should use creative language to make the article interesting for your reader, and you can ask the reader direct questions to engage them. You should write 140–190 words.

2 **Read the exam task. What should you write an article about? What points should you include? Where will people read your article?**

You see this notice in an English-language magazine.

Articles wanted

My hobby

Write an article about your hobby. Say what it is, how you started doing it, and why you enjoy it.

The best articles will appear in our magazine next week.

Write your **article**.

3 **Study the model answer and answer the questions.**

1 Does the article cover all the points in the task?

2 How many paragraphs does it have?

3 How many direct questions does it ask the reader?

4 Is it written in a formal or an informal style?

MODEL ANSWER

[1]The thrill of the stage

[2]I'll never forget the first day I stepped onto a real theatre stage. I knew immediately that this was my hobby for life! I'm now a member of my local drama club. We put on two shows every year and have a lot of fun while doing so!

[3]I first started acting by chance. A friend of mine was interested in joining a drama club, and I agreed to go along with her, to give her a bit of support. [4]And I loved it from the first day!

First, drama is [5]incredibly challenging. [6]Not only do you have to learn what you're going to say, but also understand the character you're playing, their role in the play, and then communicate that to the audience.

[7]Another thing I love about drama is how sociable it is. I've made so many good friends at the drama club, and spending time with them, working towards a shared goal, is extremely rewarding. And in addition to all of this, [8]what could beat the thrill of appearing under the lights, in front of a cheering crowd?

[1] has an interesting title

[2] has a first sentence which interests the reader and encourages them to read more

[3] is organised into clear paragraphs, each with a topic sentence

[4] gives the writer's opinions

[5] uses creative language with strong meanings

[6] gives examples to support the ideas

[7] uses structures to add emphasis

[8] try to end with a question or a lively final sentence

4 **Read the tips.**

Remember, to get a good mark for your article:

- you must include all the points in the input
- you should choose an interesting title for your article
- your ideas should be organised into clear paragraphs, which each focus on a clear topic
- you should make the reader feel interested by asking them questions
- you should use a wide range of creative language and language structures
- you should include your own opinion and experiences.

5 **It is important to choose a title and first sentence which will engage your reader and encourage them to read more. Choose the best title and first sentence for an article about Nelson Mandela. Why is it the best?**

A Nelson Mandela
I really admire Nelson Mandela because of everything he achieved in South Africa.

B A peaceful transformation
Can you imagine one person bringing peaceful change to a whole country?

C An important figure in South Africa
Nelson Mandela is a very important figure in the history of South Africa.

6 The first sentence in each paragraph (the topic sentence) gives the topic of the paragraph. Match the topic sentences (a–e) to the paragraphs from an article about a favourite place to visit. There are two topic sentences you don't need.

a The people here are incredibly warm and welcoming.
b This is a lovely, relaxing place.
c I first discovered this place about five years ago.
d One thing I really love is the stunning scenery.
e If you love good food, this is a great place to visit.

1 .... When you look in one direction, you can see the beautiful beach and the clear blue sea. In the opposite direction, there are lovely views of the mountains, which have snow on their peaks all year round.

2 .... You can find delicious local cheeses, and plenty of fresh fruit and vegetables. And of course there's fresh fish which the fishing boats bring in each day, and which is perfectly cooked in the restaurants by the beach.

3 .... They always have time to stop and chat and they seem genuinely keen for you to enjoy your stay. There is always someone to help if you have any problems, too.

7 In an article, it is important to use creative words with strong meanings to make your writing more interesting. Replace the bold words and expressions in the sentences with the creative words with similar meanings from the box.

> absolutely   essential   fascinated by   freezing
> huge   packed   terrifying

1 Like a lot of people, I was **interested in** the castle's history.
2 The city centre is always **crowded** with tourists.
3 His first film was a **big** success.
4 I always enjoy watching my local football team play, even when the weather's **cold**.
5 The drive up the narrow mountain road was quite **scary** at times.
6 A good fitness programme is **really necessary** if you're serious about losing weight.

8 You can use structures to emphasise your ideas and opinions in an article. Complete each second sentence so it has a similar meaning but has more emphasis.

1 I admire his determination.
   What ....I admire is.... his determination.
2 I like the freedom you get when you go hiking.
   The thing .... the freedom you get when you go hiking.
3 Her honesty really surprised me.
   One thing .... her honesty.
4 I will never forget our evening barbecues on the beach.
   What .... our evening barbecues on the beach.
5 I noticed how happy everyone looked.
   The thing .... how happy everyone looked.

9 Study the words and expressions in the *Key language* box.

KEY LANGUAGE FOR ARTICLES

Catching the reader's attention:
Have you ever …? I want to tell you about … It's the best …

Ordering ideas:
First(ly), Second(ly), Finally,

Linking similar ideas:
moreover, in addition to this

Linking contrasting ideas:
while, whereas

Linking results:
therefore, which means

Emphasising ideas:
What I love/admire the most is …, The thing I like best is …

Giving your opinion:
In my opinion, For me, as far as I'm concerned

10 Complete the sentences with one word in each space.

1 .... me, sailing is definitely the best sport in the world!
2 Painting is relaxing, creative and fun, and .... addition to this, you can earn a bit of money by selling your paintings.
3 As far .... I'm concerned, cooking is the best hobby.
4 Hiking isn't expensive, ... means that anyone can do it.
5 .... I love most is watching live shows in a theatre.
6 I want to .... you about something amazing that happened to me last year.

11 Read the exam task and plan your article.

You see this notice on an English-language fitness website.

Articles wanted

Staying healthy

How important is your health to you? What do you think are some of the best ways to stay fit and healthy?

The best articles will appear on our website next month.

Write your **article**.

12 Write your article in 140–190 words. Use the checklist on page 213.

STORY

1 Read about the story in Part 2 of the Writing paper.

In Part 2 of the Writing paper, you choose a task from three possible ones. One of the tasks might be a story. The task will give you the first sentence of the story, and two ideas that you must include. It will also tell you who the story is for, e.g. a school magazine or an English-language website for young people.

You should make sure you use the first sentence correctly and include the two ideas you are given. You should organise your story into paragraphs, and make sure your story has a clear beginning, middle and end. You should use a range of past tenses, and a range of words and expressions to show when the different events of the story happened. You should write 140–190 words.

2 Read the exam task and answer the questions.

1 What should the first sentence of your story be?

2 What two ideas do you need to include?

3 Where will people read your story?

You see this notice on an English-language website for young people.

> We are looking for stories for our English-language website for young people.
>
> Your story must begin with this sentence:
>
> *Feeling slightly nervous, Emma walked up the steps and onto the plane.*
>
> Your story must include:
> – bad weather
> – a surprise

Write your **story**.

---

3 Study the model answer and answer the questions.

1 Does the story start with the first sentence in the task?

2 Does it include the two ideas from the task?

3 Does it have a clear beginning, middle and ending?

4 What past tenses does it use?

5 Does it include descriptions as well as actions?

MODEL ANSWER

[1]Feeling slightly nervous, Emma walked up the steps and onto the plane. She [4]'d never been to America before, but now [2]she was on her way for a one-month exchange visit to an American school.

[3]As she [4]was waiting for the plane to take off, questions [4]went through her mind. Would she get on with the other students? Would they accept her? Would it be difficult? Emma sighed. It was too late to change her mind now!

[3]An hour later, Emma was looking out at the [6]clear blue sky as they flew over the ocean. Then, [5]all of a sudden, the sky darkened. There was a roar of thunder and the pilot told passengers to put on their seat belts. [5]Two minutes later, the plane was in the middle of [8]a fierce storm. Lightning flashed, and the plane bumped and shook [6]violently. Terrified, Emma closed her eyes.

After what felt like hours, the plane landed. As she walked out into the terminal building, Emma saw a big colourful sign: *Welcome Emma!* [9]What an amazing surprise! Her host family were there, smiling and waving, and Emma knew immediately that [7]everything would be fine!

[1] starts with the first sentence from the task

[2] includes some background to the events

[3] is organised into paragraphs

[4] uses past simple, past continuous and past perfect verb forms

[5] uses a range of time expressions to say when the actions happened and what order they happened in

[6] uses descriptive adjectives and adverbs to make the story interesting

[7] includes a clear ending

[8] includes the idea of bad weather, specified in the task

[9] includes the idea of a surprise, specified in the task

4 Read the tips.

Remember, to get a good mark for your story:
- you must use the first sentence and the two ideas in the input
- your story should be organised into paragraphs, and it should have a clear beginning, middle and end
- you should use a range of past tenses for the events in the story
- you should use a range of words and expressions to show when the different events happened
- you should include descriptions as well as actions
- you should use descriptive adjectives and adverbs to make your story interesting
- you should think of an interesting ending.

5 Read two beginnings of students' stories. Which one is better? Give three reasons why.

A When Laura sat down on the train, she noticed a bag on the seat opposite her. She waved goodbye to her mum, and the train started moving. Laura started reading her book, then the phone in the bag rang.

B When Laura sat down on the train, she noticed a bag on the seat opposite her. There was no one else in her part of the train, so she guessed someone had probably left it there by mistake. It was a very modern, fashionable bag, and looked expensive. Laura opened her book to start reading, when she heard a phone ringing. It wasn't hers – it was coming from inside the bag.

6 Choose the best ending for the story in Exercise 5. Why is it better than the other one?

A Laura stepped down from the train, holding the bag. A woman immediately ran towards her. 'I'm Kirsty,' she said, 'the owner of the bag. Thank you so much for all you did for me today!' Laura handed her the bag. 'No problem,' she said, smiling. 'It certainly made my journey a lot more interesting!'

B When Laura reached her station, she picked up the bag. She wasn't sure what to do with it, so she decided she would take it to the lost property office. Then, all of a sudden, a woman came running onto the train. 'That's my bag!' she said, and grabbed it out of Laura's hands.

7 We often use words and expressions in stories to make it clear when the different actions happened. Choose the correct option in *italics*.

1 Sam was watching TV when *eventually / suddenly* the door burst open.

2 *By the time / Until* they got home, it was completely dark.

3 *While / As soon as* the letter arrived, Max picked it up and opened it.

4 No one spoke *during / meanwhile* the journey.

5 *At first / In the end*, everything turned out to be OK.

6 *Before long / Just then*, they were chatting as if they had known each other all their lives.

8 Study the words and expressions in the *Key language* box.

KEY LANGUAGE FOR STORIES

Past simple verbs for the main events:
went, found, saw, decided, helped

Past continuous verbs for longer actions or descriptions:
was waiting, were sitting, was raining, was feeling

Past perfect verbs for earlier actions:
had forgotten, hadn't told her, hadn't noticed

Time expressions:
after, as soon as, at first, before, by the time, during, eventually, in the end, finally, gradually, meanwhile, just then, later, suddenly, while, when

Descriptive adjectives for feelings:
determined, enthusiastic, nervous, optimistic, puzzled, relieved

Descriptive adjectives for the weather:
bitter, damp, frosty, mild, misty, stormy

Descriptive adjectives for places:
busy, crowded, peaceful, picturesque, stunning

Descriptive adverbs:
angrily, fiercely, gently, quietly

Adverbs to comment on what happened:
fortunately, luckily, sadly, unfortunately

Direct speech:
'Hi,' she said. 'Where are you going?' he asked. 'Go away!' she shouted.

9 Add the correct punctuation to the direct speech.

1 Will you come with me he asked.

2 Don't worry he said.

3 Get out she cried.

4 It doesn't matter she said.

10 Read the exam task and plan your story.

Your teacher has asked you to write a story in English for a school magazine for teenagers.

Stories wanted

We are looking for stories in English for our new school magazine for teenagers.

Your story must begin with this sentence:

When he saw the postman coming up to his door, Matt ran to open it.

Your story must include:
– a mobile phone
– a new friend

Write your **story**.

11 Write your story in 140–190 words. Use the checklist on page 213.

1 Read about the review in Part 2 of the Writing paper.

In Part 2 of the Writing paper, you choose a task from three possible ones. One of the tasks might be a review. The task will give details about what you should review and what aspects of it you should discuss. It will also say where people will read your review, e.g. on a website or in a magazine or newspaper.

You should make sure you cover all the points in the task, and structure your review in a suitable way. You should talk about your personal experience of a product or experience, give your own opinion of it clearly, and make a recommendation for your reader. You should write 140–190 words.

2 Read the exam task. What should you write a review of? What points should you include? Where will people read your review?

You see this notice in an English-language magazine.

> **Film reviews wanted**
>
> What films have you seen recently? Write a review of a film you have seen, explaining what it was about and whether you enjoyed it or not. Tell us whether or not you think other people would enjoy it.
>
> The best reviews will be published in next month's magazine.

Write your **review**.

3 Study the model answer and answer the questions.

1 Does the review cover all the points in the task?

2 Did the writer enjoy the film?

3 Who does the writer think will enjoy the film?

4 Is the language in the review formal and neutral, or informal and friendly?

MODEL ANSWER

[1]*Black Panther*

I watched the film *Black Panther* for the first time last week. [2]It's a superhero film, in the same genre as *Superman* and *Spider-Man*, and has been extremely popular around the world.

[3]Although I am not usually a big fan of superhero films, [4]I was really impressed with this one. The story is fairly traditional, with the hero T'Challa (Black Panther) defeating the evil Killmonger, who is trying to gain power over the whole world. [5]But the action is gripping and the special effects are spectacular. Chadwick Boseman, who plays T'Challa, acts superbly, and really brings the comic-book character to life. The brilliant costumes and music also really help make the film a real spectacle.

[3]On the negative side, [6]I felt that there was sometimes a bit too much violence, which makes it unsuitable for young children, and of course you have to accept that the plot is slightly predictable because the good guy will always win.

In spite of this, [7]I loved the film and [8]anyone who enjoys fantasy movies will definitely like it.

[1] includes the name of the film as the title

[2] briefly describes the film in the introduction

[3] is organised into clear paragraphs, which focus on positive and negative aspects

[4] uses a range of phrases to express a personal opinion

[5] praises positive features and says why the film is good

[6] includes some negative features, to give a balanced view

[7] clearly states the writer's opinion in the conclusion

[8] includes a recommendation, saying who would enjoy the film

4 Read the tips.

Remember, to get a good mark for your review:
- you must include all the points in the input
- your ideas should be organised into clear paragraphs, which each focus on a clear topic
- you should state clearly whether you liked or didn't like the product or experience
- you should include a recommendation
- you should use descriptive language to make your review interesting
- you should use an informal, friendly style.

5 Read the review task. Then look at the two student plans. Which plan is better? Why?

Reviews wanted!
What shopping websites have you used recently? Write a review of a shopping website that you have used. Say what you bought, how pleased you were with the product, and talk about any problems you experienced. Say whether you would recommend the site to others.

A

Introduction
name of website TechWorld, and basic information (what they sell).
What I bought (a new tablet)

My experience
The website – why I like it (easy to use – good prices)
The product – why I was pleased with it (good quality)

A few problems
slow delivery, missing case, but they dealt with this quickly

Recommendation
great website for anyone who is looking for a low-priced tablet or other device

B

Introduction
why I chose to use this website (looking for a cheap tablet, easier to buy online than go into town)

The website
how I found out about it, how I chose my tablet, problem of slow delivery

Games
why I like it (I needed a new tablet for playing games)

Conclusion
I'm very pleased with my new tablet and it was very cheap

6 Using descriptive adjectives and adverbs in a review makes it interesting to read. Choose the best adverbs to go with the descriptive adjectives.

1 The action scenes in the film were *a little / incredibly* gripping.
2 The food in the restaurant is lovely, but it is *absolutely / ridiculously* expensive.
3 The basic plot of the book is *rather / mildly* predictable.
4 This is a *completely / brilliantly* entertaining show.
5 The device that I bought is *totally / extremely* useful.
6 The holiday flat is small but *very / highly* well equipped.
7 Our hotel room was *absolutely / very* perfect.
8 All the staff were *a bit / really* welcoming.

7 We often use adjectives or phrases to give our opinion about something in an indirect way. Match the beginnings and endings of the sentences.

1 I was disappointed to
2 We were delighted that
3 I'm absolutely thrilled with
4 The tent isn't as big
5 The food was even better
6 There weren't enough

a my new camera.
b seats around the pool for all the guests.
c find that the screen was cracked.
d than I expected.
e as it looked on the website.
f we had a room with a view of the sea.

8 In a review we often use words to express contrast. Complete the sentences with words from the box.

| although | despite | however | spite | though |

1 The weather was terrible, but in .... of this, we thoroughly enjoyed our stay at the resort.
2 Even .... it was rather expensive, we really enjoyed our time at the museum.
3 I would advise anyone to check out this website, ... the problems that I experienced.
4 .... the service was quick and friendly, the food was a little disappointing.
5 The website stated that the bag was made of leather. ...., when it arrived, it was clear that it was not genuine leather.

9 Study the words and expressions in the *Key language* box.

KEY LANGUAGE FOR REVIEWS

Praising something:
It is one of the best … I have ever …
the … was absolutely perfect
the … was even better than I expected
I was pleased/delighted to find that …
It was a nice surprise to find that …

Criticising:
The … was rather disappointing
The advertisement said …, but in fact …
I was a little disappointed to find …
There weren't enough …

Recommending:
Anyone who likes … will really enjoy …
Don't miss the chance/opportunity to …
I'm sure everyone will really enjoy …
If you get the chance to see/buy/try …, you should definitely do it
I would advise anyone to …

Advising someone against something:
I would suggest finding a better … than this.
I would strongly advise against eating/reading/watching/buying this …
My advice is to avoid this …

10 Choose the correct words in the sentences.

1 This show was even better *than / as* I expected.

2 The dessert was rather *disappointed / disappointing*.

3 Anyone who enjoys crime novels *will / can* love this book.

4 Don't *lose / miss* the opportunity to visit this theme park.

5 I would suggest *using / to use* a different website.

6 I would strongly *advise / suggest* against staying at this campsite.

11 Read the exam task and plan your review.

You see this advertisement on a travel website.

Reviews wanted!

What holiday resorts have you been to recently?

Write a review describing the resort, explaining why you did or didn't enjoy your stay there and saying if you would recommend it

The best reviews will be published on our website.

Write your **review**.

paragraphs	ideas	useful phrases
Description of the resort		
Why I enjoyed/ didn't enjoy it		
Good value for money?		
Recommendation		

12 Write your review in 140–190 words. Use the checklist on page 213.

WRITING CHECKLISTS

ESSAY CHECKLIST

- Have you answered the question in the task?
- Have you included the two ideas in the task and added your own idea?
- Have you included only relevant information?
- Have you started with an introduction and ended with a conclusion?
- Have you ordered your ideas into paragraphs?
- Have you given reasons for your ideas and opinions?
- Have you used words and phrases to link ideas?
- Have you used between 140 and 190 words?

EMAIL / LETTER CHECKLIST

- Have you covered all the points in the task?
- Have you used an appropriate formal or informal tone?
- Have you used a range of phrases for giving advice, making suggestions, etc.?
- Have you used a suitable opening phrase, and a suitable ending?
- Have you used a wide range of language?
- Have you used between 140 and 190 words?

ARTICLE CHECKLIST

- Have you covered all the points in the task?
- Have you organised your ideas clearly into paragraphs?
- Have you got an interesting title and first sentence?
- Have you given your own opinions clearly?
- Have you used creative vocabulary with strong meanings?
- Have you used structures to add emphasis?
- Have you used between 140 and 190 words?

STORY CHECKLIST

- Have you included the two ideas in the task?
- Have you organised your story into paragraphs?
- Have you given some background to the story?
- Have you finished with a clear ending?
- Have you used a range of different past tenses?
- Have you used time words and expressions to say when the actions happened?
- Have you used descriptive language?
- Have you used between 140 and 190 words?

REVIEW CHECKLIST

- Have you covered all the points in the task?
- Have you organised your ideas clearly into paragraphs?
- Have you given your own opinion clearly?
- Have you ended with a recommendation?
- Have you used descriptive adjectives and adverbs to make your writing interesting?
- Have you used a friendly tone?
- Have you used between 140 and 190 words?

VOCABULARY

1 ARRANGEMENTS

Prepare, arrange and organise

When you **prepare** for something, you get ready for it.

The students are preparing for their exam.

You **arrange** or **organize** an event or an activity.

✓ *The school **arranges** visits to local museums.*

✗ *The school prepares visits to local museums.*

✓ *The festival is **organized** by local people.*

✗ *The festival is prepared by local people*

When you prepare food, you get it ready to eat, for example, by chopping vegetables, etc.

*Can you help Ed and Annie **prepare** the food for the party?*

You can also say you **made** lunch or you **made** some sandwiches, especially when the preparation process is less important than the finished food.

✓ *I've made us some sandwiches for lunch.*

✗ *I've prepared us some sandwiches for lunch*

1 Choose the best option to complete the sentences.

1 Lisa is .... a party for her sister's birthday.
   A preparing   **B** organizing   **C** making

2 The tourist office can .... boat trips along the river.
   A arrange   **B** prepare   **C** prepare for

3 The hotel .... activities for guests with children.
   A makes   **B** prepares   **C** organizes

4 Jack is in the kitchen .... some food for the picnic.
   A preparing for   **B** preparing   **C** arranging

5 Let's .... another meeting for next week.
   A prepare   **B** make   **C** arrange

6 What's the best way to .... a job interview?
   A prepare   **B** prepare for   **C** organize for

7 One of my friends .... me a lovely cake for my birthday.
   A prepared   **B** made   **C** organized

8 Everyone is busy .... the festival next week.
   A organizing for   **B** preparing   **C** preparing for

Which preposition?

2 Choose the correct preposition to complete the sentences.

1 We're meeting the others *at/to* the restaurant.

2 On Friday, we're going *in/on* a trip along the river.

3 Don't worry, we can buy drinks and snacks *in/on* the train.

4 Our flight leaves at 4 o'clock *in/on* the afternoon.

5 I'll meet you *at/in* the top of the steps, *out of/outside* the café.

6 Are you going to Lyon *during/for* the whole weekend?

7 You can buy tickets online or you can get them *in/at* the theatre.

8 This weekend, I was *at/in* a music festival with some friends.

Pronunciation: Words ending in R

Remember, the letter R is not normally pronounced at the end of English words. Words like *offer*, *later*, *better* and *visitor* end in the weak sound /ə/.

3 Listen and repeat the sentences. Focus on pronouncing the /ə/ sound at the end of the words in bold.

1. I'll see you **later**.
2. It's **cheaper** to get the bus.
3. We're leaving **after** breakfast.
4. Do you **offer** discounts for students?
5. Let's meet at the **visitor centre**.
6. It's **better** in the **summer**.
7. **Remember** we're in room **number** 26.
8. The **weather** can be a **major factor**.

Before and after

To talk about time and sequences, we use:

before/after + noun: *I'll meet you **after** <u>lunch</u>.*

before/after + clause: *Get a ticket **before** <u>you get on the train</u>.*

You can use **early/earlier** or **beforehand** to talk about a time before something:

✓ *Amy arrived for the class 20 minutes **early**.*

✗ *Amy arrived for the class 20 minutes ~~before~~.*

✓ *The meeting will last all through the lunch break, so have something to eat **beforehand**.*

✗ *The meeting will last all through the lunch break, so have something to eat ~~before~~.*

You can use **later, then** or **afterwards** to talk about a time after something:

✓ *You fill in the form online and a few minutes **later**, you get a confirmation email.*

✗ *You fill in the form online and a few minutes ~~after~~, you get a confirmation email.*

✓ *The match finishes about 8pm. **Afterwards/Then**, we could get a pizza maybe.*

✗ *The match finishes about 8pm. ~~After~~, we could get a pizza maybe.*

4 Read the sentences carefully. Underline the action or event which happens first.

1. Let's meet outside the sports centre after <u>the training session</u>.
2. Before each match, we usually spend about 15 minutes warming up.
3. Anyone can come to the workshop, but you need to book your place beforehand.
4. You have to choose a username now, but you can change it later if you want.
5. The talk starts at 7.30pm, but most people arrive a bit earlier.
6. The talks usually last about 45 minutes and there's time for questions afterwards.

5a Find and correct <u>one</u> mistake in each comment.

1. Every Saturday, I go to the cinema with my friends. The film starts at 4pm, so we usually meet for a coffee ~~before~~. Then afterwards, I go home for dinner with my family.
   beforehand

2. Tomorrow morning, the bus will pick us up at 9.30. Can you all be in reception at least ten minutes before the bus leaves, please? We'll visit the National Museum in the morning and after there'll be time to walk around the city.

3. I'm really excited about our trip to Australia. We fly to Sydney on the 12th, then two days after, we're heading to Melbourne. We'll spend 10 days staying with friends in Melbourne before we go back to Sydney again for the last few days.

4. I go to a yoga class on a Wednesday evening after college. The class starts at 6, so I generally leave college at about 5.30. It only takes me 15 minutes to walk, but I like to arrive a bit before so I've got time to get changed.

5. On Friday, I've got a meeting in London. It starts at 10 o'clock, but I'll get the 8.30 train which is due to arrive at 9.15. I'll probably be at the office before, but I want to allow time for delays. The meeting finishes at lunchtime and then I'll stay in town to do some shopping.

About you

5b Describe something you do regularly or some future plans. You could say:

- What time you leave.
- What time you arrive.
- What you do beforehand.
- When the event starts.
- What you do afterwards.

Collocations: verb + noun

6a Complete the dialogue using the best form of the verbs from the box. Think carefully about the verb + noun collocations. One verb is used twice.

> do   give   have   make   take

Mark: You look a bit stressed. Is everything okay?

Anna: Yes, I'm fine, just busy. My cousins are visiting from the US next week and I'm **(1)** ......*making*...... all the arrangements for their stay. You know, sorting out accommodation and transport. I said I'd **(2)** .... care of everything for them so they can just relax and **(3)** .... fun.

Mark: Can I help at all?

Anna: Actually, I wonder if you could **(4)** .... me a favour?

Mark: Yes, sure. What?

Anna: Would you be able to **(5)** .... me to the airport on Saturday?

Mark: Yes, of course. No problem.

Anna: Oh, that would be great. Thanks!

Mark: What time do you need to be there? I think their flight arrives about midday, but I'll check later and I'll give you a call to let you know.

94 **6b** Listen and check your answers. Then complete the verb + noun collocations.

1 make .... for something
2 take .... of something
3 have ....
4 do somebody a ....
5 take somebody to the .... /station, etc.
6 give somebody a ....

Verb + preposition

Some verbs are typically followed by a phrase with a preposition:

look forward to sth, wait for sb/sth, reply to sb/sth, apply for sth, talk to sb

✓ You'll need to **apply for** a visa to visit India.

✗ You'll need to ~~apply a visa~~ to visit India.

Some verbs can be followed by an object + a phrase with a preposition:

provide sb with sth, explain sth to sb, describe sth to sb

✓ Your travel agent will be able to **provide you with** all the information.

✗ Your travel agent will be able to ~~provide you all the information~~.

Some verbs are typically just followed by an object:

answer sb/sth, contact sb, phone sb, call sb

✓ Or you could **contact** the Indian embassy.

✗ Or you could ~~contact with~~ the Indian embassy.

7 Are these sentences correct? Add any prepositions that are missing or cross out any that are not needed.

1 Did the travel company reply ^*to* your email?
2 No, I'm still waiting an answer.
3 Have you contacted with the hotel about arriving late?
4 Yes, I phoned to them last week and they said it was fine.
5 I'm happy to answer to any questions.
6 Can you explain the application process to us again, please?
7 Can the club provide us rackets and other equipment?
8 Yes, just talk to a member of staff when you arrive.

8 Complete the email using words from the box. Not all the words are needed and some gaps can be left blank.

> afterwards   arranged   beforehand   give
> in   make   prepared   to   with

```
● ● ●
To:        Andy
Subject:
```

Hi Andy,

I'm really looking forward **(1)** .... the kayaking trip next week. I just wanted to contact **(2)** .... you with a few questions.

According to the schedule, we finish kayaking at 4.30 **(3)** .... the afternoon on Saturday. Have you **(4)** .... anything else for **(5)** .... or are we free once it has finished?

I was also wondering about what to bring. I presume you'll provide us **(6)** .... all the kayaking equipment. What sort of clothes do we need?

Perhaps you could **(7)** .... me a call and let me know. I'm at college during the day, so it's best to call **(8)** .... me in the evening.

Thanks,

Isabelle

2 LIFESTYLES

Life

Remember the plural form of the noun *life* is *lives* /laɪvz/.

✓ Mobile phones are now part of our daily **lives**.

✗ Mobile phones are now part of ~~our daily life~~.

To talk about how someone lives and the things they typically do, you can refer to their **lifestyle** or their **way of life**. *Lifestyle* (written as one word) is often used about individual choices, especially in the modern world. *Way of life* is often used to talk about a group of people and commonly refers to traditional ways of doing things.

✓ We need to encourage more healthy **lifestyles**.

✗ We need to encourage more healthy ~~life styles~~.

✓ The **way of life** in this mountain village has barely changed for hundreds of years.

Someone's **standard of living** is how well they live: how much money they have, how much they can afford to buy, etc.

✓ We enjoy a higher **standard of living** than previous generations.

✗ We enjoy a higher ~~level of life~~ than previous generations.

The **cost of living** is how much money people need to spend to live, eat, etc., especially in a particular country or area.

✓ The **cost of living** in big cities is much higher.

1 Match the comments to the ideas they illustrate.

A lifestyle   **B** way of life   **C** cost of living
D standard of living

1 Fares on public transport have really gone up recently.
....

2 I don't often have time to cook, I mostly just grab takeaways. ....

3 I moved to this country, because my kids will receive a better education. ....

4 He gets up at 5am every morning to move the cows out into the fields. ....

2a Complete the sentences using the words or phrases from the box.

| life   lifestyle   lifestyles   lives   living |

1 We all want to earn enough money to maintain a good standard of ....

2 My grandparents spent their whole .... in the same house.

3 The problem is the cost of .... has risen, but wages have stayed the same.

4 People will always be interested in the private .... of the rich and famous.

5 Nowadays, the internet is just part of normal, everyday .... for most people.

6 This traditional way of .... is slowly disappearing as people adopt more western ....

Collocations: everyday activities

3 Complete the descriptions using the best form of a verb from the box. Some verbs are not needed and some verbs may be used more than once.

| change   check   control   do   exchange   go
have   know   make   meet   take |

I use my mobile for just about everything. If I want to **(1)** .... my email, it's on my phone. If I want to **(2)** .... a photo, I reach for my phone. I use it to play games, to listen to music, to send messages to my friends. The first thing I do when I **(3)** .... someone new is **(4)** .... mobile numbers. Sometimes, I even use my phone to **(5)** .... a call!

I think I have a fairly healthy lifestyle. I generally eat quite healthily and if I **(6)** .... a snack between meals, it's usually some fruit or nuts. I **(7)** .... quite a bit of exercise. I **(8)** .... running at least twice a week and I **(9)** .... an effort to be active during the day. So I always walk up the stairs rather than taking the lift, for example. It all **(10)** .... a difference to how I feel.

Which preposition?

4 Choose the best preposition to complete the sentences.

1 I don't understand why people take pictures *in/of* their food to post on social media.

2 Some of my friends spend a lot of money *in/on* new clothes and the latest trainers.

3 All the girls were dressed *in/with* brightly-coloured traditional outfits.

4 Of course, my tastes and interests aren't the same *as/with* my parents'.

5 I think there's a need *for/of* better education around healthy eating.

6 Some people just aren't very good *at/in* team sports.

Take part in and take place

When you **take part** in an activity, you participate.

✓ *Over 40,000 people **take part** in the London Marathon every year.*

✗ *Over 40,000 people take part of the London Marathon every year.*

When an event **takes place**, it happens.

✓ *The Football World Cup **takes place** every four years.*

✗ *The Football World Cup takes part every four years.*

You typically use *take place* to talk about an organized event. To talk about everyday or unplanned events, you use *happen* or *be*.

✓ *Something really embarrassing **happened** yesterday.*

✗ *Something really embarrassing took place yesterday.*

✓ *The meal **is** at 8pm in Pizza Workshop.*

✗ *The meal takes place at 8pm in Pizza Workshop.*

Expressions with *take*

5 **Choose the best phrase to complete the sentences.**

1 The festival **takes part / takes place** in August every year.

2 Several things **have happened / have taken place** recently that have made me think more about my health.

3 We **took part in / took part on** a competition between local schools.

4 It's important to **take care about yourself / take care of yourself** and stay healthy.

5 Remember the price doesn't **take in account / take into account** spending on food and drink.

6 The kids **took their shoes off / took out their shoes** to play in the water.

Exercise and sport

Exercise is an uncountable noun used to describe all kinds of physical activity.

✓ *Cycling to school or to work is a great way to **get some exercise.***

✗ *Cycling to school or to work is a great way to do some exercises/some sport.*

An exercise (countable) is something you do and repeat in order to practise a particular skill. You can do a grammar exercise in a language class and you can do a physical exercise, for example, to strengthen your muscles.

✓ *At the start of a training session, we always do **some** stretching **exercises**.*

Exercise is also a verb.

✓ *You should **exercise** for at least 30 minutes, three times a week.*

Sport is usually an organized physical activity. You can **do sport** or you can **play sports** that involve games and scores, such as football, tennis, basketball, etc.

✓ *We're trying to encourage children to **do** more **sport**.*

✗ *We're trying to encourage children to practise more sport.*

✓ *I prefer **playing team sports** like football and volleyball.*

When you **practise** something, you try to improve your skills, for example, by doing exercises.

✓ *In my tennis lesson, we were practising serving the ball.*

Practice is a noun, e.g. *football practice, a practice session*

6a Complete the dialogue using the best form of the words from the box. Some words are used more than once. More than one answer may be possible.

> do   exercise   go   play   practice   practise

Katie: Did I tell you I'm training at the moment to take part in a marathon next year?

Ella: Wow! I didn't even know you were a runner.

Katie: I wasn't! I only started running last year. When I was at school, I **(1)** .... a lot of team sports. You know, I used to be part of the volleyball team and I'd go to **(2)** .... sessions after school. But then when I started work, I didn't have the time any more.

Ella: Yeah, I know what you mean. I used to **(3)** .... quite a bit of sport when I was a kid. I really loved swimming. I went to lessons and I spent hours in the pool **(4)** .... my technique, but I haven't been for ages.

Katie: Exactly, same here. So anyway, I realized I wasn't doing any **(5)** .... and I was getting really unfit. So I joined a running club.

Ella: That sounds fun.

Katie: Yeah, I tried to **(6)** .... running on my own, but it's more fun **(7)** .... with other people. We meet at the local park and we usually start off with some stretching **(8)** ...., then we go for a run together.

Ella: So why did you decide to do a marathon?

Katie: Well, some of the people from the running club had signed up and I thought it would be good to have a goal to work towards.

Ella: Wow, good luck!

6b Listen and check your answers.

Spelling: y

7 Find and correct three spelling mistakes in each paragraph.

I'm thinking about getting a bycicle. I've noticed that a lot more people are ciclying around the city recently and there are more and more cycle lanes. I think it's better for the environment and it's a good way to stay phisically active too.

I've started wearing a device to track how much exercise I do as I'm walking around town. It allows me to analise how many steps I've done and how many calories I've burned each day. So, on a tipical day, I do about 8,000 steps. Although sometimes it seems to record steps when I'm sitting on the bus too which is a bit misterious!

A few years ago, my city hosted the Winter Olimpics. It was an amazing event and it encouraged me to take up skying. I loved it and now I go up into the mountains most weekends during the winter. It's great fun and a fantastic way to keep fit; much better than going to the gim!

Pronunciation: /ɪ/, /iː/ and /aɪ/

96 **8a** Listen and practise saying the three vowel sounds.

	/ɪ/	/iː/	/aɪ/
1	bit	beat	bite
2	hit	heat	height
3	sit	seat	sight
4	Tim	team	time

97 **8b** Now listen to these phrases and tick the underlined sound.

		/ɪ/	/iː/	/aɪ/
1	my whole life			✓
2	our daily lives			
3	a healthy lifestyle			
4	the cost of living			
5	a live concert			
6	the type of person			
7	a typical day			
8	a strange feeling			
9	a filling meal			
10	download the file			
11	read a book			
12	get rid of it			
13	ride a bike			
14	cycle to school			

97 **8c** Listen again and repeat the phrases. Pay special attention to the vowel sounds.

9 **Find and correct one mistake in each sentence.**

1 We all have busy, modern ~~ways of living~~ and we seem to spend less time together as a family. *lifestyles*

2 I work full-time and so does my husband, so that our children can have a good level of life.

3 On a tipical day, I don't get home from work until around 7 o'clock in the evening.

4 Even in the evening, I still control my email on my phone, so I don't really relax properly.

5 If one of the kids is taking place in a school play or a sports competition, one of us will always go along.

6 We do an effort to eat together as a family at least two or three times a week.

7 Because we're always busy, we tend to drive everywhere which means we don't get as much exercises as we should.

8 I know I should do a bit more phisical activity and take better care of myself.

3 PLACES

Place, space, room and area

Place is a useful word to describe a town, a building etc., but there are other words which better describe specific places.

Room and **space** both refer to a place that is empty or available to use.

✓ We don't have enough **room** to store all our things.

✗ We don't have enough ~~place~~ to store all our things.

✓ There's a big garden and plenty of **space** for the dogs to run around.

✗ … plenty of ~~place~~ for the dogs to run around.

Space is often used with another noun: *office space, storage space*. It is also used to refer to an area you are free to enjoy: *open space, green space, public space*.

Part of a town or a piece of land is an **area**.

✓ The neighbourhood has plenty of parks and playground **areas**.

✗ The neighbourhood has plenty of parks and playground ~~zones~~.

You can also say that something **is located** or **is situated** somewhere.

✓ The hotel is **located/is situated** on the top of a hill, above the beach.

✗ The hotel is ~~placed~~ on the top of a hill, above the beach.

Note that *located* and *situated* are quite formal, it is common to just say:

The hotel is on the top of a hill, above the beach.

1 **Choose the best option to complete the sentences.**

1 Is there **place/room** for one more chair at the table?

2 Living in the countryside, there's plenty of open **room/space** for children to run around and play.

3 Clifton is a small seaside town and it's a **great place/zone** to live and work.

4 Many people have left the countryside and moved to urban **areas/places** to find work.

5 Their offices are **located/placed** on the outskirts of the city, close to the motorway.

6 In the centre of the island, there's a large **area/zone** of forest.

7 Write on every second line, so you leave **place/room** for changes and corrections.

8 There's a lovely new kitchen with plenty of storage **area/space**.

Car park / parking space

A **car park** is a building or an area where people can park their cars. In American English, this is called a parking lot.

✓ There's a large car park behind the shopping centre.

✗ There's a large ~~parking~~ behind the shopping centre.

A **parking space** is a place in a car park or by the side of the road where you can park a car.

✓ We drove around for ages looking for a **parking space**.

✗ We drove around for ages looking for a ~~parking~~.

car park

parking space

False friends

2 Complete the sentences using a word or phrase from the box. Not all the words are needed.

> camping campsite car park choice election
> exhibition exposition facilities installations
> parking parking space

1 We had trouble .... near the hotel.
2 The hotel .... only has space for a handful of cars and it was already full.
3 It took us nearly 30 minutes to find a .... in a street near the port.
4 Have you visited the new Van Gogh .... at the City Museum yet?
5 We could either go to the museum or visit the park. It's your ....
6 I went .... with my friends last summer in the mountains.
7 We stayed at a great .... on the edge of a forest.
8 It had really good ....; nice showers, a small shop and barbecues.

Go, get to and arrive

When you **go** somewhere, you travel to that place. You usually use **go to** + a place.

✓ We're planning to **go to** Paris next week.
✗ We're planning to ~~go Paris~~ next week.

When you **arrive** or **get** somewhere, you reach that place.

✓ What's the best way to **get to** your house?
✗ What's the best way to ~~get your house~~?
✓ Sam **got back** about an hour ago.
✓ The match had already started when we **got there**.

Arrive is used especially to talk about transport and journeys. The preposition after **arrive** depends on the type of place; *in New York, in Italy, at the cinema, at work*

✓ Her flight **arrives** at midday.
✓ We finally **arrived** at the station nearly 20 minutes late.
✗ We finally ~~arrived to~~ the station nearly 20 minutes late.

3 Complete the sentences using the best form of go, get or arrive.

1 My sister .... to Miami on holiday last year. She said it was amazing.
2 How do you .... to college? It is close enough to walk?
3 I was meeting Sam at the cinema at 6, but I .... there early, so I grabbed a coffee next door.
4 I think the train's due to .... in Brussels at 3 o'clock in the afternoon.
5 Hey, Gemma! I thought you were in Germany. When did you .... back?
6 Sorry, I have to .... home now. Mum said I have to be back by 10.
7 How do we .... to the stadium from here? Have you got a map on your phone?
8 Give me a call when you .... at the airport.

Which preposition?

4a Complete each possible sentence ending with the correct preposition.

They arrived ...

1 ... . an old house that seemed to be empty.
2 ... . Rome on Saturday.
3 ... . the village just as it was getting dark.
4 ... . the island last week.
5 ... . train from Paris.
6 ... . a small market selling fruit and vegetables.
7 ... . foot after walking for several hours.
8 ... . Mexico 11 hours later.

4b Check your answers, then use one of the sentences as the first or the last line of a short story.

5 Match the sentence halves.

1 Finally, the ambulance arrived
2 Kim explained that she'd arrived
3 When the police arrived
4 Most children from the village get
5 When we eventually got
6 I really think you should go
7 By the time they got
8 I'll tell George when he gets

a. to the top of the hill, we were all exhausted.
b. back to the car, the ice-creams had all melted.
c. to the doctor.
d. in this country as a child.
e. on the scene, the men had already run off.
f. home from work this evening.
g. at the hospital.
h. to school by bus.

Spelling: gh

6 Find and correct <u>two</u> spelling mistakes in each description.

I live on the outskirts of the city. Although there aren't as many shops or things going on as in the city centre, it's a nice neightbourhood. Everyone's friendly and there's a sense of community.

For most of the year, my home town has a really nice climate. For a few weeks each summer thought, we experience really hight temperatures and it's difficult to keep cool.

My apartment is pretty quiet. The family who live upstairs have a young daugher. When they moved in, I thought she'd be really noisy. Sometimes I hear her laughting and playing, but she really doesn't make much noise.

I have to cycle across the city every day to get to college. The roads are really busy and there aren't enought cycle paths. I go throught a park for part of my route, which is much safer, but the rest of the journey can be a bit of nightmare.

Entering and leaving

You **enter** or **go into** a room or a building. *Enter* is a slightly more formal word.

✓ We **went into** a shop selling souvenirs.
✗ We ~~entered~~ a shop selling souvenirs.
✓ Luke **went into** the kitchen to make some coffee.
✗ Luke ~~got into~~ the kitchen to make some coffee.
✓ Please **enter** the building via the main entrance.

You **leave** a room or building or you **go out**. You **go out** especially for a purpose.

✓ We'll need to **leave** the house at about 6.30.
✗ We'll need to ~~go out from~~ the house at about 6.30.
✓ Let's go out for a walk.

You **get into** or **get out of** a car, but you **get on/onto** or **get off** a bus, train, plane, etc.

✓ A woman **got out of** a taxi.
✗ A woman ~~got off~~ a taxi.
✓ We **got off** the bus at the next stop.

7 Complete the sentences using a preposition from the box. Write - if no preposition is needed. Some words can be used more than once and some are not needed.

> in   into   off   on   out   out of

1 She went ___into___ the wrong room by mistake.
2 Anna left .... the office about an hour ago.
3 The driver got .... the car and went over to a woman standing nearby.
4 His mother only went .... the room for a few minutes to answer the front door.
5 We got .... the train at Lime Street station and went a couple of stops.
6 I need to go .... to do a bit of food shopping later.
7 They got .... the bus in the main square and walked down to the sea.
8 The pupils all stood up when the teacher entered .... the room.

8a Read the texts quickly and match them to the text types.

1 A travel blog: ....
2 A police report: ....
3 Directions: ....

A

At approximately 4.45pm, three men [1]***entered/got in*** the building. Fifteen minutes later, at around 5 o'clock, they [2]***left/went out of*** via the front entrance carrying six bags of stolen goods. The men [3]***got into/got onto*** a black Mercedes parked outside and drove off.

B

When you [4]***get out/leave*** here, you need to [5]***get out from / go out of*** the main door and turn right. Follow the path for a few metres, then turn left by the library. The Chemistry Department is right next to the library. When you [6]***go in/get into***, there's a reception desk in the lobby, they'll tell you which room to go to.

C

The next morning after breakfast, I [7]***went out/left*** to explore the city. The hotel was quite a way out of town, so I [8]***got into/got on*** a bus. I wasn't quite sure where I was going, but I [9]***got off/went out*** when we arrived at what looked like the main square. I wandered around for a while, then I [10]***got into/went into*** a small café and managed to order some mint tea.

8b Now choose the best options to complete the texts.

Noun forms

9 Write the correct forms of the <u>underlined</u> words.

1 Did you enjoy your <u>visiting</u> to the castle? visit
2 I'm stuck in traffic on my way to the airport and my <u>fly</u> leaves in 45 minutes.
3 She goes for a run in the park every morning before <u>working</u>.
4 There have been lots of <u>complains</u> about the noise from the bar.
5 I posted lots of photos of our <u>staying</u> on the farm on social media.
6 I'll send you the details a couple of weeks before my <u>arriving</u>.

Transport

Remember, **transport** is an uncountable noun and is not usually used in a plural form.

✓ Most people use **public transport** to get around the city.

✗ Most people use ~~the public transports~~ to get around the city.

You can talk about different means of transport or forms of transport.

✓ Bikes are the main form of transport on the island.

✗ Bikes are the ~~main way~~ of transport on the island.

Note: **means** is the singular and the plural form.

✓ The tram is still a major **means of transport** in several European cities.

✗ The tram is still a major ~~mean of transport~~ in several European cities.

10a Are these sentences correct? Correct any mistakes.

1 Over short distances, a bike is the cheapest mean of transport.
2 Ferries are a very common form of transport between the islands.
3 The council is encouraging people to use a public transport instead of driving into the city.
4 Lots of people go to work on bicycle.
5 The simplest means of getting from the airport to the hotel is by taxi.
6 The website has more information about accommodation, food and local transports.
7 It's only a 15-minute travel by bus into the town centre.
8 I don't mind having a 30-minute walking to work each day.

About you:

10b What are the most popular means of transport where you live?

- Do people use public transport?
- What's the quickest way to get around?
- Are there problems with traffic?

Collocations: adjective + noun

11 Choose the best adjective to complete the sentences.

1 The company's offices are in a **high / long / tall**, glass building in the city centre.
2 The journey can take up to an hour in **big / heavy / great** traffic.
3 I hate trying to park my car in a **little / small / short** space.
4 If you live in a **big / great / main** city, you expect a certain amount noise.
5 We heard a really **big / loud / strong** noise, like an alarm going off.
6 Arrive at the museum early to avoid **big / large / long** queues.

4 FACT & OPINION

Subject or theme?

The **subject** of an article, a conversation, a talk, etc. is the thing being discussed. You can use **subject** to talk about everyday things such as the topic of an email or a meeting.

✓ *Immigration is a subject that people have strong views about.*

✗ *Immigration is a ~~theme~~ that people have strong views about.*

Theme is a slightly more formal word often used to talk about the main idea in a work of art or in an academic talk or book. A **theme** can also be the idea which links together several things, such as the talks at a conference or works of art at an exhibition.

✓ *The theme of this year's conference is technology in education.*

False friends: information

1 Choose the best word to complete the sentences.

1 The economy has been a key **subject/theme** of the election campaign.
2 Has Grandpa ever told you the **history/story** of when he travelled to America by ship?
3 According to the **advert/announcement**, the new phone even works under water.
4 Recently, we received the sad **news/notice** that the club is going to close at the end of the year.
5 I went to an interesting **conference/talk** by a crime writer about how she researches her books.

Verb + noun collocations

2 Choose the best verb to complete the sentences. More than one option may be possible.

1 Students have to .... some research into a particular topic for their end-of-year project.

   a conduct   **b** do   **c** make

2 Each person is asked to .... a one-minute talk about one of their hobbies or interests.

   a give   **b** make   **c** say

3 The local mayor .... a speech at the opening ceremony.

   a did   **b** gave   **c** made

4 The tutor .... us some really good advice about preparing for exams.

   a gave   **b** offered   **c** taught

5 Last summer, I .... a course in digital photography at the local college.

   a did   **b** made   **c** took

6 Let me .... straight to the point.

   a get   **b** go   **c** reach

7 The advert for the event .... that there would be food and drink available at the venue.

   a put   **b** said   **c** wrote

8 I'll send you copies of the slides, but you might want to .... your own notes.

   a do   **b** make   **c** take

3a Complete the questions with an appropriate verb in each gap. More than one answer may be possible.

1 Have you ever .... a talk in public?
2 What's the most interesting course you've .... ?
3 Do you prefer to .... research online or in a library?
4 What's the best advice you've been .... about learning a language?
5 Do you prefer to .... notes on paper or on a laptop or tablet?

About you:

3b Check your answers, then answer the questions about yourself. Explain your answer.

Which preposition?

4 Choose the best option to complete these sentences.

1 There were a number of talks and other events all *related to/related with* art and photography.
2 The price is reasonable but in *relation to / in relation with* quality it's a bit expensive
3 No one from the company has yet been in contact *regarding/regarding to* my complaint.
4 You will be sent additional information *concerning/ concerning to* meals and accommodation nearer the time.
5 There was a welcome pack *consisting of/consisting on* a map and some information about the local area.
6 All the information about the holiday apartment was correct *apart from/apart of* the address.

Point, factor, aspect

A **point** is an idea that someone expresses. It is often an opinion or an argument rather than a simple fact.

*Sophie **made a good point about** the cost of new technology.*

A **factor** is a fact or a situation that influences something.

✓ *Education is clearly an important **factor** in encouraging people to reduce waste.*

✗ *Education is clearly an important ~~point~~ in encouraging people to reduce waste.*

An **aspect** of something is part of a problem or a situation.

✓ *Spelling is an important **aspect of** language learning.*

✗ *Spelling is an important ~~point~~ of language learning.*

5 Complete the sentences using point, factor or aspect.

1 An important .... to take into consideration when planning an advertising campaign is the age of the target audience.
2 I completely agree with the writer's .... about some adverts being misleading.
3 I think helping people is the most rewarding .... of the job.
4 Price shouldn't be the only .... in your decision about which course to choose.
5 For most people, food is still an important .... of family life.
6 His main .... was that motivation is a key .... in academic success.

Actual, current, present, modern

Actual describes something that is real or correct, especially compared with a guess or false information.

the actual + cost, number, amount, result

✓ We expected the repairs to be around €100, but **the actual cost** was nearly double.

Current and **present** describe something that exists now, especially compared with the past or the future.

the current + system, situation, level, rate

✓ There need to be changes because the **current** system is incredibly slow.

✗ There need to be changes because the ~~actual system~~ is incredibly slow.

the present + study, system, case, situation

✓ Anything would be an improvement on the **present** situation.

Modern describes something that is new and exists now, especially compared with the past.

modern + world, society, life, technology

✓ Online advertising is just a part of **modern** life.

✗ Online advertising is just a part of ~~actual life~~.

6 Complete the texts using words or phrases from the box.

> actual   actually   current   currently
> modern   present   right now

In our **(1)** .... society, it's possible to access all kinds of information about the world around you via mobile technology. Your mobile phone can use GPS to pinpoint your **(2)** .... location, then you can find information about nearby restaurants, get directions or check the local weather forecast. It can tell you about nearby events that are happening **(3)** .... and you can even book tickets.

One of the **(4)** .... issues in education is its focus on learning facts and information. Some people have suggested this is no longer what we need in a **(5)** .... world. As technology changes the world around us at an increasingly fast pace, the facts that people learnt in school a few years ago are already out-of-date. What young people **(6)** .... need to learn at school, the argument goes, is not facts, but skills.

Some estimates reckon that there are around a quarter of a million words in English, but the **(7)** .... number may be much larger. This includes words that are in **(8)** .... use as well as obsolete words that you might find in literature, for example, but which are no longer used in the **(9)** .... day. And of course, new words are being added to the language all the time to describe new technology and new concepts that have become a part of **(10)** .... life like self-checkouts, selfies and fake news.

5 PERSONAL RELATIONSHIPS

Relationships and relations

Relationship is used to talk about the personal connections between people, especially from the same family or partners (husband/wife, boyfriend/girlfriend).

✓ Chloe has a good **relationship with** her parents.

✗ Chloe has a good ~~relation~~ with her parents.

Relations (plural) is usually used to talk about the way two groups or countries feel and behave towards each other.

public/customer/international relations

*She is head of marketing and **public relations** for the company.*

A person in your family is a **relative** or a **relation**. **Relative** is the more common word.

*They had a big party and invited all their friends and **family/relatives/relations**.*

1 Complete the sentences using the best form of *relationship*, *relations* or *relative*.

1 Their .... broke up after Alice moved away to study at university.

2 Maria lives on her own and she has no close .... living nearby.

3 Since the crisis, ... between the two countries have completely broken down.

4 Josh has always had a close .... with his grandparents.

5 Some people have responsibilities caring for elderly ....

6 The company is trying to improve customer .... and reduce the number of complaints.

Verb + preposition

2 Complete the sentences using an appropriate preposition (*for, on, to*, etc.) in each gap. Two gaps can be left empty.

1 It's only natural that teenagers don't always agree .... their parents.

2 I sent Gemma a message to thank her .... the flowers.

3 When you see Rory, congratulate him .... the new baby from me.

4 Louisa finally got married .... her long-term partner last year.

5 Tom suspects .... Alex .... secretly looking at his phone messages.

6 I trust .... Lily to look after the house while we're away – she's a sensible girl.

7 Mark confessed .... taking money from his mother's purse.

8 Ruth would never lie .... her parents about something like that.

Spelling: adjectives

3 Find and correct <u>four</u> spelling errors in each story.

When I met my girlfriend's parents for the first time, I was really nervious. When I arrived at her house and her mum answered the door, I suddenly wasn't sure whether it was appropiate to kiss her on the cheek or just to shake hands. So I just stood there awkwardly smiling. Thankfully, she stepped forward and gave me a big friendly hug. I was really greatful and immediately relaxed and felt confortable as she welcomed me into the house.

My sister is married to a Canadian and they live in the far north of Canada. Last year, I visited them for the first time and I was atonished by what a beautiful area it is, with vast areas of unspoilt landscape. I was there in the spring, but the temperatures were still really low and there was snow on the ground. I'm not accostumed to such cold weather and I had to borrow extra clothes from my sister. I found it quite dificult just walking around on the icy ground and at first, I was frightenned of falling over, but I gradually got used to it.

Pronunciation and spelling: weak vowels

The weak vowel sound /ə/ can be represented by any vowel in the spelling of words. Remember not to stress syllables with weak vowels.

A: **a**gree, comfort**a**ble
E: par**e**nts, fright**e**ned
I: cous**i**n, poss**i**ble
O: c**o**nfess, fact**o**r
U: s**u**spect, nervo**u**s

4a Underline the weak sound(s) in the words in bold in each sentence.

1 Is the film **appropriate** for **children**?
2 We had a **marvellous** time **yesterday**.
3 My **parents arrived together**.
4 Sorry, it's **currently unavailable**.
5 We only meet up for **special occasions**.
6 I **suspect** Tom's **probably responsible** for the mess.

4b Listen and repeat the sentences. Be careful not to stress the weak syllables.

Nervous

If you're **nervous**, you feel slightly worried, especially about something that's is going to or might happen. You might feel nervous before an exam or another important occasion.

✓ Most people feel a bit **nervous** before a job interview.

If someone feels slightly angry or they find a situation stressful, you can say they're **agitated** or **irritable**. You might feel agitated or irritable if you're stuck in a traffic jam or you have to wait too long for something.

✓ The concert started more than forty minutes late and people were starting to get **irritable**.

✗ The concert started more than forty minutes late and people were starting to get ~~nervous~~.

✓ One man got really **agitated** and started shouting at the hotel manager.

✗ One man got really ~~nervous~~ and started shouting at the hotel manager.

Commonly confused adjectives

5 Choose the best option to complete the sentences.

1 We'd been walking around all day and the kids were getting tired and *irritable/nervous*.
2 It's natural to feel a little *agitated/nervous* when you have to speak in front of a lot of people.
3 Sam became quite *agitated/nervous* and accused his brother of lying to him.
4 I really enjoyed going surfing with Steve, it was *great fun/very funny*.
5 Isabelle was a long way from home and feeling a bit *alone/lonely*.
6 I quite enjoy travelling *alone/lonely* because I can do exactly what I want.
7 I'm very *pleasant/pleased* to hear that you can come next week.
8 Children inevitably get *bored/boring* on long car journeys.
9 I spent the whole day sitting in long, *bored/boring* meetings.

Be/get/go + adjective

You can use **get** + some emotion adjectives to describe a feeling that develops.

get tired/excited/angry/nervous

✓ Everyone's **getting excited** about the festival next week.

You use **be** + an emotion adjective to describe a reaction.

be disappointed/shocked/surprised

✓ **I was very disappointed** when I heard the news.

✗ I ~~got very disappointed~~ when I heard the news.

Some expressions use **go** + adjective; go mad/crazy, go red

✓ His parents **went mad** when they found out.

✗ His parents ~~got mad~~ when they found out.

6 Complete the stories using the best form of *be*, *get* or *go* in each gap. Sometimes more than one answer is possible.

> I recently moved into an apartment with two other university students. After just a couple of days, I **(1)** .... surprised to find that the coffee I'd bought was nearly empty. I asked my flatmates about it and they admitted that they'd been using it. I explained I **(2)** .... a bit disappointed and I'm hoping it won't happen again.

> This new girl moved into the apartment recently and she **(3)** .... mad when she found out we'd been using her coffee. I mean, it was just a bit of coffee, but she **(4)** .... really upset about it.

> TThe other day, I had to make a speech at a party to celebrate my grandparents' 50th wedding anniversary. It was awful. I **(5)** .... really nervous and I completely forgot what I was going to say. I managed to say a few words off the top of my head, then I **(6)** .... bright red and sat down as quickly as possible.

> My granddaughter, Amy, made a lovely speech at our party. I **(7)** .... really touched by what she said. I don't often **(8)** .... emotional, but I admit I had to wipe away a tear.

Don't mind, don't care, don't worry or doesn't matter?

If you **don't mind** something, it's okay with you: you're not annoyed or worried about it. It's generally a positive expression to show you're happy whatever happens.

I really **don't mind** walking to work.

If you **don't care** about something, you don't think it's important or interesting. It's often a negative expression to show a lack of interest.

✓ He's only interested in making money and he **doesn't care about** anything else.

✗ He's only interested in making money and he ~~doesn't mind about~~ anything else.

You say to someone '**don't worry**', to show that something isn't a problem and they can relax about it.

✓ If you have any problems, please **don't worry**, just give me a call.

✗ If you have any problems, please ~~don't mind~~, just give me a call.

You say something **doesn't matter**, if it isn't important.

✓ For me, it **doesn't matter** where I spend my birthday, as long as I'm with friends and family.

✗ For me, ~~it doesn't mind~~ where I spend my birthday, as long as I'm with friends and family.

7a Complete the responses with *mind*, *care*, *worry* or *matter*.

1 A: If you're late again, you might lose your job.
   B: To be honest, I really don't .... I hate the job anyway!

2 A: Would you prefer to meet in the morning or the afternoon?
   B: I don't .... Whichever's easiest for you.

3 A: I'm really sorry, I forgot to pick up your dry cleaning.
   B: It doesn't .... I can get it tomorrow.

4 A: I'm afraid I can't give you a lift tomorrow after all.
   B: Don't .... I can get the bus.

5 A: Oh dear, we've only got enough chairs for four people.
   B: I don't .... sitting on the floor.

6 A: So, you want me to get some red balloons to decorate the room?
   B: The exact colour doesn't .... Just something bright and colourful.

7 A: I'm so sorry. I'm afraid I broke one of your mugs.
   B: Oh, don't .... about it. It wasn't expensive and I've got plenty more.

99 **7b** Listen and check your answers.

6 THOUGHTS AND MEMORIES1

Commonly confused verbs: thinking

Think is a general verb to talk about having ideas and opinions.

✓ *I **think** it's a good idea.*

✗ *I think is a good idea.*

✓ *I've been **thinking about** what to do next.*

✗ *I've been thinking what to do next.*

You can use **remember + that** … when you want someone to consider a particular point.

✓ *You have to **remember that** different cultures have different ideas about personal space.*

✗ *You have to think that different cultures have different ideas about personal space.*

You can use **imagine** to talk about hypothetical situations.

✓ *It's almost impossible now to **imagine** life without electricity.*

✗ *It's almost impossible now to think life without electricity.*

You can use **wonder + if/whether/why** … when you are considering possibilities.

✓ *For a long while, I **wondered whether** I should forgive him.*

✗ *For a long while, I thought whether I should forgive him.*

1 Complete the sentences using an appropriate form of think, remember, imagine or wonder.

1 It's important to .... that everyone has different priorities in life.

2 People were asked to .... that they could only save one object as their home was burning down.

3 It's human nature to .... whether our lives would have been better if we'd made different choices.

4 When something like this happens, it makes you stop and .... about what's really important to you.

5 We should all .... that our actions have an impact on the people around us.

6 There are lots of factors to consider if you're .... of moving to another country.

7 Most teenagers .... why their parents make such a fuss about tidying their rooms.

Phrases with *think*

2a Identify and correct one mistake in each sentence.

1 I think^ *it* is very important to teach children how to think critically.

2 Whenever you read something, you should think on the source of the information and how this might affect how it's presented.

3 There's lots of information which we think it is objective and accurate but is, in fact, just opinion.

4 Some people seem to think that get qualifications is the main aim of education.

5 I think that is one of the key functions of education to raise young people's awareness of the world around them.

6 As a society, we need to think in the long-term effects of the decisions we make now, especially when it comes to the environment.

7 Before you make a decision about your future studies, you need to take your time, get some advice and think about carefully.

8 There's lots of really useful information online for anyone thinking in studying abroad.

About you

2b Do you agree or disagree with the statements in 2a? Explain your reasons.

Spelling: vowel combinations

3 Complete the gaps in the words using one, two or three vowels.

1 You shouldn't bel............ve everything you read on social media.

2 Just bec............se something sounds convincing, it doesn't mean it's true.

3 Sometimes, it's difficult to tell the difference betw............n fact and fiction.

4 Her latest article rec............ved hundreds of comments.

5 Do the ideas that people read online directly affect their beh............viour?

6 Most of us focus on ideas we agree with inst............d of trying to seek out opposing arguments.

7 The magazine always has such b............tiful photos to accompany the articles.

8 I love writing about issues that matter to me so I'd like to pursue a car............r in journalism.

Commonly confused verbs: notice, realize, see

When you look at something, you **see** it.

✓ As soon as I opened the box, I could **see** it was empty.

✗ As soon as I opened the box I could ~~notice~~ it was empty.

When you see or hear something and you consciously think about it being there, you **notice** it.

✓ At first, I didn't **notice** the security guard standing in the corner.

✗ At first, I didn't ~~notice of~~ the security guard standing in the corner.

When you think about a situation and you understand something new, you **realize** it.

✓ When I got in the taxi, I **realized** I didn't know the address of Jack's apartment.

✗ When I got in the taxi, I ~~noticed~~ I didn't know the address of Jack's apartment.

100 **4a** Complete the text using the best form of *notice*, *realize* or *see* in each gap.

Last week, I had to travel to a business meeting in another city. I chose to go by train so I could do some work on my way. When I got on the train, I didn't **(1)** .... it was quieter than usual. I got out my laptop and started some work. After about 30 minutes, we stopped at a station and I looked out the window to **(2)** .... where we were. I didn't recognize the name of the town at first, then I suddenly **(3)** .... I was on the wrong train and going in the opposite direction! I quickly gathered up my things and jumped off the train. On the platform, I checked the times of the trains going the other way. I could **(4)** .... that the next train was going to be another half an hour and I **(5)** .... I was going to miss my meeting.

Pronunciation: final /s/ and /z/

101 **4a** What is the final sound in the words below?

1 notice /s/ /z/ ....
2 realize /s/ _ /z/ ....
3 choose /s/ _ /z/ ....
4 lose /s/ /z/ ....
5 miss /s/ /z/ ....

4c In the text in 4a, circle four words that end with /s/ and underline eight words that end in /z/.

Commonly confused verbs: remembering and forgetting

When you **remember** something or **remember doing** something, it is still in your mind from the past. When one thing **reminds** you **of** something else, it makes you think about it again.

✓ I remember playing on the beach with my brothers as a kid.

✓ The smell of sun cream **reminds me of** family holidays at the beach.

✗ The smell of sun cream ~~remembers to me~~ family holidays at the beach.

When you **remember to do** something, you don't forget to do it. When you **remind someone to do** something, you tell them about it, so they don't forget.

✓ Can you remember to get some more milk on your way home?

✓ Can you **remind me to call** Alex this evening?

✗ Can you ~~remember me to call~~ Alex this evening?

When you **forget** an object, you don't remember to bring it with you.

*Oh no, I **forgot** my swimming stuff.*

If you mention the place, you say you **left something somewhere**.

✓ I suddenly realized I'd **left my keys in my other trousers**.

✗ I suddenly realized I'd ~~forgotten~~ my keys in my other trousers.

When you **lose** an object, you don't know where it is.

*I've **lost** my phone. I can't find it anywhere.*

5a Complete the anecdotes with the best form of a verb from the box. Add me or myself where needed.

forget   leave   lose   remember   remind

I'm really bad at **(1)** .... people's names. I meet a lot of people for my job and it can be really embarrassing when I know I've met someone before, but I've completely **(2)** .... their name.

I've always had a terrible memory. I used to write notes on the back of my hand to **(3)** .... to do things. Nowadays, I set reminders on my phone. So, my phone beeps to **(4)** .... about a dentist's appointment or someone's birthday.

When I was a young kid, I **(5)** .... playing in the fields behind our house with my sister on long summer days. We always used to come home covered in grass stains and now the smell of grass always **(6)** .... of that time.

I always leave the apartment in a rush in the morning and several times recently, I've got to work and realized I've **(7)** .... something important like my phone or my keys. The other day, I thought I'd **(8)** .... my wallet. I thought maybe I'd dropped it on the tram or perhaps that it'd be stolen. It was only when I got home that I discovered I'd actually just **(9)** .... it on the kitchen table.

About you

5b Answer the questions about yourself.

- What kind of things do you find difficult to remember?
- How do you remind yourself to do things?
- What's your earliest memory?
- Which sounds, smells and tastes remind you of your childhood?
- Do you often forget to take things out with you?
- When was the last time you left something somewhere?

Collocations: lose, miss and waste

6 Choose the best option to complete the sentences.

1 The exhibition is only on for another week, so don't *lose/ miss* the chance to see this unique collection of artworks.

2 Unfortunately, I *lost/missed* the last train and had to get an expensive taxi home.

3 I don't understand why people *lose/waste* their money on expensive designer clothes.

4 The only way to *lose/take off* weight is to eat less and do more exercise.

5 If you drop out of your university course now, you'll have *lost/wasted* all that time and effort.

6 Yes, the tickets are expensive, but it would be a pity to *lose/miss* the opportunity to see my favourite band play live in my home town.

7 Read the conversation between two old friends. Complete the dialogue using the verbs from the box.

> leave   lose   notice   realize   remember   remind
> think   think of   wonder

Steve: Look, I found this old photo when I was clearing out some stuff. Do you **(1)** .... that summer?

Emma: Oh wow! Look, there's my yellow teddy bear. If I still had it then, we must've been about five or six years old.

Steve: Oh yes, I didn't **(2)** .... that. I remember when you **(3)** .... that bear. You were so upset!

Emma: Yes, we looked everywhere for him. My mum **(4)** .... I'd just **(5)** .... him somewhere, so we spent ages searching. When I **(6)** .... we weren't going to find him, I cried and cried. I **(7)** .... what actually happened to him.

Steve: I guess we'll never know! That does **(8)** .... me though, I need to buy a birthday present for my niece. I was **(9)** .... getting her a book, but I **(10)** .... if she'd like a teddy bear.

Emma: That's a great idea. Every little girl should have a bear!

GRAMMAR

1 PEOPLE & SOCIETY

Plural nouns: groups of people

When you talk about a whole group or type of people, you usually use a plural noun.

✓ *The hotel offers special rates for* **students**.

✗ *The hotel offers special rates for* ~~student~~.

✓ *Most of their fans are* **children and teenagers**.

✗ *Most of their fans are* ~~child and teenager~~.

Remember, some common nouns to refer to people have irregular plural forms, e.g. *people, children, men, women*

1a **Choose the correct noun form to complete the sentences.**

1 We don't know whether animals have emotions in the same way as *human being / human beings*.

2 On public transport, passengers should give up their seats for mothers with *babies / babys*.

3 In the future, *scientist / scientists* will probably find a cure for diseases like diabetes.

4 It's important for *children / childrens* to develop healthy eating habits at a young age.

5 I think you can tell what kind of *person / people* someone is within the first few minutes.

6 Although *tourist / tourists* bring money into a country, they can also cause problems.

7 I don't believe that *policeman / policemen* should carry guns.

8 It's shocking that a *child / children* born in Spain can expect to live to 83 years old compared to some African countries where life expectancy is just 50 years.

About you

1b **Do you agree or disagree with the comments in exercise 1? Give a brief opinion on each topic.**

The + plural noun

When you talk about a general group of people, you don't need **the** before the noun.

✓ *Lots of junk food advertising is aimed at* **children**. *(=all children)*

✗ *Lots of junk food advertising is aimed at* ~~the children~~.

When you talk about a particular group of people, you use **the** before the noun.

✓ *At some schools,* **the children** *have to wear a special uniform. (=the children at those schools)*

Some nouns to describe groups of people are typically used with *the; the police, the public*

✓ *They reported the incident to* **the police**.

2 **Is *the* needed in each sentence below? Cross out any that are not needed.**

1 It's important to have green open spaces where **the** people can relax.

2 Nowadays **the** students are more likely to search for information online than in a library.

3 Most of **the** people inside the stadium were singing and having a great time.

4 We called **the** police as soon as we realized the money was missing.

5 In most restaurants, the menus are also written in English for **the** tourists and other visitors.

6 Museums are trying to appeal more to the young people with interactive exhibits.

7 She didn't have a microphone and **the** people at the back couldn't hear what she was saying.

8 After the wedding ceremony, **the** guests all gathered together for photographs.

Which preposition?

3 **Complete the sentences using one preposition from the box in each gap. Some prepositions are used more than once and some are not needed.**

at	by	from	in	of	under

1 The university has students .... all over the world.

2 Some of the people .... my class have taken the exam before.

3 I read a really interesting book .... an Australian writer.

4 One of the women .... our tour group had her bag stolen.

5 I don't think I've ever met anyone............... Slovakia before.

6 Obviously, ... his point of view, the situation seems unfair.

False friends: people

In English, you can refer to people in general as **the public** (*always singular*).

✓ *As a police officer, I have to deal with the public every day.*

The people at a performance (at the theatre, a concert, etc.) are the **audience** (*usually singular*).

✓ *At the end of his speech, **the audience** stood and clapped.*

✗ *At the end of his speech, the ~~public/the spectators~~ stood and clapped.*

The people at a sporting event are **spectators** (countable noun) or fans.

✓ *The sports stadium can hold 30,000 **spectators**.*

You can refer to the people who live in a particular place as **residents** or **inhabitants** (both fairly formal). Local people would be more informal/neutral.

✓ *It's a small town of about 12,000 **inhabitants**.*

✗ *It's a small town of about 12,000 ~~habitants~~.*

✓ *Local **residents** have complained about the plans for the new road.*

4 **Choose the best word to complete the sentences.**

1 The *audience / public / spectators* sang along with the band's most well-known songs.

2 The younger *habitants / inhabitants / neighbours* of the village are leaving to find work in the city.

3 Local politicians answered questions from members of *the public / public people / publics.*

4 The museum is open to the *audience / public / spectators* on Tuesdays and Fridays.

5 It's difficult for *young people / youngs / youths* to find places to live in the city.

6 The race was watched by hundreds of cheering *audience / publics / spectators.*

7 I think the best bit about going to new places is meeting the local *inhabitants / people / residents.*

8 She works in a small software company and she's popular with her *classmates / colleagues / companions.*

Someone, everybody, nothing + verb

Remember, this group of pronouns are all followed by a singular verb.

everybody, everyone, everything + *is/has*, etc.

✓ ***Everything seems*** *more difficult when you're tired.*

✗ *~~Everything seem~~ more difficult when you're tired.*

somebody, someone, something + *is/has*, etc.

✓ *The bus only stops at the next stop if **someone presses** the button.*

✗ *The bus only stops at the next stop if ~~someone press~~ the button.*

nobody, no one, nothing + *is/has*, etc.

✓ ***Nobody knows*** *how the fire started.*

✗ *~~Nobody know~~ how the fire started.*

anybody, anyone, anything + *is/has*, etc.

✓ *I don't know if **anyone** else **has** a better suggestion.*

✗ *I don't know if ~~anyone else have~~ a better suggestion.*

5 **Are these sentences correct? Correct any mistakes.**

1 When I arrived for the meeting, nobody ~~were~~ there. ✗ *was*

2 Not everyone thinks the new policy is a good idea.

3 This problem concerns everybody, but nobody want to take responsibility.

4 The lights go on automatically when someone enter the room.

5 They promised to improve things, but nothing have changed.

6 If no one answers the door, the delivery person just leaves a card.

7 Just call me if anything go wrong.

8 Everything were going okay until it started to rain.

We all …

We + all + main verb

✓ ***We all want*** *to have clear air to breathe.*

✗ *~~We want all~~ to have clean air to breathe.*

We + be + all

✓ ***We are all*** *aware of the health problems linked to eating fatty foods.*

✗ *~~We all are~~ aware of the health problems linked to eating fatty foods.*

We + auxiliary/modal + all + main verb

✓ *I'm sure **we could all** do more to help.*

✓ ***We've all met*** *someone who talks too much.*

6 Add *all* to each sentence in the best position.

1 Of course, we ^all^ want our children to grow up in a healthy environment.

2 To be honest, I'm sure we have done things we're not proud of.

3 At the end of the day, we are able to make our own decisions about what we buy.

4 The students stood in silence for a moment, then they started clapping.

5 In an ideal world, we would be treated equally.

6 People in different jobs might find it strange if they were paid exactly the same.

7 As a society, we should contribute to looking after the elderly.

8 The coach reminded the players that they had a responsibility to behave well.

Uncountable nouns: abstract concepts

Many general concepts are described using uncountable nouns; society, *education, health, pollution, tourism, technology*, etc. These nouns are not usually used with *a* or *the*.

✓ *In **modern society**, we accept that families come in many different forms.*

✗ *In the ~~modern society~~, we accept that families come in many different forms.*

✓ *Some people worry that **education** has become too focused around exams.*

✗ *Some people worry that ~~the education~~ has become too focused around exams.*

7 Read the Q&A. Delete any articles (*a, an, the*) that are not needed.

WHAT DO YOU THINK ARE THE MOST SERIOUS ISSUES FACING THE MODERN SOCIETY?

Personally, I think the health is a big issue. Although the medical technology has improved enormously, people are living much less healthy lifestyles. We all eat a fast food and drink sweet, fizzy drinks and we spend all day sitting at a desk. That means that the obesity is becoming a massive problem.

· ·

For me, it's the environment that I worry about. The pollution is a huge issue, especially in big cities. To solve it, we need to look at the transport. More people need to leave their cars at home and use a public transport. We also need to have tougher regulations on the industry.

· ·

I worry about the pressures on young people. I think the social media is having a negative influence. There's too much pressure to post perfect photos of yourself and to get lots of 'likes'. Plus, the education nowadays is all about tests and grades. Children are under enormous pressure to do well at the school.

Noun-verb agreement

8 Complete the sentences using the best form of the verb in brackets. Think carefully about the noun which agrees with the verb.

1 Young people typically ....*watch*........ (watch) TV on their phones or laptops.

2 Modern technology .... (allow) us to access news almost as it happens.

3 Most of the company's employees .... (work) at their main office in Milan.

4 My parents .... (live) in a small apartment on the coast.

5 In the winter, the weather sometimes .... (affect) the public transport system.

6 At the university, students all .... (have) a card that gives them access to the library.

7 Local people usually .... (hang) their washing to dry outside.

8 All this information .... (be) available via our website.

9 Of course, tourism .... (create) jobs in the area.

10 Visitors to the region .... (spend) thousands of euros every summer.

Spelling: double letters

9 Find and correct one spelling mistake in each sentence.

1 There will be plenty of oportunities for people to try out different sporting activities.

2 If people in the community all work together, then anything is posible.

3 Everyone agrees that major changes are necesary to improve living conditions.

4 We need to comunicate our ideas more effectively to the general public.

5 Health officials recomend that people eat five portions of fruit and vegetables a day.

6 Local people are very unhappy about the decission to close the public library.

7 To be honest, it's embarrasing to see our politicians behaving in this way.

8 The audience were dissapointed when the concert was cancelled at the last minute.

Noun + verb form

opportunity/right/decision + to do

✓ A handful of students had **the opportunity to spend** a year at an American university.

✗ A handful of students had the opportunity ~~of spending~~ a year at an American university.

---

danger/idea + of doing

✓ Many people like **the idea of cycling**, but find the roads are too busy.

✗ Many people like the idea ~~to cycle~~, but find the roads are too busy.

But: **be a good/bad/great idea** + to do

✓ It isn't **a good idea to use** your date of birth as your password.

✗ It isn't a good idea ~~using~~ your date of birth as your password.

---

have problems/difficulty/trouble + doing

✓ Some people **have difficulty sleeping**.

✗ Some people have difficulty ~~to sleep~~.

10 Complete the texts using the correct form of the verb in brackets. Add any other words that are needed.

According to the Universal Declaration of Human Rights, all children have the right **(1)** ...._to get_.... (get) a free elementary education. However, children in some countries have difficulty **(2)** .... (access) even basic schooling. For example, in countries that are hit by war or natural disasters, children may have problems just **(3)** ....(reach) the nearest school safely. In other cases, parents may make a decision **(4)** .... (not send) their children to school because they need them to work to help support the family.

The internet has opened up the opportunity for students **(5)** .... (search) for information from a huge range of sources. Whilst the idea **(6)** .... (have) access to all this information sounds great, are we in danger **(7)** .... (be) overloaded? We're constantly being told that it isn't a good idea **(8)** .... (trust) everything you read online. If you have trouble **(9)** .... (decide) what's fact and what's fake news, these simple guidelines might help …

11 Find and correct <u>four</u> mistakes in each paragraph.

children
I think it's a great idea for ~~child~~ and young people learning about politics at school. It's an important part of the education. And, of course, the decissions that politicians take now will affect young people in the future.

I strongly support the idea to have plenty of parks and green spaces in urban areas. In areas where most local habitants live in apartments, it's the only oportunity they have to relax and exercise outdoors. They are especially important for family with young children.

Modern technology makes it posible for people of all over the world communicating very cheaply and easily. Family members who live in different countries now have no trouble to keep in touch with instant messaging and video calls.

On holiday vs in the holidays

A **holiday** is a time when you are not working or studying, especially when you can travel or relax.

✓ *We had a great holiday in Sicily.*

✗ *We had a great ~~holidays~~ in Sicily.*

✓ *I really need a holiday.*

You can go somewhere **on holiday**:

✓ *Kate's not here, she's **on holiday** at the moment.*

✗ *Kate's not here, she's ~~on holidays~~ at the moment.*

✓ *We're **going on holiday** to Greece next month.*

The holidays are a time when children and students are not at school or university, e.g. during the summer.

✓ *What did you do **in the summer holidays**?*

1 Complete the sentences using *holiday/holidays* and any other words that are needed.

1 You've been working a lot lately. I think you need to take
....

2 George is .... from 15th July for a week.

3 As children, we often spent .... with our grandparents.

4 Emily said she had a really good .... in Jamaica.

5 Hotel prices are always higher during the school
....

6 Our neighbours are away .... at the moment.

Adjectives and adverbs

Remember, you can use an adjective before a noun.

✓ *Our trip along the Amazon was **a real adventure**.*

✗ *Our trip along the Amazon was ~~a really adventure~~.*

✓ *The holiday was a **total disaster** – it rained every day.*

✗ *The holiday was a ~~totally disaster~~.*

You can use an adverb before an adjective or with a verb.

✓ *It was an **incredibly hot** day.*

✗ *It was an ~~incredible hot~~ day.*

✓ *The weather can **change** very **quickly**.*

✗ *The weather can ~~change very quick~~.*

2 Choose the appropriate adjective or adverb form to complete the sentences.

1 Most people go on holiday to have a break from their ***normal/normally*** lives.

2 There's a ***direct/directly*** flight from Madrid to San Francisco.

3 Several people complained they were treated ***bad/badly*** by the travel company.

4 The website gives a ***brief/briefly*** description of each hotel along with some photos.

5 Problems can often be solved ***easier/more easily*** if you speak to someone right away.

6 The hotel is much better after some ***recent/recently*** changes to the restaurant and pool area.

7 Restaurants in the main tourist resorts can be ***terrible/terribly*** expensive.

8 All the day trips were very ***good/well*** organized.

9 For many people, the ***main/mainly*** reason for visiting the Maldives is to go snorkelling.

10 Would you go away on holiday with a ***complete/completely*** stranger?

Which preposition?

3 Complete the description using a preposition from the box in each gap. Some words are used more than once and some are not needed.

along	at	by	from	in	of	on	to

Last year, we visited the island of Dominica in the Caribbean. We stayed **(1)** .... an amazing eco-hotel **(2)** .... the centre of the island. Our room was **(3)** .... the second floor and from our balcony we had a fabulous view **(4)** .... the surrounding area. Dominica has a tropical climate, so it's slightly cooler and dry for the first few months **(5)** .... the year, but then there's a hot, rainy season **(6)** .... mid-June to mid-November, which is why the island's so green. We were there **(7)** .... late April and it was lovely and warm. We did quite a bit of hiking through the forest. We saw loads of wildlife and we came across some spectacular waterfalls where we swam **(8)** .... the refreshingly cold water. We also hired a car and drove **(9)** .... the coast. One day, we stopped at a tiny village that wasn't even marked **(10)** .... the map and had lunch from a local fried chicken stall, sitting under a palm tree, looking out at the ocean.

Parts of the day

You mostly use **far** to talk about distance in questions and negatives.

✓ *How far is it to the city centre?*

✓ *The apartment **isn't very far from** the beach.*

✗ *The apartment isn't very ~~far of~~ the beach.*

You say something is **5 kilometres/10 minutes away**.

✓ *The apartment is **two kilometres away from** the town centre.*

✗ *The apartment is ~~two kilometres far from~~ the town centre.*

✓ *The hotel is about **30 minutes away from** the airport by bus.*

You can also say something is **a long way**.

✓ *We were **a long way from** the nearest village.*

✗ *We were ~~far away from~~ the nearest village.*

4 Choose the best option to complete the sentences.

1 I live quite a *long way/far* from where I work.

2 Do you know how *far/long* the station is from here?

3 The castle is about 20 minutes *away/far* by car.

4 There's a great restaurant that isn't too *far away/far* from here.

5 The university is only about five minutes *away/far* from my apartment.

6 We've travelled a *long way/far* in the past few days.

Reflexive verbs

These verbs can be used with a reflexive pronoun (myself, yourself, etc.):

enjoy yourself, take care of yourself, introduce yourself

✓ *I think everyone really **enjoyed themselves** at the beach.*

✗ *I think everyone really ~~enjoyed at the beach~~.*

These verbs aren't usually used with a reflexive pronoun:

apologise, relax, feel + adjective

✓ *When I'm on holiday, I just want to **relax** and forget work.*

✗ *When I'm on holiday, I just want to ~~relax myself~~ and forget work.*

✓ *We want all our guests to **feel comfortable** here.*

✗ *We want all our guests to ~~feel themselves comfortable~~ here.*

You can say that someone behaves themselves when they behave well. This is usually used about children or to compare adults to children.

✓ *The kids mostly behaved themselves on the flight.*

You don't usually need a reflexive pronoun when talking about behaviour in general.

✓ *If you keep **behaving** that way, of course people will get annoyed.*

✗ *If you keep ~~behaving yourself~~ that way, of course people will get annoyed.*

5 Choose the best option to complete the sentences.

1 The guide .... to the group and ran through the schedule for the day.

   a introduced   **b** introduced him   **c** introduced himself

2 The hotel manager .... and moved us to a different room.

   a apologised   **b** apologised herself   **c** apologised for

3 If you see someone ...., speak to a member of airport staff immediately.

   a behaving strangely   **b** behaving themselves strangely   **c** behaving him strangely

4 Lots of people .... about flying.

   a feel nervous   **b** feel themselves nervous   **c** feel oneself nervous

5 Make sure you .... while you're away.

   a take care yourself   **b** take care of you   **c** take care of yourself

6 If you ...., you can have ice cream for pudding.

   a behave it   **b** behave you   **c** behave yourself

7 The kids really .... at the ski school.

   a enjoyed   **b** enjoyed themselves   **c** enjoyed them

8 I'm looking forward to .... by the pool and reading a book.

   a relaxing   **b** relaxing me   **c** relaxing myself

Names of buildings

You use *the* before the names of most buildings; *the Hilton Hotel, the National Museum*

You usually use *the* before names with … *of* …; *the Tower of London, the Museum of Modern Art*

But, you don't usually use *the* when the first word is the name of a place; *Edinburgh castle, Berlin Zoo*

6 Complete the sentences with *the* or – in each gap.

1 The couple were staying at .... Grand Hotel.

2 Thousands of tourists visit .... Royal Palace in Phnom Penh.

3 We did a tour around .... Cambridge University.

4 I took a great photo of .... Prague Castle.

5 It's really worth visiting .... Science Museum.

6 Have you been to .... Colosseum in Rome?

7 .... Milan Cathedral is an amazing building.

8 If you visit Istanbul, you have to go to .... Blue Mosque.

9 I'd love to see .... Leaning Tower of Pisa.

7a Choose the best options to complete the dialogue.

Dan: Have you got any travel plans this year?

Nina: Yes, we're going ¹***on holiday/on holidays*** to the US ²***in/on*** May.

Dan: Wow, that's really exciting. Where are you going?

Nina: We're flying to San Francisco. We've got a ³***briefly stop/brief stop*** there for a couple of days, to see all the famous sights, like ⁴***the/a*** Golden Gate Bridge. Then we're going to drive inland to Yosemite National Park.

Dan: That sounds amazing. Are you going on an organized tour?

Nina: No, we're travelling ⁵***independent/independently***, but Hannah's got everything pretty ⁶***good planned/well planned***. All the hotels are already booked and she's planned out the route ⁷***in/on*** the map.

7b Listen and check your answers.

3 PROBLEMS & SOLUTIONS

Adjective + verb form

difficult/easy/important/impossible (for someone) to do something

It is easier/cheaper/better to do something (=to make a suggestion)

something is **suitable/better for** doing something (=to describe the reason/purpose of something)

concerned/excited/worried about doing

interested in doing something

1a Match the problems, 1-3, to the solutions, A-C.

Problem 1: I've just got a new job, but it's difficult for me **(1)** *to get* (get) to the office from where I live because it's not on a bus route.

Solution: ....

Problem 2: I'm going to Africa on holiday next month. I'm really excited **(2)** .... (go), but I'm a bit worried **(3)** .... (get) sick.

Solution: ....

Problem 3: I've seen a holiday apartment online that I'm interested **(4)** .... (rent), but I'm a bit concerned **(5)** .... (give) my credit card details to the owner for the deposit.

- -

Solution A: It's sensible **(6)** .... (not / give) your payment details to someone you don't know, especially via email. Secure online payment systems, like Paypal, are much safer **(7)** .... (make) online payments. Alternatively, you could check whether it's possible **(8)** .... (pay) the deposit using a bank transfer.

Solution B: It really depends on how far away it is. A scooter might be a good option. They're cheap to run and it's easy **(9)** .... (get through) traffic. Scooters are only really suitable **(10)** .... (get around) the city though. If you need to travel further out of town, it's probably better **(11)** .... (buy) a car. Or would it be possible for you **(12)** .... (get) a lift with a colleague who lives nearby?

Solution C: If you're travelling to a tropical country, it's important **(13)** .... (visit) your doctor for advice before you go. Your doctor will advise you about any vaccinations you need. When you're there, you should be careful about what you eat and drink. It's always better **(14)** .... (drink) bottled water and **(15)** .... (avoid) ice in your drinks. It's easy **(16)** .... (get) sick from ice made from unclean water.

1b Now complete the texts using the best form of the verbs in brackets. Add any other words that are needed.

Which preposition?

2 Choose the best preposition to complete the sentences.

1 The airline didn't tell us anything about the reason **for/of** the delay.
2 You should contact the person responsible **for/of** maintenance and they'll sort it out.
3 I'm afraid, there's no simple solution **of/to** the problem.
4 I don't have enough information **about/for** the risks to make a decision.
5 This is a typical example **about/of** poor management.
6 Most people aren't aware **about/of** their rights when it comes to online booking.

Spelling: *-ing* forms

3 Find and correct three spelling mistakes in each paragraph.

We had a nightmare journey to Rome. Our flight was delayed and we spent nearly four hours waitting in departures. It was really frustrating because no one was giving us any information, so we didn't know what was happenning. Some passengers were begining to get really angry.

My cousins are visitting next month from the US and I've been planing what to do with them. They're really difficult to please though. Everything I suggest they say they're not interested in. They don't like sightseeing and they don't want to go to the beach. To be honest, I'm starting to wonder why they're comming!

Last year, I started writting a blog for a cycling club I'm part of. At first, I just wrote about the trips we went on and posted a few photos. Over the past few months though, it's been developing into something a lot bigger with links to social media, advertising what we do and trying to attract new members. It's good for the club, but it's almost becomming a full-time job now and I don't really have the time.

Make it easy and find it difficult

find/make something + adjective
✓ Technology should **make our lives easier**.
✗ Technology should ~~make easier our lives~~.
✓ Some people **find it very difficult** to talk about their feelings.
✗ Some people ~~find very difficult~~ to talk about their feelings.

4 Complete the sentences using the verb make or find plus the words in brackets. Put the words in the best order and add any other words that are needed.

1 The kids ate so much ice cream, they *made themselves sick* (sick / themselves).

2 People don't mind going to work if they .... (interesting / their job).

3 The noise from the road outside .... (impossible / to sleep).

4 It's quite a good website, but I .... (annoying / slightly / the adverts).

5 Losing weight seems like a simple task, but lots of people .... (difficult).

6 There are lots of things we could do to .... (more attractive / the apartment).

7 Having a qualification in English language .... (easier / to find a job).

Worth, worthwhile and worthy

Worth, meaning 'having a particular value', is only used after verbs such as *be*, *seem* and *look*. It is always followed by an object; **be worth something**.
✓ Some of the items stolen were **worth a lot of money**.

If something **is worth doing**, it is useful or important enough to do.
✓ It's definitely **worth getting** travel insurance.

If you say that something is **worth it**, it is useful or enjoyable enough to make the cost or effort acceptable.
✓ Getting a car with air-conditioning was slightly more expensive, but I think it **was worth it**.

If something is **worthwhile**, it is worth the time, effort or money involved in doing it. **Worthwhile** can be used before a noun or after a verb such as be, seem or look. It can be used at the end of a clause or sentence.
✓ It was **a worthwhile experience** and it's taught me a lot.

✓ I think all the hard work has been **worthwhile**.

Worthy is a more formal adjective to describe something that deserves respect or support. **Worthwhile** is a more common and natural word in most contexts.
✓ They're raising money for **a worthy/worthwhile cause**.

5 Match the sentence halves. Think about both meaning and grammar.

1 She's involved in a really worthwhile …
2 Some people believe it isn't worth …
3 European countries give humanitarian aid worth …
4 This project is a huge investment, but it's worth …
5 Health education projects are especially worthwhile …

A it because it could save hundreds of lives.
B millions of euros to development projects every year.
C project to encourage reading skills in young kids.
D because they can help prevent future problems.
E giving money to charity because it gets wasted.

Comparative and superlative adjective forms

6 Are these sentences correct? Correct any mistakes.

1 Some people find it ~~more easy~~ to travel as part of a group. ✗ *easier*

2 It's always more safe to carry any cash and your credit cards separately.

3 By putting your bag across your body, you make it more difficult to steal.

4 They might find it simplier just to get a taxi from the airport.

5 Remember, the rules about what you can take on board may be stricter with some airlines.

6 It's probably more nice and more comfortable to visit in September when it's slightly cooler.

7 The beaches are certainly much more clean than they were a few years ago.

8 Probably the strangest way I've ever travelled was by camel.

9 Generally, you'll find it quickier to buy your ticket from one the machines.

10 The castle is quite small, but combining it with a visit to the nearby historic town make it a worthy trip.

Pronunciation: words ending in /v/ and /f/

Remember, /v/ is a 'voiced' sound so there is a vibration in your throat as you make the sound.

Put your hand on your throat and say 'save' – you should feel the vibration at the end.

Now say 'safe' – the air escapes from your mouth with no vibration in your throat.

Listen to the dialogues and underline the word you hear.

Ben:	I got my tickets online. It's much cheaper.
Zak:	How much did you (1) **safe/save**?
Zoe:	We mostly travelled on the metro in Mexico City.
Matt:	Really? Is it (2) **safe/save**?
Lily:	I don't think we've ever been to Lisbon.
Suzie:	Yes, we (3) **half/have**.
Leo:	I think it'll take about two hours.
Nick:	I'd say two and a (4) **half/have**.
James:	Will the interview be recorded?
Sophie:	No, we're doing it (5) **life/live**.
Anna:	I wish we didn't have so many exams.
Ella:	Ah, it's just a fact of (6) **life/live**.
Molly:	Did you hear that the café's going to close down?
Rory:	No! I don't (7) **belief/believe** it!
Tom:	Apparently, the team have sacked the manager again.
Jake:	Oh no, that's almost beyond (8) **belief/believe**!

7b Check your answers then work with a partner to repeat the dialogues. Focus on the pronunciation of the underlined word.

Condition or conditions?

Condition can be an uncountable noun used to describe the state of something. *in good/bad/poor condition*

✓ *The car's a few years old, but it's still **in good condition**.*

✗ *The car's a few years old, but it's still in good ~~conditions~~.*

Conditions is a plural noun used to describe a situation.

✓ *The flight was cancelled due to the extreme **weather conditions**.*

✗ *The flight was cancelled due to ~~an extreme weather condition~~.*

✓ *There are concerns about low pay and unsafe **working conditions**.*

Countable and uncountable nouns:

8 Complete the sentences using the correct form of the noun.

1 The apartment was in very poor **condition/conditions** and needed a lot of work.

2 The doctor gave him some **advice/advices** about how to improve his diet.

3 Everyone agrees we need to cut waste, but no one wants to change their **behaviour/behaviours**.

4 People living in remote areas sometimes find it difficult to access medical **care/cares**.

5 We need to improve the living **condition/conditions** of some of the world's poorest people.

6 Several local residents complained about the **noise/noises** from the event.

7 Mass tourism in the area has done a lot of **damage/damages** to the environment.

8 The police couldn't find any **evidence/evidences** that it was anything but an accident.

9 The course is suitable for students with no previous **knowledge/knowledges** of the language.

10 You can avoid being bitten at **night/nights** by sleeping under a mosquito net.

11 Animals are often scared of loud **noise/noises**, like fireworks.

12 Some people had **trouble/troubles** getting to the stadium because of traffic jams.

Word order: wh- clauses

When a verb phrase is followed by a wh-clause, remember the word order is:

… what/why/how/whether + subject + verb

✓ I don't know **who I can ask** for help.

✗ I don't know ~~who can I ask~~ for help.

✓ No one explained to us **where the meeting point was**.

✗ No one explained to us ~~where was the meeting point~~.

✓ Let me know **how long the work will take**.

✗ Let me know ~~how long will the work take~~.

9 Complete the sentences using in the words and phrases in brackets.

1 I just can't understand why .... (are / so selfish / some people).

2 Several people have asked when .... (reopen / the station / will).

3 I'm trying to find out where .... (can / get / I / more information).

4 I read an article discussing whether .... (be banned / plastic bottles / should).

5 You can imagine how upset .... (a lot people / by the news / were).

6 You mustn't forget how important .... (is / it / plenty of water / to drink).

7 We all know how hard .... (a parking space / be / can / it / to find).

8 I wonder what .... (about the problem / do / the new government / will).

Negative adjectives

10 Choose the correct adjective form to complete the sentences.

1 The man was badly injured and **inconscious/ unconscious**.

2 It's totally **inacceptable/unacceptable** that people have to wait so long to see a doctor.

3 The accident left her **incapable/uncapable** of working.

4 At the moment, it's **impossible/unpossible** to say how long he'll take to recover.

5 It's very **inusual/unusual** for someone so young to suffer a heart attack.

6 I thought it would be **impolite/unpolite** to ask too much about her health problems.

11 Choose the best option to complete the sentences.

1 The college has made a number of changes to make …
   A it easier for disabled students to get around.
   B it more easy for disabled students getting around.
   C easy for disabled students to get around.

2 The course aims to make participants more aware …
   A about some of the challenges blind people face every day
   B of some of the challenges blind people face every day.
   C some of the challenges blind people face every day.

3 For everyone, I think learning a bit of sign language …
   A is really worth.
   B is really worth to do.
   C is really worthwhile.

4 People with dyslexia sometimes find …
   A better text on a coloured background to read.
   B it better for reading text on a coloured background.
   C it better to read text on a coloured background.

5 It's important that young people know where …
   A can they find information about mental health issues.
   B to find information for mental health issues.
   C they can find information about mental health issues.

4 CHOICES

Verb + preposition

Some verbs are often followed by a preposition:

✓ There are several different dates available to **choose from**.

✗ There are several different dates available to ~~choose~~.

✓ They finally **decided on** the larger TV.

✗ They finally ~~decided~~ the larger TV.

Some verbs are followed by a thing or a person, with no preposition:

✓ The changes will only **affect final year students**.

✗ The changes will only ~~affect to final year students~~.

✓ A young man with a clipboard **approached me** in the street.

✗ A young man with a clipboard ~~approached to me~~ in the street.

You can **ask someone** something. You can **ask a question** or **ask permission**.

If you **ask about** something, you want information. If you **ask for** something, you want someone to give it to you.

✓ Please **ask** a member of staff **about** our special offers.

✗ Please ~~ask to a member of staff~~ about our special offers.

✓ Have you **asked for** a discount?

✗ Have ~~asked a~~ discount?

❶ Read the sentences. Some sentences need a preposition added, some gaps can be left empty.

1 As you approach .... the city centre, look out for signs for the university.

2 If you're not sure which option is best for you, then ask .... advice.

3 You can listen .... the show online or via digital radio.

4 I asked .... the sales assistant which camera would be best for wildlife photography.

5 When you enter .... the station, you either turn left for the regular trains or right for the metro.

6 It's possible to pay .... your ticket in cash or by card at the ticket machine.

7 Customers can choose .... a list of different colours.

8 Please tick which course you would like to attend ....

9 In the afternoon, you can either visit .... the museum or you can go shopping.

10 Excuse me, can I ask .... you .... a question?

Commonly confused word forms

choose (verb) – **chose** (past simple), **chosen** (past participle)

choice (noun)

✓ Students can **choose** between full-time and part-time courses.

✗ Students ~~can choice~~ between full-time and part-time courses.

lose (verb) – lost (past simple and past participle)

loss (noun)

loose (adjective)

✓ Be careful not to **lose** you key.

✗ Be careful not to ~~loose~~ you key.

fall (verb) – **fell** (past simple), **fallen** (past participle)

feel (verb) – **felt** (past simple and past participle)

✓ The baby quickly **fell** asleep.

✗ The baby quickly ~~felt~~ asleep.

✓ It's easy to **feel** confused by all the different options.

✗ It's easy to ~~felt~~ confused by all the different options.

❷ₐ Complete the sentences using words from the box. Not all the words are needed.

> choice   choose   chose   chosen   falling   feeling
> fell   felt   loose   lose   loss   lost

1 My second .... of film is by a Spanish director.

2 Are you .... okay or do you want to sit down?

3 I didn't want to .... my place in the queue.

4 You can .... to travel by train or by bus.

5 If the factory closes, it'll mean the .... of hundreds of jobs.

6 I'm really glad we've already .... the venue for our wedding.

7 To keep cool in hot weather, wear .... clothing and drink plenty of water.

8 Perhaps your keys .... out of your pocket when we were playing volleyball.

104 ❷ᵦ Listen and check your answers. Then repeat the sentences paying special attention to the pronunciation of the key words.

English for Spanish Speakers   243

Past simple and past participle forms

3 Complete the sentences using the correct form of the verb in brackets.

1 Originally, we .... (plan) to stay for four days, but we decided to stay on for an extra day.

2 After I'd .... (read) a few online reviews, I changed my mind about the hotel.

3 What .... (happen)? Did you get the job or not?

4 When she was younger, she .... (prefer) to be called Kate rather than Katherine.

5 Yesterday, I .... (hear) that Louis has changed his mind about moving.

6 We've .... (write) a list of possible venues for the meeting.

7 Most of us walked to the beach, but Max and Zoe .... (catch) the bus.

8 There are only two seats .... (leave). Which one do you want?

Relative pronoun + verb

When a relative pronoun is the subject of the following verb, look back to see which noun the relative pronoun refers to. This will help you use the correct form of the verb.

*This is a **decision** <u>which</u> **affects** everyone in the neighbourhood.*

singular noun   singular verb form

✗*This is a decision ~~which affect~~ everyone in the neighbourhood.*

*There are some **people** <u>who</u> **prefer** to live alone.*

plural noun   plural verb form

✗ *There are some people ~~who prefers~~ to live alone.*

4a Underline the noun which the relative pronoun refers back to.

4b Choose the correct verb form.

4c Tick the final sound of each verb.

1 I'm looking for <u>a job</u> **which** doesn't/~~don't~~ involve too much travelling.

2 It would be good to work with people **who** *are/is* as passionate as me about design.

3 I'd like to find a role **which** *use/uses* my language skills.

4 Everyone wants a manager **who** *listen/listens* to their employees.

5 There are lots of people **who** *wish/wishes* they could work shorter hours.

6 As a mother, I'm interested in jobs **which** *finish/finishes* in time for me to pick the kids up from school.

7 I'd never work in an industry **which** *cause/causes* pollution or *create/creates* a lot of waste.

		/ɪz/	/z/	/s/	/ʃ/
1	uses		✓		
2	listens				
3	wish				
4	finish				
5	causes				
6	creates				

4d Listen and repeat sentences 3-9. Pay special attention to the verb endings.

Spelling: adverbs

5 Find and correct one spelling mistake in each sentence.

1 Personaly, I prefer to buy fruit and vegetables from the market rather than the supermarket.

2 As a family, we regulary do our food shopping online because it's so much easier.

3 I absolutely hate shopping for clothes so I'd much rather order stuff online.

4 I think it's extremly sad that so many bookshops have closed down because of competition from the internet.

5 As a single parent on a low income, I have to think very carefuly about what I spend money on.

6 The cost of living has really risen recently, petrol has become particulary expensive.

7 My two sons like totaly different kinds of food which makes cooking for them impossible.

8 I stopped eating meat a couple of years ago and now my diet is completly vegetarian.

Word order: adverbs

6 **Choose the correct option to complete the sentences.**

1 There's a café on the first floor and visitors .... snacks from the ground floor shop.

    A can also buy   **B** also can buy

2 I was disappointed that there .... parking space for disabled guests.

    A was one only   **B** was only one

3 To choose which option you prefer, ... touch the screen.

    A simply you have to   **B** you simply have to

4 The centre is open late on a Wednesday and Friday for those who .... after work.

    A can only get there   **B** only can get there

5 If there's a choice, ... a room on the top floor.

    A I'd probably prefer   **B** I'd prefer probably

6 The university library has lots of areas for quiet study, it .... a space for group study.

    A has also   **B** also has

7 There's a coffee stall outside if you .... a quick coffee to take away.

    A just want   **B** want just

8 You .... drinks brought to you in your cinema seat.

    A even can have   **B** can even have

7 **Choose the best options to complete the text.**

Teenagers have a lot of (1) *choices/chooses* to make which potentially (2) *affect/affects* their future lives. They have to (3) *choice/choose* which subjects to study at school and then whether to go on to university or college. When you (4) *decides/decide* on a subject to study, of course, you (5) *have to think also/also have to think* about what career that might lead to. It's not surprising then that many young people (6) *feel/fell* unsure and slightly stressed. That's why it's so important to (7) *ask about/ask for advice* from people who (8) *know/knows* about study options and careers.

5 STATISTICS

A lot and a few

You use **a lot of** or **lots of** (*informal*) + ***plural or uncountable noun*** to talk about a large number or amount of something.

✓ *There were **a lot of people** in the square. /There were **lots of people** in the square.*

✗ *There were ~~lot of people~~ in the square. / There were ~~a lot people~~ in the square.*

You use **a few** + ***plural noun*** to talk about some or a small number of something.

✓ *Only **a few people** left comments.*

✗ *Only ~~few people~~ left comments. / Only ~~some people~~ left comments.*

You can use ***the last/past/previous/next few days/ years***, etc.

✓ *Numbers have increased suddenly in **the past few months**.*

✗ *Numbers have increased suddenly in ~~the past months~~.*

1 **Choose the best option to complete the dialogues.**

A: Are you nearly ready for the move? Have you got (1) ***a lot/a lot of*** things still to pack?

B: No, we're almost ready, I think. There are just (2) ***a few/a few of*** boxes which Tom will take in his van today. Then I'll take (3) the last ***a few/few*** things in my car with me on Tuesday.

A: How was your journey? Was there (4) ***a lot/a lot of*** traffic?

B: No, it wasn't too bad actually. There were (5) ***a lots of/lots of*** cars going the other way, but we were quite lucky. We had to slow down (6) ***few/a few*** times, but mostly it was fine.

A: How's work?

B: It's been pretty busy lately. Over (7) ***the past few/the past weeks***, we've had (8) l***ots of/lots*** new orders. Which is great for the business, but it means I've had to work long hours and (9) ***few/a few*** weekends too.

Spelling: vowels

2 **Find and correct one spelling mistake in each sentence.**

1 Recently, there's been an encrease in the number of people taking holidays in their own country.

2 Avoiding unnecessary flights is one exemple of a way in which people are becoming more eco-conscious.

3 Those who travel abroad are also choosing hotels and resorts that are more environmentally responsable.

4 In many parts of the world, eco-turism is now becoming the dominant model.

5 Many more hotels are involved in projects to help conserve wildlife in the sorrounding area.

6 Some hotels make it more convinient for guests to avoid waste, such as by providing refillable water bottles.

7 For most, a hotel's eco-credentials are secundary to its location and facilities, but nonetheless, it's something they now take into account.

8 For conservationists, just the existance of eco-resorts which contribute to conservation efforts is a positive step.

This/these

3 **Choose the best option to complete the sentences.**

1 At the sports club, the tennis courts are in bad condition, the showers don't work and there aren't enough coaches to run training sessions. The majority of **this**/**these** problems could be solved by more investment.

2 Heavy traffic in towns and cities puts poisonous gases into the air and **this**/**these** kind of pollution directly affects human health.

3 More than 150 students at the university reported their phones stolen last year. In around 50% of **that**/**those** cases, the phones later turned up and had not been stolen at all.

4 Recently, our local museum hosted a special exhibition of paintings by Salvador Dali and more people visited the museum in **that**/**those** five days than in the whole of the previous year!

5 The new housing development would cause an increase in traffic and put pressure on local services. For **this**/**these** reasons, the council has refused permission for it to go ahead.

6 Local residents would like to know more about the size of the planned business park and the type of businesses it might include, but **that**/**those** information isn't publically available yet.

7 In feedback, college students have asked for more study space, a better wi-fi signal and longer lunch breaks. Some of **this**/**these** things, of course, are much easier to fix than others.

8 People post hundreds of photos of themselves on social media every day, but what percentage of **this**/**these** pictures have been edited or filtered to create a better image?

Which preposition?

4 **Choose the best option to complete the sentences.**

1 These statistics are **based in**/**based on** a relatively small sample of just 150 people.

2 The majority of people are **capable for**/**capable of** scoring at least 70% on these kinds of tests.

3 The **key of**/**key to** achieving a high score often lies in understanding the format of the test.

4 We collected a lot of information about the 30-50 age group, but we **lack**/**lack of** data about younger and older people.

5 The article **concentrates in**/**concentrates on** the figures for the past 12 months.

6 She just picked out a few statistics to support her view **instead**/**instead of** giving the overall picture.

7 Which type of graph you choose will **depend in**/**depend on** the type of information you're presenting.

8 She was positive about the future of the business **despite**/**despite of** the disappointing sales figures.

Word order: a lot/very much

After a transitive verb(a verb that requires one or more objects), **a lot**, **a bit** or **very much** comes after the direct object.

like/enjoy + something + very much

✓ Most employees **didn't like the changes very much**.

enjoy/use/miss + something + a lot

✓ Stephanie **missed her family and friends a lot**.

You can also use **much**/**very much** before some verbs.

✓ We all **very much want** the project to succeed.

✓ Most customers **much prefer** to pay by card.

5 **Read the comments. Are the words in bold in the correct position? Edit any that are not correct.**

I'd like to thank ~~very much~~ you all for your help over the past few weeks. We couldn't have completed this project without you. I **very much** appreciate your hard work. Now hopefully, you can relax and enjoy **a bit** the summer before the next big project starts in September.

To be honest, I didn't enjoy **very much** school. But that was nearly 20 years ago. I think education has changed **a lot** now. From what I see at my kids' school, I think I'd much prefer to be at school nowadays. They use **a lot** technology to make learning more fun and engaging.

Losing my sight has changed my life **a lot**, but not all the changes have been negative. Of course, being visually impaired has affected **very much** the way I do things. I rely on the people around me **a lot** to help me get about, but in many ways, that's brought me closer to people. I've realized what good friends I have.

6 Being polite

Verb forms 1

1 **Choose the best verb form to complete the sentences.**

1 If you're able to come at the weekend, we'd be delighted *see*/*of seeing*/*to see you*.

2 I really don't mind *pick*/*picking*/*to pick* you up from the airport.

3 Would you like *go*/*going*/*to go* anywhere particular while you're in London?

4 Please don't hesitate *get*/*getting*/*to get* in touch again if you need more details.

5 I'm sure Greg would be happy *look after*/*looking after*/*to look after* the children for a few hours.

6 Would you rather *sleep*/*sleeping*/*to sleep* in the room on the ground floor or the room upstairs?

7 I'm really looking forward *see*/*to seeing*/*to see* you both soon.

8 Thank you so much *for feed*/*for feeding*/*to feed* the cat while we were away.

9 I'm keen *start*/*of starting*/*to start* classes as soon as possible.

10 I was glad *hear*/*of hearing*/*to hear* that everything went well.

11 Many thanks for letting me *stay*/*staying*/*to stay* at your place overnight.

12 It would be really nice *meet up*/*meeting up*/*to meet up* while you're in Madrid.

2 **Choose the best option to complete the messages.**

The flowers you sent were (1) *absolutely*/*totally* beautiful. I was (2) *absolutely*/*so* surprised when they arrived.

Thank you so much for helping me decorate the apartment last weekend. It looks (3) *absolutely*/*completely* different now. I'm (4) *really*/*totally* grateful for all your help.

Congratulations on getting a place at university! I know the entrance exam was (5) *very*/*so* difficult and you worked (6) *really*/*totally* hard. I'm (7) *absolutely*/*very* delighted for you.

As you know, I was (8) *absolutely*/*very* sad when you decided to leave. The office just isn't the same without you! I'm (9) *really*/*totally* pleased that you're enjoying your new job though.

Which preposition?

3 **Complete the sentences using prepositions from the box.**

> by   for   from   of   to   with

1 Unfortunately, we were not completely satisfied .... the service we received.

2 I'm incredibly grateful .... everyone .... their support.

3 The hotel staff were very kind .... me when I was unwell.

4 We were all very impressed .... the quality of the food.

5 Personally, I do not see the need .... any further changes.

6 I look forward to hearing .... you again soon.

Spelling: double letters

4 **Find and correct one spelling mistake in each sentence.**

1 I'd like to wellcome everyone to today's conference.

2 All food and accomodation is included in the cost of the trip.

3 If you could just complete your full name and adress, please.

4 Could I just draw your atention to the safety information?

5 It may be necessary to wait a little longer during bussy periods.

6 The staff we dealt with were polite and profesional.

7 There are extra toilet facilities on the first floor in adittion to those in the reception area.

8 The hotel is especially popular with bussiness travellers.

9 I'm writting to you regarding your recent enquiry.

5 **Choose the best options to complete the messages.**

Thank you for (1) *getting*/*got* in touch about our introduction to photography course. I'm delighted (2) *for telling*/*to tell you* that we still have a number of places available. However, the course is (3) *very*/*so* popular so we recommend booking your place as soon as possible. You can (4) *book*/*booking* a place online via our website or if you prefer, I'd be happy (5) *sorting out*/*to sort out* your booking over the phone. I look forward to (6) *hearing you*/*hearing from* you again soon.

I'm getting in touch to cancel my booking for next month's yoga course. As you know, I injured my ankle recently and it's still (7) *completely*/*very* painful. The doctor has told me I need (8) *resting*/*to rest* it for a few weeks. It was very kind (9) *of*/*to* you to offer to switch my booking to the following course, but (10) *I don't think*/*don't think* I'll recover in time. I'm still keen (11) *for doing*/*to do* the course at some point in the future, so I'll get in touch again when I'm (12) *absolutely*/*so* certain that my ankle's okay.

Acknowledgements

The authors and publishers acknowledge the following sources of copyright material and are grateful for the permissions granted. While every effort has been made, it has not always been possible to identify the sources of all the material used, or to trace all copyright holders. If any omissions are brought to our notice, we will be happy to include the appropriate acknowledgements on reprinting and in the next update to the digital edition, as applicable.

Key: U = Unit, SB = Speaking Bank, ESS = English for Spanish Speakers

Text

U10: The Telegraph for the adapted text from 'Sharecycling: Our family and friends took everything we owned' by Jennifer Rigby, *The Telegraph* 13.11.2015. Copyright © 2015 Telegraph Media Group Limited. Reproduced with permission; **U13**: Paprika Patterns for the adapted text from 'Daily Life in a Yurt: Winter'. Copyright © 2015 Paprika Patterns. Reproduced with kind permission.

Photography

All the photographs are sourced from Getty Images.

U1: Niedring/Drentwett/MITO images; FatCamera/E+; Eric Audras/ONOKY; Jupiterimages/Stockbyte; Nikada/iStock/Getty Images Plus; Caiaimage/Chris Ryan; SW Productions/Stockbyte; AntonioGuillem/iStock/Getty Images Plus; JGI/Jamie Grill; DGLimages/iStock/Getty Images Plus; ViewApart/iStock/Getty Images Plus; Alex Tihonov/Moment; Kohei Hara/DigitalVision; **U2:** moodboard/Cultura; piskunov/E+; isitsharp/E+; Davizro/iStock/Getty Images Plus; Ryan McVay/Photodisc; Caiaimage/Trevor Adeline; Aksonov/E+; Letizia Le Fur/ONOKY; Hero Images; ranplett/E+; FatCamera/E+; Westend61; Nancy Ney/Photodisc; Cavan Images; Moelyn Photos/Moment; **U3:** LuckyBusiness/iStock/Getty Images Plus; Sol de Zuasnabar Brebbia/Moment; Westend61/Brand X Pictures; Janie Airey/Cultura; Westend61; joci03/iStock/Getty Images Plus; Sijori Images/Barcroft Media; theJIPEN/iStock Editorial/Getty Images Plus; valentinrussanov/E+; Gina Pricope/Moment Open; Jenny Jones/Lonely Planet Images; xavierarnau/E+; horstgerlach/iStock/Getty Images Plus; Jose Luis Pelaez Inc/DigitalVision; SolStock/E+; Jupiterimages/Stockbyte; Flying Colours Ltd/Photodisc; Nigel Fennell/EyeEm; **U4:** Batel Shimi/Kari Feinstein PR/Handout/WireImage; NosUA/iStock/Getty Images Plus; SeventyFour/iStock/Getty Images Plus; luknaja/iStock/Getty Images Plus; Eugene Mymrin/Moment; Caiaimage/Robert Daly; Tetra Images; Mike Harrington/DigitalVision; Westend61; ahirao_photo/iStock/Getty Images Plus; PNC/DigitalVision; Image Source; gerenme/E+; Janja Milosevic/EyeEm; wundervisuals/E+; brittak/E+; Andersen Ross/Cultura; StefaNikolic/E+; d3sign/Moment; **U5:** Hill Street Studios LLC/DigitalVision; Compassionate Eye Foundation/Steven Errico/DigitalVision; Klaus Vedfelt/DigitalVision; Compassionate Eye Foundation/Robert Kent/DigitalVision; Alistair Berg/DigitalVision; Maskot; Stockbyte; Patrick Kunkel/MITO images; LeoPatrizi/E+; Hero Images; Monty Rakusen/Cultura; bo1982/iStock/Getty Images Plus; Daisy-Daisy/iStock/Getty Images Plus; Tim Macpherson/Cultura; James Woodson/Photodisc; monkeybusinessimages/iStock/Getty Images Plus; caracterdesign/E+; UygarGeographic/E+; **U6:** Indeed; Christine Schneider/Cultura; Highwaystarz-Photography/iStock/Getty Images Plus; GCShutter/E+; John A. Rizzo/Photodisc; Stuart Ashley/DigitalVision; Wavebreakmedia/iStock/Getty Images Plus; asiseeit/iStock/Getty Images Plus; Kelvin Murray/Photodisc; i love images/Juice Images; Alistair Berg/DigitalVision; Echo/Juice Images; Doris Beling/Folio; South_agency/E+; Jose Luis Pelaez Inc/DigitalVision; Steve Debenport/E+; Hero Images; spooh/E+; Johner Images; **U7:** Kacey Klonsky/Image Source; Hero Images; Steve Debenport/E+; CasarsaGuru/E+; Oliver Furrer/Photographer's Choice RF; Image Source; dannicolae/iStock/Getty Images Plus; Joanne Hedger/Moment; Mario Widmer/EyeEm; Brett Froomer/The Image Bank; Graiki/Moment; Kamran Jebreili/arabianEye; FatCamera/E+; **U8:** Hill Street Studios LLC/DigitalVision; igor_kell/iStock/Getty Images Plus; joshblake/E+; elkor/E+; SensorSpot/E+; quavondo/iStock/Getty Images Plus; Hero Images; Maskot; Robyn Beck/AFP; Caiaimage/Martin Barraud/OJO+; Dmytro Aksonov/E+; satori13/iStock/Getty Images Plus; Matt Roberts/Getty Images Sport; Philippe Turpin/Photononstop; Jack Taylor/Getty Images News; aluxum/E+; Caiaimage/Robert Daly; vgajic/E+; Caiaimage/Martin Barraud; **U9:** kali9/E+; Caiaimage/Sam Edwards; Philartphace/iStock/Getty Images Plus; Rayman/Photodisc; Layland Masuda/Moment Open; Eric Audras/ONOKY; Ryan McVay/Stockbyte; Jupiterimages/Pixland/Getty Images Plus; numbeos/E+; ArtMarie/E+; Flashpop/DigitalVision; gpointstudio/iStock/Getty Images Plus; PNC/DigitalVision; YinYang/E+; Cultura/Seb Oliver; Cyndi Monaghan/Moment; Johner Images; Adie Bush/Image Source; dszc/E+; **U10:** Foodcollection; scanrail/iStock/Getty Images Plus; vnlit/iStock/Getty Images Plus; Sung Yoon Jo/iStock/Getty Images Plus; Glowimages; Robert Daly/OJO Images; bonetta/iStock/Getty Images Plus; baibaz/iStock/Getty Images Plus; kali9/E+; Simon Potter/Cultura; Ben Pipe Photography/Cultura; lolostock/iStock/Getty Images Plus; Tony Anderson/Taxi; Juanmonino/iStock/Getty Images Plus; blue jean images; **U11:** Westend61; jacoblund/iStock/Getty Images Plus; kali9/E+; m-imagephotography/iStock/Getty Images Plus; Barcin/E+; REB Images/Blend Images; Caiaimage/Sam Edwards/OJO+; izusek/iStock/Getty Images Plus; Andrew Brookes/Cultura; Tang Ming Tung/DigitalVision; imagenavi; anouchka/iStock/Getty Images Plus; Claudia Goepperl/Photodisc; PeopleImages/E+; Corey Jenkins/Image Source; Emilija Manevska/Moment; Nlauria/iStock/Getty Images Plus; **U12:** Zocha_K/E+; XiXinXing/iStock/Getty Images Plus; Ariel Skelley/DigitalVision; moodboard/Brand X Pictures; Rosmarie Wirz/Moment Open; Frans Lemmens/Corbis; Chris Minihane/Moment; Robert Cinega/500px Prime; 101dalmatians/E+; Huntstock/Brand X Pictures; Westend61; Keren Su/Corbis; kajakiki/E+; Konrad Wothe; Kryssia Campos/Moment; Barbara Bergmann/EyeEm; Ioannis Tsotras/Moment Open; Estersinhache fotografía/Moment; Mike Kemp; Monty Rakusen/Cultura; Jose Luis Pelaez Inc/DigitalVision; Santiago Urquijo/Moment; **U13:** Mario Gutiérrez/Moment; sbossert/E+; Martin Barraud/Caiaimage; LuisPortugal/E+; ImagineGolf/E+; Jon Bower at Apexphotos/Moment Open; Melissa Ross/Moment Open; malerapaso/E+; RDImages/Epics/Hulton Archive; moodboard/Cultura; skynesher/E+; Pascal Broze/ONOKY; Marco Bottigelli/Moment; George-Standen/iStock/Getty Images Plus; shan.shihan/Moment; kali9/E+; Hoxton/Martin Barraud; dbvirago/iStock/Getty Images Plus; **U14:** Glow Images; filmfoto/iStock Editorial/Getty Images Plus; Sunnybeach/iStock/Getty Images Plus; Flavio Vallenari/iStock/Getty Images Plus; Anik Messier/Flickr/Moment; FooTToo/iStock Editorial/Getty Images Plus; Klaus Vedfelt/Taxi; Glowimages; VLIET/iStock/Getty Images Plus; Ira Heuvelman-Dobrolyubova/Moment Open; ambaradan/iStock/Getty Images Plus; Feverstockphoto/E+; martinedoucet/E+; Pekic/E+; Hero Images; Martin Dimitrov/E+; Toshiaki Ono/a.collectionRF; Image Source; **SB**: Tim Graham/Getty Images News; George Rose/Getty Images News; JOKER/Gudrun Petersen/ullstein bild; Tetra Images; Monty Rakusen/Cultura; Daniel Mihailescu/AFP; **ESS:** Todor Tsvetkov/E+; Ben Pipe Photography/Cultura; Westend61; Alistair Berg/DigitalVision; Carol Yepes/Moment; Topic Images Inc.; Alon Ceng/EyeEm; Chuck Ortego/EyeEm; Alexander Spatari/Moment; Jesse Kraft/EyeEm; Hero Images; Image Source/DigitalVision; Tetra Images - Rob Lewine/Brand X Pictures; khoa vu/Moment; Jordan Siemens/DigitalVision; Digital Vision/Photodisc; fontina/Moment; RichVintage/E+; Michal Gutowski Photography/Moment; David Hastilow/Getty/Stockbyte; mikeuk/E+; Rene Frederick/DigitalVision; Evan Reinheimer/Moment; Livinus/iStock Editorial/Getty Images Plus; Image Source; Jesús Argentó Raset/EyeEm.

Front cover photography by ultraforma/E+/Getty Images; Josef Lindau/Corbis/VCG/Getty Images.

Audio

Audio production by Leon Chambers.